VAUDEVILLE AND THE MAKING OF MODERN ENTERTAINMENT, 1890–1925

Vaudeville and the Making of Modern Entertainment, 1890–1925

DAVID MONOD

THE UNIVERSITY OF NORTH CAROLINA PRESS
CHAPEL HILL

This book was published with the assistance of the Anniversary Fund
of the University of North Carolina Press.

© 2020 The University of North Carolina Press
All rights reserved

Designed by April Leidig
Set in Garamond by Copperline Book Services, Inc.
Manufactured in the United States of America

The University of North Carolina Press has been a member
of the Green Press Initiative since 2003.

Cover illustration: Everett Shinn, *The Vaudeville Act* (1902–1903);
courtesy Palmer Museum of Art, Pennsylvania State University.

Library of Congress Cataloging-in-Publication Data
Names: Monod, David, 1960– author.
Title: Vaudeville and the making of modern entertainment, 1890–1925 / David Monod.
Description: Chapel Hill : University of North Carolina Press, 2020. |
Includes bibliographical references and index.
Identifiers: LCCN 2020015418 | ISBN 9781469660547 (cloth) |
ISBN 9781469660554 (paperback : alk. paper) | ISBN 9781469660561 (ebook)
Subjects: LCSH: Vaudeville—United States—History—20th century. |
Vaudeville—United States—History—19th century. | Popular culture—
United States—History—20th century.
Classification: LCC PN1968.U5 M66 2020 | DDC 792.70973—dc23
LC record available at https://lccn.loc.gov/2020015418

This research was supported by the
Social Sciences and Humanities Research Council of Canada.

SSHRC≡CRSH

TO NEW YORK CITY
FOR THE MEMORIES YOU HAVE
GIVEN OUR FAMILY

CONTENTS

Acknowledgments xi

Introduction 1

ONE
The Vogue for Vaudeville:
Urbanity, Comfort, and Celebrity 21

TWO
Ragging Style:
Presenting the Modern American 51

THREE
Grabbing Attention:
Making Good with the Distracted Audience 91

FOUR
Vaudeville Modernism 119

FIVE
The Business of Mass Entertainment 149

SIX
The Hook:
Vaudeville Makes Its Exit 187

Notes 227

Index 261

FIGURES

Harry Lauder and Imro Fox portrait 15

Koster and Bial advertisement 26

Tea being served at Proctor's Pleasure Palace in 1905 30

Annette Kellerman advertisement 40

Valeska Suratt portrait 74

Billy B. Van publicity still 79

Bob Cole and Rosamond Johnson portrait 82

William Glackens sketch 84

Postcard of Detroit's Orpheum Theater 102

Nora Bayes portrait 108

Postcard from 1906 with sketch of blackface act 127

La Sylphe portrait 138

Advertisement featuring Gilda Gray 142

Fred Proctor portrait 159

B. F. Keith's New Theatre, Boston 164

Marcus Loew portrait 193

Advertisement for "Grasping an Opportunity" 203

Gallagher and Shean sheet music cover 220

ACKNOWLEDGMENTS

ALTHOUGH STUDYING in an archive is undeniably *work*, it's worth acknowledging how much pleasure I take from doing it! I enjoy the intensity of research: the drive to read through the material you've called up before traveling home, the concentrated energy of other people mining for evidence, the oppressive quiet. There's even something beguiling about the watchful curators who survey the room, charged with protecting records from clumsy and dishonest visitors. It seems so magically antique in our digital era. Many of us develop bonds with the people we are researching, and we want to know what happened to them. Reading through an archival collection becomes a kind of prospecting, where every researcher knows that somewhere, buried in one of those brittle documents, is an important discovery waiting to be found. And each one of us is convinced that his or her great discovery will be of seminal importance, even if the topic is the century-old vaudeville theater.

Archives are personally important in other ways. I've never thought of books as milestones, but I realize that researching them has influenced not just my working life but also the life of our family. Archival study drew us to specific locations, often for months at a time. During the almost fifteen years I worked on this book, our family spent many months in New York City. Adam, Emma, Michaela, and I grew to feel wonderfully attached to that remarkable, insistent place. Many of the moments in our children's growth to adulthood, and in our relationship, glow more intensely because they occurred during one of our visits to New York. The city backgrounds and defines some of our most important memories about the people most precious to us.

Archives, then (the physical ones, not their increasingly virtual selves), were at the heart of this study. If I offer my strongest thanks to Doug Reside and the archivists and staff at the New York Public Library for the Performing Arts, that doesn't mean that visits to other institutions were less rewarding. I simply count those other experiences in weeks rather than in years! My appreciation goes to the staffs at Special Collections, the University of Arizona; the Library of Congress; the Georgetown University Archives; the Harvard

Theatre Collection, Houghton Library; the Archives of Traditional Music, Indiana University; the University of Iowa Archives; the National Archives; the Institute of Jazz Studies, Rutgers University; the Archives Center, Smithsonian Museum of American History; the Harry Ransom Center, University of Texas; and the Hogan Jazz Archive, Tulane University. I am really delighted that the University of Iowa Archives, home to the singular Keith-Albee Collection, has agreed to be the repository for the digital collection created out of the research done for this study.

Doing research in archives (and living in New York) is expensive. As a Canadian scholar, I was fortunate to have the Social Sciences and Humanities Research Council support my work. A pair of five-year research grants made possible not only this book but also the population of the database that will hopefully make vaudeville research less expensive for future historians. The digital resource is designed to whet the appetite of the curious and make studying vaudeville easier, but I would not want its convenience to supplant the pleasure of archival research. Wilfrid Laurier University, where I have been teaching for over thirty years, provided me with a substantial grant that allowed me to create the infrastructure for the vaudevilleamerica.org database. The Office of Research Services wasn't required to do this, and I am very grateful for the vote of confidence it made in my work.

Decades spent as part of a scholarly community means relationships that nurture and sustain ideas. A collective thank you goes to friends and colleagues, some of them now departed, who have inspired me through conversation and the critical reading of portions of this manuscript. The two anonymous readers for the University of North Carolina Press will see their imprint on the pages that follow; a special thanks is due them not just for improving this work but for doing a job that is underacknowledged yet essential to scholarship. I am honored that the Press has granted this book publication assistance from its Anniversary Fund, which was established in 1997 to celebrate the Press's seventy-fifth anniversary. UNCP and its amazing staff have been everything an author could desire in terms of support and efficiency. Charles Grench is my image of an editor: realistic, enthusiastic, funny, and a tiny bit intimidating. Dylan White was a masterful assistant editor who kept everything moving at the right pace. Julie Bush did an exemplary job copyediting the manuscript; I marvel at her ability to identify inconsistencies and untangle prose. Jay Mazzocchi, who carried the manuscript through the stages of production, was unfailingly positive, effective, and encouraging. For many readers, the index will be the doorway to the book, and a good index should show readers what an author is trying to get across. My special thanks to Michelle Johnston for disassembling my work and then reconstructing it in point form with such uncanny insight.

I'll wrap up by thanking the students who entered over 35,000 reviews on the vaudeville database and created what I hope will be a lasting resource for historians. Heartfelt appreciation goes to my most stalwart research assistants: Lyndsay Rosenthal, Taylor Surnam, Jordan Desai, and Julianne Scott. I was very privileged to have such a disciplined, hard-working, and meticulous team of researchers. And warm thanks go to the all the students who contributed their energies over the last six years: Cameron Baer, Lee Barich, Hannah Hancock, Laila Hawrylshyn, Breanna Kettles, Matthew Morden, Kyleigh Poultney, Eliza Richardson, Jordan Roberts, Trevor Stace, Chelsea Telfer, and Alex Wharton. I hope each of you will find time for a little vaudeville in your lives, no matter where your future takes you.

VAUDEVILLE AND THE MAKING OF MODERN ENTERTAINMENT, 1890–1925

INTRODUCTION

"SIMPLE STUPIDITY" was how the researcher and reformer Michael Davis described vaudeville in 1911. To be plain, he believed "no person of moderate intelligence can attend a dozen vaudeville performances without being disgusted at their vapidity." Davis might have been thinking of an act like the Talking Tea Kettle, which seemed better suited to a country fair than an entertainment in a big theater in New York City. The kettle's "operator" carried the "famed piece of kitchen ware" through the audience where it "perceive[d] thoughts in the human mind" and offered "intelligent insight into the future." He could also have been thinking of Colonel Gaston Bordeverry, who in 1905 toured an act in which he used a rifle to shoot away the clasps on his assistant's gown, gradually undressing her. She was, noted one critic, "a very slim target." As columnist William Grimes, who reviewed a television documentary on vaudeville for the *New York Times* in 1997, enthused, "From the 1880's to the 1930's, a man with a singing duck could find good, steady work at vaudeville theaters all across the United States, sharing the bill with jugglers, singers, dancers, comedians, contortionists, magicians, female impersonators, famous sports figures—anybody, in fact, who could hold the attention of an audience for 10 minutes."[1] How mystified Michael Davis would have been, had he lived long enough, to see this kind of material become the topic of serious scholarship.

And there is no point denying it: considerable stupidity could be found in vaudeville. But there is also no reason to allow that fact to obscure the entertainment's significance. In this chapter, I want to make a case for vaudeville as a worthy subject of academic study, summarize the arguments of scholars who have written about the theater before, and highlight how my approach differs from theirs. For readers who consider vaudeville as Michael Davis did—as the quintessence of stupidity—this introduction may not seem like a lot of fun. While I hope enough of that fun returns in subsequent chapters, it isn't my goal to reproduce the sprightly mayhem of the variety show, as works by Donald

Travis Stewart and others have done.[2] In partial atonement for this, I would say that there was less slapstick and nonsense in vaudeville than we generally imagine. Joe Weber's oft-repeated remark that the way to make people laugh was for one comic to stick a finger in another comic's eye and the way to make them laugh harder was to stick two fingers in is a misrepresentation of vaudeville performance in its totality. Comics did not make up vaudeville's most common act—singers did—and there were plenty of straight-faced illusionists, acrobats, dancers, instrumentalists, animal trainers, and shootists as well.

Despite the banality of some of its acts and the lunacy of others, vaudeville is an important topic for serious study for no other reason than because it was the United States' first modern mass entertainment. Vaudeville was different from the concert saloons, dime museums, and variety theaters that dominated popular amusement at the time of its birth. Those entertainments certainly appealed to "the masses," but they were not mass entertainments in a modern sense of the word. Vaudeville, in an era before technology allowed acts produced in one location to be transmitted to other places at the same time, delivered amusement through national networks of theaters. Performers traveled from theater to theater, allowing people across the country to experience the same things, though at different times. Traveling shows had, of course, done the same thing in the nineteenth century, but on a much more limited scale. Vaudeville was the first organized national amusement.

There was, however, more to mass entertainment than widespread distribution. Vaudeville offered an easily understood product marketed as extraordinary because of its wealth, its celebrities, its trendiness, and its casual atmosphere. It was the first entertainment built around the mass appeal of its "stars." Moreover, vaudeville was the first entertainment designed to make going out less an "event" than an everyday activity for men, women, and children. It was intended to be consumed unthinkingly. Perhaps most important to defining it as a modern mass entertainment, vaudeville presented itself not just as an escape from the workaday world but as a form of mental and emotional reinvigoration. Mass entertainment, I suggest, can be characterized as therapeutic. In keeping with this, vaudevillians presented their theater as affirmative, wholesome, and modern rather than as countercultural, raunchy, or subversive.

This study looks both at distribution practices and at performance to prove that vaudevillians advanced cheery ways of perceiving and experiencing modern life. The "modern" attitude performers communicated was pleasure seeking, down to earth, hostile to conventions, and "authentic." Mass entertainment became what I call a "democratizing" force, not only because it made commercialized culture accessible but because it presented a reasonably coherent vision of how ordinary Americans should experience modern society. Although "Americanization"—the promulgation of a national identity among a diverse population, many of whom were recent immigrants—did result from this promotion of modern attitudes, that was not the objective. Vaudevillians concerned themselves with style, not content; behavior, not identification. I believe "democratization" is a better way of conceptualizing vaudeville's performance horizon than Americanization is because it implies a less nationalistic project, one that involved forms of communication and image making that touched on national identity in only indirect ways. Moreover, democratization was not an exercise in making working people, immigrants, or African Americans invisible but instead centered, to a considerable extent, on the appropriation of forms of expression commonly associated with them.[3] That does not mean that vaudeville promoted equality. It did not transcend the racial, regional, class, or gender inequities that characterized American democracy at the turn of the century. But it did hold out the possibility that every American could make good and get rich if they had talent or personality, and it associated mobility with conspicuous consumption. In this sense, democratization works as conceptual mortar joining mass entertainment as an organizational form with the cultural project of celebrating modernity: vaudeville was at once a way of providing an entertainment to the "masses" and a means of reconfiguring the public who would consume that product into a forward-thinking taste community, a coherent "mass" of people.

The contours of vaudeville's expansion are elusive, but at its peak, in 1910, there were roughly 1,600 variety theaters in the United States. In that year, New York had 48 vaudeville houses, Chicago 41, and San Francisco 20; smaller centers like Milwaukee, Portland, St. Louis, and Atlanta had 4 theaters each. At least 5 million Americans attended vaudeville shows every week.[4] For a few years, before radio and movies attracted a truly heterogeneous audience, vaudeville was the cultural experience most commonly shared by Americans. To deliver the variety format nationally, entrepreneurs created chains of theaters and worked together to pool their bookings and establish cartels in order to better secure the supply of acts and restrict competition. The circuits they established became the basis of film distribution, and their influence continues to resonate in retail entertainment today. Vaudeville was the first leisure industry designed to relax and rejuvenate tired people; it was the first to be structured around transportation and marketing; and it was the birthplace of the modern celebrity performer.

Paradoxically, for an industry that innovated so impressively, vaudeville delivered a product that was surprisingly old. Vaudeville refers to a particular way of distributing live entertainment nationally, but the product it featured was originally called "variety" and, as a theatrical entertainment, it dated back to the mid-nineteenth century.[5] The variety show offered in a vaudeville theater consisted of a wide range of unconnected acts of relatively brief duration that followed one after another, without a break (though some theaters did have a single intermission). The range of acts changed over time, but the most common ones were singers, monologue comedians (we would call them stand-up comics), one-act plays (called sketches at the time), acrobats, dancers, instrumental musicians, and magicians. With the exception of sketches and monologuists, all of these act types would have been familiar to audiences attending nineteenth-century concert saloons, carnivals, tent shows, and the intermissions of plays in legitimate theaters. Variety shows would continue as features on the radio and on television for decades following vaudeville's demise.[6] In this sense, vaudeville was simply one of a series of ways used in the nineteenth and twentieth centuries to distribute variety entertainment.

The business culture in vaudeville was also cut from older cloth. Although many of the theater chains were very large, they were closed corporations, owned by individual proprietors or a few partners. None of the chains sold public stock until the early 1920s. Few businesses in the golden age of vaudeville maintained sinking funds or adequate cash reserves.[7] The theater chains also allowed their individual houses to run with little oversight, and theater managers behaved much like independent operators. Head offices tended to restrict their activities to their firms' overall direction and managed the booking side of the business. Although most of those booking offices had press departments, which prepared the advertising and promotional material for the individual theaters, it is fair to say that while buying and (to a lesser extent) marketing were coordinated centrally, over-the-counter sales were not. Senior executives with the chains, such as Martin Beck and Fred Proctor, were even absent for months at a time, hunting up acts in Europe.

It is peculiar thing, but despite their involvement in the new business of selling entertainment to a national audience, the mindset of vaudeville entrepreneurs remained supply-oriented. The main corporate innovation occurred at the buying (or booking) end, and head officers were content to allow considerable local independence in sales. Some, like Fred Proctor, did not even think print advertising was important. The owners of the vaudeville chains believed that if they could secure appealing acts, the variety show would sell itself. Furthermore, many of the industry's leading entrepreneurs, including the owners of less expensive theaters, like Marcus Loew, thought that vaudeville would be improved by raising its "quality" and ignoring the preferences of those consumers they deemed low-class. Since they sensed the audience was not infinite, managers also sought to grow sales in their individual theaters in a very old-fashioned way: by destroying the competition and establishing territorial monopolies.[8] In sum, even though vaudeville launched mass entertainment in the early twentieth century, a good deal of its business culture looked backward to the Gilded Age.

Vaudeville was an intriguing mix of old and new, chaos and trailblazing, but in areas where entrepreneurs and players did innovate, their interventions were truly revolutionary. They created mass entertainment because they were the first show people to treat commercial amusement as something millions of spectators might consume as an everyday activity. Like the owners of chain stores (also relatively new things in 1900), they brought entertainment into residential neighborhoods to make its consumption more convenient. They adopted a low-price policy, not because they were catering to poor people (the initial market for vaudeville was reasonably representative of the urban population, at least in terms of class, ethnicity, sex, and geography) but because they wanted to remove the pocketbook stress from going out to a show.

Low ticket prices made manifest a management belief that the same spectators were going to attend vaudeville regularly, preferably once or even twice a week. They also reflected managers' conviction that the audience was not seeking an occasional escape through leisure so much as regular reinvigoration. Unlike the amusement parks or dime museums that tried to excite, or the medicine shows and concert saloons that used entertainment to sell ancillary products, or the melodramas that rubbed emotions raw, vaudeville aimed to make people feel relaxed and happy. It did not force Americans to look at things they might find dispiriting. While vaudeville lacked those other entertainments' range of programming, it sold itself, in the same way radio and television would later do, as a way for worn-out consumers to recharge.

Surprisingly, for an industry of vaudeville's historical significance, relatively little (compared, for example, with early cinema) has been written about it. In fact, for the first half of the twentieth century, scholars tended to disparage mass culture and to see it as a placebo that masked the alienating effect of late capitalism. Marxist scholars, for example, thought popular entertainment served to advance modern capitalism's commodification of desire and its objectification of the physical body. But there were always a few who dissented. As early as 1937, the idea that vaudeville might serve as a force of emancipation from modern capitalism had been introduced by Herbert Marcuse, a critical theorist otherwise fairly scornful of popular culture. His view gained ground in the 1960s as vaudeville began to attract scholarly attention as a manifestation of urban diversity and irreverence. It was hailed by historians as a multifaceted, heterogeneous entertainment (a place where ordinary Americans could "get a glimpse of themselves," according to Gunther Barth) that appealed to immigrants and natives, rich and poor, men and women—the ideal embodiment of the American urban mosaic. While some labor historians disputed the entertainment's universality, arguing that vaudeville was essentially a working-class immigrant theater, they accepted that it reflected its audience and that variety acts were best read as expressions of the vibrancy of "low" culture.[9]

Almost before the ink was dry on this interpretation, scholars like David Nasaw and Richard Butsch were countering that vaudeville played a critical role in "disciplining" audiences by not only "refining" amusement but also imposing rules of spectatorship on the once rowdy popular theater. This inspired some historians to interpret the variety show as a contested space where self-conscious spectators pushed back against corporatizing owners. Since the 1990s, "contestation" and its more benign sibling, "negotiation," have moved to the foreground. To Alison Kibler, writing in 1999, vaudeville was an early example of a "midcult" entertainment, something that uplifted less refined audiences by presenting them with digestible versions of elite amusements even as it exposed highbrows to popular forms of fun. In Nicholas Gebhardt's recent study, vaudeville performers are described as mediating between an audience that wanted the theater to represent their tastes and interests and a management that sought to turn leisure into a business.[10]

By the early twenty-first century, then, scholars had become less interested in what vaudeville said about urbanization, nativism, class struggle, or the development of mass culture and more intrigued by what was happening on the stage itself. The study of vaudeville as a site of contestation or negotiation shifted attention from "objective" processes, like urbanization or assimilation, to what actors did and how they were understood.[11] It was only logical, perhaps, that as neoliberalism seemed to triumph at the end of the Cold War, that interest in how disempowered people perform resistance, and therefore express their dissidence, would grow. The attention of many scholars shifted from institutions, collectivities, and structural categories to the dissent of individuals and groups, and this led some to look anew at vaudeville, a form of theater described by many historians as popular among the poor, immigrants, and working women.

Variety acts were now studied not as manifestations of a rich, if conflicted, urban culture but as expressive works of performer and spectator transgression. Subversive performance provided an effective counter to the view that mass entertainment functioned as escapism, brainwashing, or social control. Performers, scholars argued, were able to manipulate narcotizing cultural forms to create a dynamic and disruptive art. For example, while variety actors commonly employed stereotypes that were racist, nativist, and sexist (and in so doing reinforced sexual, economic, and racial hierarchies), theater scholars argued that the demeaning images could be exploded onstage, with liberating results for spectators. Henry Jenkins's highly influential work characterized comedy in vaudeville as "anarchistic," and Rick DesRochers built on that idea to show how immigrants and first-generation Americans used nonsensical humor to contest the values of the host society by discombobulating it. Similarly, Susan Glenn, Andrew Erdman, and Sharon Ullman argued that vaudeville served as a forum for the expression of disruptive attitudes to sex, attitudes that theater owners, progressive reformers, and the courts struggled unsuccessfully to contain.[12]

Beneath many recent interpretations of variety performance is the conviction that marginalized people naturally enjoy subverting the authority of elites and "transgressing" hierarchical boundaries. "One of the primary pleasures of popular culture," writes visual arts educator Paul Duncum, "derives from its transgressive nature." Many of those who have recently written on individual vaudeville performers depict them engaging in a kind of carnival, an ironic, anarchic, grotesque assault on authority. The idea of vaudeville as carnival is derived from Mikhail Bakhtin's notion that popular festivals in the early modern period temporarily shifted the "world order" for their participants. According to Bakhtin, carnival was a bawdy, irreverent form of communitarian excess where reason and decorum were put aside and eating, excreting, and penetrating reigned supreme. Carnival sets performance in a realm of fantasy and aspiration, not real life, making vaudeville into what historian Kathleen Casey calls "a safe space" in which the powerless "could experiment." Popular variety performers like Sophie Tucker and Eva Tanguay became, in performance, destabilizing sexual "icons." As Casey explains of the outrageous Tanguay, "by linking white womanliness to animalistic savagery at a time when both race and gender were undergoing considerable reconstruction, Tanguay presented audiences with a new ideal of racialized masculine femininity."[13] This would certainly help explain why staid critics like Michael Davis considered vaudeville offensive!

Of course, all art is to some degree "transgressive," and all representation allows for "multiple and resistant readings." For historians—whose subject is change through time—the fascination with such "discursive notions of performativity" as the "interpretive agency" of audience members or the "negotiations" of actors as they "navigate" the "configurations" of "embodiment" can be a bit unnerving. Change is messy, there's no doubting that, but it must involve motion. The historian's job is to explain how, why, and what changes are produced by people as time passes. Negotiations, contestations, and agency should result in change, but these terms are often used in performance and media studies to describe synchronic relationships rather than a diachronic process.[14]

Admittedly, drawing any conclusion about the historical meaning of a performance that occurred a century ago or more is a challenge. To show this by example, consider the vaudeville comedian Bertie Herron, who marketed herself as the first "female minstrel." Herron broke into vaudeville in 1903 performing a blackface role (the Tambo in a minstrel lineup) that was traditionally reserved for men. After setting out on a solo career, Herron became a stand-up comic who wore burnt-cork makeup and showed off her legs. Herron's was a novel act because she challenged a number of variety show conventions. As the critic in *Variety* snorted, "It's pretty hard for a girl in short skirts to make people believe she is a [comic] monologist." Another reviewer complained that her act was so "dizzying" that he felt what he saw onstage was "like what a man sees after he has had too many rickeys." But while this all may seem pretty subversive, Herron also operated within the minstrel tradition and performed soubrette roles. She employed "baby-talk," wore a racist mask, deferred to her manager ("He won't let us talk," she complained to a reporter who wanted an interview), wore short skirts, and played the part of the innocent, exuberant, and engaging kid. She did not come up with the idea of an all-female minstrel troupe (the producer Ned Wayburn did), and many of her most popular routines were lifted from other people. Acknowledging the negotiations and contestations here doesn't help us prioritize or determine what Herron "meant" or why she might be historically significant. Was Bertie Herron an agent of change or even a manifestation of changes that were taking place, and if so, which ones?[15]

Trying to figure out what Herron did onstage, how she was perceived, and what audiences took away from her act is especially difficult because she worked in vaudeville. One of the peculiarities of vaudeville is that unlike in the legitimate theater, music, or cinema, almost no texts survive. Contemporary recordings of performers or the scripts of acts are exceedingly rare. What we know about the majority of performances is only what the press reported or what theater managers told each other. Rarely did performers themselves—and then often in potted interviews—reflect on what they were trying to achieve onstage. These absences force historians to deduce the practices of players from the reactions of those professional reviewers and employers watching them. The difficulty, it goes without saying, is that spectators constructed the narrative of the performance, interpreting the players' design, intent, and address in their own ways. Similarly, reviewers were not neutral observers, and those writing in the trade press (for example, *Variety*, *The Player*, the *Dramatic Mirror*, and the *New York Clipper*) and in the reports managers prepared on their weekly shows were writing for industry insiders (other performers and employers) or a public looking for advice. Moreover, only a few papers in larger cities even employed critics who reported on vaudeville; the majority simply reprinted press releases supplied to them by press agents.

While all of these factors place the student at some remove from the actual performance, there are advantages to reviews and professional assessments, if we ask the appropriate questions. Contemporary observers do tell us what they apprehended to be the most important parts of an act. Managers and critics serving the trade press, in particular, wanted to identify controversial elements and to point out those features that most pleased (or seemed to disappoint) audiences. These reviews present performances in "shoppy" ways, as acts that were prepared, rehearsed, and delivered with the goal of engaging spectators. Volume in using reviews is helpful, as it can serve to counterbalance the biases in individual contributions. Approximately 35,000 reviews, compiled from various trade, business, and newspaper sources, underlie this study. Statistical treatments of these data are presented in the pages that follow in order to document change over time and draw conclusions based on the massed material. Transcriptions of the reviews used are available to researchers at the website vaudevilleamerica.org.[16]

What, then, does this study argue about vaudeville and its role in temporal relationships, structurations, and experiences? Although to do so would have been enticing, I don't employ contemporary reviews to locate acts of resistance, and I don't see vaudeville as transgressive in the sense that it violated moral conventions or sensibilities. Instead, this study focuses on how popular culture encouraged the values and attitudes that helped Americans accommodate and enjoy the development of a modern urban consumer society. Vaudeville's fundamental cultural contribution, I suggest, was that it made people feel optimistic about change itself: urbanization, modernization, consumerism, assimilation, and democratization. I arrived at this conclusion by asking three basic questions. First, what made vaudeville popular? Second, what differentiated it as an entertainment from earlier amusements? And third, why did it ultimately fail to maintain its audience and influence?

Given that variety shows had been performed for decades, it is important to ask why such an old-fashioned amusement should grow into the most popular entertainment of the early twentieth century. This study looks beyond those elements that would have been familiar to the nineteenth-century variety audience—the inanity, the fragmentation, the carnival—and concentrates on what was new: the celebration of commodities, fashions, and styles. For roughly two decades, vaudeville provided Americans with positive, upbeat insight into the latest trends in music, clothing, language, and humor. It exerted enormous influence over style because it democratized the chic. Vaudeville presented performers as ordinary Americans who, by dint of personality and talent, became stars. It then marketed those headliners as models of fashion and taste, if not always onstage (where some of them did outrageous things) then in their private lives. In selling this image of itself and its players, vaudeville helped to create modern celebrity culture and to link success to personality, pluck, and conspicuous consumption.

Today we see vaudeville as somewhat tawdry, its performers old, wrecked, and alcoholic, like Harry Greener in *The Day of the Locust*. That's a misleading view that ignores the spectacular and fashionable theaters that, quite rightly, later became known as "palaces." In its prime, before World War I, vaudeville was America's "in vogue" entertainment, an amusement regarded by its customers and operators as trendsetting, witty, and unconventional. Some great actresses, such as Sarah Bernhardt, appeared in vaudeville, as did a few opera stars, including Emma Calvé and Fritzi Scheff, and most of the leading singers of operetta, such as Dorothy Jardon and Fay Templeton. In its prime, vaudeville was known for the stars it featured, and the celebrities were its primary draw rather than the variety. Celebrities were not only at the center of vaudeville's self-image but also one of the entertainment's lasting contributions to modern American culture.

For a public that had few opportunities to observe commercialized life represented in a positive, cheerful, and actual way (as opposed to in print or through a shop window), the variety show filled a niche. It became, before World War I, a way for consumers to hear new jokes and songs, pick up amusing slang, and watch the parade of fashions and styles. And, unlike the musical comedies or naturalistic dramas filling the legitimate theaters (an area of entertainment known as "the legitimate"), vaudeville democratized those fads and made them accessible. It presented ostensibly ordinary people—speaking directly to their own kind—as glamorous, talented, popular, and rich. They were embodiments of a consumer goods revolution that brought seasonal fashion changes and popularized beauty and health products to ordinary Americans. For example, the singing dancers Ruby Norton and Sammy Lee, who in 1919 returned to vaudeville after three years spent performing in revues and cabarets, attracted a warm reception in part because their numbers were now all "jazz" (a relatively new music in 1919) but also because Norton's gowns were all new. The performer made five costume changes during the act, leading the reviewer to note that "her dressing" was at intermission "the sole topic of conversation."[17] The democratization of what had once been the preserve of the wealthy—a claim on contemporary style and fashion—was vaudeville's most powerful transgression.

This helps explain why modernist artists like Charles Demuth, Marsden Hartley, Ernest Hemingway, Kurt Weill, and John Alden Carpenter turned to vaudeville as a metaphor for modernity. In their minds, the variety theater was not so much a subversion or disruption as an ideal representation of their age. Other more cynical observers, like the writer Edmund Wilson, considered the pointlessness and disunity of the variety show to be a manifestation of the bewildering confusion of urban life and the "enfeeblement of the faculty of attention." But more positive commentators, such as Gilbert Seldes or the art critic Henry McBride, believed they were living in an age where "everything was vaudeville." By democratizing success, talent, and style, vaudeville assaulted nineteenth-century privilege. To Mary Cass Canfield, the modernist playwright and producer, vaudeville was "The Great American Art," and she praised it as a "throwing away of self-consciousness, of Plymouth Rock caution.... Here we countenance the extreme, we encourage idiosyncrasy." And the painter Marsden Hartley rhapsodized that "if you care for the iridescence of the moment you will trust vaudeville as you are not able to trust any other sort of performance."[18]

Like its modernist fans, I interpret vaudeville's irreverence—the convention-busting purpose of many of the acts—as a playful expression of early twentieth-century modernity. The variety show may have been decades old, but what vaudeville offered was very new. Vaudeville figured itself as the most democratic of industries—one in which anyone with "personality" could gain success—but also one that helped forge a new society in which leisure and style were themselves democratized. Variety artists communicated this message through a distinct approach to performance that involved demystifying entertainment and presenting it as something people might drop into on their way home, or when they were bored of a Thursday night, or when they wanted to do something fun in the afternoon with friends. And they presented these ideas not using the language of the theater but of the street. This helps explain why so many of the country's avant-garde artists saw vaudevillians expressing ideas and employing techniques they found inspirational.

Successful vaudeville players tried to simultaneously do something novel or weird while making themselves appealing to audiences, or to put it another way, they tried to be both unusual and familiar. This made them singularly well-suited to communicating the idea that the new was positive and exciting, which they did in part by presenting novelty in lighthearted tones. What differentiated vaudeville was that its performers acted as though they were simply real people showing off their talent; their movements, accents, stunts, and songs seemed appropriate to everyday life. Roller skaters and stunt bicyclists showed ordinary people what might be done on the rink or the road; animal trainers held out the possibility that everyone could get their dogs or cats or birds to do clever things. The singers and dancers and divers and acrobats often presented their clothes and figures as appropriate to the dance hall, restaurant, beach, or gym. Monologuists who delivered their confessional comedy routines hoped to influence attitudes to relationships, society, and the urban environment. Significantly, almost all vaudeville acts were set in the present (only 3 percent were not), and performers wanted, for the most part, to appear contemporary in their attitudes, appearance, and style.

Vaudeville theaters were very large (even the "small-time" ones sat 1,000–2,000 spectators), but despite the size of the space in which they performed, players wanted to provide audiences with an impression of intimacy, a sense that spectators were friends having a good time together. Except for those acting in sketches, they tended to employ a style that disguised the performance itself. Just under 20 percent of vaudeville acts between 1902 and 1922 featured players inhabiting a fictional "character" or impersonating someone else. Naturally, most players employed stage names and they were all "performing," but they tried to look as though they were not. In a variety show, acting was not a way of becoming someone else; it was a means of presenting oneself.

Kathryn Oberdeck referred to this as vaudeville's "aesthetic of realism," and I modify her phrase to describe it as an aesthetic of "actuality." Vaudevillians strove to achieve something more than the realism of the conventional theater because they wanted to model usable forms of behavior, talent, humor, or taste. They wanted to convey the impression of "authenticity"; they weren't just performing reality but were the real thing. Vaudevillians attempted this through discursive devices, the most common among them being the direct address to the audience (called the "direct appeal" at the time). Performers maintained the illusion of actuality by doing things that would appear untheatrical in other contexts: laughing at their own or each other's jokes, talking to their piano accompanists or the orchestra directors, ad-libbing, or explaining to the audience what they were going to do next. Even acrobats and athletes often had an accompanying attendant who would crack jokes, comment on what was happening, and generally get in the way. The direct appeal was the essence of "that vaudeville something," the entertainment's defining feature, and it would remain central to mass entertainment. In radio and TV it was used to humanize commercialization and mechanical reproduction, and especially in formats like "talk shows," it conveyed what radio and television producer Sylvester Weaver referred to as the all-important "marriage of spectacle and intimacy."[19]

Why did the direct appeal become the defining convention of variety? Partly it was a legacy of street busking and concert saloons. Variety, after all, developed as an entertainment for spectators who were convivial but distracted (whether because they were on the street or because they were drinking and socializing in a bar) and whose attention to the stage had to be earned. Saloon performers, in particular, took themselves seriously at their peril. But the tradition survived because it continued to have relevance, despite vaudeville's huge theaters, tiered seating, and distant balconies. Managers and performers were convinced that their audiences were as distracted as the saloon's and that they needed to be "woken up" and engaged. Odd though it may seem, vaudevillians saw their audiences as passive and tired, and they believed it was their job to not only excite them but arouse in them a feeling of community.

The fiction that vaudevillians were not performing a role made their challenge to expectations, traditional tastes, fashions, and manners all the more significant. Where carnival was a temporary inversion, permissible only because it was contained and unnatural and limited to the stage, the vast majority of vaudevillians normalized and demystified the novelties they incorporated into their acts. They presented an earlier form of what cinema historian Larry May called "the consumption allure" of film entertainment, an allure that inspired consumer behavior as a form of "mimetic rivalry" with the stars. As market researchers later discovered about television, audiences (and particularly female spectators) found "formal or super-sophisticated" performers less appealing than those who looked ordinary but "radiated grace and naturalness."[20]

Vaudevillians, like television's early stars, wanted to be seen as models of style without making their glamour inaccessible. This was not something one would say about their forebears in commercial entertainment: saloon performers, blackface minstrels, museum curiosities, or even the most popular actors of the legitimate, such as Edwin Booth or Helena Modjeska. Mass entertainment, in its variety format, presented supposedly ordinary Americans (albeit with talent or personality) offering a vision of how their contemporaries should look, feel, and act. Its popularity was in large part due to its role as a showcase for a modern urban lifestyle.

It may seem odd that a theater based on verisimilitude and selling modernity made such productive use of stereotypes. For example, around 3 percent of vaudeville acts featured blackface, and roughly the same proportion included "Hebrew" impersonators. All stereotypes are falsehoods, even when positive or empowering, because they collectivize traits and assign people to groups that may exist only through the stereotype itself. So why did a theater positioned as "actual" make such rich use of hoary representations? One reason the stereotypes survived was that they were frequently employed in vaudeville by entertainers who, in real life, identified with the group they depicted. In the early twentieth century, players like the Scottish singer Harry Lauder or the Irish comic Charles McAvoy intensified their accents, used an unfamiliar vocabulary, and sported ethnic signifiers (Lauder wore a kilt). African American performers began appearing in vaudeville in the 1890s playing stereotypically blackface characters. This authentication of types made them seem more real. And many of those performing "types" made a point of maintaining their onstage persona in private life. For example, 60 percent of illusionists pretended to be either Native Americans or Hindu fakirs or from somewhere in a "Mysterious Orient," and almost all of them maintained their stage identities offstage as well. In their case, a remarkable talent like "second sight" could not be a pose, it had to be "true," and this meant the stage character had to be made actual.

Consequently, vaudevillians were interested in enhancing the authenticity of their racial or ethnic performance, and they did so by using stage techniques. Some African American performers wanted their humanity to peak out from beneath the burnt-cork makeup, and they dressed or spoke in ways that subverted the crude racism of their racialized disguise. Other players layered one stereotype on top of another, actualizing their own racial or ethnic identity by placing it in an absurd context. Charles Hoey and Harry Lee, for example, were popular "Hebrew comedians" open about their Jewish heritage. Hoey maintained that the accent he used onstage was the one he learned growing up on

The Scottish singer Harry Lauder, outfitted in glengarry and kilt, with the German American magician Imro Fox, dressed in outrageous "yellowface." Ethnic and racial impersonation was variously used to enhance the perception of an authentic identity, to draw attention to the falsity of appearances, or to ridicule the people depicted. (Collection of James Marturano)

the Lower East Side. The trade magazine *Variety* referred to them as portraying "genteel Hebrews." Both performers dressed, however, in everyday clothes rather than in the conventional comedy togs—big hats and oversized shoes—of the slapstick Jew. And yet Hoey and Lee chose to perform their own ethnicity using many of the stereotypical tools. They twisted their sentences and laced their dialogue with malapropisms, as Jewish impersonators had done for decades. They also layered the stereotypes by performing in blackface when they told Jewish jokes. Imro Fox, the magician, did the same thing when he appeared in outlandish "Chinese" guise but spoke with a heavy German accent.

Absurd acts like these reminded audiences of the theatricality of the impersonation, but the transparently phony racial mask also strengthened the impression of the reality of the underlying "identity" of the player.[21]

Lending contemporary "reality" to nineteenth-century racial, ethnic, class, and gender stereotypes would prove to be one of vaudeville's more pernicious contributions to American culture. By playing their own race or ethnicity using stage conventions, performers made aspects of those stereotypes appear more authentic. But "naturalizing" them had another inadvertent effect. As stage falsehoods gained credibility as true, performers assimilated elements of them—a walk, a manner of speaking, a look—into acts that were not intended to be impersonations and used them as shorthand for values or ideas. For example, white jazz musicians who wanted to pay homage to black musicians appropriated the sounds, movements, and speech they associated with African Americans and made it part of their own "authentic" performance. Sophisticated dancers like the Astaires similarly "naturalized" the buck-and-wing and soft-shoe, even though those dances were initially made popular by performers in blackface. Nineteenth-century stereotypes, or facets of them, therefore continued to exert a baleful influence in entertainment because performers were able to draw usefully from their cultural or emotional associations. Unfortunately, through vaudeville, they now appeared not to be theatrical conventions but expressions and appearances that were "true."

The ability of vaudevillians to breathe new life into old forms, to market modern fashions and styles, and to provide entertainment that seemed to have use value to spectators in their daily lives made the variety show into a craze. Which brings us to my third question: If vaudeville was so functional and effective, and so representatively modern, why didn't it retain its place at the pinnacle of American entertainment? The obvious and most common explanation is that cinema killed it. The timing here makes that conclusion sensible, as vaudeville's contraction came in tandem with the nickelodeons' expansion. Considered from inception to death, vaudeville lasted from the mid-1870s through the late 1930s. But as the dancer Pat Rooney told a government inquiry into the business, it had really only "come to the front" around 1900. According to Rooney (who lived through it), the late nineteenth century should be seen as a time when the public was "gradually educated to appreciate the vaudeville shows."[22] Although the entertainment staggered into the 1930s, it had lost its leading position by 1922. A typical night of vaudeville in the mid-1920s featured three or four acts, almost exclusively comics and singers, intermixed with films. This was a far cry from the two- or three-hour bill of live performers, possibly with a film as a "dumb act" to close, which characterized the entertainment in 1910. The problem wasn't that both vaudeville and cinema were competing for the same market; it was that so many entrepreneurs gave up on live entertainment and converted their variety theaters to cinemas. They did so, either all at once or more gradually, by instituting what was called "pop vaudeville," a hybrid in which theaters offered a reduced number of acts interspersed with movies. The ever-increasing employment of film in vaudeville was critical to Hollywood's success, but why did theater owners do it?

Vaudeville had never been a homogeneous industry. By 1910, the majority of theater managers were running "small-time" houses, and only 10 percent were engaged in "big-time" live entertainment. Small-time theaters were not small theaters or theaters exclusively serving poorer people. Instead, "small-time" was a pejorative term applied by big-time competitors to those businesses that charged less for admission and featured few, if any, of the leading performers. But despite being belittled by their more pretentious competitors, the fact is that the small time was the most innovative branch of vaudeville and championed the entertainment's original business model: low prices, frequent shows (after 1905 this meant three or four per day), a weekly turnover of acts (increasingly, after 1910, a biweekly turnover or the "split week"), and neighborhood theaters. The minority of enterprises that called themselves "big time" broke away from this form of mass entertainment in the late 1890s and attempted to move upmarket. They offered two shows per day, charged significantly more than their small-time rivals, featured an "all-star" bill, and tended to locate downtown or on major streets near middle-class residential areas. The difference between the small and big time was similar to the one that separated chain and department stores: both were mass merchandising, but one sold itself on convenience and the other on the services and quality of goods it had to offer. What differentiated vaudeville from retail is that the owners of the big-time theaters created the cartels that before World War I dominated bookings in the industry.

The failure of live entertainment to compete with film wasn't simply a matter of ticket prices or the narrative appeal of the movies. While it is true that the price difference between big-time vaudeville and movies was large (a dollar or two compared to a nickel or quarter), it was much less in the case of the small-time (which charged a maximum of thirty-five cents in 1910). The problem, I argue, was that the industry's cost structure and its collusive practices made it difficult for vaudeville managers to provide affordable live entertainment centered on celebrities and fashion. The cartels that controlled bookings were a major factor in vaudeville's inflexibility. Central booking offices were by necessity less sensitive to regional or neighborhood tastes than local managers, and this led agents to be conservative in the shows they organized. Because the cartels controlled competition in terms of the salaries members paid to performers, the richer theaters were able to block rivals from featuring the artists they employed. High salaries became a way in which the richer chains maintained their monopoly over the biggest stars. Because the big-time theaters relied on their headliners (rather than on price or convenience) to keep vaudeville in vogue, they pushed up wage costs, tied themselves to a stable of aging artists, and became less attentive to emerging talent.

Rising salaries and promotional costs led a great many entrepreneurs (in both the small time and the big) to invest in larger theaters to keep relative overhead under control. Big-time owners, however, raised ticket prices as well, and they derived prestige from their one- and two-dollar seats. They also colluded together, and the cartels they formed prevented rivals (including small-time houses) from entering their "territory." By 1912 vaudeville had become, from the booking side at least, an oligopoly. When the big-time cartels were threatened by the small-time theater chains, they tended to increase wages for loyal stars while blacklisting performers playing the competition. In short, the competitive strategy pursued in vaudeville drove up costs as competition increased rather than reduced them. Only during the war would the big-time cartels briefly return to the ideals of mass merchandising and lower prices. But by then feature films were on the market, and the competition from other entertainment providers was growing. Vaudeville's ability to shape the overall amusement industry was at an end.

Collusion was, however, only one of the reasons for vaudeville's decline. In its prime, the entertainment was the cutting edge of modern leisure and offered a vision of a democratized style of pleasure seeking. Because of the attractiveness of the modern values it communicated, it became trendy, or what early twentieth-century people called a "craze." As newer forms of amusement moved to capture what vaudevillians had first discovered—the increased market for leisure activities—they staked a claim on that cultural preeminence. It wasn't just the movies; revues, cabarets, and musicals also competed for consumers' dollars. Revues were a new genre in the second decade of the century, and they presented themselves as smart, chic, and risqué. Cabarets, in the meantime, played on the popularity of dancing and jazz and provided unique opportunities for interracial contact. It was to the cabarets, rather than to vaudeville, that consumers went to hear jazz, the new music of the postwar era. Believing that audiences attended vaudeville because it was fashionable, vaudeville entrepreneurs scrambled to maintain their leadership over style. They did so by emulating what their rivals were doing—introducing more narrative elements in the form of films and one-act plays, hosting dances, and featuring mini-revues and jazz bands. Playing catch-up after 1910 was a sign that vaudeville had lost the swagger of an entertainment giant and increasingly appeared to be a business struggling to contain other, more vital, forms.

Vaudeville's achievements and failures were therefore both economic and cultural. Strangely, in view of the industry's importance as a pioneer in mass entertainment, the commercial side has received even less scholarly attention than the performative.[23] The economics of the industry did, however, influence what happened onstage. In particular, the reliance on celebrities to sell their shows led vaudeville managers to collude together as a way of securing the supply, and these strategies increased overhead and provided leverage for performers in their wage demands. The adjustments that were made did not save vaudeville but debilitated it.

Until the movies and magazines were colorized and films had sound, live theater provided audiences with unique opportunities to observe, admire, and hear the newest products. Although vaudeville developed as a way of relaxing patrons assumed to be exhausted by urban living, it did so by making modern urban culture appear upbeat and fun. Historians generally, and rightly, focus on the wounds caused by the social and cultural upheaval of the Gilded Age and Progressive Era. Few focus on the pleasures, but that does not mean they were unimportant. Variety show performers frequently complained about streetcars, fashions, women's rights, the hectic pace of business, and their domineering mothers-in-law, but they did not let modern life overwhelm or depress them. Theater chains marketed their positive, plucky attitudes in truly innovative ways. They pioneered the idea that commercial amusement was something to be enjoyed in the idle daytime moments or the evening downtime. They sold entertainment as a way of relieving stress, in part through relaxation but also by improving one's mood. As Michael Davis and other critics knew, the standard variety show was devoid of educational or spiritual value, and some of it was completely inane. But it helped define twentieth-century American culture by laying the foundation on which film, radio, and television would build. Drawing out the entertainment's contribution to making America a modern democracy will, I hope, bring us a few steps closer to understanding this ephemeral amusement as a transformative force, both economically and culturally.

CHAPTER ONE

THE VOGUE FOR VAUDEVILLE

URBANITY, COMFORT, AND CELEBRITY

TEN THOUSAND fifty-cent tickets were sold for the opening night of Oscar Hammerstein's Olympia Variety in New York in 1895, a theater seating six thousand. The doors opened two hours before the show, at 6 p.m., and in a short time the crowd was choking Broadway and the crush at the doors became alarming. "A well-dressed mob" pushed and jostled for admission, a journalist reported; "puffed sleeves wilted and crimped hair became hoydenish in the crush and rain: toes were trampled and patent leather and trousers were splashed, dresses torn and still the crowd pushed on." The audience packed the foyer in a dense mass and the stairs became impassible. Those wanting to get in jammed the doors open, and although Hammerstein shouted at the ushers to close them, he might have been directing them to stop the tide for all the good it did. The show continued until 1 a.m. so that the maximum number might see it, but when it finally ended, people were still waiting to get in. Hammerstein, needless to say, was delighted. "I have always liked this life; I have always liked this world," he told the audience, "but this life and this world have never looked so beautiful before as they do to-night."[1]

As Hammerstein knew, turn-of-the-century vaudeville was more than an entertainment; it was, in the words of comic monologuist Lloyd Spencer, "a craze." Managers and publicity agents came to believe that the United States had entered a new era, one characterized by the voracious pursuit of pleasure, and many attributed that appetite to vaudeville. Commentators were at a loss to explain just what it was about the amusement that made it so popular, and even insiders offered different explanations. Edward F. Albee, who managed the most powerful chain of big-time theaters, the B. F. Keith circuit, thought that vaudeville drew audiences because it perfectly suited an age when everyone was in a hurry: "The people that build great office buildings in a few months and change the skyline of a city every year have no time for long dragged-out entertainment," he explained. In contrast, a Boston journalist felt vaudeville "appeals to the impromptu impulse. Seized by a sudden thirst for entertainment, you pull out your watch, find it's 8 o'clock, know you'll spend an evening wondering who's who and what's what if you go late to a play, and so you decide on vaudeville." More critical observers worried that vaudeville succeeded because it was sensational and satisfied a materialistic people's thirst for sensual (rather than spiritual) gratification. Others insisted it all came down to economics: vaudeville was popular because it was cheap, though that didn't explain why so many well-heeled spectators jostled and shoved their way into Hammerstein's Olympia on a rainy November night.[2]

What made vaudeville a craze?

It's a complicated question to answer. The popularity of any leisure activity depends on a host of consumer preferences: perceived quality, novelty, price, availability, timeliness, and more. In the case of vaudeville, however, I believe its sparkling success can be preeminently attributed to the way it made glamour accessible and the rewards of modernity tangible. It wasn't just mass entertainment that was new in the 1890s; also new was the idea of mass consumption.[3] It was a time when people were adjusting to the idea that once unaffordable products—products that had hitherto been markers of class distinction—were becoming cheap enough and plentiful enough to be affordable, or at least desirably close to it. Many vaudeville players, as we'll see in the next chapter, displayed aspects of a contemporary style that they intended audiences to emulate. They offered modernity as a commodity. Of course, the number of acts was too great for a single, undifferentiated message to emerge through performance. As Sam Goldwyn reportedly said of the movies, people interested in sending a message should use Western Union. But the promotion of modernity as affordable luxury was less an overt message than a style communicated by things Goldwyn knew well: the performers onstage, the marketing that made them stars, and the physical space in which they worked.

Vaudeville was the ideal entertainment for the dawn of the age of mass consumption, when the ready-made revolution was making fashions more available. On a cultural level, the variety theater's appeal resided in the way it transformed modernity into a fantasy of consumption and achievement, a place middle- and working-class Americans could go to applaud success and laugh at failure, to gawk at the fashionable and snicker at the unstylish. And nothing symbolized that place more than the celebrities (or headliners, as vaudevillians called them) who onstage and off embodied the public fascination with success, fame, taste, and fashion. The stars did not just model style onstage; they lent their names to it by promoting products. The diver Annette Kellerman sold self-help books and a line of swimwear; singer Nora Bayes's face appeared on cigarette packages; and fashion icon Valeska Suratt lent her name to face powders and creams.[4]

Sophisticated critics, and those looking through the glitter-gauze that soon enveloped Hollywood, often rated vaudeville as tawdry and low-class. That image has endured, in such accounts as the 1960 film and 1975 television remake of *The Entertainer*, and not without reason. Even though many of the lavish picture palaces of the 1920s began life as vaudeville theaters, what marked variety entertainment was that it was a barroom amusement that had been dolled up and made family friendly. Its tawdriness was part of its charm: it was a little rough-edged (and therefore pure fun) for the well-to-do and a rather upscale pleasure (with truly highbrow moments) for ordinary folks. It marketed itself as at once exceptional, especially in terms of its theaters, the salaries it paid, and the talent it featured, yet marvelously ordinary. Linking these two was an emphasis on reproducible cultural goods: fashions and skin products one could buy in shops, jokes and songs one could learn, slang words one could use. The explicit use of advertising in variety acts was prohibited by management in 1905, but before that date, the connection between pitches from the stage and consumer goods had been overt. In 1903, for example, the plate-smashing jugglers Bedini and Arthur traveled with a set "supplied by the Uneeda Biscuit Co., and given over entirely to the advertising of that product."[5] But even after the ban on direct advertising, the idea of a "contemporary" style as a product that could be acquired was essential to vaudeville's popularity. Many women went to vaudeville shows to see the fashions, couples watched the dancers and learned how to shake their bodies, sports stars and retired politicians told spectators how to win competitions, and audiences picked up new ways of kidding each other.

Although vaudeville managers and performers promoted and commodified modernity, they were not consciously attempting to engineer, control, or assimilate the public. Managers, booking agents, and performers did not engage in market research, and they took it for granted, as Edward Albee put it, that "public taste does not have to be taught. It grows by itself." Vaudevillians used simple observation in determining what they thought went over well with audiences. There is no reason to doubt that they really believed what they said in their press releases on this issue: "Success in vaudeville depends on results. Do you or do you not attract and hold audiences? That is the only question asked."[6]

Vaudeville theaters, like chain and department stores, supplied a wide variety of Americans with ready-made cultural and material goods, tailored to their budgets and tastes. It did not offer them only what they already owned but instead what they might possess; in fact, it made them self-conscious about old-fashioned values, clothes, and ways of speaking. Down-at-the-heels characters were generally the butt of jokes, and managers and critics commonly criticized performers whose costumes showed excessive wear or were outdated. But even though they helped shape tastes, vaudevillians convinced themselves that they were supplying only what they thought the public wanted. They could maintain this because, at the turn of the century, when the whole idea of an in-vogue entertainment addressing all Americans was new, the public eagerly consumed what was placed before it. In giving audiences what they hoped to have and become and suggesting that anyone with spunk could make it, vaudeville expressed the promise of an emerging consumer democracy.

BECOMING FASHIONABLE

In the 1860s, variety shows were considered raunchy entertainment. While some of the "museums" that offered variety shows, like Kimble's in Boston or Barnum's in New York, were respectable places for families, most charged a dime (or less) and featured startling "freaks" and suggestive displays of dancing and posing women. Concert saloons, the other venue where variety shows were on offer in the postwar years, were barrooms with stages that served food and liquor to male customers while (generally female) performers danced, sang, and told jokes. In most towns and cities, concert saloons and dime museums clumped together in quasi-theater districts, a practice that both provided protection from the law and allowed customers on a night crawl to move easily between them. Brothels and gambling dens filled in these districts, as various entrepreneurs tried to cash in on the early variety theaters' clientele.[7]

Only in the late 1860s and 1870s, when changes in state law forced theaters and saloons to separate, did some saloon owners decide to move their barrooms into basements or adjoining buildings and to prevent customers from bringing drinks into the concert halls. A few entrepreneurs then seized on this as an opportunity to "uplift" variety entertainment by inviting women and children into their theaters. The process was fitful, hinging on law enforcement, location, and the individual managers' perception of his market, but by renovating, raising prices, eliminating explicit material, and closing their bars, "vaudeville," as the respectable form of variety entertainment became known, gradually emerged.[8]

A vogue, however, depends on more than just respectability. As early vaudeville entrepreneurs like Oscar Hammerstein and Fred Proctor knew, what really drew audiences was the excitement produced by performers whom spectators were eager to see and acts with spectacular novelty or (better) a little notoriety. It was not the conservative Benjamin Franklin Keith or Edward Albee, men whose horizon was gentility, who created the vaudeville craze; they were developers who refined what others invented. It was instead entrepreneurs like Hammerstein and Proctor and John Koster and Albert Bial, owners who in the 1880s and early 1890s understood that a modicum of raciness could be glamorous, who brought variety entertainment into vogue. They transformed variety by making a saloon entertainment into something chic.

Koster and Bial made their money running a restaurant in the basement of the New York Tribune Building, but in 1879 they moved aboveground to a music hall in the former home of Bryant's Minstrels on 23rd Street. Because New York law allowed liquor to be served during concerts but not in a theater, Koster and Bial featured only dumb acts (nonspeaking performers such as acrobats and dancers) and musicians. What helped Koster and Bial's become a fashionable institution were the high-quality imported European acts it presented, such as the celebrated Hungarian violinist Ede Reményi. Moreover, Victor Herbert, America's most famous civilian conductor and composer, led the house band. Spectators to the first music hall listened to the music while sitting around small tables as wine, beer, and food were served. It was all terribly cosmopolitan—"a little German, a little French, a little Russian" was how one patron described it—and a symbol of New York's urbanity. Visitors to New York were sometimes scandalized to find that women attended the music hall, despite the booze, in large numbers. At Koster and Bial's "you will see as many women as men enjoying a foaming cup. Again, I am not referring to common women, but women of respectable position," wrote a bemused visitor. A gossip columnist who attended an evening at the music hall in 1886 noted that "the dresses were a la mode, many were wholly modest, and several were expensive, and a few were in excellent taste and beautiful to look upon. At least half the men were in full dress." Even the inspector for the Society for the Enforcement of the Criminal Law had to admit that "the people who go there are very respectable."[9]

For many affluent women in the 1880s and 1890s, music halls were a guilty pleasure. When rendered by entrepreneurs like Koster and Bial into something sophisticated and European, the amusement took on a frothy naughtiness that cosmopolitans found exciting. What one critic visiting Koster and Bial's said of the "wicked" Barrison Sisters, a notoriously sexy singing group, could be applied to the whole enterprise: it was "pretty, charming, and not overpoweringly

An advertisement for a "family matinee" at Koster and Bial's Music Hall in New York, ca. 1893. The theater promoted itself as offering naughty but sophisticated amusement to high-class patrons. The idea of entertainment nurtured here and at other variety theaters and roof gardens in the 1890s helped turn vaudeville into a craze. (Houghton Library, Harvard University, MS Thr 625, Vaudeville by Town: New York City)

wicked. At all events, [its] wickedness has not yet been proved to any great extent. Koster & Bial's . . . is high-class."[10]

Although few fashionable Americans would count themselves "wicked" bohemians or decadents, that countercultural movement influenced their tastes, leading a significant number among the elite and middle class to challenge nineteenth-century social conventions in ways small and large. The cultural "rebellion" they launched in the 1880s against what one called the "gray-drab age" that "stretched round" them "like the pale blanket of a London fog" could take the form of unconventional clothing, manners previously viewed as outrageous, riding a bicycle, smoking, buying art nouveau bric-a-brac, or going out to a variety show. Variety shows, with their dancing chorus girls and European associations, were an especially safe form of rebellion. How deliciously fun it must have seemed when, one 2 a.m. at Koster and Bial's in 1886, some of the well-dressed female spectators started tossing the top hats of their male companions under the feet of the dancers doing a cancan onstage. "In some cases the owners objected to the ruin of their hats," a witness observed, "but no row occurred over the matter, as everyone saw that any resentment would surely involve one or more women in a disagreeable scene."[11]

The sheer frivolity of music halls such as Koster and Bial's inspired an invention that was uniquely American: the roof garden. The first rooftop theater in the world opened above the Casino Theater in New York in 1883. The Casino was a legitimate playhouse and concert hall, owned by the composer and impresario Rudolph Aronson. Aronson knew that the theater business collapsed in the hot summer months because people were unwilling to sit in poorly ventilated playhouses. He therefore conceived of moving the audience to the theater's roof in the summer and took advantage of a loophole in New York's anti-saloon legislation that prohibited liquor being served in theater auditoriums but allowed it outdoors. Women, he gambled, would not stay away from a bar with a show if it was under the stars. He was right. As a craze for Austro-German operettas enveloped the city, wealthy New Yorkers and affluent tourists took to sitting at tables on the Casino roof, drinking wine and beer and watching a musical. Like Koster and Bial, Aronson maintained he was offering only musical entertainment, though he lost his liquor license several times for running a theater.[12]

Aronson's magnificent idea was quickly imitated. Koster and Bial opened their own garden atop their elegant new music hall on 34th Street in 1892. But the most spectacular roof garden was the one constructed above the Madison Square Garden, a vast and spectacular amphitheater, built in 1890. The roof had a seating capacity of 1,200, with standing room for 400 more, which made it three times bigger than the Casino's. According to the Garden's management, entertainment taken on the roof was like an aperitif: "Here one can dine from 6 to 8 while listening to entrancing music, amid flowers and fountains, and then descend at will in huge elevators, taking a choice of the various amusements below."[13]

Since open-air entertainment was conceived as a light start or close to the evening, the roof gardens' move from operettas (which were expensive to mount) to variety show song-and-dance skits seems almost inevitable. The Madison Square Garden first made the move in the summer of 1892, and the other rooftop oases followed suit. Aronson, at the Casino, declared his roof would model its variety entertainment on the Parisian café chantant, and he began securing French cabaret performers in the same summer that the Madison Square Garden adopted variety entertainment. By the start of the 1893 season, all four of Manhattan's roof gardens featured some form of variety show.[14]

The roof gardens appealed to rich people interested in unconventional fun. They also became major tourist attractions. The spectators, one journalist observed, "generally appear in negligé costume, straw hats being the rule and it is only rarely that evening dress is seen among the gentlemen and never among the ladies. . . . At the Madison Square Garden, ladies sometimes appear without bonnet or hat, having evidently come in a carriage from some dinner party. The delightful unconventionality and the general coolness of dress add greatly to the refreshing gayety of the scene." As Oscar Hammerstein explained it, the roof garden at his Olympia Theater was "not a sailors' boarding house. The best people in town come here. . . . They order drinks, and are jolly and happy." The rooftop playgrounds of New York were the country's most celebrated ones, but other cities soon got their own theaters under the stars. In 1895, the first roof garden in Chicago opened on the twenty-first floor of the Masonic Temple building, and it adopted a variety show as its eating-and-drinking accompaniment. Atlanta saw its first roof garden built in the summer of 1895, above Harry Frank's New Variety Theater, and in 1898 Union Station in Washington was graced with one.[15]

Music halls and roof gardens helped release variety entertainment from its associations with seedy barrooms and dime museums and made it stylish. Entrepreneurs like Fred Proctor and Percy Williams, who were looking for a moneymaking popular amusement but who were uninterested in running saloons, seized upon variety's new, modish associations. Ultimately, what they did with their respectable neighborhood and downtown theaters was take an entertainment that was regarded as delightfully naughty and high-class and make it appealing to more conservative audiences. They achieved this by prohibiting alcohol and smoking and promoting the respectability of their theaters. As Percy Williams, the Brooklyn theater owner, remarked, music hall customers were "the sporting element," and those who patronized roof gardens had "Bohemian taste." His audiences, in contrast, consisted of everybody else.[16] But entrepreneurs like Williams and Proctor and Hammerstein nonetheless profited handsomely from the chic associations that late-night and rooftop ramblers gave to variety. Where the decadents and the out-of-towners partied al fresco on the roof or in the music halls, ordinary Americans consumed the now fashionable entertainment in more conventional surroundings.

The businessmen who created vaudeville did their best to preserve some of the glamour of rooftop variety. Though they catered to what were often working-class audiences, they insisted on conveying the impression of European elegance. Richly decorated surroundings were crucial to maintaining the idea of a fashionable entertainment. Vaudeville houses, as a rule, provided comfortable armchairs in the orchestra section, boxes, and dress circle, and many even had upholstered seats in the upper balcony. This was a change from the benches and wooden chairs that prevailed in nineteenth-century concert saloons and in many legitimate theaters. In vaudeville, comfortable seating was considered essential. At the Majestic Theater in Chicago, the seats sat on rubber-mounted ball bearings so that audience members could get up during the show without causing disturbing squeaks. The chairs at the Orpheum in Los Angeles were described as "big [and] cozy" that one "sank" into, while those at Hurtig and Seamon's in Harlem were apparently "supremely cozy" and "most comfortable." At the Orpheum in Kansas City, even the upper balcony, which was "for the exclusive use" of "colored patrons," had "comfortable stuffed leather seats" finished in mahogany.[17]

Vaudeville theaters offered other amenities. The practice in the Keith chain was to hire fifteen-year-old high school students as ushers, which gave the theaters a fresh-faced and informal atmosphere. Remodeled in 1901, the lobby in Chase's was outfitted with wicker furniture in the summer and gilded upholstered chairs and sofas in the winter. Flowers and trailing vines decorated the halls, and the auditorium had Japanese silk tapestries on the walls as well as little Japanese umbrellas and screens in the corners. There was a reading room for those who got tired of the show and a café that served ice cream sodas. Some theaters served tea to those sitting in the boxes during matinees. The Majestic in Chicago, which opened in 1906, had a marble floor in the lobby with walls of soft gray, olive green, and old rose. There was a smoking room for men, designed in nautical style, and a women's restroom painted heliotrope, gold, and white, like "a little parlor." The enormous auditorium, the biggest in the city, was decorated and designed to convey an impression of "coziness and intimacy, despite the largeness of the room." Most of the larger theaters, including small-time houses, such as those in the Loew's circuit, had powder rooms, libraries, cafés,

Tea being served to women occupying the box seats during a matinee at Proctor's Pleasure Palace in 1905. Both conventional plays and variety shows were presented in this innovative space. Proctor was not interested in lavishly decorating his theaters. The photograph shows the main auditorium's simple but elegant fixtures and furnishings, as well as the type of patrons buying the highest-priced seats. (Museum of the City of New York, 93.1.1.15643)

and a variety of subsidiary spaces for rest or conversation. Edward Albee insisted that amenities could make a silk purse from the sow's ear of the variety show: "I get people to come to my theaters to see vaudeville acts," he later explained, "and when they get there they find themselves surrounded by beautiful paintings, by architectural beauties, rare pieces of furniture, tapestries and objects of beauty. At first the layman may not appreciate or understand these things, but he gradually becomes familiar with them and learns to understand them. I feel that beautiful thoughts are fostered by aesthetic surroundings, and that many lovely spirits have been crushed by mean, sordid surroundings, and that a poor soul with mean degrading thoughts loses them when he is in beautiful surroundings."[18]

Variety's fashionable, quirky, mildly bohemian associations were a central part of its appeal as some of the naughtiness of the music halls and roof gardens carried over into vaudeville. Managers like Oscar Hammerstein were among the first to recognize this and to use it as a way of building enthusiasm for his theater. Hammerstein's Victoria in New York was especially known as providing "a man's idea of good entertainment," even though, as the manager insisted, "nine-tenths of the tickets sold from the box office are in pairs, and nine-tenths of these pairs of seats are occupied by representatives of the opposite sexes."[19] Vaudeville showcased what were considered, at the time, scantily clothed performers, especially women (though male acrobats also wore tights), and it was not averse to presenting moderately risqué situations in skits. The way performers undertook this work and the feeling they projected that everyone was in on the fun were part and parcel of the music hall/roof garden performance tradition.

What vaudeville managers accomplished was to turn the music hall into an entertainment that appealed to a majority of Americans. Although they managed to keep vaudeville at the forefront of American entertainment for a relatively short time—perhaps twenty-five years—it was nonetheless an impressive achievement. They did it by pursuing customers into their neighborhoods, making their stars important enough to be regularly showcased in the press, ferociously expanding their theaters, and advertising energetically. They also delivered on the inside what they promised on the tin: a hint of raciness, a dose of glamour, a comfortable atmosphere, luxurious surroundings, and a feeling that if you wanted to be up-to-date on the latest fads, you had to go to vaudeville. Theater owners boasted that they were improving tastes through the refined surroundings and quality performers they featured, but this was a rationalization. What they were doing was linking luxury and modernity to fun and frivolity and consumerism. It proved, for several decades, a delightful combination for millions of American spectators.

AUDIENCES

Vaudeville was not the first popular entertainment to attract female consumers and families—minstrel shows, circuses, and fashionable music halls already did so—but it was the first to draw a diversity of them on a national scale. In order to ensure that women felt safe going out to an entertainment formerly associated with saloons and dime museums, vaudeville theaters not only offered amenities but also imposed rules. The Gem Concert Hall in Missoula, Montana, for example, informed vaudevillians in 1904 that "performers playing in this house must bear in mind that they are playing to an intelligent audience and that 'any old thing' don't go." The Gem prohibited the use of profane language and banned smoking and drinking in the auditorium. A generation ago, the Keith publicity department explained, the variety saloon was not safe for women and children. Progressive managers, however, "emancipated" vaudeville from "peanuts, profanity and pugnacity" by enforcing rules of decorum. Keith's quite accurately described the process as a "domestication" of the theater. Even the Orpheum chain, which grew out of a San Francisco concert saloon, ordered managers to excise all "unclean lines, oaths, profanity, double-meaning jokes, suggestive songs, improper dances and offensive situations.... Under no circumstances should religious ridicule or the irreverent mention of or reference to the Deity be countenanced."[20]

Managers tried to ensure that seedy customers didn't offend the respectability they wanted to maintain. In Cleveland, the Empire Theater refused to sell tickets to men "in red flannel shirts and a growth of beard you could scratch a match on." Male patrons at the Empire, as at other theaters, had to be "well dressed and scrubbed" for admission. Those sitting in the cheapest seats, which were located on the uppermost balcony, or gallery as it was called, were also subject to policing by special officers wielding canes that were used to knock the hats off individuals blocking the view of others or to subdue raucous crowds. As late as 1904 in a theater in San Francisco, an enthusiastic Scot was removed by security when he began to hoot during a performance by the Kilties Highland Band. Special officers had the power of arrest, and spectators who were considered disorderly or who interrupted a show were removed to the nearest police station and often wound up with a court fine.[21]

These activities had an impact. As early as 1899, the *Buffalo Courier* remarked on "the important position the vaudeville theater has obtained among the better class of people" and the degree to which the legitimate houses were suffering. It opined that of all theater audiences the vaudeville one was "the most refined and cultured." The term "polite vaudeville" was coined in the mid-1890s to draw middle-class women to the theaters, and many, like Chase's in Washington, advertised themselves as presenting "polite vaudeville and polite environments to polite people." But in Boston, the *Globe* maintained, the word "polite" was unnecessary: "an entertaining [vaudeville] program needs no such qualification"; in Boston it was always "polite."[22]

Managers like Keith and Proctor energetically pursued female customers, but as vaudeville became a craze, even theater owners who did not expect them began to see more women in their halls. Sam Jack, a veteran of the saloon business whose variety theater specialized in lightly clothed female dancers and singers, found the increasing number of women attending his shows in the 1890s a source of wonder: "I cannot understand why this should be so, for I do not see that Jack's young women should attract the [female] sex, no matter what fascination they may exercise upon the men."[23] It did not take the wily entrepreneur long, however, to realize that women in the audience meant money in the till, though he made his theaters more respectable without jettisoning the pretty chorines that were his trademark.

The reorientation of variety entertainment toward women does not mean that they made up a majority of the spectators in vaudeville theaters. The presence of women at shows attracted comment in the 1880s and 1890s, but their numbers varied according to the place and the time of day. A Boston study revealed that matinee audiences were composed mainly of women and children, and in her 1914 study of vaudeville Caroline Caffin reported that over 60 percent of the average matinee audience in New York was female. Most afternoons, "women will arrive alone and in parties, especially at the uptown houses or in Brooklyn." A few men did go to matinees—visitors, college students, and "businessmen with an hour to spare before an appointment"—and observers noted that there were far more men at vaudeville matinees than there were at afternoon shows in the legitimate, but women were always in the majority.[24]

Evening audiences, however, were evenly balanced. In 1899 a Brooklyn reporter who spent some time studying vaudeville thought a little under 50 percent of the balcony and orchestra audience was female and the gallery overwhelmingly male. Caffin, who went out to shows regularly in New York, thought that unlike the audience in the legitimate theater, in vaudeville "usually more than half is composed of men." Similarly, Michael Davis's 1910 survey of New York theaters found two-thirds of the evening audience was male. But location influenced attendance. Francis North's 1913 survey of leisure in Waltham, Massachusetts, found that women outnumbered men by a ratio of almost two to one at the evening shows. This may have been due to the large number of young women working in the city's light manufacturing industry; Waltham had 30 percent more women than men between the ages of fifteen and forty-four in 1910.[25]

One group of women that generated a considerable amount of press in the early twentieth century were the "matinee girls." These reasonably affluent teenagers, with extremely large hats and bags of chocolate creams, reportedly sat in clumps close to the stage and talked more or less continually through the show until the star they had come to see appeared. The matinee girls were presented as the performers' most avid fans. They were said to read about their favorite stars;

collect autographs, photographs, and programs; and linger in groups around the stage door after shows. In other words, they modeled fan behavior. In the legitimate theater, favorite actors like E. H. Sothern and Forbes Robertson, the heartthrobs of the 1890s, were closely associated with matinee girls. But because male stars rarely played their kind of romantic roles in vaudeville, there were few who attracted this level of adulation. Still, some vaudeville performers were promoted as idols of the matinee girls, and not all were males. Women were particular fans of the all-female Fadette Orchestra, for example. In fact, some reporters understood that the matinee girls attended vaudeville not to see men but to observe the clothes and hats of the women onstage and in the audience. "The matinee girl," one critic noted in 1902, does "not pay close attention to the stage.... She found it intensely interesting to watch the women at this vaudeville show."[26]

The women who attended vaudeville came from diverse social strata. Watch the lines that form outside theaters at 1 p.m., wrote a Brooklyn drama critic in 1908;

> is there a dashing young miss at the head of it[?] ... Perhaps there is, but just as likely there is a woman fifty-two or fifty-three years old, in a neat but old-fashioned ready-made suit.... In back of her are three youngsters from high school laughing and giggling over their "really truly lark." Then see the tall handsomely dressed woman, in a broadcloth suit of the latest cut ... searching for a half-dollar to pay her ticket.... Next a tired little woman carrying a baby.... Three well-dressed young society girls are next. They have probably had luncheon ... and are out for an afternoon's enjoyment.... Behind them, smiling at their chatter, is an old, old, old, old lady.

Vaudeville matinee audiences did tend to be younger than those at the legitimate, and the "foreign element" was better represented. But the vaudeville fan was as broad as the society itself: "young and old, pretty and plain, rich and poor."[27]

In large cities most neighborhoods had a vaudeville theater by 1910. Smaller towns generally had two or three theaters in central locations. The leading vaudeville theaters in large cities were also located in the downtown, and these tended to draw a higher percentage of middle-class patrons. At the fancy downtown theaters, a journalist declared, "you will never see a poorly dressed woman among those who wait in the lobbies for their friends. They seem as well supplied with furs, feathers and hair puffs as the girls who patronize the more fashionable theaters." The women in the matinee audience at downtown houses, another commented, "seem mostly to have stepped in after shopping, as many of them have packages, and a rainy day brings them out in force." In order to help unwind, they chewed gum during the show. Gum was sold at the entrance to the auditorium, and "nearly everyone buys [it]. . . . It is part of vaudeville show etiquette, just as peanuts are at a baseball game." For many of its matinee patrons, vaudeville remained "a secret vice" as women were seen hurrying into their wraps and hats when the program was prolonged, "evidently with the desire to reach home before the dinner hour." Nearly all came with friends, and a critic remarked that "as you catch the drift of their talk in regard to the various acts you realize that they are vaudevillers of long standing, knowing the names of the entertainers and not objecting in the least to sitting for a second or third time through the same sketch."[28]

The limited statistical data supports the impressionistic evidence. A survey of vaudeville houses in Scranton found that the downtown audiences were overwhelmingly middle-class: 35 percent were "leisured" (wealthy) or had business or professional careers; 40 percent were from clerical occupations; and only 25 percent were working-class. This made the downtown houses different from neighborhood theaters or those in most factory towns. The survey of those attending vaudeville in Waltham, for example, found 8 percent of audience members "leisured," 18 percent business and professional, 10 percent clerical, and 63 percent from the working class. Only one study of the entire vaudeville audience in a big city was prepared, but in 1911 this survey of New York theaters found 40 percent of the audience to be professional or clerical and 60 percent to be working-class.[29] These figures were fairly reflective of local demographics, suggesting that, taken as a whole, and considering both the neighborhood and downtown houses in the small towns and the big cities, vaudeville drew a reasonably representative urban audience, at least in its prime.

While social researchers did not count them at the time, immigrants were in all likelihood a significant element in the vaudeville audience, especially in cities like New York and Chicago. Between 1890 and 1910, when vaudeville was at its peak in popularity, over a million immigrants came to the United States. By World War I, first-generation immigrants made up 15 percent of the population, with another 22 percent being native-born children with at least one immigrant parent. Because immigrants and their families were clustered in cities, their presence in places where vaudeville was strongest is almost certain. At the start of the century's second decade, 40 percent of New Yorkers were foreign-born, and two in three were either immigrants or children of immigrants; Chicago was only marginally below New York in the proportion of immigrants and their children living there, while 34 percent of San Francisco's population was foreign-born. This diversity was reflected among vaudeville players, who the anecdotal evidence suggests included a sizable number of immigrants and first-generation Americans. Around 5 percent of all entertainers between 1900 and 1920 were ethnic impersonators, and many of these came from the ethnic groups they portrayed onstage. But many new Americans and children of immigrants used assumed and transliterated names onstage, making their origins difficult to trace.

How important were immigrant communities to vaudeville ticket sales? It depended on where one lived. For example, around 1.2 million Jews lived in New York City in 1910, and of these almost 900,000 listed Yiddish or Hebrew as their mother tongue. Many saw Jews as "among the chief supporters of theaters in New York." Jews certainly made up the majority of spectators in most East Side vaudeville houses. Their patronage was so important that New York managers were extremely worried about insulting them and policed acts to make sure they gave no offense. Managers were relieved to find that Jews and Germans, unlike the Irish, tended to take "good humoredly the poke of fun at their peculiarities."[30] The Jewish audience in New York was not homogeneous, however, and while several vaudeville houses served the more affluent in the uptown East Side neighborhoods, even in 1910 the working-class Lower East Side (below Houston and east of the Bowery) did not have any English-language theaters. This was because the Jewish "Theatrical Trust" and the "Hebrew Branch" of the White Rats actors' union blocked English-language vaudeville's penetration of the Lower East Side.[31]

For first-generation working-class New Yorkers with limited English, there was foreign-language neighborhood vaudeville. Jews in New York supported an estimated twenty Yiddish variety theaters in the Lower East Side. Most of these houses were cafés or music halls, which allowed free admission with the purchase of a glass of beer or a soda. The largest of these theaters was the Oriental Music Hall, which opened on Grand Street in 1902. Similarly, there was an Italian-language vaudeville in New York, with theaters clustered around Spring Street. The evidence suggests that the fare offered in these theaters was similar to that provided in English-language vaudeville. The Oriental featured short sketches, acrobats, singers, monologuists, blackface minstrels who sang "darky melodies with Hebrew words," Jewish dialect comedians, and, on one night in 1903, a pair of Irish comics who "wore long red whiskers trimmed in Hebrew fashion" and sang Irish songs. When one of those Irish comics tumbled over, the other said, "I vill dell you der choke. . . . Dot was an Irish descendt." According to a reporter who attended that show, the young spectators were more identifiably working-class than most New York vaudeville audiences, apparently composed of tailors and sweatshop girls: "The girls come in without hats and the men wear their working clothes. . . . Among the crowd may be found, however, a small number of middle-aged men and their wives, most of whom come to see what the place is like, and leave it with the feeling that the sons and daughters of Israel have surely fallen from their high estate when they find amusement and recreation in such trivial and ungodly amusements." The most popular song in the show was "Sadie," presumably a setting of the Anna Held hit of 1902 (the reporter noted that the song was all the rage on Broadway), relocated to a tenement and featuring a sweatshop girl "who aspires to be a lady and has some difficulties in her attempt." In other words, vaudeville in Yiddish seems to have employed many of the same acts and songs as conventional vaudeville, though it did so in another language, to a neighborhood audience, applying locally meaningful references.[32]

Still, just because there was Yiddish or Italian-language vaudeville in New York does not mean that it was everywhere popular with all new immigrants. In 1913 neither of Scranton's most crowded working-class wards, its 14th and 16th—the former an area of Poles and Italians, the latter "almost wholly Jewish"—had vaudeville theaters, though both had several cinemas. In fact, in 1910, Sylvester Russell, critic for the African American papers the *Chicago Defender* and the *Indianapolis Freeman*, asserted that movies were the real "craze" among immigrant and black consumers, and he reported "stampedes" of people outside the cinemas, not the vaudeville houses.[33]

No group was more visible or less welcome in "mainstream" vaudeville than African Americans. Most owners believed that because white patrons did not like sitting near black ones, admitting African Americans meant a loss of white patronage. Jim Crow laws in the South allowed black and white customers to attend the same theaters but stipulated that their seating, entrances, and even ticket windows be segregated. When the Black Patti company played the Jefferson Theater in St. Augustine, Florida, in 1912, for example, the audience was black in the parterre and gallery but all white in the balcony. In other places, one side of the theater would be reserved for whites and the other for blacks. Most theaters outside the South also segregated their seating, but some, including the Lyric in New York, refused to admit African Americans altogether, even when black performers like Bert Williams were on the boards. Loew's theaters would not sell anything other than a gallery seat to African Americans, and they required black customers who did manage to get a seat elsewhere in the house to move. Only a very few theaters allowed black and white customers to sit anywhere they chose, and due to racial antipathy the theaters sometimes suffered because of it.[34]

Discrimination pushed African American customers to support "colored vaudeville" theaters in both the North and the South. By 1912 there were a reasonably large number of "colored vaudeville" theaters: Memphis had 5, as did Atlanta, while Hot Springs had 3, as did Richmond and Norfolk, and there were also theaters in northern cities that served African American neighborhoods, such as the Pekin, the Grand, and the Monogram in Chicago, the Walker in Indianapolis, and the Crescent and the Lincoln in New York. By 1922 there were reportedly 115 theaters in the United States catering largely or exclusively to African Americans. Unfortunately, most of the owners of black houses were white, and they did not feel black patrons were any more capable of enjoying high-quality acts than did managers of white theaters. Some critics complained that it was not black audiences who had uncouth tastes but the white owners of black theaters who "stifle progress along the lines of art" by assuming that "any kind of show is good enough for a colored audience and their only desire is to have a comedian and a few half naked girls on hand to keep the doors open." But in the South, especially, Jim Crow theaters were considered raw establishments by many touring performers. Henry "Gang" Jines, a diminutive singer and dancer, thought that the people he played for in segregated southern theaters were contemptible: "You give them class and refinement[;] it is not appreciated. You give them 'smut' and the manager hollers his head off, but the audience howls with laughter. . . . I am not writing what I think, but what I see daily." Jines was a New Yorker and had probably imbibed Washingtonian ideas regarding racial uplift, but others also complained about the audiences in southern theaters. According to a comic who toured the Jim Crow circuit in 1908, "The people down here don't want refined music and comedy; the majority of them want low comedy and we can't give it to them." Audiences may have varied according to the show, of course. S. Tutt Whitney, a performer with the Smart Set, commended black spectators at the Majestic in Nashville "for their intelligence, refinement and culture."[35]

Although poorer customers and African Americans often watched vaudeville in their own theaters, the fact remains that at its peak of popularity, in the decade before World War I, vaudeville remained popular with almost every demographic. Its audience did vary according to the location of the theater and the time of the show, but taken as a whole, it was popular with the middle class and the working class, men and women, white and racialized, immigrant and native. Mae West, the sexy comedian who played the vaudeville circuit, later recalled, "I usually found that one night a week you would get a top society crowd, and another night you'd get mostly working class people. Other nights there would be family groups." It all depended on where and when one played. The comedian Trixie Fraganza made a similar point: "You've got so many different kinds of people to be funny for that, believe me, it's rough going sometimes."[36] The attempt to appeal to all Americans was innovative and rested on the public's belief that vaudeville was a trendy entertainment. What made it into a craze was its atmosphere, its comforts, its fashions, its convenience, its frivolity, and its success at conveying the impression that it was modern and hip. Managers expressed vaudeville's entertainment culture in the design of their theaters and in the rules they imposed; players conveyed it through the clothes they wore and the jokes they told; and agents and promoters advanced it through the celebrities they marketed.

HEADLINERS

Vaudeville was the first entertainment to feature not just famous performers but "stars," in the modern sense of the word. There had been many well-known actors in the nineteenth century, but until the end of the century they weren't "stars." Modern stardom was ideally suited to the aesthetic of vaudeville, one that owed much to the entertainment's origins as a chic "European" amusement. In keeping with the performance tradition of the music halls and concert saloons, variety performers presented themselves as entertaining people in whose company the audience was sharing an afternoon or evening of fun. Rather than performing a role, most players spoke directly to the audience and often talked about their costumes, the events of the day, or the business of vaudeville. Even in skits, performers frequently broke character to ad-lib to the audience. This placed spectators in the curious position of feeling on friendly, even intimate, terms with a performer about whom they actually knew nothing. Artists' agents, booking offices, and theaters moved to fill this intimacy gap by providing audiences with the missing context, informing them about the private lives, tastes, and experiences of the stars. Where theatrical fame through most of the nineteenth century rested on the successful marketing of the individual's public achievements, modern celebrity involved the private being made public.[37]

The advertisements for products that vaudevillians marketed tried to make this case. Annette Kellerman declared openly that people who bought her

An advertisement for a self-help book ostensibly written by the diver and vaudeville star Annette Kellerman. Vaudevillians were commonly employed to sell consumer goods, and the publicity helped make them celebrities. The advertising featuring them often adopted the kind of conversational, even intimate, tone employed here. (*New York Times*, 30 March 1913)

self-help books would become her friend. Similarly, Valeska Suratt beauty products were sold in newspapers through advertisements that adopted a convivial tone. They featured the vaudeville star answering questions from worried fans, which culminated in her recommending one of her creams or powders. The tone of the star's answers were intensely personal: "Most face powders are too chalky for me," she wrote; "that's why I had my own made after my own formula." Or "[My] formula makes the skin delightfully plump and youthful.... Use liberally every day and soon crow's feet, deep lines, big and little wrinkles, and flabbiness of flesh will disappear.... Save your precious time by laying aside all the so-called wrinkle creams you have been using and try this. You will never regret it."[38]

This was something new, and it developed in the 1890s. Famous people had always risked having intimacies explode into scandals, and they resisted those moments. Edwin Booth came under close personal scrutiny after his brother John Wilkes Booth shot President Abraham Lincoln in 1865 and the family closed ranks. Similarly, intimate details of actor Lillian Russell's love life splashed over the newspapers when she moved to England with her lover, composer Edward Solomon, in 1885. But making the news because of a scandal or because of a public success or failure was tangibly different from media attention to a star's everyday lifestyle. Apart from the scandal, for example, and reviews of her performances, Lillian Russell—the country's most famous entertainer—received almost no coverage in the daily press in the 1880s. But "stars" of the modern kind, and this category includes Russell, who became one in the 1890s, had their private lives publicized even when they weren't transgressing social norms.[39]

Modern celebrity emerged in part because vaudeville audiences wanted to get to know the headliners better and in part because of the development of the print media in the late nineteenth century. The single greatest change to affect mass circulation newspapers in the antebellum period was the growth in the amount of content being devoted to society news, leisure, and "women's issues." Profiles of stars fit into these categories as coverage of how they set their dinner tables, how they exercised and dieted, how they kept their skin soft, and what they liked to read proliferated. Content for women grew in importance because advertisers wanted women to buy their products. The companies that funded press expansion pushed newspapers to increase their reporting beyond the Sunday women's pages of the 1880s and to provide more fashion and society news. Vaudeville was at the center of this push not just because it was at the time the only national entertainment but also because its press agents were able to provide copy to the newspapers. In stories about celebrity lifestyles, to paraphrase Ellen Gruber Garvey, fiction and advertising were enmeshed. Not surprisingly, as vaudeville press agents produced the stories and sold lifestyles, the image of celebrity they generated affirmed the entertainment culture of the theater in which they worked.[40]

Vaudeville celebrities were products of a culture that prized self-made wealth at a time when wealth was still associated with merit-based achievement, and this influenced the creation of celebrity. Headliners in vaudeville presented the projection of talent and personality onstage as hard work that was deserving of financial reward. "Every time I walk out on the stage," a vaudeville violinist explained in a press release, "I know that it's going to be absolutely about me. I work alone, if I fall down, I know just who is to blame.... My one idea is that I will show my spirit, or my temper, or grit, or whatever you call it, and get away with it.... That's probably what you mean by 'personality,' as it appears to the audience." Celebrity reporting became, paradoxically, a way of authenticating the headliner's personality and validating that his or her talent and common touch were actual. Celebrity was designed, then, to further break down the barrier separating the performer from the audience and to make the exotic lifestyle of the famous performer both real and, because it was derived from hard work and personality, available to everyone with the pluck to go after it.[41]

If advertisers in the 1890s were pushing for more leisure and society news, spectators familiar with vaudeville performers were interested in seeing that reporting take the form of stories about the performers they watched. The character of the reporting shows that readers were interested in making the illusion of intimacy less fanciful, by learning how much of a performance was actual and how much was acting. Because the turn-of-the-century media was not equipped or inclined to dig for information on the personal lives of actors, reporters got most of their information, over cigars and drinks, from press agents. The theater press agent, one journalist smirked, "must know everything, must have an unlimited supply of ingenuity, an unbounded amount of nerve, and the ability to hide two grains of advertising under two bushels of chaff." The volume of material they got into the papers was the measure of their success, and much of the copy they supplied was what some today might call "fake news." Theaters and artists' agents were generally able to have stories printed according to their own dictation "with the newspaper as simply a receptive sponge, glad enough to print a live, readable story, if it is well written and does not contain too much free advertising." This allowed performers, theaters, and agents to control the discourse and use the media to sensationalize an individual's life. The boundary between actuality and advertising therefore blurred, as Valeska Suratt's purported answers that sold skin care products in response to the "real" letters of "actual" fans make clear.[42]

At the turn of the century, entertainment publicists so abused their influence by releasing spectacular and specious reports—the most notorious one being the story of Anna Held's daily milk baths—that the papers became distrustful of *all* press releases. Press agents responded by making their stories more believable and supplementing them with potted interviews. Only a few—Alexander Pantages's vaudeville publicity office being one—were thought to offer reasonably factual write-ups on their performers. Other press agents used interviews and press releases to create colorful pasts or false identities for those players who needed the boost that a touch of the exotic might provide. In this way, theaters and artists' agents were able to advertise by providing what was ostensibly true information about a star's private life. In the case of more bizarre headliners, like the extravagant and oddball Eva Tanguay or the jazz dancer Joe Frisco, press "exclusives" served the opposite function: to inform the public that they were just ordinary folks and not the characters they played onstage. Frisco may look like a "rakish gunman" onstage, wrote one journalist, but in reality he was "soft-spoken, clean-cut and far from what he appears to be," while "if there was ever a lone female person who tried to mind her own business and live decently, it's yours truly," according to Tanguay. Once she removed the grease paint, an interviewer reported of Tanguay, she "becomes the quiet and lovable woman of everyday life. Her one thought then is for her home."[43]

The star interview or feature, often written by a theater press agent or the player's professional representative, helped to create modern celebrity. Stories about performers new to the public often sensationalized their life stories, while those dealing with established vaudevillians presented them as ordinary people and focused on their pets, home life, and taste in food. The childhood of the star and his or her discovery or rise was a recurrent feature of these interviews. This made sense because the mythology of vaudeville stardom was that anyone with talent could move from obscurity to fame through the mechanism of "discovery." It was a rare interview with Eva Tanguay that did not cover her family's impoverishment following the death of her father. Tales of hardship were especially appealing to publicists. Belle Baker, a headlining singer, explained in a 1915 interview that she started out singing in "Jewish music halls" in the Lower East Side for three dollars a week and had "an uphill fight" to stardom. Baker claimed she never went to school and that she was put out to work as a child in a shirtwaist factory. At night, she said, after work, she would hear music "drifting up" from the theaters below, and it "made me dream of the stage." When she was twelve (Baker said she was born in 1897, but she was actually born in 1893, so dates were as fanciful as everything else) she was given a "break" by the manager of a music hall around the corner from her family's tenement. A short time later, she claimed she was spotted by a talent scout who gave her a job in a dramatic stock company. In another interview, though, she declared that her big break came when she met Irving Berlin, "just springing into fame," who allowed her to "introduce" his new song "Alexander's Ragtime Band" in 1911 (she didn't, though she did introduce his "Cohen Owes Me Ninety-Seven Dollars" in 1915). At still other times, press releases claimed Berlin was a childhood friend of Baker and that "they promised each other, no matter what success the other might achieve, the other would share it." The contradictions and fabrications are less important than the general thrust of the narratives offered by stars like Tanguay and Baker. As with many other celebrities, they wanted to be seen as having triumphed over adversity, whether to justify the high salaries they were now being paid or to link themselves to the popular dream of wealth and fame.[44]

Although some stars *were* "discovered," others faked their own success. In 1909, *The Girl from Childs*, a musical about a sarcastic fast-food waitress, premiered at the Wonderland amusement park in Indianapolis. Childs was the country's first cafeteria-style restaurant serving inexpensive meals to working people. Irene Franklin, a popular vaudeville comedian and singer, turned parts of the musical into a solo act and brought it to New York. In 1912, the theatrical agent Raymond Hitchcock made plans to launch the complete musical on a national tour featuring an actual "girl from Childs," he claimed, in the lead role. "I've hardly got back my breath," the supposed waitress, Gertrude Clancy, explained in a press feature; "I feel as though my old world has been shattered and I had risen on an aeroplane into undreamed of heights.... A week ago I was a waitress at eight dollars a week at Childs restaurant. To-day I am a vaudeville star. A very short time ago I earned eight dollars a week and worked twelve hours a day. Now I sing for twenty minutes and earn $500 a week. I'm sure Cinderella herself!" Clancy went on to explain how Hitchcock discovered her and how Sophye Barnard trained her voice. The article promoted Barnard as a famous voice coach with a swanky apartment on Riverside Drive in New York City, a star who mixed with the world's "great singers and players." Yet Hitchcock never placed *The Girl from Childs*, and Clancy never appeared in vaudeville. It is quite possible she never existed. Barnard, however, was one of Hitchcock's clients, and she broke into the big time soon after the newspaper articles extolling her elegant lifestyle and prodigious talents as a teacher appeared.[45]

The narratives offered by headliners or their agents were tailored to what they thought were spectator expectations. The publicity was integral, for as historian Daniel J. Boorstin observed, it was the "well-knowness" that made people into celebrities. In fact, some vaudevillians admitted that celebrity itself was mostly hokum and that actors rarely received fan mail or had young women accost them at the stage door. What is interesting about the creation of stardom, then, are the ideas agents communicated to make their performers intimately known. These tell us something about the way in which vaudeville presented itself as both democratic and exceptional. Vaudeville performer Marshall Montgomery, for example, was born in 1886 and grew up in a middle-class Brooklyn home. He seemed interested in a performing career, though at twenty he was still selling advertising for a newspaper and performing ventriloquy at church picnics. In 1907, however, he developed a trick piano act where he played backward while standing on his head, and it got him into small-time vaudeville. Interviewed in Atlantic City at the start of his career, Montgomery claimed to be a student at Cornell University and to have played the piano (right-side up) before President Roosevelt and his cabinet. He also said he was the son of a "merchant prince" and quit university and a career in business "in spite of parental objections and gloomy predictions of friends" to launch his career in vaudeville. Later in life he retold his personal history, claiming to have been a sickly youth who doctors predicted would not survive. He now said that his family put him out to work and that he had quit his job for the hard life of touring "the tank circuits . . . through some of those one-horse cities in Massachusetts." It was a manager, he now related, who told him to add a ventriloquy act to his trick piano routine. Neither of Montgomery's personal narratives appears true, but each suited his purpose.[46] At the start of his career he wanted to claim instant stardom and to seem a curiosity because of his wealthy background. Like Sophye Barnard, his sudden appearance on a vaudeville stage demanded explanation. Ten years later, Montgomery's success had to appear hard-won, so his background became more humble and his fame seemed deserved.

Vaudeville stardom, like mass entertainment itself, originated in the public's faith in the democratic, open society. Combining a hard-luck past with current riches touched all segments of the audience, appealing to the aspirational clerk, the middle-class patron admiring the jewels and the gowns, and the working-class or rural spectators envying the success of one of their own. The riches, however, were especially important in substantiating a star's celebrity status. In repeated "interviews," Tanguay, for example, emphasized the fact that she had risen from poverty to extreme wealth: "from $4 per week to a salary of $3,500 per week." Publicists encouraged the talk of huge salaries because it created an aura around vaudeville, reinforcing the impression that it was an industry in vogue. The reading public, at least from the volume of material published on the topic, seemed fascinated with the salaries of vaudeville headliners. Imagine it, the publicists chortled, salaries in vaudeville were even higher than those paid in grand opera, the most refined and exclusive of all the performing arts! Every week there was at least one act in one's neighborhood theater earning a four-figure salary, and three figures for a week of work was the minimum. "This isn't fiction," declared a press release; "no wonder vaudeville is popular with the masses." As Eva Tanguay sang, emphasizing her extraordinary salary to the audience at Hammerstein's,

> My voice may be funny,
> But it's getting me the money,
> So I—don't—care.[47]

Vaudeville star salaries were a source of wonder for good reason. In 1910 the average American nonagricultural wage earner was paid around $700 a year and a successful traveling salesman about $1,500. Ten years later, white-collar workers in clerical positions earned an average of $1,000 a year, and employees of banks and financial services averaged $1,500–$2,000. Even white-collar workers and professionals reported working an average of eleven hours a day. By comparison, a starting salary for an act in big-time vaudeville was around $300 a week in 1910. How many people "do you know who earn $5,000 a year?" the vaudeville actor and writer Will Cressy asked a reporter in 1910. The "cheapest" act in a downtown house, he boasted, earned at least that.[48]

The salaries of headliners like Tanguay and Baker were the source of apparently endless public fascination, which appears to have contributed to pushing those salaries up, as income was a measure of the headliner's celebrity. This was why new stars, whom the theaters were marketing, were paid considerably more than those who made a name for themselves in the pre-celebrity era. A high salary was itself proof of star status, and this gave new headliners the leverage to bid up their pay faster than established ones. Consequently, older stars who entered the business around the turn of the century did not see their pay increase very quickly. The trick juggler W. C. Fields increased his pay from $400 to $500 a week between 1904 and 1910; nut comics Raymond and Caverly saw their pay rise from $200 to $250 over the same period; and ventriloquist A. O. Duncan's pay grew from $150 to $200 per week. Additionally, at the turn of the century only a handful of vaudevillians earned extravagant salaries, and all of them were men. One newspaper reported in 1902 that the highest paid vaudeville stars were George Fuller Golden and Ezra Kendall, who were being paid $500 a week.

But the number of performers in the upper salary reaches increased as the big time emerged and the craze for vaudeville took hold. Moreover, women, whose identification with consumer goods, advertising, and style best suited vaudeville's image, were now the ones who enjoyed the biggest salaries. In 1906 the French chanteuse Yvette Guilbert was paid $2,000 a week, and the Foys earned $1,500. At that date, singer Emma Carus was earning $800 per week, as was Sophie Tucker. Salaries of headliners appear to have risen quickest for female headliners entering vaudeville after 1905. Comedian Irene Franklin's salary increased from $300 to $1,000 a week between 1907 and 1910; Annette Kellerman, who broke into vaudeville in 1908 with her diving act, was earning $1,350 a week within a year. Most of these performers were onstage twenty minutes for the matinee and the same at night. To make a decent living in the big time, Edward Fay, who ran an independent theater in Providence, estimated a headlining act needed only ten weeks of bookings a year.[49]

Of course, celebrity players were exceptional. In 1902, the *Chicago Tribune* reported that a performer in neighborhood vaudeville started at $25 a week, and four years later the *New York Times* cited $100 a week as a starting salary. A typical small-time theater in 1918 still paid an average of $35 a week per actor. Expenditure sheets for two small-time theaters in 1921—Keith's in Woonsocket and Pawtucket—provide insight into salaries at more high-end small-time houses. Each theater employed around eight performers a night and paid them an average of $90 per week, with a range of $50 to $125. In a neighborhood theater, players were onstage anywhere from an hour and a half to three hours per day. It was generally agreed that a performer would need to cobble together twenty to thirty weeks of work in the small time a year, which would be a good run of employment, to earn a decent white-collar income. It is also important to remember that out of performers' salaries railroad fares and hotel accommodations had to be deducted. It was a tough life, and most small-time performers did not manage to work enough or had to endure costly jumps between jobs. As one former booking agent noted, "I should judge ninety percent of them are just four days ahead of the sheriff always."[50] Not surprisingly, performers flowed in and out of the small time. If they scored a hit and migrated to the higher-paid big time, they were winners; if they didn't, they eventually moved on to something else.

But the appearance of good wages, and the possibility of stunning ones, still drew thousands into the industry, though no one really knew how many performers worked in vaudeville. The Vaudeville Managers' Protective Association estimated that in 1915 there were 20,000 players, roughly half of whom worked in any individual week in one of the 6,000 acts employed. In 1919 the White Rats vaudeville actors' union claimed a membership of 15,000 (it grossly exaggerated its membership as it collected dues for only 3,000–4,000 members), which suggests that it also estimated the total number of players to be at least 20,000. Actual numbers, if one includes small-time and local talent, those trying to break into the business, and those who played vaudeville occasionally, would have likely been higher than either of these estimates. Since only around 5,000–10,000 vaudevillians were employed onstage in any one week, it appears likely that roughly two-thirds of actors formed a surplus pool of labor. Even popular acts spent a lot of the season not working. The dancer Pat Rooney, who was a solid feature rather than a headliner, estimated in 1919 that he worked between nineteen and twenty-five weeks most years.[51]

No matter what the reality, the image of vaudeville was created by its headlining celebrities. Increasingly, vaudeville's most influential managers (those who ran the big-time theaters) marketed their entertainment as offering actual stars performing live. So closely were the leading theaters associated with celebrities that the whole entertainment shifted to turn around them. Their popularity seemed the best way of keeping vaudeville in vogue. Consequently, shows were organized to gradually build excitement around their appearance (generally toward the middle of the show). The variety of acts became less important than the singularity of the star. This had a decisive impact on the industry as a whole. Less affluent or well-placed managers who could not secure celebrities were disadvantaged by the image of vaudeville that the big-time theaters cultivated. They had to find ways of competing in price or convenience or through less-expensive ways of drawing customers. This was one of the factors that led small-time managers to feature movies. Initially, films were a novelty item, but in short order they began to feature their own stars, celluloid celebrities whose appearances could be purchased at a much lower price than live ones.

Among the stars that big-time vaudeville promoted, Eva Tanguay was for several years the biggest. She was manic onstage, romping and twirling about, firing off funny lines, and acting gleeful, impudent, and childlike. The *New York Dramatic Mirror* dubbed her "miss tantrum," the "girl-who-wouldn't-grow-up," and a "peter pan in real life." But female fans, especially, were reported to crowd around her, packing the stage door to catch sight of her as she departed the theater, "crazy for a look or word" from the woman who blew kisses at them and called out "God love you." Journalists struggled to identify just what it was women liked about the star. She touched "a subconscious chord," thought one, a secret admiration for "irresponsible impudence and anarchy," while another believed she captured the frivolity and excess of the fin de siècle itself. Tanguay had equal trouble explaining her popularity, as she told the gossip columnist Dorothy Dix, "I am not beautiful. I cannot sing. I don't know how to dance. I am not even graceful." What she thought she had was "personality." Pinning down the quality of that personality was difficult, and the star said it amounted to being "always cheerful" and expressing the "spirit of youth." Another critic hypothesized that her "exaggerated ego" was not "the ego of [her own] individuality" but a realization of the dream life of the women in the audience "reflected in her." More important might have been Tanguay's preoccupation with her own vulnerabilities. According to a critic, "No other artist—it is an art to do as she does—would dare to ridicule herself as Eva Tanguay does." In an age that scrutinized and judged women and pressured them to conform to standards of behavior and appearance, Tanguay's extravagant defiance of proprieties may have struck a chord. In any case, what reflections on her stardom demonstrated is that people at the time believed performers achieved celebrity because they embodied the aspirations of their fans. As Tanguay explained, "They like my assimilated egotism because I say about myself things that every one would like to say about one's self if he dared."[52]

Female stars like Tanguay, as much as male ones like Gene Greene, made actual the fantasies of their audience. Onstage Tanguay may have appeared crazy, but when interviewed in her home she presented an image of fashionable elegance, refinement, and supreme wealth. In one potted interview about the Tanguay "the public does not know," an interviewer visited her "magnificent home" on Morningside Drive in Manhattan. Here she was a genteel "hostess ... careful and circumspect in her attention to every detail of housekeeping." Her library had mahogany furniture, upholstered in red Morocco leather, and rare books stacked the shelves. She often sat there, the reporter observed, "engrossed in good literature." The bedroom was lavender and gold, with the bed draped in a French canopy, and a tiger skin lay on the floor. There was a boudoir, a music room, and a dining room, which displayed her "refinement and good taste."[53] Homes and cooking were favorite subjects of star features, but so too were hobbies, lifestyles, and health. Stars had their exercise regimes, diets, hobbies, and cosmetics profiled in the press. Anna Held was regularly found interviewed about keeping one's skin beautiful and Adele Rowland about racing cars. Vaudeville stars wanted the public to believe they had risen from poverty, but their goal was to demonstrate, through their lifestyles, that every American could live like royalty.

The celebrities whom vaudeville featured can be considered emblematic of the factors that made the entertainment a "craze." Variety show headliners were at once ordinary and extraordinary, down-to-earth people from humble backgrounds who now earned vast incomes and enjoyed fantastic lifestyles. The star was the successful everyman (or everywoman), someone audiences were able to identify with because they could imagine themselves in the celebrity's place.

Vaudeville's creators built their industry on a fundamentally different principle from previous commercial amusements. By the late nineteenth century, patrons and proprietors in the conventional theater treated a night out as a luxury, one that was relatively expensive and where spectators were required to show up at a specific time, sit quietly, and dress appropriately. Vaudeville was an affordable entertainment designed for everyone that nonetheless sold itself as stylish. The theaters were palatial and the headliners' salaries were gargantuan, but beneath it all were ordinary people working hard to bring the public happiness from stages close to home. This was the foundation of vaudeville's pitch to the public, its effort to be at once modish and down-to-earth. And it was on this foundation that performers built their appeal as agents of change, exponents of a contemporary urban style. Their modern chic was something more natural and liberating than the hidebound conventions of the past. It was the behavior and art of the common people elevated by attitude and personality and handed back to the audience in the form of mannerisms, products, lifestyles, words, and movements that spectators could deploy in their own lives to keep themselves fashionable and hopping.

CHAPTER TWO

RAGGING STYLE

PRESENTING THE MODERN AMERICAN

VAUDEVILLE SHOWCASED the aspirations and prejudices of turn-of-the-century Americans. It connected leisure with comfort and luxury, made naughtiness and irreverence into lighthearted fun, found ways of including (even as it demeaned) members of minorities, and featured, in its headliners, ordinary people who became fantastically wealthy thanks to talent and chutzpah. In different cities and towns across the country, entrepreneurs initially tailored this theatrical experience to local tastes, but the underlying formula they followed—luxury and leisure twinned with a fluid connection between performers and audiences—was everywhere pretty much the same. Vaudeville players communicated the theater's approach to entertainment through a performance style that was direct, flippant, and unpretentious. Many of them sought to present themselves as exemplars of success in the modern world and were sassy, sharply dressed, quick on the uptake, and yet casual. Most importantly, the great majority of them made a point of trying not to appear stuffy or conventional; their moto was "act naturally."

Granted, actors in every generation believe they are making the characters they play natural or "real," even though when we watch or listen to recordings of artists from the past, they often sound stilted and rehearsed. What explains this strange phenomenon is that our understanding of what is "genuine" in a performance and our sense of how to appear "natural" in any given situation have changed over time. The ways people speak to each other, their body language and their sensibilities, and their sense of what type of behavior is appropriate to which relationship are continually in flux. Acting naturally in vaudeville had a distinct meaning that was both peculiar to the times and specific to the medium.

Naturalness in vaudeville was not designed to arouse sympathy or make people forget that they were watching a performance. Vaudeville provided audiences with a highly artificial entertainment experience that made them aware at all times of the space and functioning of the theater. Performers were announced by a board placed onstage, and acts changed every ten or fifteen minutes; players by custom acknowledged the presence of the audience and often addressed it directly; if the house had a band, the musicians and conductor were visible to spectators; the house lights were kept on so that audience members could see and talk with each other; and people entered and left the auditorium throughout the show. The "suspension of disbelief" that conventionally prevails in the theater—the pretense that the audience doesn't exist for those onstage and that the spectators are eavesdropping on something "actually" taking place—did not apply in vaudeville. Instead, in place of an imagined actuality, vaudeville offered the impression that its players were real people doing actual things in real time. For example, audiences were made to feel that Houdini really was sealed in that submerged trunk, that the singer actually felt the emotions she was expressing, and that the comedian's talk was spontaneous and the personal information true. Authenticity was the measure of the vaudeville experience, even if the acts featured relied on their own kind of suspended disbelief.

"Authenticity" is an ambiguous word for students of popular culture. In the nineteenth century, folklorists established the basis of our contemporary understanding of the term by using it to describe cultural practices that they believed remained unaffected by modern or commercial influences. This use of the word, while common today, is not well suited to the study of mass entertainment, a medium that is both commercial and modern. A more pertinent form of authenticity is that which flows from a performer's identification with, and acceptance as belonging to, a particular group. For example, country musicians who share some identity with their audience are generally seen as more authentic (think of Johnny Cash at Folsom prison). This form of authenticity was certainly important in vaudeville, but it was not the whole story. Japanese acrobats, French singers, and German strongmen did not share characteristics with most of the people in the audience. Rather, it was a third type of authenticity, one associated with performers who appear not to be acting or who are performing themselves, that most suits the vaudeville case.[1] Today, we see the survival of this form of "existential" authenticity in the rock musician's seemingly uninhibited, emotional engagement, in the daredevil's feats, or in the conversational style and autobiographical content of the stand-up comic's routine.

This chapter focuses on vaudeville's existential naturalism and how it underpinned the theater's modern urban style. It begins with a discussion of the emergence of ragtime, which I see as vaudeville/variety's defining style. Ragtime infused music, speech, movement, and racial ideologies. Because vaudevillians presented themselves as real people doing actual things, rather than as "actors" performing roles, they were able to make their ragtime-inflected forms of address, songs, clothing, and ways of moving seem appropriate to everyday situations. They were engaged in a performance of authenticity. But it wasn't just the actuality of daily life; it was the hyperreality of the trendsetting acting life. Just as vaudeville theaters provided luxury and leisure to the masses, many vaudeville players exemplified success, personality, pizzazz, and style for their fans. This chapter, then, examines the way vaudevillians used authenticity to turn style into a commodity for mass consumption.

Although we tend to remember vaudeville for its eccentricities and inanities, between 1900 and 1925 the largest groups of performers were singers, instrumentalists, and dancers (over 30 percent). Comedians made up another third of all vaudeville acts, and of these only about 8 percent were what were called "nut" comics and 10 percent engaged in "acrobatic" or "knockabout" comedy. The vast majority of comedians told jokes (or used malaprops or solecisms as comedy), with 10 percent being monologuists. Other than comedians and musicians, the largest groups were acrobats, jugglers, bicycle riders, roller skaters, and the like, making up 15 percent of all acts. There were numerous other act types—magicians, animal trainers, impersonators, lecturers—but none made up more than 1 or 2 percent of the total. One might conservatively estimate that between a half and two-thirds of all vaudeville performers hoped to be taken "seriously" by audiences, to the extent that they were mostly interested in demonstrating their expertise or talent. Although a majority of vaudevillians cracked jokes, engaged in comic banter, or sang funny songs, most of them wanted to be seen as amusing and talented rather than ridiculous. A verbal comedian or singer who did the odd inappropriate thing was different from a nut comic; their actions served to validate, not marginalize, irreverence and goofiness. The true eccentrics represented a small minority of vaudevillians, and their slapstick humor can be understood as providing a break from the singers, dancers, comic conversationalists, acrobats, magicians, and sketch actors.

Vaudeville's marketing and self-image and, in particular, its emphasis on rooting the people performing on this most artificial of stages in actual experience influenced the nature of the talent that players modeled. Had vaudeville targeted bohemian or elite audiences, as roof gardens or the Ziegfeld Follies did, it would have communicated more poise, cleverness, and sophistication. But since vaudeville presented itself as an amusement for ordinary Americans (even as it discriminated against the racialized and the poor, among others), its vision of a usable, attainable style had an off-the-rack feel to it. Performers were less inclined in vaudeville to disguise their regional accents, and they liked to talk about their favorite baseball teams or fondness for cold beer. Their version of the real was what they imagined would appeal to urban Americans who dreamed of looking like they had succeeded and who wanted to be seen as having "personality." This chapter documents some of the ways their idea of an authentic cosmopolitan style and personality changed over the course of two decades. I am not trying to explain here why that change happened—to do so would require discussions of purchasing power, urbanization, and the fashion industry, among other topics—but to document how it manifested itself in the vaudeville theater in terms of performance practices. My goal is to show that vaudeville performers tried both to be on the cutting edge of taste and to naturalize and democratize the very idea of "style." They wanted to model for members of the audience the idea that every one of them could be an up-to-date consumer, humorous, free from conventions (or their mothers-in-law, as vaudevillians often symbolized the oppressively conventional), and ready to enjoy life and make money. This was turn-of-the-century America's democratic promise.

EVERYBODY'S DOIN' IT

Vaudeville's impact was nowhere more pervasive than in popular song. Before vaudeville, listeners had few places to hear music performed by "professionals" other than those performing in opera or art music genres. Museums did feature singers, as did concert saloons, but few of the former, and even fewer of the latter, attracted women or families. In the age before recording, the primary way in which songwriters or publishers made money was through sheet music sales. Since women and children made up much of the market for sheet music, the connection between the producers and the biggest group of consumers was obstructed by propriety. Women did attend old-time minstrel shows and legitimate theaters, where they heard operettas, which helps explain the popularity of waltzes and blackface songs in the post–Civil War period. But outside of the largest cities, the professional musical theater and the minstrel show were seen only when touring companies visited town. This is why vaudeville was so important to American song. It was vaudeville that first provided popular singers with a national stage and that secured the link between the writers and publishers of music and the mass of consumers.

Popular song is therefore a good place to look for the cultural influence of vaudeville and to evaluate its approach to authenticity. This section describes the centrality of vaudeville to the growth of the popular music industry and some of the ways in which the variety theaters' naughtiness helped loosen sexual mores and reshape racial ones. Songs communicated messages to the audience about how acceptable it was to laugh and have fun, to express feelings of love or sexual desire, or to be free from inhibitions in public. Singers helped to normalize and make public (essentially, commodifying) movements and appearances and feelings that more conservative Americans believed should remain private.

Singing acts made up almost a quarter of all vaudeville performances, and they became increasingly important as time went on. Between 1902 and 1906, 15 percent of all acts featured singers; over the next five years that number jumped to 25 percent; and from 1912 to 1922 it stood at 36 percent. The steady concentration on singing evidenced variety's role as the primary venue for listening to live popular music. Because vaudeville played such an important role in the development of what we now know became modern popular music, it is worth taking a little time to chronicle the emergence of the new style. My objective here is not to provide a comprehensive narrative of popular music's emergence—that has been expertly done elsewhere—instead, I am interested in illustrating how popular singing became intertwined with new attitudes to authenticity and a contemporary style.[2] What makes the story so peculiar is that blackface song was where popular music took shape, meaning that performers had, at one and the same time, to impersonate and caricature a racial minority and reveal their "actual" selves.

Broadly speaking, in the third quarter of the nineteenth century, commercial song was divided between the lugubrious and sentimental ballads that were sold as sheet music, largely for domestic performance in middle-class homes, and the ironic, often ribald, songs that were sung in theaters and saloons. Waltzes, such as Charles K. Harris's best-selling "After the Ball," were also popular, as were sentimental minstrel songs of the Stephen Foster variety. Until the 1890s, more bawdy songs tended to be printed in "songsters" containing lyrics but no music, suggesting that they were not meant to be faithfully reproduced or that they were published for sing-along purposes. In the early 1890s, however, music publishers—inspired by the popularity of "Ta-Ra-Ra-Boom-De-Ay," an American minstrel song that became a runaway hit in British music halls before being reimported to the United States by English singers—began to produce more risqué, comic material with words and music intended for home performance. The success of these songs was related to the growing popularity of variety shows, which made a hint of naughtiness more acceptable to middle-class music consumers. For example, Feist Music Publishers' 1892 release "Her Golden Hair Was Hanging Down Her Back," a song made popular on the variety stage by Eunice Vance, told the story of a country girl who went to New York and contained such playful lyrics as

> When she left the village she was shy,
> But alas, and alack! She's gone back
> With a naughty little twinkle in her eye.[3]

What made songs like this, which winked at promiscuity, acceptable as parlor entertainment was that singers were able to distance themselves from the material through their narrative approach. The lyrics are in unidiomatic, refined English and do not require the singer to become the working-class girl they depict. The pathos, or comedy, came from the third-person narration itself. Telling a risqué story (sometimes from a reproachful perspective) was different from seeming to become a naughty person, and it was through narrative that genteel people were able to cross boundaries of respectability without impugning their own reputations.

The naughtiness of a song like "Ta-Ra-Ra-Boom-De-Ay," which celebrated flirting, became several degrees hotter when, in the mid-1890s, a new type of risqué song began to be sung in vaudeville, one that featured stories about African American murderers, drunks, and prostitutes. Minstrel songs had been sung in America since the 1830s, but they had generally dealt with rural southerners (which is why they were called "plantation songs" in vaudeville). The new type of racialized music was called the "coon" song or "coon" shout, and it differed from the dominant minstrel form in depicting the black urban underclass. Songs about poor people and criminals had appeared in saloon songsters for decades, but they did not tend to show up in middle-class sheet music, and "coon" shouts succeeded thanks to their popularity on the variety stage. The evidence from performances at glees and charity events suggest that well-to-do people not only were happy to buy the "coon" sheet music but also performed the songs in public (the most recorded singer of "coon" songs was just such an amateur, the Washington lawyer Arthur Collins).

Many factors contributed to late nineteenth-century white interest in African American poverty, crime, and violence, but concerns over what an emancipated black population would do with its freedom and how white people would maintain their racial supremacy were paramount. The possibility that African

Americans might move away from the rural South in large numbers worried white urban people, in all parts of the country. Hundreds of African Americans were lynched between 1880 and 1900, and while each of these killings had its specific character, all were an exercise of white communal power. Industrialization, urban crowding, and the growth of a diverse working-class population motivated new laws to segregate and subdue African American residents and migrants. Depictions of black criminality or poverty or sexuality helped to justify white beliefs in African American inferiority and the necessity of repression.[4] For those in the entertainment business, the development of African American commercial theater and the presence of black performers on white stages made these issues even more salient. It was a small step at the time, though it seems a large one today, to heighten the authenticity of slightly risqué minstrel tunes like "Ta-Ra-Ra-Boom-De-Ay" by grounding the narrative in white fear of black behavior.

The term "coon" was pejorative, and the lyrics of "coon" songs demeaned African Americans, just as the "shouting" style of their delivery separated them from other types of songs. The first of the new "coon" songs was written by an African American minstrel, Ben Harney, who was in the process of moving from the touring minstrel show into the more lucrative variety business. Like many black performers before him, Harney gained acceptance in the predominantly white entertainment business by caricaturing African Americans. Harney's first "coon" song was, in all likelihood, a transcription of a "bad man" song he heard in a saloon or brothel. According to his publisher, when Harney came to him in 1893 with "You've Been a Good Old Wagon but You Done Broke Down," he could play the music but had "no more idea than a monkey as to how to write" it. If the statement about notation is true, rather than a continuance of the racist slur—and we do know that Harney worked with John Biller, the music director of Macauley's vaudeville theater in Louisville, to create a score for the song—then the composer may have heard it performed somewhere and had difficulty transcribing it because it used pitch variably.[5]

Harney produced a number of "coon" songs that he sang in his vaudeville act, and they sold reasonably well as sheet music. Not surprisingly, their success inspired others to take up the genre. The first "coon" shout to become a phenomenal hit was the "Bully Song" by the white composer Charles Trevathan, published in 1896.[6] Trevathan offered the song to the popular singing comedian May Irwin, who first performed it in a musical comedy, "The Widow Jones," before bringing it to vaudeville. Here it achieved runaway national success, both onstage and as sheet music. The words of the "Bully Song" depict a primitive struggle on the streets as one tough guy (or bully) murders a rival who challenges him for control of the neighborhood:

> I went to a wingin' down at Parson Jones'.
> Took along my trusty blade to carve dat nigger's bones.
> Just a-lookin' for dat bully, to hear his groans...
>
> When I got through with bully, a doctor and a nurse
> Wa'n't no good to dat nigger, so they put him in a hearse.
> A cyclone couldn't have tore him up much worse.
>
> You don't hear 'bout dat nigger dat treated folks so free.
> Go down upon the levee and his face you'll never see.
> Dere's only one boss bully and dat one is me.[7]

So popular with vaudeville audiences did the "Bully Song" and music modeled on it become that one publisher declared in 1898 that in his business "everything is coon!" That may have been the perception, but "coon" songs in the later 1890s remained the musical property of variety performers and those who wanted to sound like them as they sang at the parlor piano. According to historian Karl Hagstrom Miller, of roughly 100,000 songs published in the United States in the late 1890s, only 600 or so were "coon" songs. Still, thanks to vaudeville, "coon" songs became big sheet-music sellers (Ernest Hogan's "All Coons Look Alike to Me" of 1896 earned the hefty sum of $26,000 in the first six months of its release), and they revolutionized American music. "Coon" shouts provided mainstream writers, performers, and consumers with new ways of exploring taboo themes and marginalized characters. In doing so they smashed conventional boundaries and proprieties in popular music. When they performed "coon" shouts in the parlor or in a glee, respectable white people were singing in lighthearted ways about murder, theft, gambling, and sex.[8]

Ben Harney may have performed the first "coon" song, but by the late 1890s the most popular "coon" singers were white, and a majority were women. Ashton Stevens, the eminent critic, noted that until 1898 he "used to think that what is called the modern coon song was entirely the invention of the white person and that only the white person could sing it with the real fancy flavor and the light pumpkin-colored insinuation." Stevens's reference to the color of the singers' "pumpkin" tone is important, because "coon" singers, unlike their blackface forebears, made little effort to engage in an over-the-top characterization of black speech or manner. May Irwin, the "coon" song's premier white exponent, for example, had a big voice and clear diction, as did contemporaries like Clarice Vance and Billy Golden. But judging from the recordings they made in 1905–7, they almost never "broke" a line to emphasize some point in the narrative, and they did not accent the upbeat, which would have added characteristics from African American song. As a white columnist observed, "until you hear" Harney or another African American render a "coon" song, "you will never know the true essence of the song" and in particular its "subtle emphasis," or what he called its "rag ripple." Rather than appropriating African American musical style, what characterized the performance of "coon" songs by white vaudevillians was their extreme volume and wild use of pitch. For good reason, their work came to be known as shouting. "Nobody sings well—is supposed to sing well ... only loud," a manager explained to a would-be "coon" singer in a 1914 comedy sketch. Sophie Tucker, a leading "coon" singer in the first years of the new century, admitted that she never "sang" her songs: "You don't have to sing.... You tell 'em the sad story of Mistah Napoleon Brown an' Miss Carolina Anastasia Jones.... But you don't sing." Tucker made this comment in 1915, by which time she was comfortably ragging tunes, but her point remained valid: "coon" singing was about the characterization and the story, not the music.[9]

It was the piquant stories that "coon" shouters told that audiences seemed to most enjoy. In vaudeville, "coon" singing was less about racial impersonation than it was about depicting exotic characters and situations. In this way, as we shall see below, "coon" songs served to transfer possession over aspects of an imagined "blackness" to white people. Elizabeth Murray, for example, a popular Irish American singer, was called a "storyteller and singer of coon ballads." Telling stories in song was nothing new, but "coon" shouters broke with conventions of the ballad by rejected sentimentality and even empathy. It was, after all, hard to project empathy with the characters in a story when one was bellowing. As Sophie Tucker explained, the "coon" song "has given a wonderful spur to music hall specialties—both in music and dancing—lively, gingery and full of red-blood humor. What a contrast to the popular songs of a generation ago— 'She Sleeps under the Willows,' 'A Flower from My Angel Willie's Grave' and all that lugubrious stuff. I wonder that they lived through that teary epidemic." "Coon" shouts were delivered in a drop-anchor-and-sing way, without much emotional engagement or nuance. The evidence of recordings from early in the twentieth century by stars like Marie Cahill and May Irwin suggests that "coon" shouters had lots of volume, but they were lacking in spontaneity. Rhythmically, they march rather than swing, and they employ diction designed to reveal the text as clearly as possible. This was not because sound technology at the time demanded stiffness (Enrico Caruso, for example, sounds impulsive in his early recordings) but because of the peculiarities of largely untrained singers shouting in a 1,500-seat vaudeville theater. Crisp pronunciation was considered more important than a melodious voice or emotion and was necessary so people could understand the story that the singer was booming to the gallery.[10]

There were also gender- and race-based reasons for the unempathetic nature of "coon" singing at the turn of the century. In shouting "coon" stories, singers were describing African Americans, but the women had to be careful to limit their racial impersonation to vocabulary and modest accenting. It is notable that Sophie Tucker was one of very few "coon" shouters to paint herself black or attempt to emulate the undulating vocalizations associated with praise songs and field hollers. Female singers needed to be seen as people telling someone else's story, not their own. Sung "in the white man's dialect," a critic remarked in 1899, the lyrics of most "coon" songs "would be positively objectionable . . . but when couched in the flash nigger's lingo even the frankest of these songs seems [to be made] humorous and harmless."[11] Making the song harmless by grounding it in a vocal caricature without going so far as to risk being taken for the "racialized other" was essential for white vaudevillians.

Marie Cahill, for example, employed a stilted, transatlantic accent in the verse of "Under the Bamboo Tree" (Victor 45125), switching to the conventional "black" dialect only in the chorus. Even Bert Williams, an African American performer, who billed himself as a "real 'coon,'" distanced himself from the content of "coon" songs with a ponderous tone, clear diction, and formal, Anglicized pronunciation. In Williams's case, the effect is ironic, but there was no irony in the singing of his white female contemporaries. "Coon" songs were absorbed into the nineteenth-century narrative tradition, and telling an amusing or piquant story with modest African American characteristics was more important than trying to sound "authentic."[12]

The stentorian style of singing and depersonalization of the story carried over into other aspects of "coon" performance. Shouters like Irwin, Cahill, Tucker, and Emma Carus did not move much onstage and generally described what they did as "swaying." Valeska Suratt, considered the living embodiment of the Gibson girl, did nothing more than a "walking step" when she sang "coon" songs. Irwin and Cahill and Bert Williams and Anna Held used their eyes and hands for emphasis rather than moved their bodies. Very few performers at the turn of the century—Etta Chapman, who enjoyed a brief career as a "coon" shouter in vaudeville was an exception—moved onstage. Chapman, who had the conventional "voice like the edge of a newly sharpened knife," was considered a novelty because she wiggled her hips slightly while she sang, to the apparent delight of the gallery audience. Generally speaking, however, whatever titillation or joy white people derived from singing "All Coons Look Alike to Me" came from the text.[13]

In the case of female "coon" singers, the stiffness of the clothing and the size of the performer contributed to their immobility. Fat was considered an asset to female performers in the 1890s, and most "coon" shouters were big. Today we are predisposed to see fat as unrestrained flesh, "soft, loose, or wiggly," in the words of Susan Bordo. But the sexy plump body of the 1890s was very much bound, constricted, manufactured, and constructed. The ideal theatrical legs of the 1890s had to be "stout legs, massive legs," and they were often padded with lamb's wool "symmetricals" so that they appeared more rounded at the thigh and calf and the ankles looked small and dainty. Similarly, a good corset maker, as a Jewish monologuist explained, knew "what he can do with your fat. . . . Where there isn't too much, he makes it more, where it advances he makes it retreat, he pushes it from where it ain't wanted to where it should be." Stout vaudevillians squished their waists into corsets and padded their breasts and hips because "massiness, as a general thing, passes for perfection of form and the [singer's] voice . . . is welcomed if only it emanates from a mountain of flesh."[14] It was hard for players to move freely when they were encased in layers of fabric and rigidly bound in stiff corsets. Gliding, trotting, and shaking demanded less structured clothing, which helps explain why early vaudeville singers tended to remain immobile.

The "coon" song phenomenon therefore introduced new features while remaining firmly grounded in older ones. Although it was the first type of popular song to be closely linked to vaudeville and embodied the variety theater's slightly naughty, racially intolerant aesthetic, it remained within the narrative song tradition. Vaudeville shouters struggled to preserve their respectability even when singing about, and in the character of, poor, violent, and promiscuous African Americans. This allowed them, though, to keep the focus on themselves rather than on the characters they depicted, and they were among the first popular artists to be strongly identified with particular songs. Audiences demanded that May Irwin sing the "Bully Song" whenever she appeared, which became such an annoyance that in 1898 she announced she would never sing it again.[15] But the most important change initiated by the "coon" shout, although it was more subtly musical, would spark a music revolution within a few years.

Once again, it was Ben Harney who launched the movement among vaudevillians. The sudden hit status of the "coon" song marginalized its creator, and

Harney countered by drawing attention to elements in the new form that white composers and singers neglected. In 1896, he introduced an influential variety act in which he lectured, played the piano, and sang while a partner illustrated buck-and-wing dancing, an old favorite in minstrel shows but an apparent novelty in vaudeville. In the talk Harney gave to explain the songs and dances, he declared himself the creator (perhaps "translator" is a better term, as he said the style was already "known among Southern darkies") of a new music he called "rag time." According to many commentators, the term came from the fact that Harney syncopated his "coon" compositions as well as plantation tunes, the effect "being to make the melody ragged."[16]

Around 1900, white composers picked up on the syncopation Harney and his ragtime dancers demonstrated in vaudeville and began adapting it to various song types. Marches had been a staple of the song repertoire for some time, but "coon" songs, also in 2/4 time, had an unusual bounce that implied dancing. This drew even more notice when the cakewalk, an African American march, was first featured in vaudeville in 1896. The origin of the cakewalk is unclear, though by 1870 it was known as an African American festive march used in community gatherings, such as church parties, where couples walked as elegantly as possible around a hall, with a prize going to the pair that demonstrated the most grace. It was soon adopted by minstrel shows, which used the walk as a closing number because it allowed the various performers to parade around the stage and be individually applauded. In these shows, the march was made funny, and it was here that the tradition started of accompanying the walkabout with a jerky, amusing tune. The cakewalk came to vaudeville as part of a wave of minstrel show–inspired dances and songs introduced in the late 1890s by performers like Harney, Ernest Hogan, George Fuller Golden, and Lew Dockstader, all of whom hoped to profit from the new interest in things African American sparked by the "coon" song. Songs in 2/4 time became standard, many of which had the cakewalk meter of short-long-short-long-long. Even waltzes were turned into two steps, which were increasingly being called rags, either by hesitating on or taking two short steps on the first beat. Although the "coon" songs that white people composed in the early twentieth century tended not to be syncopated, the cakewalk did spread the idea of stressing the offbeat.[17]

It wasn't just the syncopation that distinguished the new ragtime music. As Sophie Tucker explained, getting the new music across meant communicating a "raggy, snappy swing that makes a person want to dance." One Indianapolis fan, interviewed a lifetime later, recalled people in that city called ragging "clogging" in recognition of its foot-stomping quality. The Chicago ragtime composer, publicist, and teacher Axel Christensen admitted in 1915 that there was no "exact and proper definition of ragtime" and instead put the emphasis on its physical impact. It was "the kind [of music] that makes the heart throb and the blood tingle—that makes the feet shuffle and the mouth pucker—that makes you forget your troubles and worries and feel at peace with the entire universe."[18] It was this that made ragtime such a useful tool in vaudeville performers' efforts to make audiences feel peppy.

RAGTIME

The impact of the variety theater on popular song was already becoming apparent in the "coon" shout. Although "coon" singers were storytellers, they were also the focus of audience attention. They were not simply communicating material; the song was communicating their personality. The importance of actuality in performance encouraged musicians, and the songwriters who wrote for them, to shift from telling stories in song to offering a more personal statement that ostensibly expressed their feelings and experiences. In so doing, singers redirected attention from the narrative elements toward their own personalities. This reinforced the illusion of truth and intimacy in the variety theater and fed the celebrity culture that vaudeville was nurturing.

The individualization of songs sometimes created a tension between the performer and the material. Unused to the link forged between personality and material that celebrity brought, some performers complained of the chains that bound them to a particular song or gag. The comedian DeWolf Hopper, for example, like other headliners who wanted to act "naturally," had a "catchy way of taking an audience into his confidence." The public, one reporter noted, "take naturally to a man whose native sense of humor is so strong." Hopper's manner, however, was dominated by the same struggle between respectability and salaciousness that characterized "coon" shouting. In the 1890s Hopper would appear before the curtain and declare that he was going to say what he really thought "and then proceeded to say what was probably just opposite," as the *Chicago Tribune*'s critic remarked. His manner was that of the late nineteenth-century elocutionist—pompous and artificial—and he delivered his lines in a "mock-egotistical style well known to listeners." But Hopper had a star vehicle, one that seemed at odds with his manner of delivery. "It is a cruel fate that drives him to Casey and the audience has no pity. Indeed they like it, and they want more," according to a San Francisco reporter. For Hopper, like Irwin, was best known for a story that brought him to the level of the street: the baseball poem "Casey at the Bat."[19]

For many older vaudevillians in the 1890s—Hopper was born in 1858 and Irwin four years later—"naturalizing" their contact with the audience pulled them away from traditions of the parlor and the theater that they had grown up with. They were not just expected to deliver material; they had to occupy it or own it. Some were concerned that respectable spectators might think less of them, and many in the 1890s worried that playing vaudeville might hurt their careers in the legitimate theater or in musical comedy. It fell to the next generation, those born in the 1870s and 1880s, to embrace vaudeville's theater culture and make the performance into a less inhibited expression of their "actual" personality. Strong character was increasingly a prerequisite for a distinct musical personality. Elizabeth Murray, one of the first "coon" singers to move energetically about the stage (she was known for her "ragtime walk"), for example, announced proudly that she was "unmanageable.... I'm not an insect and it's a good thing to let managers know it. I'm a human being. Treat me like one and I'll work my Irish head off; but try to 'put one over' and it's goodby." During the First World War Murray would perform suffragette songs like "She's Good Enough to Be Your Baby's Mother and She's Good Enough to Vote with You."[20]

For musicians, the revolutionary impact of ragtime was to free them from the conventions that still bound the "coon" singer and to focus attention more fully on themselves. Ragtime moved mainstream popular music from a narrative art to something direct, personal, reflexive, and even therapeutic; it was a way of lifting spirits and expressing feelings that normal words inhibited. Instead of telling a story about others, ragtime composers used the first-person point of view, and singers presented the music as expressing their own feelings. This encouraged publishers to connect the songs they produced ever more closely to the vaudevillians who premiered them, and after 1900 they were paying them to have their pictures on sheet music covers. The songwriter Irving Berlin, who was just emerging as one of vaudeville's premier composers, said that it was no longer necessary to tell a story in songs, and he wrote lyrics in the first person so that the singer "talks directly to the auditors."[21] This change in music reflected the growth of celebrity, personality, and a vaudeville performance culture that rested on a direct appeal. Authenticity flowed from "naturalizing" the delivery and making the song more personal, and this individualization, paradoxically, enhanced the song's marketability. All of this resulted from the critical shift in the singer's role from storyteller, where the real identity of the performer was erased, to a melding of the performer's emotions with those of the character in the song.

Among the first to personalize her delivery of ragtime songs was Ohio-born Clarice Vance. Originally known as a "tough girl" who stomped onto the stage and sang in a stentorian way, "hard, loud and faultless in articulation," in 1900 Vance tried a more subdued approach. At Keith's Bijou in Philadelphia, Vance surprised audiences with a performance of ragtime songs free of shouting. She was one of the earliest "coon" singers to shift attention to her vocal quality, rhythm, and lyricism. In this sense, she was among the first to navigate the shift from "coon" shouting to ragtime singing. Her lightened, sweetened sound did not excite the gallery as it did when she bellowed a story, but she claimed to be more satisfied with her work. "I find my audience enjoy the quiet, modest way in which I sing my songs more than they do the blustery, knockabout shouting style generally used in the rendition of coon songs," Vance explained. In her view, "ragtime songs should be sung on the stage like they would be in the parlor." Younger singers like Nora Bayes, Gene Greene, Adele Rowland, Bobby North, Belle Baker, and Rae Samuels adopted Vance's highly personal approach. Nora Bayes proved a big hit with vaudeville audiences with her "forward," highly personal approach to song, something more suited, one manager initially thought, to a club or cabaret. Her style was "not particularly pleasing to an older theater goer," a manager explained when she broke into vaudeville in 1904, but she worked in a "gingery way" and gained "really good applause."[22]

By 1905 many performers had assimilated ragtime's emphasis on accented rhythm and were blending it with more individualized vocalizations. They wanted to model songs for home performance, which meant more intimacy and less volume. A comparison of the 1910 recordings of Sophie Tucker and Nora Bayes in "That Loving Rag" (Edison 10360 and Victor 60023) provides insight into how styles were changing. Tucker's approach remains anchored to the "coon" song tradition. Her staccato rhythm and crisp attack bring out the clarity of the lyrics (she applies only the slightest hint of a stereotypical "black" accent), and her delivery is propulsive if somewhat jerky and stiff. Only in the last repeat does she break free of the "coon" tradition, ad-lib four bars of text, and shout a bluesy wail, making her sound African American without conventional impersonation. What the character she depicts clearly loves about the rag is the dance, and the excitement builds to the point that she becomes her own idea of a black person. Bayes, in contrast, is gentler and much more lyrical, laying emphasis on creating a romantic mood. She adds African Americanisms more overtly by adopting black stage dialect, though she is incapable of sustaining it and often slips back into a midwestern accent. The dialect is, however, the only thing reminding listeners of the blackface origins of the song. Bayes heavily ornaments the music, adding personal touches and ostensibly impromptu changes of vocal color. Although she tries to maintain minstrel-show pronunciation, her personal, conversational, intimate performance is transparently white. What is important is that both the reformed "coon" singer and the proto-crooner manage to make the song sound improvised, something older singers of ragtime songs, like May Irwin and Marie Cahill, simply couldn't manage.[23]

As singer Blanche Ring observed, the new style evolved because of the need to express one's personality in vaudeville. In the variety theater you have to "give it to them plainly. Give it to them so that they must get it whether they are listening or not," she told *Variety* in 1909. People often asked her how she was able to "swing an audience along," and Ring said the answer was getting "the gladness in circulation by being glad yourself through and through." As syncopation and ragtime's energy infused not just "coon" shouting but also romantic, sentimental, and comic songs, it seemed to modernize traditional musical genres. Popular singers continued to emphasize clarity of diction—something they thought necessary in cavernous theaters—but they tried to make their music sound less constrained and rehearsed. The idea of the direct appeal merged with ragtime's impulsive rhythms to create a new style of popular singing that was unaffected and impromptu. According to singer Adele Rowland, the way to put a song over in vaudeville was by using "a direct appeal . . . the slightest assumption of insincerity or affectation is fatal." Any artist who, when singing, would "clinch her heart, shut her eyes, or otherwise prove herself devoid of real feeling . . . would exit from vaudeville." The increased focus on the star performer was the essence of the thing to Nora Bayes: "You have to make them [the audience] forget themselves. If you can set them to thinking about *your* blues instead of their own, they are taken completely out of themselves . . . [and then] you are really entertaining them," she explained.[24]

Essential to individualizing songs was a naturalization of pronunciation, as vaudevillians made stage dialects (such as "darky" or "Hebrew" modes) and the transatlantic accents conventionally used in art and parlor song sound closer to "everyday" speech. Irving Berlin, one of the most important songsmiths nurtured by vaudeville, managed to make language sound ragged, even when it wasn't being sung. Syncopation was at the root of the change as many singers—Gene Greene and the Nichols Sisters are good examples—would distort language by placing emphasis unusually in a phrase, such as "who took the engiiine" or "I've a feeliiin'," where the stress fell on the unimportant "-ing" rather than on the "feel." The Nichols Sisters, who performed in blackface and sang in "a ragged kind of way," pronounced the name "Eva" as "E-e-e-e-vah," much to the amusement of one Indianapolis critic.²⁵

The syncopation of speech was accompanied by new ways of pronouncing words. The most characteristic feature of this was the prevalence after 1900 of a nasal tone. The tone was popular with singers because of its projection and clarity, but it was often criticized by the classically trained as unlovely, metallic, and harsh. Voice instructors said it was an "undignified" way of speaking that suggested a "whadda you want?" attitude, one they urged young female vocalists, in particularly, not to emulate. Classically trained singers noted with despair the unusual stress vaudevillians laid on short vowels, which popular singers hung on to, according to the dramatic soprano Margarete Matzenauer, "as a puppy hangs on to a bone."²⁶

Popular theater relied, throughout the nineteenth century, on stereotypical characters who revealed their identities through different ways of speaking. The Irish character, the Scot, the Bowery Boy, the Yankee, the rube, the African American, and the Jew all had their dialects. After 1900 specific vaudeville characters, including wise guys, comedians, "midgets," tough girls, and many singers adopted a different way of speaking that soon become associated with modernity itself. It was a fast, slang-filled speech, ostensibly based on that of New York's Bowery (whose denizens served the same apocryphal role on American stages in the nineteenth century as the London cockney did on British). This way of pronouncing became vaudeville's argot, and it was widely used to render ragtime songs. Unlike the slang associated with specific groups in the nineteenth century, vaudeville's slang floated away from impersonation. Its distinctive features were the nasal tone, a flat *a*, and a pronunciation of the *i* or *e* before an *r* as though it were an umlauted *o* combined with a *y*, as in g*oey*l for girl. By 1903 even sophisticated performers like the sketch actor Valerie Bergère were using this form of slangy speech. A short story writer, imagining a conversation between a vaudeville star and her agent, inscribed their conversations as "Lissen! You keep them contracks by you and you don't do nothin'." And the blonde star whispered back, "You can count on me straight; I won't do nothing for nobody till I hear from you."²⁷

In actuality, vaudeville's quasi–New York accent was as artificial as any of its other stage dialects. The writer Owen Kildare, who spent his life in the Lower East Side, once read some vaudeville-style slang to longtime Bowery inhabitants, and they could not understand or identify any of it. Bert Leslie, an actor who specialized in playing Lower East Side characters ("his slang is a perfect marvel and his manner of delivering it is great," according to one manager), admitted in 1904 that practically all the slang in circulation originated on the stage. "It is sheer invention," Leslie said, but "an audience takes up an expression and in a few days it is on the lips of every newsboy in the city." Many of the new words and phrases vaudevillians invented entered ordinary parlance, like "jazz it up," "shine," "bonehead," "cut it out," "the limit," "savvy," and "peachy." Because the use of slang expressions became a characteristic of the vaudeville type, different performers had to continually invent their own new words and expressions in order to provide an element of novelty. "Flivved," "flopped," "did a Brodie," and "bust" were all coined by vaudevillians to describe failure. "You cannot keep up with the demand for slang," Leslie observed; "the moment a slang expression comes into common use about the street it loses its novelty," and the up-to-date performer had to invent something else. For good reason the monologuist Fred Niblo dubbed it "Broadway slang."[28]

Even though vaudeville's slangy idioms were fabricated, they still served to make the entertainment seem more closely connected to real life. Unlike the legitimate theater, there was no need to put on linguistic airs in vaudeville. The paradox, as H. L. Mencken pointed out in *The American Language*, was that the drive to create new words and expressions arose from a desire to make the speaker's language more "pungent" and "picturesque." Slang was, essentially, a theatricalization of speech, even though it had the odd effect of making it sound more true-to-life. Vaudeville performers maintained that because they were onstage only briefly, they needed words that condensed complex thoughts, but there was more to it than speed or convenience.[29] It was no faster to say someone had "done a Brodie" than "he failed." Colorful and unusual expressions are, of course, more interesting, and their employment made sense in a theater demanding novelty. But the sassy implications of vaudeville slang, which denoted the persona of players, was something else. It spoke to the image of vaudeville as the democratic, up-to-date, streetwise, urban entertainment that gave Americans ragged songs and the ragged words to go with them.

NO BONES

As ragtime percolated through popular song and speech, the two-step sparked a sudden and unprecedented craze for dancing. By 1915 there were around 800 dance halls in New York, while Chicago had an estimated 700 catering to 70,000 people per night. Most dance halls did not serve liquor and charged two or three cents for admission, making them particular favorites with young, single working people. But everyone, it seemed, was bitten by the dancing bug. "Men who have hitherto scorned to appear on ballroom floors . . . and girls who formerly eschewed waltzes and two-steps have now tossed aside their prejudices . . . and are by the thousands taking lessons in order that they may enjoy the turkey trot and its kindred rhythmic genuflections," a Washington newspaper reported in 1913. Ragtime dancing involved less intricate movements of the feet than waltzes or polkas but more mobility in the body. After watching the Boston dip danced at a New York dance hall in 1912, an investigator noted, "Men and women held each other in a tight grasp, the women putting their arms right around men. Almost all walked the two step in a combination bunny hug and nigger. Several couples danced the shivers and some the dipping varieties. . . . One couple had a distinct houchi couchi [sic] movement."[30]

As the dance craze caught hold, ragtime dance acts became an increasingly popular feature in vaudeville. In 1903–5, 5 percent of acts featured dancing, either on its own or in conjunction with singing or comedy; in 1910–12, the figure had grown to 12 percent. More than a third of all singing acts before World War I had a dance component. As with song, vaudeville became a venue where new dances were introduced to a mass audience. Ragtime singer Blossom Seeley began "toddling" onstage in 1908 (the steps to the todolo were similar to the fox-trot's but were accompanied by a bounce; it was considered shocking because women lifted their feet high off the floor when dancing it), and in 1911 she turned the Texas tommy into the latest sensation when she performed it on a table during a show.[31]

Just as ragtime personalized and naturalized song, ragtime dancing helped inspire a change in performers' body ideals. To vaudevillian Bee Palmer, ragtime was the perfect cure for obesity. She couldn't carry "an extra ounce of flesh on my body . . . and I have never worn a pair of stays. Syncopation—that's the answer." The singing comedian Bert Williams stood in one spot and used his hands and face for emphasis when singing. But African American ragtime singers accompanied their songs with a slow rotation of the hips: the "Elgin Movements" made popular by vaudeville comedian and singer Butler "String Beans" May in 1910–11. The movement most commonly associated with popular song was the shimmy, which burst over vaudeville in 1919. The shimmy was variously described as Indian, Hawaiian, or African in origin, though the shoulder wiggle had been associated with female flirtation for decades. The greater freedom provided by the shirtwaist and the elimination of corset stays made the movement of the breasts more pronounced when one shimmied, according to Gilda Gray, which is what people liked to watch. Gray, who became the country's most famous shimmy dancer, and by her own account its originator, said that "you've got to accent that syncopated stuff with your body.... Nobody could stand still and do that." Gray did the shimmy rooted in one spot, hardly moving her feet, and shaking her shoulders and breasts by rocking on her pelvis. She insisted it wasn't a dance at all but "more of a physical exercise."[32]

Because women's bodies were openly commodified and assessed in the early twentieth century, changing tastes were unselfconsciously inscribed on them. At the turn of the century, weight had been a positive attribute among performers in both the popular and the legitimate theaters. Plumpness was not just sexy; it also suggested good health and humor. Stage women were admired for their fat, and those who didn't have enough were often seen as unfeminine. In 1888, for example, a review of a variety show that a critic called "the worst in America" singled out the "pathetic... undersized and unshapely girls" of the chorus. One spectator, the reviewer noted, was apparently so put off by their skinny legs that he yelled, "Why don't you wear pants?" Substantial breasts and sturdy calves were especially admired, and Charmion the acrobat boasted that although her bust normally measured thirty-six inches onstage she was able to "expand" it to a more appealing thirty-nine inches, and her calves measured fourteen inches each, roughly double the size of her ankles. Chicot (the pen name of Epes Sargent), writing for the *New York Morning Telegraph*, expressed his admiration for voluptuous women. He thought Louise Dresser, sometimes considered Lillian Russell's successor as America's blonde idol, had a particularly "good figure" and in 1899 wrote of one vaudeville show that it had been a great "relief... to the men at least" when "the plump figure of Louise" replaced the "skinny" one of Cissy Loftus. According to Chicot, the only people who liked Loftus were scrawny, unattractive girls. May Irwin, the "coon" singer, was never thought to have a beautiful face, but her body was widely admired for its corpulence. Her "avoirdupois is prodigious.... She is radiant," one fan wrote. Irwin worried in 1899 that if she lost weight she might sacrifice some of her popularity. "Plump, jovial, laughing May" is how Irwin described herself. According to a Minneapolis critic, the popularity of stout women in vaudeville was only natural. "Go to the Columbia [Theater]," the reporter wrote, "and see for yourself the unusual number of fat persons who are attracted by the words 'May Irwin.'... They consider her one of them."[33]

Ragtime and the dance craze, however, inspired fashions designed to liberate the body from stiff corsets and padding. As Joe Watson, the Jewish comedian, complained in a 1915 monologue about his wife, who had been bitten by the dance craze, "All she's got in her mind is Tommy Texas, the Bummer Hug, the Thirsty Trot, the Capsule Walk, the Orangeine, the Brazilian Makes-itchy. Always I knew she was crazy in the head. Now she's crazy in the feet.... She says she's going to be like Peter Pants and never grow up. I tell her it would be better for her if she would grow up—and stop growing sideways. She says, 'Dancing brings my weight down.' And it does—right on my foot."[34] Already, in the 1870s, thinness was becoming fashionable among the elite (the empress of Austria starved herself to attain a sixteen-inch waist), but it took time for the ideal to reach the American popular theater. By the time it did, early in the new century, natural thinness was starting to be preferred to the constructed and corseted kind, as movement became more integral to fun.

In order to demonstrate women's freedom from artificial constraints, dress designers rather maliciously constructed the gowns of the early twentieth century to be form-fitting. It was the new style in dresses that vaudevillian Fay Templeton said first drove her into the gymnasium. "I am the happiest thing in town," the once-weighty star declared after slimming down in 1904. "Do you know I have simply pined to wear a tight-fitting widow's gown?" Like many other female stars, Templeton was known for the fashionable clothes she wore. But the rising value of thinness stranded voluptuous performers as their bodies seemed unsuited to sheath gowns and hobble skirts. Some, like Templeton or Valeska Suratt, were able to compress their bodies into the required shape by wearing gut-wrenching corsets. But not everyone could, or wanted to, squeeze down. When Sophie Tucker appeared in a sheath (a very tight dress slit down one side so the wearer could walk), a critic mocked her "great larded voice" and the "monstrous spectacle" made by "her full tonnage" moving about in such a tight dress. According to a Jewish monologuist, fashions were becoming a "skirt tight here, to make the shape stick out, and a big hat with a plume flying in the air, and a Schlitz down the side so the men will look downstairs." Vaudeville celebrities sold themselves as paragons of style, but with the newspapers unhesitatingly reporting that stars once considered beautiful, like Emma Carus, were now "fat like a baby elephant" or, like Eva Tanguay, "too fleshy to show her torso," they had limited room to protest when it came to physique. One Minneapolis critic observed of Tanguay that she was "rather too buxom to do much dancing of any kind" and "doesn't attempt anything more than a few prances." Sophie Tucker, a paper declared, became a "thinner and better woman" when she lost weight in 1915. According to singer Blanche Ring, "I belong to the public and the public doesn't want a fat woman, and I've just got to keep my flesh down."[35]

In the first decade of the new century, thinness, new fashions, and freedom of movement were connected to both ragtime and modernity. Performers who did not embrace the new values and body ideals—such as Eva Tanguay—had to carve out a niche for themselves by being outrageous. Fat vaudevillians in the first two decades of the century needed to establish their personalities in defiance of fashion—as a still heavy Clarice Vance did when she introduced her satire of thinness, a Salome song which she sang while doing a mock contortion dance. Fat performers Trixie Friganza and Eva Tanguay also added comic dances to ridicule the new fashions. When bathing suits became the rage, Friganza introduced a diving act where she belly-flopped into a pool, sending the water flying everywhere. But even as they made fun of the rising popularity of thinness, many gave way. Friganza, for example, dropped fifty pounds in 1908 after George M. Cohan told her to "get rid of the excess baggage."[36]

In 1914 even Emma Carus announced that she was on a diet. The singer was thirty-five at the time and said that she weighed 197 pounds. This was no more than Lillian Russell had weighed at the peak of her career, some twenty years before, when she was considered America's most beautiful woman, but since then attitudes had changed. Directors of shows, Carus complained, were no longer considering her for many of the parts she used to play. She blamed it on her weight. She also suspected that criticism of her singing, which grew as she gradually eliminated her "manly basso," was connected to her size. Shouting was what fat singers were supposed to do, and when Carus adopted a more subtle ragtime style, critics didn't think it suited her. Only after she lost weight did they consider voice and body to have moved into harmony. By 1915 her voice was in favor again, and directors started giving her the kind of work she wanted. "The sacrifice to the Moloch of art has been made," a trimmed-down Carus sighed in 1918, not altogether happily.[37]

Adapting to the growing association of the unaffected, the slangy, and the physically liberated with the modern was not easy for the heavyweights of vaudeville. They complained that managers were embarrassing them by insisting they continue to dress in revealing ways at a time when thin was becoming more fashionable. Before losing weight, Emma Carus scrapped with several managers over their insistence she wear tights. Taken to court by Oscar Hammerstein in 1904, she defended her decision to break her contract by arguing that "I can't wear tights. I am too big." Carus felt that she could no longer "reconcile" revealing clothing with "my healthy robustness. . . . An actress [who] develops an ankle more than ten inches in circumference and the remainder of her limbs in proportion, should think twice before adopting tights."[38]

The woman considered the "handsomest in vaudeville," Valeska Suratt, also protested against the changing body ideals. Suratt first attracted notice when she appeared in a sketch with Billy Gould in 1905. Within months, she'd achieved star billing because of her corseted hourglass shape, beautiful gowns, and colossal pile of hair. Soon she was a real celebrity who offered beauty tips to women, had a line of cosmetics, and wrote an advice column for several newspapers. Press releases mixed stories of her humble Terre Haute, Indiana, beginnings with descriptions of her thousand-dollar gowns. Reviewing an appearance in 1906, a critic observed that her décolleté rig "fashioned of cloth of gold which enveloped a Venus de Milo figure in glittering snake-like folds . . . made the women gasp and the men give vent to a chorus of expressive 'whews.'" Suratt couldn't stay on the cutting edge of fashion for long, however. The demise of the tight-laced corset as a fashion item in the early twentieth century left her painfully exposed. She lashed out against the new style. "Nakedness is not nice," she exclaimed; "a woman's body is too sacred—or should be—for every leering male to gloat over and fondle with his sneering eyes. Get under cover, you young girls, for the sake of your own souls."[39] Suratt was only twenty-eight when she condemned the new, less structured fashions, but taste and body mass had already made her an artifact of a passing era.

She was right, of course. Men ran the entertainment industry, and they determined who would appear and the kinds of acts women would perform. But this was also an age when women's expectations and roles were changing, and removing corsets and wearing new fashions were as liberating for many of them as employing slang, expressing emotions in song, or dancing the grizzly bear. Sophye Barnard, who was marketed as a high-class singer with a wealthy background, caused a stir when she appeared without a corset in a fitted gown. She wore clothes for their stylishness, not their sexiness; "I want it distinctly understood," Barnard told a reporter, "I'm not frivolous."[40]

A great many of the slender young women whom men most liked to ogle declared their professional and personal independence. To the dancer La Sylphe, there was "no harm in the nude figure [onstage]," and she also had unconventional views on marriage. Being single, she told an interviewer, "is a good idea. . . . Marriage is fine for a man, but it's rotten luck for a woman. In my opinion." Other vaudeville women expressed the same view. Charmion, an acrobat who did a striptease on an aerial swing, said, "It would not make me happy to know that I had a husband hanging around in the lobbies of the theaters where I was working with nothing to do but wait for Saturday night and the salary I earned." The real obstacle to marriage, she added, was that "one couldn't use

Valeska Suratt, considered in 1905 "the handsomest in vaudeville." Her heavily structured hourglass shape and mountain of hair would fall out of fashion before World War I. (Wisconsin Historical Society, 69348)

physical violence to force one's own husband to work." Young female vaudevillians often said they were not trying to be slim or to shimmy for the sake of voyeuristic men but because they felt healthier and more confident. The svelte teenage dancer Evelyn Law pointed out that she wore tremendously high heels onstage because "a high heel and an arched instep make a girl's foot look very much prettier, you know. It tends to make the ankle slimmer and the leg more shapely. We have to exhibit our pet vanities to best advantage." But, she maintained, she wasn't interested in what men thought of her, she didn't believe in love, and she had no intention of marrying: "I don't think about it at all. I prefer to think about my dancing and singing career."[41]

Performing women who had freed themselves from swathes of cloth, padding, and bone defiantly described their undress as a form of emancipation. This was especially true of the bathers, who became a hit in vaudeville largely because they appeared in swimsuits. Lalla Selbini, who started her career doing a disrobing act on a bicycle, switched over to swimming, apparently for the suit. Selbini was a real headliner, and the press agents built her up with stories of shocked audiences (she does "not wear a corset and she assumes positions that leave little to the imagination," according to one). Responding to a complaint about her risqué appearance, Selbini reportedly said, "Some of the prudes seem[ed] to think the bathing costume in which I appear in my act was a trifle too scant." But she "faced these women" and brought them over to her side. Annette Kellerman, the Australian athlete who dove into tanks of water on vaudeville stages, similarly provoked women to reveal themselves as a way of declaring their independence. Appearing before a New York audience in 1909, she made clear that "the only bones about me, girls, are the ones nature gave me." And, in order to prove this, she removed her "tight-fitting black velvet gown ... and revealed herself in her black swimming suit." Making the point even clearer, as if such a thing was necessary, she then announced, "I'll just rip this thing (the suit) down the side and show you that there is nothing underneath but—but me," and she did that too.[42]

In the early twentieth century, vaudevillians forged novel connections between the liberated body, personality, and commodified cultural products such as clothes, ragtime songs, slang, and animal dances. Female headliners, one vaudevillian explained, "used to depend upon tonnage to put them across. Those days have slipped into the discard. Now patrons want to see and hear ... leading women ... who can sing."[43] Through vaudeville, slang words and supposedly working-class idioms became a sign, not of a poor education, but of authenticity. Similarly, discarding the corset or dancing the turkey trot came to evidence not sexual dissipation but personal freedom, naturalism, and contemporary sensibilities. Songs shifted under the influence of vaudeville to become less narrative and more personal. Styles and manners once specific to a class or ethnicity or place were commodified and adopted by people unassociated with that group or place. To many traditionalists, there was something dangerous in all this, an attack on the idea that the more refined one grew the more polished were one's sensibilities. The exposure of middle-class people, and especially young women, to democratic entertainment would, many cultural conservatives argued, have a corrosive effect on the traditional idea of femininity, gentility, and taste. As one conservative writer presciently griped in 1910, "There are certain standard subjects that are used almost every night on vaudeville stages through the country. An audience, composed of many persons mentally fatigued after a day's work, learns a philosophy that embraces such precepts as: marriage is an unfortunate institution to which the majority of us resign ourselves; women are fashion-crazy, spend money heedlessly and believe that their husbands are fools; politics is all bunk[;] . . . clandestine affairs of most any sort between at least one married person and another of the opposite sex are comical; and finally nothing in life really matters." Summarize the vaudeville formula for happiness, the writer added, it came down to "Get all the money you can and keep your mother-in-law as far off as possible."[44]

Some might complain, but vaudeville had imbued its invented Lower East Side dialect and its ragged rhythms with authentic and irreverent associations that proved too exciting to be kept onstage. In an era that prized authenticity, consumerism, and novelty, it was just what the public wanted.

NATURALIZING STEREOTYPES

In 1898, Billy Rice, the corpulent former blackface minstrel, decided to put together "an old fashioned minstrel show." Rice was distressed by the post–Civil War transformation of blackface performance into a variety act and dreamed of reviving the original art with its eight-man cast of comedians, clog dancers, and sentimental singers. Until the 1870s, minstrel shows had been America's most popular and distinctive light entertainment, but the variety show had supplanted it. Like vaudeville, the minstrel show consisted of unrelated comic and musical skits, but it was by convention organized into three parts, beginning with solo turns by members of the eight-man lineup, who were called upon individually to perform by the interlocutor, or master of ceremonies. Part two was the most like vaudeville with comic and musical acts by the various performers (and after the Civil War this expanded to included acrobats, animal trainers, and female dancers and singers, none of whom were members of the eight-man company). The third part consisted of a comic skit. All of the actors performing in the first and third parts, and some of those in the second, wore blackface and pretended to be African Americans.[45]

It was the war with Spain that inspired Rice to revive the minstrel show, as he thought "money will be circulating more than it has since the civil war and business of all kinds, including the show business, will be great." But it was not to be. The war was short, and although Rice's minstrels successfully opened at Lothrop's Opera House in Worcester, they never got out of Massachusetts. As a *Washington Times* critic snarled, the problem with Rice was that "his efforts to be funny are pathetic" and everything about him "is antiquated—including the jokes." Three years later, impoverished and nearly blind, Rice died. "Where now is Billy Rice?" Mark Twain lamented in his autobiography. "He was a joy to me, and so were the other stars of the nigger shows... [all] departed to return no more forever."[46]

In the nineteenth century, minstrels pretended to be African Americans because they associated black skin with a childlike innocence, emotional freedom, and pathos. Minstrelsy combined nonsense and slapstick humor with tender, sentimental music that dwelled on loss and longing. In the minds of minstrels, their characterization was close to the truth because they believed real African Americans were both condemned to suffer by their race and unsophisticated in their joy and anger. According to Dan Emmett, one of the founders of minstrelsy, "The old time minstrel did nothing but what the negro could and did do.... The old-time interpretation of dialect and mannerisms was... true to life." Traditional minstrels claimed to have picked up their songs and dances directly from actual black people; Dan Rice said he learned his "Jump Jim Crow" dance from a black stable worker (or bootblack) in Louisville, and Emmett maintained he composed "Dixie" to a tune he heard "negro laborers singing on a levee while loading a steamboat with cotton" in 1847. For these mimetic minstrels, getting the "negro character" right required research and "training." This was why the old-time minstrel pair McIntyre and Heath said authentic blackface was a matter of study and research, and they boasted that they had acquired their mannerisms and accents by close acquaintance with black people in North Carolina. Needless to say, these performers were presenting a fantasy image of African Americans, despite their claims. Like Billy Rice, however, they were convinced that the kind of blackface they saw in vaudeville was completely phony.[47]

The old-time minstrels had a point. Blackface performers in vaudeville rarely performed the stereotype "straight." Blackface was reasonably rare in vaudeville; between 1902 and 1922 only 3 percent of acts featured a blackface character, and managers believed the traditional methods "do not go with the public any more." Of the small number of blackface acts, about two in five were performed in ways that made apparent the falsity of the racial performance. Many variety performers removed their makeup onstage to show that they were white, while others employed burnt cork in ways that made it ludicrous, as when Lew Dockstader did blackface impersonations of presidents Theodore Roosevelt and Grover Cleveland. Mixing up the stereotypes was especially popular. The Frank Wilson Trio, for example, performed in blackface, singing "nigger songs" in German. "At first blush one might fail to realize the effect of hearing a rag-time negro or coon song rendered in German," a critic observed. "But to hear 'Back, Back to Baltimore' in the unadulterated vernacular of Schleswig-Holstein, or yet again in the colloquial of Saxe-Coburg, is something one cannot forget." In the South, even the "the colored audiences before which the trio have appeared are sent into screams of ungovernable laughter." Similarly, Howe and Scott, who did a Jewish sidewalk comedy act, made a big hit in 1902 with their self-styled "Hebrew cake-walk." Other performers just switched from one stereotypical character to another with abandon. The Flying Dancer, rated "a sensation" on the small-time stage in 1912, sang two songs in French, then performed a "coon" song, and then closed with a "tough-girl" turkey trot. No wonder minstrels like Rice and Emmett were appalled by what they saw in vaudeville; where they had performed their impression of black people, the subject of the variety show's humor was traditional minstrelsy itself.[48]

At first glance, it may seem odd that vaudevillians, who prized actuality, set out to expose the phony "authenticity" of the traditional minstrels. But there were good reasons why vaudevillians made fun of blackface. In part they were demonstrating their modernity by breaking with a tradition, but more importantly they were affirming their own whiteness by rendering the burnt-cork disguise transparent. Their goal was not to make the black characters they portrayed more real but to show that an authentically funny white person was working behind the black mask. That did not mean that the blackface itself was irrelevant; the funny white person was still playing a black character rather than portraying a character of what was considered dubious whiteness, such as a Jew or an Italian or an Asian. They could not, therefore, ignore the conventions of minstrelsy or transgress racialized boundaries entirely by, for example, having the black character engage in sexual banter with a white one, even though audiences knew that both performers were white.[49] Vaudevillians were making fun of the disguises, not eradicating them.

Knowing that the performer in blackface was white became especially important when African Americans began to appear in vaudeville. Black performers made the white impersonation problematic, in part by doing it better.

Billy B. Van looking pathetic before a confident portrait of himself. This publicity photograph reminded audiences that the comedian was white while inviting questions about those aspects of the performer's character that the disguise revealed—or might hide. (New York Public Library, Billy Rose Theatre Division, T-Mss 1984–005, Robert Benney Research Materials, box 6)

Eddie Leonard, a blackface comic, was a bust at Keith's in Cleveland when he came on after the actual African American company with which Bert Williams and George Walker were touring in 1905. "While this is a good act," the manager lamented of Leonard, "it didn't have a chance on earth following the Williams and Walker Glee Club. The two acts should never have been placed one to follow the other on any bill. They conflict and that does not express the half of it." Similarly, Sophie Tucker said she abandoned blackface in 1909 when she found out that black people did not really sing and move as she did when shouting "coon" ballads. But the presence of black performers also meant that anyone who did blackface convincingly might be mistaken as an actual African American. To avoid this possibility, white vaudevillians took to peeling away their mask so that their actual race was not in doubt. For example, in her 1905 routine the flirtatious singing comedian Artie Hall would joke about having impulses "as black as her face" while showing white skin under her glove to reveal her true color. Since everyone knew Hall was white, the *Variety* reviewer thought she did this for reasons of self-image as "no one appeared to care about the matter save herself."[50]

Black comedians, singers, and dancers gained access to mainstream popular entertainment when they began touring with white minstrel companies in the 1870s. To win acceptance there they painted themselves a deep and unvariegated black and played absurdly grotesque, comic types. But when African American performers entered vaudeville in the 1890s, many of them abandoned the grotesque, and all maintained that their impersonations were more authentic than anything one might see in a minstrel show. Ernest Hogan promoted himself as "the real thing" and an "unbleached Afro-American" (he later changed his moniker to the more pointed "unbleached American"). Avery and Hart called themselves "the original zulu babies," while Bert Williams and George Walker said they were "two real coons . . . two genuine blackies." As Williams and Walker explained in their promotional material, "We shall sing as you might hear people sing in the South and Southwest," and their buck dance was promoted as "a regular darkey hoe-down." Black vaudevillians, in keeping with the theater's culture of actuality, also claimed authenticity by sometimes connecting their act with nontheatrical signifiers of racial "uplift." In the "Evolution of the Negro," which toured the Keith circuit in 1904, eight black dancers appeared first as African "natives," then in a scene on a southern plantation, and finally dressed as waiters in a hotel restaurant.[51]

Only a very small number of African American performers, Avery and Hart being the best known, continued to play grotesque types—"perpetuating the ancient slanders which their race has long been trying to live down"—while still claiming authenticity. Most attempted to "naturalize" blackface by metaphorically removing it. Bert Williams, for example, attacked the white fantasy of sentimental blackface by arousing mock pity. In signature songs like "Nobody" and "Constantly," he accompanied his musical chronicles of woe with such minstrel-show allusions as rolling eyes, "drooping glances, [a] turning down of mouth corners and graphic gestures of those huge but eloquent hands."[52] By making fun of an empathy he did not believe he, as a black performer, could ever win from white audiences, he undermined their preconceptions about African Americans and exposed the lie of the burnt cork he wore. In other words, both white and black vaudevillians commonly employed the black mask in order to draw attention to its falsity.

Williams and Walker were pioneers in the art of donning blackface and then refusing to play the expected part. As a *Variety* critic in 1908 perceptively wrote, "Realizing, perhaps, that the white public is chronically disinclined to accept the stage negro in any but a purely comedy vein and having at the same time a natural desire to be something better than the conventional colored clown whose class mark is a razor and an ounce or two of cut glass, Williams and Walker have approached the delicate subject from a new side." That new side was to concentrate on musicianship, more low-key humor, and personal grace. Their popularity was closely tied to the cakewalk routine they used to end their act, which they returned to its origins, with Walker emphasizing the sophistication of the dance while Williams hammed it up. Other African American performers emulated their approach. Bob Cole and Billy Johnson, who headed a big minstrel troupe of thirty black performers when the "coon" song-wave broke, adapted their production for a white urban audience. In 1897 they mounted "A Trip to 'Coontown,'" which featured ragtime songs and "a clever travesty on 'cullud' fads and customs," according to one white critic. After bankruptcy split the "Coontown" company in 1901, Cole paired up with J. Rosamond Johnson and entered vaudeville. The pair focused on singing and playing ragtime and added only a little conversational comedy. Even more than Walker and Williams, the novelty with Cole and Johnson, at least for white spectators, was that they were genteel performers. They wore evening dress and acted with understatement; Johnson would even play some light classical music to emphasize their sophistication. Cole and Johnson said their goal was to express "the finer feelings of the colored race." Most "coon" songs, they said, "are rough, coarse and often vulgar"; in their songs, they wanted to show that "the negro has his sentimental side, just as the white man has." In keeping with the general trend toward naturalism, Cole and Johnson said they were displaying "their racial traits" without "any exaggeration," and "instead of using 'dis' and 'dat'... [they] indulge in the choicest language, it being their aim to appear on

The sophistication of Bob Cole (*right*) and Rosamond Johnson was an implicit attack on racial stereotypes. By refusing to mug for the audience, they made their act appear more natural and true to life. (Museum of the City of New York, F2013.41.8282)

the stage as they do in every-day life."[53] It was the appearance of black performers performing in a less grotesque fashion, albeit sometimes in blackface, that pressed white performers away from the "black-on-black" minstrel tradition.

For black vaudevillians, authenticity had ramifications beyond the theater. "We don't have to dig up old questions or appeal to any one's prejudices to draw our public," George Walker maintained; "if you admire Bert Williams you ain't a-going to inquire whether he is black or white," his partner added. Other racialized performers expressed the same feelings, arguing that working within the "coon" stereotype and making it more true-to-life was a way of undermining bigotry. Like Walker, they hoped that audiences would be color-blind and that they would be appreciated as performers, not as racial representatives. Was their goal achieved? Tellingly, when Bert Williams died in 1922, his longtime employer Florenz Ziegfeld commended him for being "the whitest man I ever had the honor to deal with." It was a troubling tribute to an actor who tried to deconstruct racial stereotypes from within; the best his employer could say of him was that he had transcended his racialization by achieving virtual whiteness.[54]

African American performers were not the only racial impersonators struggling to balance vaudeville's culture of authenticity with the conventions of the popular theater. The first "racial" depiction to be challenged was that of the Irish, in part as a result of community protest. By the turn of the century, most Irish character depictions had abandoned many of the stereotypical associations, though Irish impersonators continued to present the character type as sentimental, impulsive, and overly fond of liquor. However, like the Quigley Brothers, a comic pair, they maintained that they were now depicting the type of people "you would meet on the street any day." It is a curious thing, but racial and ethnic stereotypes were increasingly being assumed by people coming from the group represented. They then critiqued the stereotype by humanizing archetypical behaviors and mannerisms and revealing the transcendent humanity of their characters.[55]

In a great many "Hebrew" routines, the "character impersonator" became an everyman with ordinary joys and troubles who strove to have the audience laugh with him rather than at him. In Joe Watson's "Solly the Salesman" monologue, he complained that "if I would never have been born I would be a happy man today." Although fitting into the conventional stereotype of the stingy Jew ("If my best friend came to me for help and he only had one dollar in the world—I would share it with him"), Solly lived in a world where everyone was exploiting somebody. What made him lovable was the sense that he wasn't nearly as callous and materialistic as he pretended to be. Watson was among a number of Jewish performers—including Hoey and Lee, Joe and Ben Welch, Nora Bayes, Bobby North, and Lillian Shaw—who did "authentic" Jewish acts. As Joe Welch explained, he thought that crude depictions of ethnic minorities were being produced only by "unthinking and usually untalented performers." True vaudevillians, he continued, were inclined to provide accurate depictions of "racial eccentricities," "mannerisms and tricks of speech" that were "close to nature" and therefore praiseworthy.[56]

William Glackens's 1899 sketch of two "Hebrew" comedians captures the efforts of vaudevillians to make their impersonations more "authentic" without eschewing the stereotypical gestures, costumes, and makeup. (Library of Congress, Prints and Photographs Division, CAI—Glackens, W. I. no. 31)

No one exemplified the "naturalizing" trend in racial and ethnic impersonation better than the German-born, Brooklyn-raised Welch. The comedian was known for providing not a caricature but a "study from real life" in his monologues. He was understated and offered "homely humorisms," and he famously ended each turn with the ostensibly ad-libbed line "'Nuf said." Welch's character was supposed to be a Polish Jewish small businessman with a wife anxious for status and children pushing to enjoy the luxuries of modern American life. Welch insisted he was not "burlesquing a race" but offering "a character study" of an admirable, likeable, self-deprecating, ordinary mensch. To Welch "there is no finer class of men than the sturdy old men of the old generation of Jews of the East Side of New York, with their love of home and family." In the monologue "I Got Troubles," Welch told of renting a dress suit to go to the opera house because his wife wanted "to mix in the highest circles." The suit fit him "like the skin around a frankfurter sausage," and of course it burst when he tried to sit down. In another monologue, he explained that one of his daughters wanted "to have a good shape. And then dress so everyone can see it." In this gentle diatribe on modern fashion, Welch explained how "in the morning she walks eight miles for her shape. And she wouldn't walk a half a block to the grocery store for her mother." When she did exercises, he recounted saying, "'Becky... stop that or you'll kill yourself.' She says 'I can't stop. I got too many hips. Hips is gone out this year.' I says 'What's the matter with hips?' She says 'swell women ain't wearing them this season.' . . . I tell you that girl is crazy." In 1909 Welch launched a vaudeville skit in which he depicted an Italian immigrant gone to Ellis Island to collect his newly arrived wife and child. Although some critics trashed his dialect as inauthentic, the skit still demonstrated his interest in humanizing his characters. The act was a pathetic rendition of his anxious waiting, his heartbreak when he learned his wife would not be cleared for immigration, and his joy when he finds out that there was a mistake and she was free to enter the United States.[57]

The naturalization of racial and ethnic impersonation allowed performers like Welch to portray character types with more subtle affect and humor. Unlike minstrels such as Billy Rice, who tried to make white audiences laugh at the caricatures they portrayed, vaudevillians tried to show that the individuals they depicted shared the same humanity with the audience. They did this by revealing the real person doing the impersonation, thereby undermining the stereotype. In so doing they made themselves, rather than their stock characters, appear more authentic. This is not to say that the pernicious "othering" of different races or ethnicities went away. The classy African American singers and the lovable Jewish comedian were showing that they were likable people despite their use of offensive racial or ethnic characteristics. Although made more real, the racial and ethnic stereotypes remained in circulation. Actuality in impersonation meant revealing the difference between the acting subject and the character assumed; it made the performance transparent in order to connect the players with the audience through knowledge of the deception that was their impersonation.

NATURALLY MODERN

As we have seen, the individualization of song performance whereby musicians started expressing what appeared to be their own feelings in ragtime was a turning point in popular music. But it was also part of a broader trend in impersonation whereby the conventional signifiers of identity (a Chinese conical hat, blackface paint, or a "Hebrew" beard) were effectively communicating an image without the need for full immersion in a role. In contrast, the white "coon" singer Emma Carus sang in whiteface with a German accent, and the Castles co-opted African American movements and made them a part of a ballroom dance routine. Because prewar vaudevillians blasted apart the stereotypes of the nineteenth-century theater, a singer like Marion Harris, who was tall and blonde and who never donned blackface, could nonetheless be praised for her ability to transform herself, simply through flattened sevenths and "moaning[,] . . . [into] a black lady whose man has walked out on her." As minstrel Willis Sweatnam protested, the "old minstrel material" had simply been "appropriated" by performers who had "rubbed off the burnt cork and used it with complete success in whiteface."[58]

Composer George Antheil enthusiastically declared that ragtime had provided white musicians with a "gigantic blood infusion" from Africa. Indeed, many white performers seemed to feel that they were able to become what they considered black, not as a performance but as a release of some inner impulse. As a Baltimore fan wrote of Nora Bayes, "She seems to put the coon song swing into everything she does." So personal did ragtime songs become that when Emma Carus opted not to sing Harry von Tilzer's "coon" ballad "I Just Can't Help Lovin' Dat Man" at a society party at the Savoy Hotel in New York in 1902, it was because she was worried that the well-to-do audience would assume that the racialized emotions she expressed were her own. Other performers, however, were proud that they had internalized burnt cork. Clarice Vance was famous for her cakewalk and ragtime songs, but she never painted herself black and she used a dialect that she maintained was white southern rather than black. Other performers never thought enough about it to realize what they were doing. Vi Shaffer, a small-time vaudeville crooner, told a reporter that "coon" songs were just those "sung with a southern accent, containing a slight wailing note." The African American origins of the style may have been detectable in Shaffer's performance, but she didn't seem aware of them.[59]

In the first two decades of the century, the conventions of blackface and whiteface blended on the variety stage.[60] As African American, Irish, Dutch, and Jewish players blasted apart and humanized the masks they wore, performers seized some of the loose shards and assimilated them into their acts. Billy Van was equally content to perform his act in blackface or white, depending on who else was on the bill. Similarly, Gene Greene, the highest paid male singer in vaudeville in the second decade of the century, who regularly painted himself black and would "twist his face and lips after the style of the real negro," offered much the same performance when singing an Irish song or a ragtime one. Greene always employed a bright, speech-based, straight-tone production, but he ragged words and phrases (he described it as "fooling along in the middle of a song") and used different timbres to represent different speakers or better express individual words. One reviewer noted in 1916 that he had "more personality when in white face than in black," evidence that the connection between African American impersonation and musical improvisation had significantly weakened. In fact, when Lew Sully took off his black paint once and for all in 1903 and performed his usual act, one manager remarked that his "first impression was, that I was not going to like him in white face, but he seemed to go just as strong as he ever did in black, and I am going to let him continue that way." This was why the old minstrel Dan Emmett could complain in 1902 that in vaudeville "the minstrel is not black at all."[61]

The whitewashing of ragtime also affected popular dance. According to one observer, the two-step turkey trot "hadn't the faintest taint of the negro." In 1908, the African American newspaper the *New York Age* blamed the disappearance of black performers from white vaudeville on the fact that whites were stealing their material. This happened in "coon" singing and in buck-and-wing dancing, the journalist observed, as the racism of white performers and the complicity of theater owners eliminated black talent. "Result: there are more first-class buck and wing and eccentric white dancers to-day than there are colored." White people tolerated black performers only as comedians, African American theater critic Lester Walton complained. "Ragtime singers are possibly to blame—they are now all white and have pushed black performers aside. Only the comics survive." White performers taught white audiences to appreciate the imitations so much that spectators had come to regard the original "with disdain."[62]

It was in vaudeville that the cultural connection between minority groups and modernity that continued to characterize modern popular entertainment through the twentieth century was forged. Performers expressed their contemporary, urbane sensibilities by adopting characteristics that they associated with working-class people, some immigrant groups, and African Americans. This connection arose not because vaudevillians were reflecting their audience but because of the traditions, conventions, and stereotypes they inherited from the nineteenth century. Poor Americans and black Americans were linked in the popular theater with sexual freedom, uninhibited movement, and the unself-conscious enjoyment of pleasure. They were believed to be less constrained by social norms, so adopting elements of what had hitherto been associated with them became liberating. Many white performers employed the slang, style, and movements of "othered" peoples and naturalized them in performance. Even if inauthentic, appropriating styles associated with less genteel people came to seem self-actualizing.

Vaudeville pushed the ideas and manners that it associated with modernity: that the new was superior to the old, that spontaneity was preferable to the routine, that the funny trumped the serious, and that leisure was better than work. The modern American was presented as slim, limber, and ready to move to the ragged pulse of the city. Employing slang was associated with being unconventional and natural; singing or dancing a rag was an expression of an easygoing, fun-loving attitude. The players' rejection of the past was sometimes expressed in vaudeville in the adoption of personae—"coons," ethnic characters, wisecracking Bowery types, and Salomes—that were associated, in the public mind, with unconstrained feeling. Spontaneity was often, but not always, equated to performing a racial, cultural, or historical "other." Annette Kellerman, for example, was a model of the new liberated woman, but she never wore blackface, employed ethnic dialects, or used slang onstage. She did, however, exemplify, in her lack of inhibitions, a modern approach to life that other performers expressed by using racialized musical forms and class-specific speech. Like many vaudevillians, Kellerman connected personal happiness with a spontaneous, unpretentious, and authentic attitude. Moreover, many of those performers who did employ stereotypically racial traits made them so innate that they were no longer obviously imitative.

By promoting new attitudes toward pleasure, sex, clothes, language, bodies, and ways of moving, vaudeville came into vogue. Just as the decadents had done in attending rooftop theaters, audiences watching vaudeville were connecting the idea of modernity with a liberation from inhibitions and conventions. They achieved this in the context of a theater that promoted its own respectability and its comfortable surroundings, prohibitions on uncouth behavior, and freedom from liquor. Victorianisms (especially in the guise of one's mother-in-law) were depicted in vaudeville as constricting, stupid, and artificial; modern behavior was portrayed as natural, spontaneous, and actual. In act after act, performers presented the idea that kidding around, singing songs, using slang, dancing the grizzly bear, employing an African American or Jewish turn-of-phrase, or wearing fewer clothes were ways of being hip. The paradox of this was that vaudeville's ideals of authenticity were being delivered to the public by performers who repeated their acts over and over in prepackaged ways. Mass entertainment sold itself as offering a style that anyone wanting to liberate themselves from conventions should adopt. Vaudevillians encouraged people to buy it all without thinking and transform themselves just by going out, consuming, and having fun. Thinness, good humor, advertising, sexiness, success, and freedom all came together on the vaudeville stage and in the body of the celebrity. What Gilda Gray said of the shimmy could be said of all the modern styles, fads, and fashions that rippled through vaudeville: "There isn't anything to it at all, you know. Any one could do it if they would just relax."[63]

CHAPTER THREE

GRABBING ATTENTION

MAKING GOOD WITH THE DISTRACTED AUDIENCE

IN THE FALL OF 1906, a German strongman named Marino appeared at Hammerstein's promising to let a three-ton car with four men inside drive over him as he lay on his stomach. He declared himself an "auto-defier." Needless to say, Marino got top billing that week, with point-size lettering equal to that advertising Thompson's Elephants. Hammerstein made clear that Marino, who would "laugh at death," was going to be "crushed alive" by the motorcar. Oddly enough, that was something New Yorkers were eager to see.[1]

On opening night an announcer worked the audience into a "thrilling frame of mind," and then, with plenty of "noise, bustle and preparation" and accompanied by the "snorting chug-chug" of the automobile, the act began. Suddenly, just as the car was passing over Marino's body, two women (likely planted in the auditorium) shrieked, "startling the already terrified audience." An emergency ensued onstage, the announcer called for calm, people rose from their seats and a few rushed for the doors, and then, suddenly, Marino got up from the stage unharmed. For "spectacular effect and nerve wracking qualities," one critic declared, Marino could not be beat. He did, however, go rather too far in frightening the audience. It was "more dangerous than Looping the Loop, more death-defying than Looping the Gap, more daring than the Dip of Death," a critic wrote disapprovingly, referring to acts recently banned in vaudeville, because "everyone knows the danger of being run over by an automobile." But Willie Hammerstein (Oscar's son) was overjoyed; he kept Marino on the bill for four weeks, confessing the theater "never did such business as it did during his engagement."[2]

Death by motorcar touched a nerve among spectators. And so it should have. Speeding vehicles were a new reality for turn-of-the-century Americans who found themselves having to adjust to the cross-cutting movements of commuter trains, subways, elevated railways, electric streetcars, and automobiles. Their perceptions were not structured to accept the new level of attentiveness required to operate or dodge fast-moving machines, and accidents were common. Drivers frequently became distracted maneuvering unwieldly cars and buses, and they protested that it was the business of pedestrians to get out of their way. "Drivers are continually tempted . . . to forget that their machines have weight as well as power and therefore develop great momentum even when going at a moderate rate of speed," Frederick Crum, an investigator for the insurance business, observed in 1912. Crum's investigation had been commissioned because insurers were concerned over the rising number of collisions and fatalities. The year he began his work, there had been a reported 1,300 deaths caused by automobiles and a further 1,900 street railway deaths in the United States. "You don't see half the poor people now that you used to," a vaudeville comedian joked; "half of them have already been run over and the other half is afraid to come out."[3]

Auto-defying wasn't the only act trying to shock spectators by pitting people against modern technology. Volta, the electrical marvel, let killing currents of electricity pass through his body, turning electrocution into lighthearted fun. Wearing an "electric suit," Volta lit a gas burner and a cigarette with the tip of his tongue, set fire to handkerchiefs from the soles of his feet and the ends of his hair, and set sparks flying from his body in all directions. He showed, according to a Keith house manager, "perfect immunity from electrical voltage." He even claimed to have sat in the electric chair at Sing Sing prison and chuckled when they flushed him with 2,200 volts. Live wires, Volta told a reporter in St. Louis, were "as harmless to him as wicks of vermicelli to other humans."[4]

Because variety showcased actual things, spectators expected to see performers who claimed to be doing dangerous stunts really risking their lives. In fact, when it came to acts based in danger (and we might add to the electrical marvels and the auto-defiers escape artists, wild animal trainers, and the human targets of shooters, among others), audiences were angry when they felt that the anxiety they experienced was misplaced. The bicycle riders who circled Culver's Loop, for example, were a brief sensation in vaudeville when they mastered gravity and speed in 1902. But early in 1903 it became obvious that the riders, who supposedly raced each other around the interior of a "squirrel wheel," eventually "defying gravity" by "looping the loop," were clamped onto tracks. "People can be seen pointing out the deception to their friends," the manager at Keith's Bijou in Philadelphia complained when the fraud was first discovered, "and I believe this fact detracts somewhat from the drawing power that the act would otherwise possess."⁵ Vaudeville audiences wanted to see an actual struggle with natural and manmade dangers, and when that didn't happen, they felt ripped off.

The disappointment of audiences cracking the Culver Loop "fraud" reiterates the point made previously about the expectation of actuality in vaudeville. But it also tells us something about the mood of spectators at variety shows. Volta and Marino engaged in stunts designed to stimulate the audience, in their cases by shock and fear. Spectators went to vaudeville expecting to have their interests aroused; they wanted something to excite them. Vaudeville put the onus on each performer to sustain audience interest for ten to fifteen minutes.

Intriguingly, vaudevillians imagined the audience to be distracted, even passive. Theatergoers, they felt, had to be "woken up," and they structured acts and shows in order to secure their attention. Already, at the turn of the last century, the idea that attention was a limited and exhaustible resource—a core principle of marketing and management in our own information age—was taking shape. Booking agents did what they could to influence things by organizing performances in ways designed to gradually engage inattentive spectators. According to George Gottleib, who booked the Palace in New York, the first two acts were there simply to get the customers comfortable and settled, and the third act had to "wake up the audience." The fourth should then "rouse" them and begin the process of "build[ing] up their interest." The language Gottleib uses is significant; audiences needed to be wakened, roused, interested, and never "let down again." Significantly, Gottleib imagined a good thirty minutes of the show being assigned to waking the audience.⁶

The idea of a show progressively attracting interest and arousing excitement may seem obvious. Not only do we take for granted that our attention needs to be husbanded, but we also tend not to want to work for our amusement, and we expect performers to entertain us. But in placing the burden of responsibility on the player and so little on the audience, vaudeville was believed to be something of a novelty. The tactics Gottleib used when organizing shows appear to contradict the widely held belief that vaudeville managed without a fourth wall (the invisible barrier separating the performers from their audience). Did vaudeville audiences enter the theater predisposed to engage with it as participants, or were they distracted observers whose interest actors needed to secure? How are we to interpret the screams of the two spectators during Marino's act or the conversations and finger pointing at the cyclists rounding Culver's Loop? How are we to read the "address" to the camera of former variety performers like Groucho Marx and Jack Benny? Were these looks and screams and gestures signs that the audience was immersed in the show, or were they products of the managers' and performers' efforts to create engagement?[7]

Postmodern scholars conceive of the relationship between entertainment and the audience as a dynamic one where spectators have considerable control over their engagement. Today this tends to be called "agency." To represent the relationship of the engaged audience with the performers, media theorists talk about such things as feedback loops, active readers, pregnant texts, and gratification-oriented consumers. These interpretations have been strongly influenced by cinema, an engrossing medium that depends on audience involvement and identification for its success and even coherence. Vaudeville is often held up as a model of how theater audiences, as opposed to cinematic ones, were similarly engaged.

But in the early twentieth century, commentators looked back fondly on the days when spectators were an integral part of the popular theater. As one Topeka, Kansas, reporter noted in 1910, the standard variety audience of two decades before was made up of "young fellers eager to see the shows once a week, loaded to the guards with enthusiasm, and riotously happy at every stage of the proceedings . . . your heart going at a dangerous pace—but you were happy!" There was a time, a Philadelphia columnist agreed in 1902, when "a lady dressed in becoming evening décolleté became the butt of coarse jokes; a gentleman in an evening suit was subjected to ridicule. An old gentleman was hooted at as an 'old geezer,' 'baldy,' 'lobster,' 'his nibs,' and other choice epithets." The spectatorial tradition inherited from such popular establishments as concert saloons and music halls and dime museums was one where the audience was rowdy, excited, and willing to shout itself hoarse. Remember the female spectators at Koster and Bial's who threw the top hats onto the stage? Going to the popular theater in the nineteenth century was what we might today call an "immersive experience," an activity where the spectators were expected to be productive participants in the show. As Frances Trollope discovered when attending plays in Cincinnati in the late 1820s, "every man seemed to think his reputation as a citizen depended on the noise he made."[8] True, post–Civil War spectators no longer had to jostle for a view in a sweaty pit, as true theater lovers had done a half-century before, but in the 1870s and 1880s they still shouted and brawled and even, on occasion, rioted.

Agency is a relative term, and while vaudeville audiences may have been more participatory than those attending legitimate theaters, they were less obviously attentive than spectators watching nineteenth-century melodramas or saloon variety shows. Uniformed security officers and the domestication of the theater helped contain the rowdy audience, and the result was a change not only in behavior but also in spectator involvement. As our Topeka reporter noted, when he looked at the spectators lining up outside the local vaudeville theater they appeared "quiet and glum" and far more jaded, "dead wise," and "haughty" than the fans of old. There was more going on here than just the control of an audience by house security. People who didn't often attend vaudeville described variety shows as repetitive and the spectators as blasé. Why, they wondered, was there no frisson of excitement similar to the one felt when the curtain went up on a traditional play? How could an entertainment so filled with novelties be mentally deadening? This chapter looks at how managers and performers explained what they believed was the singular character of the vaudeville audience and how their perceptions influenced their efforts to involve it.

Vaudeville was the first entertainment that saw itself confronting a public that appeared to be worn out by the stresses of daily life. Rather than presuming that vaudeville lacked a fourth wall, this chapter describes the efforts vaudevillians made to penetrate it. The formula that owners developed to deal with what they believed was a distracted audience was to provide comfortable and luxurious theaters to help people relax while the players set out to engage, terrify, or startle them. The challenge performers faced was one of securing attention without unduly stressing audiences or giving them too much to think about. This was considered harder than it might seem. According to one wag, variety acts were like marriages: "There are many good ones, but no happy ones." In vaudeville, players often believed that speed or loudness would capture audience attention, but the reality was that "terrific haste in movements, noise and a splurge of speech and an overstaginess in gesture" were more tiring than pleasing and "could not be tolerated." Surprise or terror were effective at waking up audiences, as Marino the auto-defier well knew, but overexposure to them risked further exhausting customers, so booking agents kept the number of shock acts to a minimum. Ultimately, the preferred approach was one of focusing audience attention on "the human note" through the "direct appeal," the strong personality, or "what is called in the profession ginger."[9] These became the heart of performance culture in vaudeville, and they were promoted as a sure antidote to audience passivity.

RELAXATION

"Ladies and gentlemen, by special request," the baritone announced on his return for an encore, "I have been asked to sing 'The Holy City.'" The spectators smiled approvingly; the baritone sang. But Owen Kildare, sitting in the audience, puzzled over the disingenuous exchange. No one, he thought, had made a special request for the song—at least not one that he had heard; in fact, baritone encores in turn-of-the-century vaudeville houses were invariably "The Holy City" or "The Palms." So why did the singer present the fiction of the "special request"? There was, Kildare mused, a presumed communality in vaudeville that encouraged this kind of effort to treat spectators as confidants rather than customers. How often, he thought, had he heard a singer begin a set by stating, "With your kind permission I will sing"? What, Kildare wondered mischievously, if someone in the audience rose and shouted, "No, I will not permit! You shall not sing it with our permission!" It was unlikely, of course; vaudeville was not that kind of entertainment. But it was worth considering.[10]

What Kildare identified was the familiarity that served as oxygen in vaudeville's atmosphere. A reporter who was attending a small-time Yiddish variety theater in New York was surprised, when a popular tune was struck up, to hear the entire audience—men, women, and children—join in the chorus. The theater was "like one big house party, as everybody seems to know every other body, and the most friendly feeling pervades the close and almost unbreathable air." This kind of conviviality was common in neighborhood theaters and was a hallmark of American vaudeville. In fact, managers worked hard to make people feel comfortable and at ease, to create what one called a "home-like feeling."[11]

But there were limits. While vaudevillians strove to make audiences laugh at their jokes or sing along at the chorus, house security was on hand to make sure it didn't become disruptive. Audiences seemed as much disturbed as the management when rowdy minorities attracted attention to themselves. This was always a danger when African American stars were on the boards in predominantly white houses, as black spectators seemed to want to resist the invisibility of the gallery, to reassure the black performers of their support, and to advertise their presence to the white spectators sitting below them. Chicot, the critic for the *New York Morning Telegraph* in an article complaining about the number of black spectators attending a Williams and Walker show at Hurtig and Seamon's music hall in Harlem, a theater that did not segregate its seating, wrote that "the worst feature of the engagement is to be found in the way the negroes overrun the audience. . . . It is their time to yell, and they yell loudly enough to disturb the slumbers of Miss Liberty in the bay. . . . It would make a rabid anti-African out of the most benevolent to see them crowd into a box and drive out the white occupants. They not only pervade the seats, but the atmosphere. . . . Arrangements should be made to wet down the audience at half hour intervals." Chicot knew that audience enthusiasm was a sign of race pride ("It is their time to yell"), which is one of the reasons he objected to it. Attitudes like his make it clear why African American spectators, even in a moderately priced theater like Hurtig and Seamon's, were so excited to see black performers onstage. It was not just a way of expressing enjoyment but a form of protest against a racist society that tried to control how their presence would be accommodated.[12]

The behavior of rowdy spectators could make vaudeville seem like the old immersive theater, but it was different. In the concert saloons and early variety houses, members of the audience felt they had no less right than the performers to be seen and heard. In vaudeville, the audience was generally receptive to encouragement and willing to join in on cue, but they knew their place. Vaudeville cultivated the idea of amusement as a form of relaxation, not as a way of letting off steam. Until mass entertainment revolutionized the concept, relaxation involved peace, escape, or oblivion: a walk in the park, a holiday, or a drunken spree. In vaudeville, relaxation still meant turning off the noise of the street, forgetting the monotonous routine of work, and shutting out unpleasant sensations, but it pursued these goals by distracting spectators through carefree fun. As one performer explained it, spectators did not want "to worry their brains with anything more serious than chuckling at merry nothings or humming lifting melodies."[13]

The goal of creating a relaxed atmosphere was made manifest in theater design. Color, light, and air were deployed to enhance the feelings of comfort. The color scheme in a vaudeville house, Edward F. Albee maintained, had to be "suave, cheerful and restful as well as beautiful." Loew's Orpheum in Boston, a small-time house, was all soft colors and delicate decorations. The interior was painted ivory with touches of old rose and gray, and "no striking or glaring colors have been permitted to intrude; the general atmosphere of the theater is extremely restful and pleasant on the eye." The New Columbia Theater in Davenport, Iowa, was painted almond and gold, and the manager boasted that $6,000 had been spent on the ornamental plaster and paint when the theater was remodeled in 1913. From the outside, wrote a reporter in 1911, the Los Angeles Orpheum was "glare and glitter, blinding light and screeching color," but inside, "after leaving the brightness and theatricism of the splendid exterior," everything was warm and pleasant. "The harmonization of old rose and gold and ivory and dainty gendarme blue was soft and restful. It appealed. You sank back in your big chair.... The lights and their reflections were soft on your eyes." According to Albee, theater lighting "must be according to the laws of optics as regards lines of sight, the concealment of all lamps in coves, and the control of color effects ... [to] avoid strain, cross-rays, glaring footlights and borders and any effects that tire the vision." Heating and especially ventilation were also considered essential to comfort, and most theaters had fans to keep the air moving. Keith's Union Square had hundreds of small electric fans placed all through the theater, and on one hot summer day in Washington, Chase's theater was so cooled by "refreshing breezes" that it "involuntarily produced chills."[14]

The construction of vaudeville as a comfortable, hospitable amusement was enhanced by the fact that the houselights were kept dimmed, not out, and spectators came and went in the middle of acts and spoke to each other in "normal" voices when their attention was not engaged. Keith's New Theater in Philadelphia had telephones in the boxes so that audience members could communicate with "their places of businesses, homes, or with friends" during the show. Not surprisingly, some spectators found the noise of conversation distracting. "It is not possible," one audience member complained, to attend a show where someone in a nearby seat "is not audibly following the movements of the players—'He looks out of the window,' 'She sees him,' etc., etc.—or slyly anticipating the obvious denouement." Caroline Caffin recalled attending a performance where two matinee girls, sitting nearby, kept up a steady stream of commentary, noting which jokes were new, explaining what was coming, and exchanging personal details about the performers. "They talk right along, no matter what happens," protested a performer; "they tell their friends the past, present and future of all actors, and when their stock of imagination gives out they conduct a running fire of criticism as to the merits of the show, sometimes favorable and sometimes not. We actors can see them nodding and making gestures, even if we can't hear." But allowing people to speak to each other, as though they were at home, was not viewed as a sign of engagement. Vaudevillians complained it evidenced distraction and a lack of attention. Vaudeville audiences, a theater critic observed in 1906, display "complete mental inactivity—not an absence of mind power, but . . . all mentality is in a state of absolute involition and relaxation."[15]

Part of the appeal of vaudeville, especially for big-city audiences, was that theaters were often located within walking distance of their homes. In a city like Chicago, in 1914, the thickly populated North Side had a vaudeville theater every few city blocks. On the city's West and Northwest Side, there was the Academy, the American, the Kedzie, the New Apollo, and the Americus. The South Side boasted the Empress, the Monroe, the Grand, the Ellis, and the Midway. In the Loop, large dinner cafés presented vaudeville entertainment with most of them being booked by the same management that handled the leading theaters. The majority of Chicago's first-class houses, like those in other American cities, were what were termed split-week theaters, meaning they changed their bills on Monday and Thursday nights. The density of vaudeville houses and the frequency with which shows changed point to an important feature of the business: the backbone of each theater's audience was its own neighborhood. Live popular entertainment was an immense but highly stratified and location-sensitive industry. There was a hierarchy of venues, and the downtown houses pulled in audiences from all over the city, as well as tourists, but they all relied on a core audience of repeat customers. Convenient locations and proximity to densely populated residential neighborhoods made a night out something people could decide to do on a whim when they just felt like a bit of amusing relaxation.

Indianapolis native Bea Walker remembered being taken by her parents to Keith's every Friday night before World War I. "Vaudeville was our regular entertainment," she recalled. The inevitable consequence of this was that people attended variety shows with "no exacting spirit.... They are wont to flip a coin for the choice of the show... and if we are let down we console ourselves on the gambler's 'better luck next time.'" Instead of seeking involvement in a show, the painter Marsden Hartley, a regular vaudeville patron, explained, audiences are "at rest as far as thinking is concerned. It is something for the eye first and last." The novelist William Dean Howells, another frequent spectator, said most people considered vaudeville a form of diversion. It "rested" one's "soul and brain," he wrote, just to sit there and "listen to the unalloyed nonsense."[16]

African American urban audiences attending "colored" theaters seem to have enjoyed vaudeville in similar ways. Commentators described black audiences in New York as sophisticated and blasé. Lafayette Theater audiences in Harlem were thought to be especially hard to please, and spectators would often walk out during the show. To succeed one had to perform with pep, "work with spirit, sing as if imperilled to by an inner force, and dance with an almost inspired rhythm." Paul Ford, manager of the Iroquois Theater in New Orleans, patronizingly explained that black customers at his theater shared many characteristics with white audiences. This was because "the colored people who patronize this theater are in the habit of going to all the white houses in the city, consequently, they see and know actor[s]." The English writer H. G. Wells, who took in a show at the Pekin Theater in Chicago in 1905, also didn't see much difference between the white people attending music halls back home and the black spectators he observed. Wells described the audience at the African American theater as working-class but not uncouth. "The audience reminded me of the sort of gathering one would find in a theater in Camden Town or Hoxton. There were a number of family groups, the girls brightly dressed, and young couples quite of the London music-hall type. Clothing ran 'smart,' but not smarter than it would be among fairly prosperous north London Jews. There was no gallery—socially—no collection of orange-eating, interrupting hooligans at all. Nobody seemed cross, nobody seemed present for vicious purposes, and everybody was sober."[17]

Commentators unaccustomed to the idea that people might go out to a show to unwind interpreted the audience's relaxed mood as evidence of the "disintegrating" cultural impact of mass culture. But performers and regular patrons had their own understanding of what was going on. Audience members weren't so much bored, they believed, as expectant; they did not want to work for their amusement as they worked for their pay. W. L. Hubbard, a theater critic for the *Chicago Tribune*, referred to a peculiar "vaudeville look," a blend of stolid, patient endurance and resignation without resentment. He knew, however, that it was merely a torpidity that saved energy for the acts that invigorated. Caffin agreed that audiences might look bored, but they were only waiting for something to happen. As vaudevillians said, audiences liked to "sit back and dare us to make them laugh."[18]

Why did vaudevillians believe that most spectators had lost their desire to shout and heckle? Why did they feel audiences were waiting for something to excite their tired interests? Most didn't blame their own house policies or security guards. Rather, those who commented on the topic maintained that it was the conditions of modern life that were most responsible for wearing people out. Americans were being exposed to a continual barrage of shocks that hammered them with "a thousand sensations each minute." Modern times arrived at high speed, and the effect was disorienting. "Everything in these days must be faster and cheaper and better than it was a decade or two ago," wrote P. B. Chase, the president of the Vaudeville Managers' Protective Association in 1902. The result was that the public had forgotten how to slow down. "Once the world knew only how to dawdle," Chase mused; "now it pines to fly. It must fly. Some time it will fly."[19] But for the moment, what people needed most was a release from the pressures of the outside world, and that's what vaudeville set out to provide.

It was not just cars and trams and electricity that were pressing on people's attentions; everywhere there was more noise, more congestion, and more dirt than ever before. Cities were daily becoming bigger, not just in breadth but in height, as skyscrapers transformed the urban landscape. The speed of the changes taking place was striking. There were 8,000 registered automobiles in the United States in 1900; by 1914 there were 1.7 million, in addition to 100,000 trucks. The first building to be named a skyscraper was Chicago's Home Insurance Building—which stood twelve stories high—built in 1884. By 1900 Chicago had over 120 buildings that were over seven stories, and the tallest one, the Masonic Temple, rose twenty-one stories. Eventually, Americans would come to take both motorization and the vertical city for granted, but many in the first generation to experience them considered them unnerving. "You lift your eyes," wrote a visitor to New York in 1895, "and you feel that up there behind the perpendicular wall, with its innumerable windows, a multitude coming and going, crowding the offices that perforate these cliffs of brick and iron, dizzied with the speed of the elevators." The skyscraper and the automobile were the most widely recognized symbols of the modern era, representing its vertical and horizontal vectors. The car became emblematic of freedom, mobility, and danger, while the skyscraper dwarfed the individual and monumentalized the power of business. Vaudeville theaters were constructed to fit seamlessly into this modern urban world.[20]

The urban environment in which Americans lived seemed to be exposing them to forces over which they had no control. As a New York coroner, after hearing a case involving a fatal automobile collision, concluded, "When you leave your homes in the morning you don't know what danger you will run into. I think it is a miracle that so many people escape." The burden that city life appeared to be placing on people's powers of concentration was thought to have grown dramatically as processes of production mechanized, urban spaces became more tangled, and congestion increased. "The age in which we live," one physician worried in 1911, "is putting an extraordinary tax on human machinery. No one who looks about at the multiplying activities of modern life can doubt that our ancestors were subject to no such strain." It was, commentators noted, quite properly dubbed "the strenuous age," for urban life was demanding of people "more energy, more concentration, more nervous force than ever before." There could be little doubt, opined the editor of the *Atlanta Constitution* in 1901, that the pressure that "modern civilization is putting on the brain is well calculated to increase the number of cases ... [at] our insane asylums."[21]

According to many contemporary observers, the cacophony of sounds, the pervasive dirt, the crush of humanity, and the density of buildings were deadening the senses of city people. After a short time living in New York, writer William Crary Brownell reported a decline in his "sensitiveness," a "progressive atrophy" of his nerves, and a tiredness that made him feel at once anxious and apathetic. The great irony was that while modern life demanded more exertion

Detroit's Orpheum Theatre. Vaudeville marketed itself as an entertainment for inhabitants of the modern city, a place of skyscrapers and automobiles. (Detroit Historical Society, 2012.046.909)

and more concentration, attention was a finite and fragile thing. "The fact that strength is lessened by continued effort, even in moderate degree, is a matter of familiar observation," reported one expert on fatigue. According to a Dr. J. H. Girdner, the hammering of modern life was producing nerve damage:

> The deleterious effect of the constant shock or concussion of unpleasant and non-musical sounds on the auditory apparatus is demonstrated

beyond question by the fact that nearly all boiler makers ... are hard of hearing.... There is a well-recognized condition of congestion, amounting sometimes to inflammation in the internal ear ... [that is] liable to occur, in all classes of persons who are exposed, as the inhabitants of the metropolis of New York are, to the continual rattle, roar, and screams which assault their ear drums at nearly all hours of the day or night.

A French tourist evidenced these sentiments, noting in his journal how isolated and preoccupied Americans seemed to be when he encountered them on the street. On the trams in France people looked at you, he observed, but in New York and Chicago "each eye seems fixed upon the inner thought—upon some business—whatever it may be."[22]

Neurasthenia, the "American disease," was widely considered the most damaging psychological effect of modernity. The disease was characterized by lethargy, inattentiveness, depression, insomnia, anxiety, irritability, and inexplicable body pains. Because neurasthenia's symptoms varied from patient to patient, it was diagnosed liberally by physicians who commonly ascribed its onset to factors like overwork, sexual anxiety, noise, and the fast pace of everyday life. Popularized by journalists, writers, and social reformers, it became what historian David Shuster calls "a cultural phenomenon," the subject of novels, plays, news articles, and movies. Shuster counted over 2,000 articles in the *New York Times* dealing with nervous exhaustion or neurasthenia in the period from 1890 to 1910. "The rush and tear and overwork, the emotional excitement connected with failure and success, the slavery to social obligations and pleasures, so characteristic of American women, sufficiently account ... for its widespread existence," a doctor explained in one of those articles. "American fashionable and business life is a continuous nerve-storm. Nor, again, is it peculiarly the rich man's disease, for it afflicts as frequently the poorer classes, on whom fall so heavily the burdens incident to battle the world."[23]

It may seem ironic that vaudevillians countered stress over the speed, crowding, and chaos of modern urban life with rapidly revolving acts, tongue-twisting language, and syncopated melodies. But restorative, distracting, and even stimulating activities, like visiting an amusement park, holidaying on the beach, or going for a vigorous walk, were far more common ways of relieving the pressures of life than rest cures. Severe neurasthenics might need to retreat to the countryside, but most people just required some regular distraction.[24]

Vaudeville became one of these distractions. Audiences, the actor Arnold Daly wrote, did not feel it necessary "to devote energy to preening or puffing themselves up at the theater." Put more simply, the singer Elizabeth Murray explained, audiences "are tired and like noise." Spectators were generally considered to be "a study in scrambled attention," and it fell to the managers and the performers to slowly reenergize their brains and enthusiasms. If booking agents or managers had done their job and the show was well organized, then an unengaged audience was the fault of the performer. Vaudeville was conceived as a balm to turn-of-the-century Americans who felt overburdened by modern life; in cities and towns filled with traffic and noise, it was a form of therapy. As the *New York Sun* reported glibly, "A spirit of relaxation, not to say abandon, pervades vaudeville, and it makes doctors send neurasthenic patients to take a course of these shows just as they might prescribe mud baths. The music, the somewhat foolish jokes, and the dancing rest the tired brain and nerves."[25]

THE DIRECT APPEAL

Naturalness of manner was critical to success in vaudeville. As we have seen, spectators responded positively to those performers who behaved like they weren't acting and whose words and movements "seem to break out spontaneously." Mrs. Konorah, who did "lightning calculations," was considered a poor performer because "she has an unpleasant manner of intonation while speaking, giving the impression of affectation." Managers described the performers' skill of connecting in a natural way with the audience as "that vaudeville something." Players generally said that the "something" began with what they called "the direct appeal." Blanche Ring, a ragtime singer, felt the way to put over a song was "to take the audience into your confidence. Try to make each hearer think that you are singing directly to him or her. All the favorite balladists I have heard have possessed this faculty to a marked degree. . . . They seem to get right at you. . . . Once a singer gets an audience humming with her, or singing the refrain, then it is easy sailing. . . . I take a purely animal, or fleshy, pleasure in getting my audience with me." Others spoke of honesty, lightheartedness, and an ability to share the pleasure they took in performing as critical ingredients. Singer Adele Rowland told a reporter that a player needed "something" to succeed with audiences. "There are girls, you know, that have real talent—sing well, dance well, look well—who never seem to get anywhere. It must be lack of personality. Perhaps my something is alertness. I'm dreadfully alert, you know." Appearing relaxed but remaining engaged onstage might sound simple, but many described it as hard work. May Robson, a musical comedy star who tried performing in vaudeville in 1904, soon quit, declaring it much easier to play a part than to act like one wasn't.[26]

The direct appeal often began with a performer acknowledging the audience and addressing it in a genial way. Press Eldridge, the monologuist, greeted the house: "Hello audience!" Eva Tanguay offered the even more familiar "Hello everybody!" Imro Fox, a big, bald magician with a thick handlebar mustache, adopted a self-deprecating approach. Fox would declare, when he came onstage, "Yes, I'm a magician like the program says. . . . I know you would have taken me for a delicatessen proprietor." Fox's famous "Waltz me again" address to the band leader was another way in which he created a bond with the audience. "Waltz me, Professor," the magician would say; "I do not wish villain music. I want something soothing." Fox would often chat with members of the orchestra or the conductor while he did his magic routine, making the performance seem unscripted and casual.[27]

Performers often talked to the audience during their acts, though managers urged them not to single out individuals. Maud Dunn, who performed in a "sister act," after cracking a joke that fell flat, would urge audience appreciation with the line "think it over." Similarly, Ching Ling Foo, vaudeville's premier Chinese magician, after producing a bowl of rice or a child from under his cloak, would ask the audience in Chinese American stage dialect, "You likee?" The singing duet Massey and Kramer, toward the close of a song that seemed to be dragging, apologized to one audience and assured viewers that the song would soon be over. It actually wasn't that uncommon for singers to request audience indulgence when they felt themselves stuck in a routine that wasn't succeeding. Emma Carus, after singing "None of Them's Got Anything on Me" to a 1908 New York audience, exclaimed, "I'm glad that's over." The audience apparently agreed. Her next song, "Under the Matzos Tree," sung in "Hebrew dialect," also bombed, but this time she had the good sense to stop after just one verse. Animals that refused to perform were common, and trainers had to manage the result calmly as audiences were hostile to those who looked like they were angry. Riene Davies, who had a performing bulldog, would apologize for the animal's "ill manners" and then offer poetic recitations to fill up the time. Kidding the audience was another common trick. Francis Wilson, the comic sketch artist, would close her performance at the turn of the century with the comment, "Ladies and gentlemen: You have behaved beautifully, you have laughed and applauded with an intelligence that is almost human."[28]

Turning a discussion of the performance into the performance itself was yet another vaudeville staple. Harry De Vine and Belle Williams, who did a singing, dancing, and comedy turn, "knocked the audience out of their seats" when they performed this routine at McVickers in Chicago in 1906:

> Williams: I'm having trouble here; the leader won't accompany me.
> De Vine: I'll accompany you. Where do you wish to go?
> Williams: I mean I want the orchestra to accompany me. All I want them to do is to play the music for my song.
> De Vine: Must you sing?
> Williams: What do you mean, "must I sing?"
> De Vine: The audience looks so happy . . .
> Williams: Perhaps you'd rather sing instead.
> De Vine: I'm capable of it.
> Williams: You look like you're capable of anything.[29]

The ostensibly unrehearsed conversations of Williams and De Vine or of Imro Fox and the orchestra conductor made their acts sound improvised, providing audiences with the sense that they were getting something fresh. Laughing at one's own jokes achieved the same effect. Naturally, many of the supposedly impromptu jokes or conversations were rehearsed, but that isn't the point. What mattered in stepping out of character, which apparently unrehearsed conversations or the spontaneous laugh implied, was the insight it appeared to offer into the person beneath the makeup. Audiences seemed to find that kind of laughter infectious. As a critic noted of the Irish dialect comic Kitty Francis, she was so "bubbling over with natural pleasantry" that "you laugh along with her, not knowing half the time what you are laughing at." Sometimes, though, performers could overdo it. Appearing at Hammerstein's in January 1906, the Nichols Sisters laughed so much at their own jokes that the reviewer for *Variety* felt they were suffering from hysteria.[30]

In variety shows, authenticity was created when the "true nature" of the performer was made visible. Although, as Walter Benjamin argued, the "spell of personality" may have been the "phony spell of the commodity" and not the "unique aura of the person," audiences in the early twentieth century appear to have regarded that "spell" as actual enough. Authenticity of an existential kind was at the very heart of vaudeville's aesthetic. It was the essence of the personality that vaudevillians maintained made them successful. It was therefore presented as something other Americans would want to cultivate. Exactly what gave a performer that "special something" was never well defined, but whatever it was did make them more real to their fans. Personality was often linked to a release from constraint and to a way of acting "naturally" or "being oneself." "Impulse takes the place of training" in a variety performer, an Arkansas critic noted, and to be a success the player had to "free herself from tradition" and say, "I am myself in this part."[31]

This kind of freedom was judged a "natural capacity," an ability to shrug off inhibitions and have fun. Her "act is simplicity itself," wrote *Variety* condescendingly of Nora Bayes, for no matter what she sang "it is the individuality of the entertainer herself that carries her offering." Caroline Caffin was astute enough to see the craft in the performance. She dissected Bayes's method, observing her efforts to disarm those in the audience by acknowledging them when she came onstage, with a sideways glance, followed by "a dimpled smile" and then a shy downward look, "as though she would hate to think you might not like her." Then, reassured by the applause, the performer faced the audience and offered "a curving smile" pursued by a sudden upward glance "to see if you caught the curving smile which followed your applause." Bayes's smiles, Caffin wrote, were offered "with an archness which flatters you that she is confident you can see the humor as well as she can," and her songs were rendered "so simply and naturally that it is hard to catch the artifice." The popular singer's likable personality, a comedian remarked, was the yeast that raised her dough, proof of the skill with which she concealed her preparation.[32]

Treating spectators as though they were all confidants, friends, and acquaintances was another popular way of making the direct appeal. "I will not call you ladies and gentlemen," singer Billie Burke told one Pennsylvania audience; "there are so many of my friends here." Harry Lauder, the Scottish singing comedian, according to Caffin, "begins to tell us, confidentially, just because we look like good fellows that he can talk to.... The words come, haltingly and cautiously at first, for he is not going to tell us if we laugh. But soon he is pouring out his whole heart.... He has told us his secret." The secret would then inspire a song, and he would break into the ballad "I Lo'e a Lassie." "He is so human and simple that we forget the art of it," Caffin concluded. In vaudeville it was glamour, humor, and geniality that were on show, and while the disruption of expectations was normal, it was introduced to lift spirits and attract attention. Intense emotions were to be shared, not inflicted on spectators. The audience, Nora Bayes, explained, comes to a vaudeville theater "to meet old friends, to spend an hour or two in pleasant company, and there is no objection to tears if they start from the hearts of their friends on stage."[33]

Among some stars, acting naturally took the form of an appealing, self-deprecating humor or even an awkwardness. Pantomime artist Joe Jackson,

Nora Bayes projected an image of glamour and down-home simplicity. Despite her success and celebrity, she tried to act onstage as though she wasn't acting. (New York Public Library, Billy Rose Theatre Division, Nora Bayes Photographic File)

for example, would come onstage in a shy, hesitating manner, making his way downstage only after several false starts. When the audience applauded or laughed, he would jump. But "in spite of the old clothes and heavy make-up one gets the sense of something very attractive," wrote one reviewer. Kindness and sensitivity radiated from the comic, and while he worked in silence "there is personality behind it." For others, however, personality was all about vim and buoyancy. What the average person calls personality, "the vaudeville manager calls 'ginger,'" wrote one, "and he means that the performer with ginger puts life and action in the work."[34]

The pretense of actuality was enhanced by performers ostensibly using their own names and by vaudeville's deployment of famous people from various walks of life. Baseball players were frequently featured in variety shows, and they talked about their experiences and revealed their pitching or batting secrets. Notorious characters like Emmett Dalton (last surviving member of the Dalton gang of bank robbers) and Lillian Graham (who shot the real estate tycoon W. E. D. Stokes in 1911) talked about themselves and the crimes that made them famous. Others, like Evelyn Nesbit, who had been at the center of America's most scandalous murder trial, tried to put the past behind them, but the "real" events of their lives always factored into their appeal. Ned Wayburn, a professional stage designer and choreographer, even put on a sketch in which he played himself hiring chorus girls for a show. "I decided to put on an act showing myself at work," Wayburn explained, "and have been getting ready for it for some time. I have been studying myself, my personal peculiarities, and my characteristic methods, and I haven't given myself the best of it, I assure you.... I shall give a practical demonstration of how I work."[35]

The direct appeal could lead performers to anger when audiences seemed uninterested. The pressure on vaudevillians to succeed by connecting with spectators led them to resent audiences that remained unmoved by their efforts to be likable or funny. "The other night," Owen Kildare wrote, when a comic in a song-and-dance team delivered a joke that went flat, the comedian "showing his displeasure in his look... stepped closer to the footlights and sent this question into the house: 'What's the matter? Can't you hear me down there, or are you afraid of splitting your gloves?'" It was an uncomfortable moment and one neither the audience nor the manager appreciated.[36]

"It is the public demand that the actor supplies," asserted Homer Mason, a skit performer. Managers carefully watched the auditorium and made notes, not just on the acts that went over but on which individual jokes or songs succeeded. Harry Miner, the Bowery theater owner and ostensible inventor of the hook (famously used to yank bad performers off the stage), insisted that he didn't "take it upon myself to dictate to the public.... They can judge for themselves. They pay their money and they take their choice." Performers knew that they would get more pay if the audience liked them, and the number of rounds of applause or the number of encores were the accepted measures of success.[37]

Ever sensitive to audience response, managers regularly cut acts, demanded changes of costume, and censored words or movements. They were pulled in two directions, anxious to secure novelties but at the same time insistent that performers do the things that patrons expected. Managers, a player complained in the *New York Sun*, "will try to keep you doing the things they think you do best," even though "this is a business in which you've got to show a little variety to get by." In one case a manager convinced a performer to deliver his monologue in blackface rather than white. Sometimes they went even further. Cissy Loftus, a brilliant mimic, wanted desperately to try her hand at conventional acting and in 1901 persuaded the manager at Keith's Boston to feature her in a sketch based on the fairy tale "Undine." The play was a flop, and after two nights Edward Albee interceded and demanded that Loftus complete the remainder of the week doing her famous imitations. When the actor refused, pointing out that she was under contract to perform in a play, Albee scheduled her subsequent performances at 1 p.m. and 6 p.m., when the theater was empty. Loftus resented Albee's efforts to kill her skit, as all performers disliked managerial controls, but they seldom complained publicly about these things, and it was never something they raised through their union. Those few who did protest, such as the mercurial Eva Tanguay, were considered difficult by those in the trade.[38]

Spectators in vaudeville did not just want a natural acting style; they wanted the real thing—the performer just as he or she was in life. George Fuller Golden, one of the first comic monologuists, pioneered the technique of appearing onstage without makeup and "simply talking to the audience" about his own and his "friend" Casey's experiences. Golden said he got laughs by exposing "the humorous part of himself." He talked of what he saw on the street, in railway trains, on trolley cars, and in hotels, lobbies, public places, and drawing rooms. The conversational address made it doubly important for audiences to "like" the performer, and spectators seemed to especially enjoy performers who were "unctuous." The English singer Alice Lloyd was one of the most popular performers in prewar vaudeville. She had a winsome, gentle manner that struck audiences as sweet. When she sang to a mirror "I'm Looking for the Lovelight in Your Eye," audiences were charmed. Her quaint mannerisms, gushed one reviewer, "make her an altogether likeable person."[39]

Vaudeville headliners insisted in interviews that they loved the connection they had with audiences—the way people seemed happy just to have them show up. The coquettish French singer Irene Bordoni, whose exorbitant salary made her one of vaudeville's great drawing cards in the second decade of the century, explained that American audiences always seemed to greet her with "big handclapping and smiles on faces and even at the opening performance everybody seems to say 'Hello, Bordoni, glad you have come back to us.'" Lucille Carter, an English performer, felt the same way. Reflecting on the "kindness of everybody" in the theater, she told an interviewer, "The American audience is . . . so sympathetic, so keen for every point that the actor may make, so expectant that he will do his best." European audiences, it was remarked, seemed to want to get their "money's worth" from a show and tended to be critical of the performers. In the United States, Caffin noted, she had frequently heard members of the audience privately denigrate a performer and then applaud him or her "from pure goodwill."[40]

But it is also true that some types of acts adapted with difficulty to the demands of actuality and the direct appeal. Because vaudeville had a seemingly limitless appetite for material, it drew in and spawned acts of all types, many of which had not been part of saloon-based variety. Before vaudeville, the country's leading magicians, for example, appeared in their own traveling shows, while local and less successful talent tended to work in museums and fairs. Magicians traditionally performed their acts slowly and deliberately, infusing their art with mystery and a hint of the supernatural. Alexander the Great's three-hour show in the 1890s featured only a few major illusions, as did Kellar's, with the intervals between their tricks being filled with magical talk and a "repertory of rabbit snatching and sleight of hand" (or in the case of the Great Hermann, his wife's dancing). While magicians had been publicly disassociating themselves from the occult since the early nineteenth century, they continued to link their craftsmanship with serious and mysterious powers. The nineteenth-century public, after all, expected magicians to be wizardly. As Jean-Eugène Robert-Houdin, the founder of modern theatrical magic, explained, "A conjuror was an actor playing the part of a magician," meaning that the performer had to make the public believe they were watching real sorcery.[41]

While magic acts became reasonably common in vaudeville, it was hard to create the required mystery, even if one was a good actor, with a turn squeezed into twelve minutes and positioned between hoop rollers and nut comics. Eva Fay, for example, the soft-voiced fortune-teller, illusionist, and mind reader who claimed to be a "daughter of India" and a student of "the famed Mahatmas," generally performed in mystical golden robes, seated on an "Oriental" dais and attended by "a big Nubian stage servant." Although she boasted that she "hobnobs with goblins" and "calls spirits of an uncanny realm at will," she nonetheless reached out to her audience to make her act work in vaudeville. At the Bronx Theater in April 1911, she had the house rocking with laughter and cheers when she grandiloquently predicted that the Giants would win the pennant.

Shekla, a "Hindu fakir" who appeared in "picturesque Oriental costume," similarly gave up trying to appear the dignified holy man and in 1907 introduced a big finish where he "cook[ed] an Oriental dish on the head of his wife."[42]

The lightening of magic acts had an impact. Spectators regularly commented, even before the war, that conjurers were becoming less common in vaudeville. While it is true that their number did decline by about a quarter between 1902 and 1914, what audiences were noticing was the ascendance of the prestidigitator who did not perform traditional magic. An increasing number of magicians were comedians who engaged in lighthearted banter while performing a few tricks. Others presented themselves as card manipulators or escape artists rather than as magicians. The "new school magician wishes to be considered clever, rather than mysterious, emphasizing the fact that the wonders he performs are the result of his own dexterity, and not—as the old style magician would have us believe—the work of some hidden, occult power," one of the country's senior conjurers acknowledged in 1914.[43]

For traditional magicians the problem was one of upholding the dignity of their craft in a venue that seemed to work against them. As an "old-timer" grumbled, the variety show artist who wanted to display his or her dexterity was a "modernist," not a respecter of tradition. Eugene Laurant, who spent much of his career playing the classy Lyceum circuit, begged vaudeville managers to prevent the "young man stunted in intellect"—with "nothing but a few dollars with which to buy apparatus and the ability to get on and off the stage without stumbling" and who "juggles the English language with the same abandon used in handling a knife and fork"—to pass himself off as a magician. The true conjurer, he insisted, had to at least be "polished and suave in his stage action" and possessed of a good education, a knowledge of chemistry, mathematics, and optics, and a commanding personality. The vaudeville magician, Laurant declared, should be no different from his forebears: he should "use his own knowledge to do, apparently, the impossible." It would undermine the craft to have him seen as "merely acting the part of the magician."[44]

The root cause of the decline of traditional magic was not hard to find. "In vaudeville," a writer in the *Los Angeles Times* quipped, "the unexpected is expected." This should have been a boon to magicians, but audiences also wanted truth and realism. It was this that disinclined them from taking conjuring seriously (audiences actually "come to scoff," one manager lamented) and put the pressure on magicians to find ways of connecting with spectators. The solution for many magicians was to emphasize explainable skill rather than supernatural power, though this increased the likelihood that some would reveal their secrets in order to show the public how clever they were.[45] Exposure (as magicians called it) had the benefit of making magic "usable"—something audience members could try at home, just like the songs and dances and phrases they saw and heard in theaters. Magicians had especial problems being both "real" and "magical," but they were not alone in having to appear "normal" to get by in vaudeville.

Magicians, by virtue of their acts or personalities, faced particular challenges appearing affable or approachable. Like many who practiced the mysterious arts, Pauline the hypnotist wanted to look intense and focused in performance. When working with a subject he preferred to ignore the audience, acting as though he was totally absorbed in the business of controlling the mind of someone else. Under his power, subjects were able to tolerate 600 pounds of weight being placed on their stomachs, and they did not die when the hypnotist drained their blood into a container and then restored it to their bodies (they would, however, go white as this was done, "proving" it was happening). But to reach a vaudeville audience, in between these sensational feats, Pauline introduced burlesque. Unwilling to compromise his own intensity, the hypnotist worked with assistants, who were often planted in the audience and who had been selected for their comic abilities. By making them do outrageous things when under his hypnotic sway, Pauline turned a serious act into one that was "hysterically funny." Audiences intuited that the act was so outrageous it had to be a sham, which was why Pauline's supposed concentration and his assistants' slapstick humor saved it. It was, wrote the manager of the Grand Opera House in Pittsburgh in 1908, "a big hit as a laughing number but it is about the fakest thing I have ever looked at."[46] By juxtaposing the serious business of mind manipulation with goofiness, Pauline became a star.

Vaudevillians with unusual or what were considered off-putting features also had to find ways of making vaudeville audiences like them. Armless painters and musicians who played instruments with their feet had been featured in dime museums, but in vaudeville they could not get by as "freaks." Many talked about their disabilities and how they compensated for them. A few brought audiences into their confidence by making light of their unusual attributes. Laddie Cliff, an eccentric dancer, scored a hit of immense proportions, finishing with encores and bows beyond count, when he was introduced at Hammerstein's in 1908. Cliff had really long legs and an "abnormally vacant countenance" and onstage he seemed to be only vaguely interested in his own act. His legs struck observers as too thin to support his languid body, and his voice was unpleasantly high-pitched. In a laconic monologue he would "recount the lack of appreciation shown by a vulgar world or make a few cynical observations on life in general." Then, by some "twitch of the eyebrow or turn of the head," he would give the audience to understand that he knew they considered him ludicrous. With amazed disapproval he would stare at his own legs as they jerked into "impossible attitudes and angles," apparently oblivious of the need for anatomical coherence.[47]

Cliff acted as though he were aware of his singular physique and mental vacuity because he wanted audiences to laugh with him rather than at him. The direct appeal was all about sharing in a common experience and reducing the separation between the actor and the audience. Nora Bayes pointed out that it was impossible for any artist to determine "how an audience is held—can the painter tell you why he paints well, or the singer why she sings well?" She archly remarked that it was all about being comfortable in oneself and making others feel the same way. "The simple truth never fails.... Be sincere.... In holding an audience... you must sustain the intensity of truth and sincerity from beginning to end." Personality, Bayes explained, was an overused word and "has nothing to do with holding an audience.... One must have heart, faith and love for one's audience. These are the elements of friendship.... I do not want an audience to laugh at me, I want them to laugh with me, just as I want my friends to do when we are together."[48]

The ability of African American stars in predominantly white vaudeville to connect with audiences was limited due to racial antipathies. White spectators, Bert Williams felt, always laughed at him, not with him. "The sight of other people in trouble is nearly always funny.... The man with the real sense of humor is the man who can put himself in the spectator's place and laugh at his own misfortune.... Nearly all of my successful songs have been based on the idea that I am getting the worst of it." His inability to appeal directly to the audience made him feel an object of humor. Like Tanguay, he complained that audiences wanted only to see and hear him do familiar work, especially his song "Nobody." "Before I got through with Nobody I could have wished that both the author of the words and the assembler of the tune had been strangled or drowned or talked to death," Williams explained. "For seven whole years I had to sing it. Month after month I tried to drop it and sing something new, but I could get nothing to replace it, and the audience seemed to want nothing else. Every comedian at some point in his life learns to curse the particular stunt of his that was most popular."[49]

Racism was central to Williams's feelings of objectification. A reporter in *Variety* confirmed that "the American public refuses to take the colored race seriously as entertainers. It wants them with a dash of comedy and consistently refuses to accept them in any other guise than the jester's motley." But racism in this case was making more apparent a problem that all vaudevillians—of all races—faced. All risked having the audience ignore them or reduce them to types. Audience members sometimes felt sufficiently comfortable in vaudeville houses to subject performers to abuse as well as to applause. Occasionally someone would call out, "Get the hook," and some would "guy" players with "catcalls." The permeability of vaudeville's fourth wall, which performers and managers worked hard to achieve, allowed a limited amount of communication from the house. But when audiences exploited their right to applaud, performers complained of the spectators' tyrannical demands. Harry Lauder, the Scottish singing comedian, performed five songs and made three funny speeches when he appeared as the second-to-last act at the Lincoln Square in 1908. But the audience could not get enough of it. At the close of his twenty-minute turn, it "stormed for two minutes to an empty stage." When Lauder returned, "the din held him speechless for minutes at several points ... [and he was] unable to make himself heard."[50] In the end he was kept onstage for an hour and fifteen minutes.

The distancing effect of celebrity could become, as in Lauder's case, something of a burden. In fact, the hype surrounding stars—the music, the fashion, the high salaries, the press releases—all encouraged totemic reverence and threatened to limit person-to-person identification. Some performers were worried enough about this to repeatedly complain about it. Eva Tanguay frequently protested that audiences would not let her leave the stage before she sang her most popular song, "I Don't Care." Since she insisted she hated the tune, audience behavior struck her as a form of abuse. "I didn't like to sing it," Tanguay whinged; "I didn't like the idea of singing about myself—but managers told me it was a good business. It was a good business for them. People got the idea that what I was singing was really true—that I didn't care, that I was conceited, that I was crazy. They came to see me because they thought I was a freak. Shall I tell you how much it hurts me to sing 'I Don't Care'? I detest it—but, perhaps, I shouldn't, because my audiences love it."[51]

A few performers bristled at the suggestion that they had to cater to the needs of their fans. Spectators had to be woken up, Marie Dressler insisted, and "you can't cuddle or jolly a vaudeville audience." She approached the task with a "come here, you" attitude, and "I grab them figuratively by the back of the neck. It's the mental effort to grab your audience quick and hold them ... interested that comes so hard. If you don't hit them right from the shoulder, you're lost."

But Dressler's shock tactics were uncommon. More usual was what Henry Jenkins calls vaudeville's "affective immediacy," the bond of fellowship that performers created with audiences. It was all right to grab attention, but not if it was done in a belligerent or threatening way. According to Caroline Caffin, it was more often a casual geniality that secured attention in vaudeville: "that feeling of good-fellowship." The audience "loves to be on confidential terms with the performer, to be treated as an intimate. It loves to have the actor step out of his part and speak of his dressing-room, or hint at his salary, or flourish a make-up towel."[52]

The direct appeal was a convention of variety saloon entertainment in the nineteenth century. In the barroom context, where audiences were male, drinking, and out for a particular kind of "good time," it made considerable sense. But that convention did not have to carry over into vaudeville, which was produced in huge theaters before men, women, and children arrayed in rowed seating and in which drinking and cursing were prohibited. It persisted as a way of reaching audiences because vaudevillians believed that spectators were exhausted and distracted and needed to be reengaged. Conveying the impression that spectators were out for an undemanding and fun evening with their friends and neighbors seemed the right way to do it.

Being among Americans, the expatriate novelist Henry James observed during a return visit from Europe in 1906, was like living among rubber people. The mental and emotional material had to be elastic, he thought, as it was constantly stretching to absorb the pressure of modern life. "Everything and everyone, all objects and elements, all systems, arrangements, institutions, functions, persons, reputations, give the sense of their pulling hard at the india-rubber: almost always, wonderfully, without breaking it." The near constant demand that people pay attention was thought to be limiting the American's ability to concentrate. "Twenty-five years ago you couldn't see an automobile on the streets of New York," explained the vaudeville comedian Lew Dockstader. "Nowadays, if you don't see it, it takes you almost twenty years to get out of the hospital."[53] At root here was not the reality but the perception. Modern urban life appeared to be more taxing and even dangerous, and Americans were believed to be having trouble coping with it. And it was the idea of a distracted, overstimulated audience in need of relaxation that determined how owners decorated their theaters and vaudevillians delivered their acts. Performers understood that they were working in a theater geared to rest and recovery from the stresses of the day, in which tired audiences were being invited to park their brains and feelings. This led them to try to connect with audiences as friends and neighbors and to impress them with their skill or talent rather than to awe them with something alien or otherworldly.

Writing in the *Yale Review* in 1917, novelist and jurist Robert Grant worried about the way the "tired and complacent" public had turned vaudeville into a craze. Overstimulated in daily life, he wrote, Americans were seeking "mental torpor," amusement rather than engagement, entertainment rather than art. Grant was hostile to vaudeville's democratization of manners and attitudes, but he recognized it arose from a therapeutic impulse. Despite the theater's popularity with women, it was men, he wrote, who controlled tastes, and the "tired businessman" had patronized vaudeville as "a gay but inane and salacious compound" from which they sought nothing but "relaxation" and were rewarded with an "atrophied imagination." It was their desire for passive pleasure that was killing meaningful theater and producing popular arts that lacked beauty, structure, and artifice. He linked the rise of mass entertainment not just to audience exhaustion but to a growing valorization of the unrefined and common. "Formalism of every kind has been dealt a death blow," Grant lamented, and "the motto of the modern world is, 'Let us get down to business and be natural. Hang appearances.'" Vaudevillians would have agreed with this assessment. But what Grant missed was the burden this new culture placed on performers. It fell to them to revive the public's exhausted interests and stimulate its appetites. Successful performers achieved this in various ways, but as Grant noted, a common one was to remove one's clothes. "Our passion for naturalness made a fetish of undress," he wrote, lamenting the disappearance of the padded and constrained Victorian body, and it threatened, in more ways than one, "to clip the wings of imagination."[54]

Vaudeville's performance culture was the product of a thoroughly modern idea: that commercial amusement could become a normal part of daily life, a form of therapy and a guide to behavior. That idea arose out of the perception that American society was modernizing at such a staggering pace that people were unnerved and distracted. Theaters would provide the comfort and escapism that the public needed. As Alexander Pantages, the theater owner, explained, "We've got enough trouble at home. When we go to the theater we want to be amused." Performers would then supply spectators with a convivial form of entertainment, the equivalent of a good joke told by a friend or a song sung with the family around the piano. The direct appeal was the essence of vaudeville performance, but it was never enough. To keep it continually fresh, performers also had to show they had strong personalities, to introduce new features, to showcase fashions, or to add new twists to make the familiar interesting. The keynote of vaudeville, noted a Brooklyn critic, was "variety. Anything and everything so long as it is different." It was this combination of novelty, glamour, and comfort that made vaudeville so appealing to tired spectators. The only worry, Willie Hammerstein admitted, was that there was only so much variety to go around. In a world of constant change and modernity, innovation can become so normative that it begins to seem commonplace. "Every vaudeville manager," he wrote, "must feel at heart a dread of that future when the cream shall be skimmed and only the milk is left, when novelty shall become tiredness, and there is no longer a new sensation left in vaudeville."[55]

CHAPTER FOUR

VAUDEVILLE MODERNISM

POET EZRA POUND could have lifted his slogan "Make It New" from vaudeville (he didn't; he got it from the founder of the Shang dynasty in China, who had it inscribed on his bathtub). Novelty was an essential feature of variety because managers and performers alike presumed that audiences were tired and restless and needed the stimulation of the unfamiliar. As comic monologuist Lloyd Spencer explained in 1907, for performers "it is a case of the survival of the fittest.... The demand for new things keep[s] the vaudeville artist on the jump continually. The oldest joke well told has no value." Writing four years earlier, a journalist agreed: "The demand for something new accounts for the increasing popularity of the houses which produce vaudeville. It is taken for granted by the public that even when 'old favorites' appear, there will be something new, but if there isn't, the turn doesn't last very long anyway."[1]

Vaudeville balanced a comfortable, convivial atmosphere with an offbeat, contemporary style. It tried to create a community of well-behaved but relaxed spectators. Vaudeville also democratized modern fashions, giving what one writer termed "the mutable many" visual and aural access to what had hitherto been the preserve of the "modish few."[2] But it did more: it made ordinary middle- and working-class Americans feel that their culture, their words, their dances, and their people were in vogue. Vaudeville's celebrities, with their shocking incomes and rags-to-riches life stories, symbolized that validation, which is what made them so vital and alluring.

The democratization of fashion and style, which vaudeville exemplified, came hand in hand with new attitudes, manners, forms of expression, and values. The slang that performers used was not cast as a throwback to tradition or a sign of stupidity, as dialect expressions had been when uttered by minstrel or rube characters in nineteenth-century farces. Instead, it was linked to the city, to social mobility, and to liberalized attitudes toward sex and leisure and family and work. Similarly, glibness about one's in-laws, boss, or wife wasn't offered up as proof of low character; it was presented as cosmopolitan. Vaudeville was clearly "modern" in its outlook. The question is: Were variety artists also "modernists"?

Vaudeville developed during a tumultuous and creative period in Western culture. The rapid transformation taking place in urban society, revolutions in science and knowledge, and the rush of technology inspired Western artists and thinkers to invent new ways of expressing themselves and new understandings of the natural world. The sensory and intellectual overload of modern life seemed to demand an art that was experimental and convention-busting. This inspired a remarkable convergence in the arts, philosophy, and science as a group of innovators, whom today we call "modernists," set out to reimagine traditional constructions and idealist philosophies.

For much of the nineteenth century, the dominant intellectual viewpoint held that science yielded truths, not hypotheses, that God's majesty was discernible in the world, and that the landscapes of nature and history made the same irrefutable sense from whichever angle they were seen. This vision of a coherently material and well-ordered universe, which needed only to be cataloged to be understood, was in wholesale retreat by the turn of the twentieth century. Modernists were critical of inherited certitudes and presented life as fractured, somewhat incoherent, random, and often cruel. Early twentieth-century (or "high") modernists used unfamiliar perspectives, dialects, technologies, and contexts to show how the senses altered the perception and meaning of objects and experiences. In place of a solid, material universe, they conceived of a nature disordered by the feelings and memories of the people occupying it.

Most vaudevillians would have been only vaguely aware of contemporary trends in art and letters, if that. There is little evidence to suggest that they employed new techniques because they were consciously reevaluating the nature of reality or the concept of the self. But they were living in the same transformative times that inspired the modernists, and they were also looking for ways of understanding and expressing them. The goal of modernism as a movement, historian Richard Pells writes, "was to force people to see, hear, and think about the world in entirely new ways." Vaudeville had the same goal. This was why a New York drama critic could say that the variety theater "represents that same let-the-conventions-go-hang tendency in the art of the theater that *vers libre* [free verse] represents in poetry and cubism in art."[3] In fact, one of the more interesting things about vaudeville is that its performers employed many of the same techniques that modernist artists were using. The high-spirited silliness of variety entertainment, its preoccupation with itself, its questioning of audience/performer conventions, its employment of dialects and masks, and its ability to assimilate new sounds and movements seemed to parallel the radical experiments modernists were undertaking in architecture, music, literature, and fine art.

A peculiarity of variety was that it was at once naturalistic and completely artificial. It offered the impression of actuality onstage only to subvert it with an environment that was thoroughly theatricalized. In this way, vaudeville manifested the inner tension within the concept of realism itself, the fact that when something real becomes art it "ceases to be reality and becomes artifact."[4] This chapter argues that many vaudevillians, like innovators in other fields, were aware of this tension and presented it ironically by making fun of the theatrical nature of the real or the actuality of the theater. Disorienting audiences was a popular technique in vaudeville just as it was in modern art, which used the physical properties of the paint or the different textures of the collage to draw attention to the contrived nature of the image.

Moreover, for both popular and "high" artists, disrupting spectator expectations seemed an appropriate way of reflecting on the times in which they lived. This involved more than just demonstrating the unpredictable impact of emergent technologies, like electrical wires and motorcars, or even using slang and syncopation. Many artists chose to disorient, surprise, and provoke because that seemed a good way of representing belief systems that were fracturing. In variety, spectators were regularly challenged by ironic contrasts or startling turns. Performers with dwarfism, for example, contrasted their size with unusual displays of strength, dexterity, or ferocity. Rossow's Midgets, the most famous company of little people, was best known for its choreographic violence where the performers "pummel and ... punch each other about, they smash and they slap each other on the face and head, all so quickly that it keeps the spectator wide awake to catch all of the action." Rossow's company was playing with cultural traditions linking little people to uncontrolled children or gremlins, and members aimed their act primarily at females in the audience. These same contradictions were deployed by composer Alexander Zemlinsky in his dissonant modern opera *Der Zwerg*.[5]

The increased speed of modern life and stunning innovations like skyscrapers, automobiles, airplanes, and telephones had a major impact on arts and letters. Less well understood is how modernity transformed popular culture. This chapter points to similarities in the ways intellectuals and entertainers approached technological and cultural change. Vaudevillians were intrigued by the same issues that attracted elite artists and thinkers: Could time and space be manipulated? Should passion, perversity, and unreason continue to be vilified? What was the relationship between personality and character? Modern life, it seemed, propelled many serious artists and a great number of popular ones to examine questions whose answers had once been taken for granted.

The parallels between modernism and variety lend credibility to the idea that America underwent a broadly based and reasonably coherent cultural shift in the early twentieth century. What vaudeville shows is that a great number of popular entertainers began looking at perception and knowledge in new ways. Vaudeville offered a democratized version of modernism. I don't want to push this argument beyond credibility by suggesting that innovative variety performers should be included in the modernist canon. But some, like Charlie Chaplin and Buster Keaton, have been described as "modernist artists," and this chapter suggests that they were not alone.[6] Many less-inspired vaudevillians than Chaplin and Keaton experimented with techniques that seemed appropriate to their questioning age, and one can divine from their work a new engagement with time and space, the nature of the self and reality itself.

But vaudevillians did not generally want to engage the spiritual or moral crisis that so troubled modernists. With very few exceptions, they did not muse on fear, obsession, pain, or the power of technology to oppress or dehumanize. There were no "desmoiselles d'Avignon" in vaudeville. Variety performers employed some of the techniques of modernist art without infusing them with any purpose beyond pleasure and relaxation. Moreover, unlike modernists, vaudevillians wanted their work to give audiences a lurch, not cut them from their moorings.

Consequently, novelty in vaudeville involved gimmicks or formulas instead of deep thinking. Even joking about offering something new could be turned into something new. As Henry Lewis, the Dutch comedian, once explained to his audience, "You know this is a new act—brand new. It reminds me of an old act—the one I did the last time I was here.... You know, by this time I ought to be doing something—I ought to sing or dance—but what's the use. There's been so much good singing and dancing on the bill ahead of me—and as soon as I start in you'd forget all about them—and they got to make a living too—so just for their sake, I won't do nothing." The juggler Edward Lavine recalled his agent telling him, after several years of performing in the small time, that he needed to update his act to make it novel. "Listen Ed," he told Lavine, "the trouble with your act is that it is too commonplace. There's a million juggler acts and yours is just like the rest of them.... What you want to do is dress your act up ... make it different. See?" Lavine took the advice to heart and made it to the big time by wearing a uniform, calling himself a "general," and setting his juggling act in an army encampment. He continued to throw the same hats, cigars, and "amusing paraphernalia," but he was now considered a "spectacular novelty." "You see," he explained to a reporter, "it isn't so much what you do, it's the way you do it."[7]

The tendency of vaudevillians to innovate in style rather than in substance encouraged reflexive habits. A great number of vaudeville acts were a pastiche of other performers' work, reworked to appear new. Sometimes, as in the case of Johnny O'Connor and Frank Dixon's performance at the American Roof in New York in 1917, the collage was so obvious as to be tedious. According to a bemused reporter, the pair opened "doing the Edna Aug scrub woman (as a man), then the Flanagan and Edwards' elusive soap, with the McIntyre and Heath palm-reading gag about the Iceman next, . . . after which there is some step-ladder business suggesting Louis Simon and many others, together with the straight man at this time talking in the rapid-fire Van Hoven delivery, while following was the goat without a nose, somewhat revised." This hadn't consumed over three minutes and the critic, thoroughly annoyed, walked out. As he explained, he had no "special desire to chance seeing the rest of vaudeville in the remainder of the turn."[8]

Vaudevillians wanted their acts to appear new, and they struggled to present some of the complex questions of their time, but they rarely sought to appear gloomy or pessimistic. In this they differed profoundly from their modernist contemporaries: where modernists exposed the disturbing dimensions of life, vaudevillians preferred to emphasize the positive.

DECONSTRUCTING PERFORMANCE

In a novelty skit of 1907, performed at Tony Pastor's Theater in New York, Fannie Van came on with a member of the house staff, Louis Schwartz. Schwartz was dressed like a seedy urban sporting type: false beard, small brimmed hat, and ostentatiously checkered clothes. He looked, according to *Variety*'s reviewer, "for all the world like a race track tout just after winning a bet, and on his way to keep an engagement with his 'lady fren.'" Fannie began arguing with Schwartz, whom she addressed as "Mr. Van." After a few minutes, she ordered him to take his trunk out of their dressing room and vamoose from her life. As Schwartz exited, Charles Van (her actual husband and partner) entered, dressed as one of the stage crew. He told Fannie that the manager wanted the disturbance stopped, and as he walked offstage, Fannie asked who he was and whether he could act. "I'm the carpenter," Charles replied, "and they keep me here because I can give the whole show if anything happens." "Do you know our act?" Fannie asked. "Sure," said the supposed carpenter. "Would you help me out with it for $10?" "For $10, I would eat the scenery," said the carpenter. The pair then went through a song-and-dance routine, with Charles slipping up now and then in order to preserve the pretense of inexperience. The Vans employed a gimmick to surprise the audience and to create interest in their decade-old routine. They staged a series of inversions: first Fannie and Louis Schwartz made it seem as though they weren't acting, entering as a real-life couple. Judging from the reviews, this produced spectator curiosity as they wondered if the actors knew they were onstage or if they were witnessing the start of a performance. Of course, Schwartz's outrageous outfit undercut the illusion of reality, raising further doubt about the seriousness of it all, even if it justified Fannie's anger at being married to such an obvious louse. The device of the carpenter then democratized the act. Anyone, it seemed, could make it in vaudeville, and the honest but poor (he'd do anything for ten dollars) carpenter was clearly a nicer guy than the oily husband. All of these inversions and complications—the apparent confusion of the personal and public and the indeterminate nature of the act—were designed to surprise and delight. But the Vans were also short-circuiting the audience's belief that in vaudeville real people played themselves, and the confusion of identities served to deny spectators a fixed perspective.[9]

Creating substance, or at least novelty, by making the audience unsure about what they were watching was surprisingly common in vaudeville. Henry Lewis, in his monologue "Squidgulum," told the audience that he would shortly be doing a sketch and asked spectators to "give me as much silence as you got. Because I'm very temperature. And when I start to act, the least bit of noise annoys.... You see this sketch is full of big moments, so big that each moment seems like an hour and a quarter, and all the way through it's very sadness, and when I start to act I'm going to act all over, up and down, side to side, with all the heart I got in me. Even my body will move." In preparation for the sketch he had announced, Lewis then called to the wings for scenery and the stage crew brought on a couch. Lewis then called for a woman, for as he explained to the audience, "no woman can be too beautiful for that couch. That's the kind of couch for a beautiful woman." A male stagehand then entered, whom Lewis made sit on the couch and whom he instructed to act like a beautiful woman. "I got a couch and the beautiful woman," he continued, addressing the house, "now I want her past. Bring in her past [nothing happens].... Can you beat that, I go to all the trouble to dig up a past for her, and then when I want to use it, it ain't there." The stage manager then entered and asked Lewis when he was going to get around to performing his sketch. Lewis asked innocently if he said he had a sketch. The manager waved to the audience: "You told them," to which Lewis replied, "What have they got to do with it?" This led the stage manager to walk off in an apparent fury as he ordered the stagehands to strike the scene.[10]

The relaxed, conversational approach of Henry Lewis turned the traditional theatrical aside into a performance in its own right. Similarly, the Vans used the "direct appeal" as a framing device, introducing themselves to the audience and at the conclusion asking spectators whether they thought they should stay together. What was it about these acts, which today seem contrived and cloying rather than "screamingly funny" (as the Vans' act was rated), that made them effective and popular? Much naturally depended on the timing and the delivery of the jokes, but the situations were popular and were widely replicated. Because of vaudeville's aesthetic of actuality, turning a performance into something that appeared real and then unsettling that perception was a common way of securing spectator attention and engaged laughter. Statistics are impossible to generate, given that parodies of reality were seldom identified by reviewers, but at least 2 percent of comedy acts and sketches can be identified as presenting real people who had stumbled onto the stage and found themselves in comic situations, while another 3 percent dealt with "satires" of stage life. In other words, this type of act was at least as common as African American performers, animal trainers, or magicians.

A number of acts also made the experience of performers—getting dressed or undressed, putting on makeup or getting hired—into an act. Audiences seem to have been intrigued by the mechanics of vaudeville and enjoyed looking behind the scenes, whether at the private lives of stars or at the process of applying makeup. The curiosity was aroused by both the novelty of mass entertainment and the promise that anyone could be in show business. Tudor Cameron and Edward Flanagan developed a skit in 1905 that was widely copied, called "On and Off," where they played two minstrel men who do a song and dance that ends in a quarrel. The fight leads the pair to "call off" their act and retreat to a dressing room (a part of the stage set up to look like one) where they continue to argue while taking off their blackface makeup and dressing for the street. The argument revolved around the mechanics of the act itself and how the routine was working, which made *Variety* worry that it might be "a bit too 'shoppy.'" But such was not the case, and theirs was "a novelty act that went very big for us," according to the manager of Keith's Pittsburgh theater. A Harlem theater manager agreed, noting that "the novelty of the act appealed immensely to our audience." What was there in Cameron and Flanagan's sketch that audiences found so new and appealing? According to a Pittsburgh manager, it was the "quarrelling, which is really funny to the audience, while they change to whiteface."[11] Washing off the burnt cork may have been particularly interesting because the personal transformation its removal represented—from black to white—was so comprehensive. But Cameron and Flanagan were simply using the blackface as a way of drawing attention to the self-referential elements, the theater behind and before the footlights.

As we have seen, the idea of turning the removal of blackface into an act originated with white female "coon" performers who didn't want audiences to think that they were actual African Americans. In 1903–4, Ned Wayburn cast seventeen Minstrel Misses in a "white face" specialty, after which they applied burnt cork to their "pretty features, (this operation taking place in full view of the audience and affords considerable fun) and give an old time minstrel" performance of plantation songs and dances. One of the stars of that show, Bertie Herron, would go on to build a very successful vaudeville career by unpacking stage conventions. Indiana-born Herron broke into vaudeville in 1903 at the age of twenty-one and first attracted positive reviews as the Tambo in the Minstrel Misses. Herron made the scandal sheets one year later when her coded love letters to Wayburn, written in baby-talk slang, were made public as part of his divorce proceedings. Recovering from the sordid publicity, she launched a rollicking comedy/singing act (one of her songs was called "Take Back Your Heart, I Asked for Liver") where, midway through, she made up onstage into blackface and told her jokes and stories "with a good deal of ginger" in African American stage dialect. In 1909 she assembled a company of chorines and put on a singing, dancing, and comedy act called "Behind the Scenes," which featured the girls and Bertie getting dressed for the show. Herron had what were considered good legs, and in 1909 she introduced a new pianologue comedy act in which she wore the short skirts of a soubrette. This too was a taunt to conventions. Finally, in 1913 she teamed up with Tudor Cameron's wife, Bonnie Gaylord, to perform a female version of "On and Off" called the "De-Corking Girls."[12]

Employing a play within a play was, of course, a time-honored dramatic technique. But what performers like Herron, Cameron and Flanagan, and the Vans were doing was different. Where Bottom or Snug were still characters in a play, vaudevillians were revealing their double identity as actors and real people. By then denying the audience the comfort of knowing what part of the performance was "true" and what part was fiction, they were implicitly

A bizarre 1906 postcard that treats the kind of uncertainty about reality and fiction, white and black, that preoccupied modernist artists. The unruly white spectator and the dignified blackface performer share racialized features and are similarly dressed. The drawing ridicules fandom and mocks the banality of commercial culture. The slippage of the real into performance is crudely, but effectively, presented. (Author's collection)

questioning people's ability to perceive reality. This was a device peculiar to variety and regarded quite negatively in the legitimate theater and in movies—media where the illusion of reality had to be preserved. In fact, Frank Woods, the Hollywood screenwriter, insisted that "remarks directly at the [audience] destroy the illusion of reality," which was undeniable.[13] But in vaudeville, the destruction of reality onstage served to enhance the authenticity of the performers by making them seem more like real people acting a part.

There was something peculiarly modern about the blurred boundary between reality and fiction. The questioning of stage conventions by vaudevillians and their habit of slipping in and out of fictional characters parallel the use of the forms of nonfiction life writing—biography, diary, memoir—by authors such as Joyce and Stein for the purposes of fiction. The first generation of modernists also sought to create a sense of authenticity by eliminating the conventions of storytelling. As T. S. Eliot put it, the modern writer had to "dislocate[,] if necessary, language into his meaning."[14] Just as writers used techniques common to documentary as a way of liberating themselves from what they saw as failed storytelling techniques and the conventional narrator, vaudevillians dissolved the line between the stage self and the everyday self in order to naturalize the performance and connect directly with the audience. The motivations may have been different, but the instruments chosen were similar.

The popularity of techniques like these suggest that spectators were willing to accept the simulacra of reality presented on the vaudeville stage as authentic. They appear to have then enjoyed having the falsehood of what they presumed to be real made apparent. As a writer in *Theater Arts* explained, "The object of the low-down [theater] is to destroy illusions, by *exposing* the *hokum* from which illusions arise," even though "any wholesale slaughter of illusions" was "disastrous to the *theater*."[15] Americans had been inordinately fond of hoaxes in the nineteenth century, as P. T. Barnum well knew. But at the close of the century they considered themselves cosmopolitan enough to want to have the falsity of those appealing hoaxes exposed, which is why automata in vaudeville generally revealed at the end of the act that they were real people, not robots, and magicians explained their tricks. In an age when science was exposing the untruth of so many nineteenth-century artifacts and beliefs, vaudevillians drew applause by destroying the fiction of their own performance.

ILLUSIONS

Gilded Age and Progressive Era Americans lived through a remarkable change in the way time and space were conceived and described. In the 1880s shutter speeds on cameras reached the hitherto inconceivable speed of 1/100th of a second, and in 1907 Yale chemist Bertram Borden Boltwood used the new science of radiometric dating to prove that the Earth was 2.2 billion years old, an impossible number to imagine. Already in 1902 one could travel by train from Chicago to New York in twenty hours, a trip that in 1870 took twice as long; the country as a whole had been shrunk from a railroad journey of almost seven days to one taking eighty-three hours. When an experimental French airplane reached the alarming flight speed of sixty-five miles an hour in 1910, experts foresaw travel times halving again. Innovations like these made tangible the sense that the physical world was losing its solidity. Physicists in the 1890s demolished the Newtonian universe of solid objects and reconceived it as a space where forces and waves interact and particles move. It was at this point that Einstein theorized that time was not an absolute but that it existed in relationship to space. The revolution in scientific understanding had a profound impact on modern art, contributing mightily to the sense of "weightlessness." It also had an influence in popular entertainment because literate Americans, even those unfamiliar with evolving concepts in physics, knew that the relationships they had grown up with between time and space were changing. Not surprisingly, many vaudevillians found ways of turning that realization into amusement.

Around 2 percent of all vaudeville performers were illusionists, and, more than any other type of act, they challenged spectator confidence in the stability of physical laws. Although a few of these mentalists continued to reference the supernatural in their work—posing, for instance, as fakirs or shamans—most presented themselves as ordinary people with minds so powerful that they could speed up time or control the natural world. The most popular illusionist act of the early twentieth century was the Zancigs, a Danish-born husband-and-wife team. Agnes and Julius Zancig framed their act as a love story. Their brains, they claimed, "vibrated in unison, moved by the same psychic forces . . . [and] wonderfully responsive to each other's emotions," and this allowed them to literally read each other's thoughts, even when they were apart. In their act, Julius moved through the audience, picking objects that Agnes could not see but would accurately identify. Crucial to the act was the idea that thoughts were a form of energy that could move through the air, unfettered by time or space; "the speed of mental telepathy is much too rapid to measure," explained one expert in 1907. "Thousands of miles are traversed instantly. It is quite possible to communicate with a person many miles distant and receive a reply; in other words, to have a mental conversation. If Mr. Zancig wished, I believe he could stand in Trafalgar Square and speak to his wife in the Broadway, New York." All it requires "is a special kind of mind," Agnes Zancig affirmed. "I open my mind," she said, "and then suddenly the message or picture goes by like a flash. If I do not catch it, it passes, and I have to try again. . . . A picture of an object is like a flash." Refusing to describe themselves as abnormal, Julius predicted that in the future everyone would train their minds to communicate with other minds without the need for words or regard to distance.[16]

Telepathy was a thoroughly modern phenomenon. Performers like the Zancigs or the Howards explained their feats by referencing telephones and telegraphs. These had "proven" that "things are not what they seem," as one critic wrote of the Howards. We think of air, a French investigator observed, as though it was not a solid body, but electricity could not pass through it; to electricity "it is a solid rock." Similarly, we can't move through an iron door, but electrical "waves" can. Our understanding of the natural world was therefore partial and misleading; "matter is only an appearance," not a universal. Why then could not thought, as some "universal dynamism," pass through space and time, defying our experience of both? Telepaths maintained that what they were doing was simply communicating across distances without the aid of mechanical devices. Their ability to do so was, they admitted, an evolution of humanity, but one that they had willed into existence. In other words, they suggested that a modern appreciation of the mind was giving birth to a new type of brain, one that no longer needed to rely on the instruments that had inspired its newfound abilities. Intriguingly, even the critics of telepathy cast it in terms of modern science and culture. Garret P. Serviss, for example, a skeptical journalist, asserted that telepathy could not work, even if thoughts did travel through space as an "ethereal wave," because the stress of modern life meant that "the mind is seldom found in the state of receptivity and passiveness requisite for the successful transmission of a message from one mind to another."[17]

Telepaths were not the only performers to challenge audience beliefs in the solidity of time and space. Horace Goldin, the Whirlwind Wizard, asserted that his mastery over "light and rapidity" was the reason why he was vaudeville's most popular magician. In the nineteenth century, magicians moved slowly and mysteriously, conveying the impression that their control over matter—their ability to make objects appear, disappear, and transform—was the result of hard and careful labor. Goldin, however, who was onstage for only fifteen minutes, worked incredibly quickly, averaging twenty-four tricks in a performance. He accomplished this, in large part, by arranging his stunts so that the results of one provided the material for the next. In one segment of a few minutes, for example, he took a bucket, placed some baby ducks inside it, and covered it with a sheet of paper. He then poured water into the bucket and the ducks vanished. One duck remained, so Goldin wrapped it in paper and tore it up, making the last duck disappear. He then drew a cloth over a table containing a number of articles, and they too vanished. Finally, he folded up the table to form a small box. Goldin did "a half dozen [tricks] in the time it usually took for the performance of one," exclaimed an excited critic in Minnesota. Goldin's appeal was that he made magic seem easy, acting as if the laws of nature were no longer an obstacle to be overcome.[18]

Quick-change artists were among the more unusual of the time-and-matter manipulators. They employed speed and control over physical objects rather prosaically but in a way that naturalized their powers even more than did Goldin or the Zancigs. The most popular quick-change artist of the early twentieth century was a Mr. Hymack. A compact, serious-looking performer who resembled a banker's clerk, Mr. Hymack (he used the title in his performance name) was born Quentin McPherson. After working for several years as an actor in England, he turned to music hall entertainment with his quick-change specialty. Mr. Hymack first appeared in the United States in 1907 and became a headliner by using speed to make an ordinary action into something extraordinary. The performer would slip his hands into different-colored gloves so swiftly that the coverings seemed to "spring into place of their own volition." He changed his necktie, collars, and cuffs at lighting speed, and for a finish, Mr. Hymack changed his entire suit of clothes in two seconds, while standing onstage in full view of the audience. In 1909, after two years of performing the same act, Mr. Hymack introduced a novelty. Setting his old performance in the context of a sketch, he now entered a stage set up like a room in a private club and, after denouncing hypnotism to a friend, agreed to allow himself to be hypnotized as a wager. Under "hypnosis" he then performed his usual act, responding to the "commands" of the hypnotist to change his clothes. The new act made clear that speed was something realized in the physical world but prompted in the mental. It was control over his mind that allowed Mr. Hymack to do things that no one should ordinarily have been able to do. His bending of time could not "be judged by ordinary standards"; it was subject to the "will" rather than to the laws of physics, according to a critic in the *Washington Herald*.[19]

The common element in magic and illusion was not the supernatural but the challenge being posed to the powers of concentration and perception. Unlike the comics who exposed their imposture, or even those magicians who revealed their tricks, the manipulators of time and matter insisted that the control they exercised over their environment was real and scientific. This is why it was Goldin's speed that was fantastical, rather than the tricks making up the act. As one manager wrote of Lo Lo, purportedly a sixteen-year-old Sioux shaman, her act "is a puzzle to anyone, I don't care how much they know about show business. . . . Not only does she describe [hidden] articles, but she does so without any apparent cue in most cases. Added to this she fills a glass to the brim with liquid poured from a pitcher without spilling any; lights a match by striking the edge with a sword and does some remarkable sharp-shooting, all while blindfolded." These were not "tricks" that could be explained, they were the product of the performer's ability to control nature through concentration. In "Konorah's Lightning Calculations" act, a female performer sat blindfolded onstage with her back to the auditorium. While in this position she offered an exhibition of mystifying mental mathematics. She squared and cubed numbers called out by audience members and even worked out mathematical problems that spectators had written on pieces of paper and kept hidden. Konorah's husband, who selected the audience members and guided them in posing their problems, secretly communicated with her through an electrical connection on a foot plate, but the audience was not aware of it, and as a result the act "mystified them." Another fine example of mental power was displayed by the "Woman of Mystery," Mrs. S. S. Baldwin. Baldwin offered a "mind-reading" act, though she made no pretense of possessing any supernatural gift. Rather, she presented herself as a marvel of memory. Two men, each carrying a novel by Hawthorne, moved up and down the orchestra aisles, inviting auditors to select any word in the book. The number of the page, number of the line, and number of the word from the beginning of the line were called out to Mrs. Baldwin, who then quoted the word selected. During the Sunday night performance at the Lincoln Square Theater in 1907, which a critic attended, she made no error.[20]

Mrs. Baldwin, Mr. Hymack, and the Zancigs exercised uncanny mental control over both their bodies and the physical space surrounding them. They offered a positive perspective on the modern experience, linking speed not just to vitality and positive energy but also to power.[21] This was modernism at its most expansive, forceful, and optimistic. Time and space and matter were being reimagined as relative properties, and as such they could be manipulated and altered. For Americans worried about being run over by streetcars or electrocuted in their homes, it was an inspiring message. But there was also an irrational side to modernism, a fascination with the forces of unreason. It was an age of skyscrapers and pistons, but also of Freud, Dadaism, and the interior monologue in literature. In order to explore the irrational dimensions of experience, modernists often employed symbols they linked with the primitive: black bodies, ritualistic murder, African masks, and jazz music. And this wild and unreasoning aspect of modernism also found a place in vaudeville.

THE WILD SIDE

Later modernists like Nathanael West and Djuna Barnes, and even some early ones, like Charles Demuth, associated the popular theater with primal energies, the erotic, and the unintelligible. Barnes, who interviewed the manager of New York's Hippodrome in 1915, said it was "something like having a nightmare," and she elsewhere presented the theater as a place of perversion and superstition. Modernist painter Reginald Marsh produced several works depicting grotesque, carnal female performers, their loose, rippling flesh observed by leering and obese male spectators. For these artists, sexual desire was an irrational impulse, and they were horrified by what they saw as the collapse of the moral center and the triumph of sensuality. Early twentieth-century modernists, following

Freud, imagined sexual appetites as universal but also obsessive and disruptive. Because of the prevailing connection of the carnal to the unreasoning, visual artists and musicians often used what they considered primitive African images and sounds in order to convey and condemn bodily impulses. Few modernists (Gertrude Stein being one) seemed to feel emotional safeguards (which Stein saw as intrinsically patriarchal) didn't need to be applied.[22]

Vaudevillians rarely dealt in an explicit way with savagery, carnality, or unreason. One rare occasion when they did was in the Thomas Ryley production of the controversial French sketch "The Submarine," which opened at the Colonial in New York in November 1908. The sketch depicted a submarine captained by an opium addict who, in a delusional state, decided to visit the bottom of the sea. The vessel's descent was seen through the portholes, which displayed moving pictures of sea creatures and then reeds as it hit bottom. The boat sprang a leak when it grounded, and the play depicts the last moments of its four crewmen as, "suffocated by escaping gas and the inrushing water," they struggle to mount a ladder to escape, fighting with each other for life. It is "harrowing in the extreme," wrote one reviewer, while another reported seeing several women "who became so nervous . . . that they hurried out and probably sought the maid with smelling salts." The spectator "grows sick with shame and horror at the fearful, humiliating scene," the *New York Sun* reported as it watched the men "die like dogs . . . without a trace of bravery or generosity." It was "entirely out of place" in vaudeville, according to most reviewers, and "caused a gloom that the performers who followed found hard to dispel." Not surprisingly, "The Submarine" quickly disappeared from the variety sketch repertoire.[23]

Given vaudeville's lightheartedness, it seems odd that modernist artists depicted it as raw and irrational; after all, theater entrepreneurs boasted that they had cleaned up their circuits and were providing good, sober fun for the whole family. The press and reformers occasionally complained that the loosening of standards had turned vaudeville into a "wolf that still wears lamb's clothing," but these never amounted to much. In fact, vaudeville did not face the kind of censorship that hit some of the novels, plays, operas, and artworks created by the modernists themselves. Naturally, there were cultural boundaries that vaudevillians would not cross: racialized people could not be portrayed having close relations of any kind with white people; sex for profit or uncoupled from love or affection was taboo; swearing onstage was never tolerated; and actual, rather than metaphorical, nudity was prohibited. But it remains surprisingly true that vaudeville theaters were not closed down even when the acrobat Charmion tossed off her street clothes from an aerial perch, or Gilda Gray danced the shimmy. In fact, vaudeville was repeatedly held up in the press as a model of "clean" entertainment, and its managers in 1911 issued a declaration pledging themselves to uphold "a higher standard of morality" on the vaudeville stage than that prevailing in all other entertainments. It is hard for us to understand how these things could be reconciled, which is why historian Andrew Erdman sees vaudeville's avowed propriety as little more than a cynical effort to sell an image. But vaudevillians drew a direct correlation between their performances and modern attitudes. Tastes, they suggested, had changed, and they were simply going along. Some people might take offense to individual things they did, but that was only because morality was relative, not absolute. And so, when some critics chastised Blossom Seeley for dancing the risqué Todolo, she responded, "If there is a public demand for [it] . . . why should not the response be considered legitimate? Modesty? Is there not a distinction, if not a difference [among people], attaching to this subject?"[24]

The prudish saw it differently. In 1908, a critic in Louisville, who normally reviewed the legitimate, was sent by his paper to watch a vaudeville show. He was disturbed by what he saw. The English singer Vesta Victoria, he wrote, appeared onstage in fleshings (a skin-colored body suit), with her arms bare and the rest of her body in feathers, and she sang a song about being captured by the king of Jujah island and being in terror lest the wind blow away her feathers and leave her nude. She then sang a song about an ice man, who was "a very nice man," but from whom all she could get was ice. After the intermission Eva Tanguay was featured, and, according to the appalled critic, she "gyrated wildly while yelling a song about the kind of fascinating girl she was." She then undid her skirt and in tights started "jiggling about the stage and screaming that no matter what anyone might say of her immodesty she was a success, success, success." The audience, he wrote, appeared to love it all, even though the journalist found it revolting. Intriguingly, critics more familiar with vaudeville reported Victoria's Jujah Island song "a first-class comedy selection" and noted that while Tanguay's costumes were "original in every sense of the word . . . she need never be afraid of the censors."[25]

What shocked observers failed to appreciate was that performers like Tanguay and Victoria and Emma Carus presented titillating material as an extravagant joke. The Gus Edwards and Will Cobb number "In Zanzibar (My Little Chimpanzee)," which Carus made a hit in 1904, dealt with a "monkey king who offers an attractive female chimpanzee a branch in his tree" as he "caressed her with chin bone chattering / His Panzie flattering." As Carus sang, a half-dozen chorines, in monkey outfits, hopped around onstage, squatted and chattered, and "finally roll[ed] over in anything but refined imitations of their prototypes." All this certainly referenced primeval lust (the monkey king sings "with twang Darwinian"), Africa, and the primitive, but it was designed to be funny in its costuming and cartoonish in its sexiness.[26]

The upbeat, comic tone most vaudevillians applied to even the most lascivious material (it might be contrasted with the earnest sexiness of Ziegfeld's chorus line) allowed managers to justify their catholic policies. Since lust was widely associated with violent passion, it followed that if the material was presented cheerfully, it couldn't really be salacious. Looking "clean and fresh," one manager explained, made a little "undress" acceptable. The singing comedian Lillian Shaw was known both for her risqué songs and for her endorsement of women's rights. Audience members sometimes took offense at her lyrics, but as a Keith manager explained, while it was true that "Miss Shaw still clings to songs that are a bit suggestive . . . her frank and wholesome manner of presenting them diverts the attention from the subject matter of the songs to her engaging personality." A smile was often all it took to get away with gratuitous displays of skin. In a dancing act, set in a school library, three smiling young women—Molly Moeller, Maud Teller, and Maud Beatty—dressed as schoolgirls came onstage, discarded their dresses, shoes, and stockings, and in their petticoats and corset covers did a barefoot dance around the library and then lay on their backs and did a "pedal dance, one part of which approaches suggestiveness." After their exit, monologuist Dan Burke entered the library and offered recitations. Was Burke there to show that high school was a place of both knowledge and hormonal surges? As Keith's Boston manager explained of such gratuitous acts, the girls were just "a bunch of broilers," but "the act is pretty and lively and the girls . . . present a cute and attractive appearance," so what was the harm?[27]

Nineteenth-century Americans were reticent about sex and used euphemisms whenever they discussed it. Commercial sex and pornography were readily available for those who sought it out, but most respectable people preferred not to talk about such vices. Breaking that silence was one of the goals of modern artists, and in the 1890s they began to make sex more explicit in their stories and plays and artworks. But despite the increased openness about sex in modern art, it continued to be seen as a morally corrosive force, and in the serious theater it was linked to vice and corruption (melodrama) or personal destruction (much modern drama). Even progressive thinkers, like the economist William Trufant

Foster, could not help feeling, as late as 1914, that the attention being given to sex in the legitimate and in movies was there "to satisfy abnormal desires," and he warned that it would lead to "lives wasted in dissipation and profligacy." In fact, in the early twentieth century, Progressive reformers fought a largely successful counterattack against sexual openness, using censorship and vice laws to prohibit sexually explicit plays, ban novels, and shut down red-light districts.[28]

This makes vaudeville's easygoing attitude to titillating material all the more remarkable, unconventional, and modern. The majority of vaudevillians approached sex as they did everything else: as something to be laughed about and demystified. As Billie Burke explained, "Right and wrong are simply matters of environment and opinion." This was a radical approach, but it clearly worked to make racy material acceptable to respectable families. Eva Tanguay, after all, was considered a particular favorite of female, not male, spectators, despite her tights and feathers. Only occasionally did managers worry about the indecency of clothing, and then only when the audience seemed to become aroused. This happened when Grace Fields and her Matinee Girls danced at Hammerstein's in 1906; as a critic reported, the young women needed "to wear something under their blouses for decency. The men in the audience are moved to make remarks about their mammillary development." Generally speaking, though, dancing vaudevillians knew they could wear revealing clothes because their act depended on both freedom of movement and the artistic effect. That knowledge prompted some of them to even tease the censors. In 1911, the dancer Sybil Maitland and her "Grecian Dancing Girls" announced in programs that their act was being sponsored by a Mrs. A. Comstock, a clear and amusing dig at the country's most famous prude. The act itself, according to *Variety*, was "simply a show of thinly clad girls cavorting about with bared legs and tootsies. . . . It is enjoyable to watch, especially since some of the girls have some looks."[29] While a number of modernists depicted vaudeville as a theater given over to depravity, vaudevillians got away with titillating material because they made sexiness funny and unspectacular.

Only a few acts made sexuality appear violent and obsessive, echoing, in their intensity, the prewar modernist imagination. It was in dance, rather than song, that the passions of sex were most often presented, possibly because dance was associated with ballet and was therefore a "serious" form where troubling subjects could be more artistically explored. Salome dances, for example, became popular following the Metropolitan's banning of Richard Strauss's opera in 1907 as vaudevillians jumped at the chance to show vaudeville audiences what the highbrows couldn't see: Salome's striptease Dance of the Seven Veils. La

Belle Dazie, a toe dancer, was the first to cash in on the notoriety of Salome, but she was sufficiently worried about it that her dance proved a letdown. We "merely saw a dancer in Oriental costume do a few languorous twists and turns," a critic complained. La Sylphe's Salome dance was different. A New Yorker named Edith Lambelle Langerfield, La Sylphe was a contortionist and dancer who did her Salome dance on a return tour of the United States in 1908, after scoring success with it in Europe. The dancer eased her audience into it with the *gigolette*, a tough-girl dance, which she performed in bare feet and wearing fleshings that stopped at her knees. Then, for the Salome dance, she wore a "picket fence skirt and gossamer bodice." She danced in a circle of white light with all the house in blackness. The lighting made it appear that she was naked under her skirt. "Her whole thin little body is outlined, and shines through the gauze and the gorgeous green and blue and yellow and red fires that flash in massed flame from the tinsel and mock gems," a critic rhapsodized. Even more tantalizingly, when she performed at Proctor's 125th Street Theater, the dancer announced that she found the bodice too warm and that she would prefer to perform topless. The police were on hand for the next performance to make sure she didn't. If she tried, Lieutenant Walsh told the newspapers, "she'll wear a bodice of bars."[30]

La Sylphe expressed a self-abasing sensuality far removed from that of Tanguay or Carus. In one of her Salome dances, the stage on which she appeared was "gloomy" and "ghostly" with a backdrop depicting a pagan temple, a "Monolith of Dead Faiths." La Sylphe entered dejected and threw herself on the ground before the altar. The setting linked the dance to primitive frenzy, as though she had been filled with some ungodly ardor. La Sylphe then engaged in a "weird, wild, ecstatic dance of abandonment," kicking her legs backward, gyrating her hips, and bending her body into her famous S curve, and "when in an ecstasy of passion and holy zeal she swayed her lithe form before the temple, the onlookers burst into applause, unable to restrain their admiration any longer." Public interest in the "undressed dance" at Proctor's rose to a high pitch. "Just how hard the public may have fallen for it may be judged by the packed houses at 125th Street this week, when most of the other New York theaters were playing to the ushers," a reporter joked.[31]

Dancers got away with this kind of thing because it was difficult to determine which movements in a routine were lascivious and which were high art. This was why managers who reported censoring dancers responded to specific movements they rated as lewd: a skirt lifted too high or a bottom wiggled at the audience. Even dancers regarded as risqué, such as Princess Rajah, a contortion

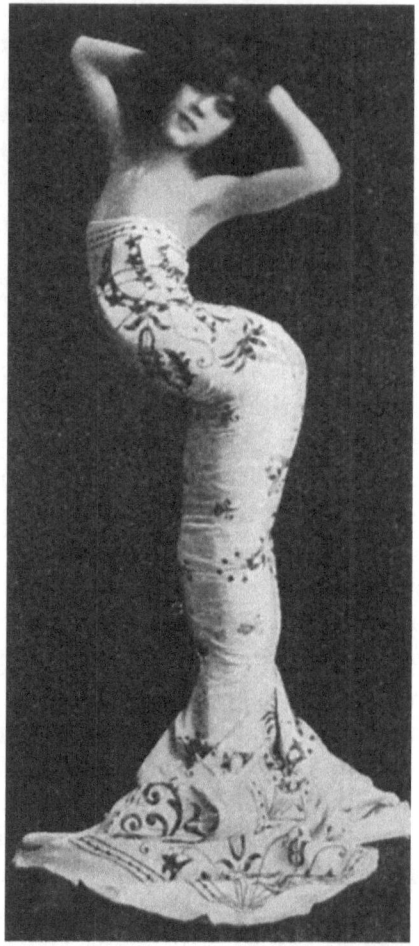

The dancer and contortionist La Sylphe, whose remarkable "bend" was briefly imitated by fashionable young women. "The State Street stores are fairly alive with La Sylphes," a Chicago reporter observed in 1905; "they float along Wabash avenue... in coveys and flocks, and in the South Side parks they may be seen strutting like peacocks or pouter pigeons." (*Chicago Inter Ocean*, 21 May 1905)

dancer who dressed even more transparently than La Sylphe, tended to get away with fairly explicit stuff. When Princess Rajah performed in Baltimore, the manager of the theater, who was on the lookout for something lewd, reported that she "performed the dance throughout without exhibiting anything in the way of a movement that I could see is the slightest off-color."[32]

Once the Salomes had broken the taboo, a number of other sexually charged dances appeared in vaudeville. Many of these, like Salome's, featured women as seductresses. The "vampire dance," for example, seemed to express a cultural unease over the growing popularity of dangerously slim, clingingly dressed young women. In the dance, a thin, pale woman, "a rag and a bone and a hank of hair" in a "snakelike gown," lures her male prey with erotic, eerie movements. She pretends to be enraptured with him and unable to resist his charms, but in fact she is trapping him by appealing to his vanity. The dance ended with the vampire biting her partner and then "falling on his bloodless form."[33] Salome and vampire dancers made apparent the curious symbiosis of thinness and dangerous eroticism. The image was of a predator's unfulfilled body, powered by a savage hunger that was at once vestigial, modern, and authentic. Although thinness was in fashion and was closely linked to athleticism and health, the misogyny expressed in many vaudeville portrayals of independent, svelte women was striking. La Sylphe's Salome was suffering from grief at having demanded John the Baptist's head and contorted herself in pain; the vampire was living death.

La Sylphe's depiction of Salome and the vampire's hunger are examples of dancers expressing the link, accepted in modernist art, between unreason, danger, and sex. But the most common way in which the theme was explored in vaudeville was in portrayals of the white underclass. New Yorkers got their first glimpse of a "tough-girl" dance in 1892 when it was staged by Edward Harrigan in his play about working-class Bowery life, *Riley and the 400*. In 1899 Ada Lewis, who had been Harrigan's "tough girl," brought the two-step jig to vaudeville and caused a sensation. Lewis's character was slim and ragged, wore an ill-hanging skirt and cap, chewed gum, and talked slang. Vaudeville managers described the character she played as a "rough soubrette." Dozens of dancers, singers, and comedians copied Lewis's character, and it quickly became a stereotype, with an accepted look and manner. But the key to a successful tough-girl depiction was for the performer to combine comedy and pathos, because the tough girl was invariably hard on the outside but soft within.[34] As with so much else in vaudeville, the tough sexuality of the poor, which modernists presented as savage, was a veneer covering a warm heart and a playful disposition.

In 1909, "toughness" took a violent turn with the importation of the tough dance's French equivalent, the "Apache." Joseph Smith, a stage director, choreographed the first Apache dance, based on one he claimed he had witnessed in a Paris café. Les Apaches was a name given to the criminal gangs of Montmartre, Belleville, and the Barrières, whose activities produced sensational stories in the French press. According to Smith, in the dance he witnessed, the man first threw a glass at "his girl," then hit her in the face, and then they danced. "Not a word did she speak," said Smith, "but her every movement, all grace and life[,] implored him to be merciful to her, to take her back and fold her in his arms." It is likely that Smith fabricated the story to cover up the fact that he stole the dance from the Moulin Rouge, which began offering a depiction of a violent, sexual fight-dance between a *gigolette* and her pimp in 1908. Smith, however, Americanized the dance by rejecting the waltz used in its Moulin Rouge staging and choreographing his Apache to the more modern, ragtime two-step. Smith hired Adele Rowland to dance with him and portray the Apache woman. Dressed like a conventional tough girl but with a beret in place of a cap, Rowland was described as his "slave" who "would steal and even murder to gratify the whims of her master." In Rowland and Smith's dance, he threw her to the floor several times and then spun her around by the legs, her head barely skimming the stage. Vaudeville Apaches are "dirty and degraded," journalists reported; "they live by crime and prostitution" in "cavernous, dingy quarters and never see daylight." In the Apache dance, the raggedy female dancer was depicted as a dangerous, dependent, and passionately hungry animal. The vulnerability of the tough girl was turned against her as she was presented as so dependent that she accepted abuse as attention. Irene Castle, the ragtime dancer, made the point beautifully when she described the Apache as a dance "in which the male dancer tries to demolish the female dancer, as spectacularly as possible, and usually succeeds."[35]

"Tough dances" were much discussed in the press, but even at the peak of their popularity, in 1909, they were seldom done in vaudeville.[36] Between 1900 and 1920 only three acts in a thousand featured a "tough" female and far fewer a dance. Salome dances were even less common. Vaudeville was never really comfortable presenting serious material, and sexual violence was just too heavy a theme for this amusement. Some managers considered the Apache dance a bit too far "from the variety idea" to be acceptable. When vaudevillians played around with ideas of the primitive, they usually did it in fun, like Carus and the monkeys or Victoria and her feathers. Comedy was a way in which vaudevillians sterilized eroticism, turning the downbeat of passion into something cheerfully upbeat. This was the case with most tough dances, including the Texas tommy. The tommy caused a stir when it was first featured in 1911 because the dancer had to be what the *Oakland Tribune* called "wiggle waisted." It had originated as a West Coast red-light district "tough dance" and was considered so indecent that it was banned in Barbary Coast and Tenderloin dance halls. But by the time Blossom Seeley first did it onstage, the dance was already becoming civilized. West Coast society balls began seeing it after Ned Greenway approved it for his elite by-invitation-only cotillion at the Odd Fellows' Hall. Seeley's wiggle was considered "cute," not erotic, and in 1912 a group of dancers were judged "graceful in execution" when they performed it in Los Angeles. The comedy was there as well. The Texas Tommy Dancers, a group purportedly from San Francisco's Barbary Coast who claimed to have originated the dance (they didn't), performed it in 1912 like a hoedown, in cowboy outfits. *Variety* thought them tame, even though the dancers believed they "went the limit."[37]

A MODERN SELF?

Scholars question whether the unitary, authentic self survived the passage to modernity. The identities people create, they point out, are only as coherent as the communities, customs, habits, and traditions that protect them and the stability of the physical world in which they operate. The sense of oneself can be destabilized when communities fragment, customs are lost, and values come under attack. Migration, environmental destruction, or a crisis of faith can lead to traumatic questioning of values and identities. Some historians and social theorists argue that the historical experience of modernity produced this kind of psychic dislocation because it created a generalized feeling of powerlessness that expressed itself in a "crisis of self." In the fast-changing modern world, they maintain, everything became contingent, and people came to expect their beliefs and values to be challenged. Communities dissolved as the lives of distant public figures became better known than those of neighbors. Merchandisers responded to the crisis by offering commodified versions of identity for mass consumption. For British sociologist Anthony Giddens, doubt became normative at the fin de siècle, and self-identity came to be associated with what remained in people's control: possessions, lifestyles, and off-the-shelf methods of self-actualization. Historian T. J. Jackson Lears argues that advertising began to define self-identity in the early twentieth century as traditional values lost their fixity; he refers to a new "weightlessness" affecting concepts of being. Susan Glenn sees a crucial "reorientation" in modern culture toward a "performative model of personality" at the turn of the century, which she suggests popular entertainers made manifest. And for Warren Susman, the nineteenth-century idea that an individual had a "fixed" and innate "character" gave way in the early twentieth century to the more fluid concept of "personality," defined as poses adopted in order to sell oneself to others.[38]

Vaudevillians worked close to the center of the cultural maelstrom that was modernity. They were the first popular entertainers to make personality

Celebrities like Gilda Gray linked the liberated female body with health, naturalness, commodities, contentment, and sex. (*Theatre Magazine* 38, no. 269 [August 1923])

paramount, and they were the first to achieve modern celebrity. Their self-promotion involved the performance of authenticity, and they commodified their success and presented character as something one stepped in and out of, at least onstage. This is why they can seem exemplars of the contingent, performance-oriented modern self. The polished English star Ada Reeve, for example, communicated the public image of a demure "gentlewoman." Her personality "is the realization of grace and graciousness and her dancing, which she indulges in slightly, is light footed and airy without vulgarity." In Caroline Caffin's view she was a model of "studied deportment." But Reeve also liked to surprise her audience by singing songs that were coyly sexual. "This young lady has leanings toward life that are not included in the curriculum of the schoolroom," Caffin added, rather disapprovingly. Some of Reeve's songs described clandestine love affairs, often "carried on under the nose of authority. And they are sung with a relish instead of disapprobation." Caffin was particularly disturbed by Reeve's rendition of her most famous song, "Do Sue Do," which, in the performance she witnessed, was accompanied by "an extraordinary wriggle of head and chest. It is a masterpiece of grotesqueness, wholly gratuitous, for the contortions have absolutely no bearing on the subject of the song. It takes the audience by surprise, with its audacity that is so entirely unlooked for. It is the climax of the surprise which commenced with the twinkle of the eyes when the first line of the first song revealed its equivocal situation." Caffin was not the only spectator to find Reeve a disturbing presence; in breaking her demure facade she was, according to a West Coast reporter, showing that she was "not disposed to comply with the demands of her admirers."[39]

Were performers like Reeve expressing a personal weightlessness or a performative approach to self? Caffin suggested as much, noting that "at the close of the performance the little grey-clad figure drops back into ladylike demeanor just as correctly as if she had never shown the unconventional humors which were concealed by the mask of decorum." There is no question that Reeve put on a good act, surprising her audience by allowing a sexy movement or naughty phrase to break the crust of her ladylike persona. But even if Reeve was trying to reveal "the lurking little devil peeping from an unexpected corner," that did not mean that she wanted her personality to appear situationally contingent or unintegrated. Like other vaudevillians, she wanted her personality to be seen as coherent and her character as authentic. Reeve denied she tried to trick her audience or present anything that was "untrue to herself." As she told Leo Levy of the *Oakland Tribune*, she was always the same whether in front of a vaudeville audience or "when I amuse two or three friends in the parlor." There was "no pose about Miss Reeve," Levy concluded, and her ostensible naughtiness was simply a misperception of her fun-loving nature. She was like Peter Pan, a prankster who "refuses to be self-conscious," and she loved practical jokes. This was the personality she insisted she presented onstage.[40]

The idea that the people appearing onstage were being "true to themselves" and to their audience was demonstrated in impersonation, a new and very popular type of act in vaudeville. Mimics, to be successful, had to replicate characters by highlighting those characteristics that made that person identifiable. Around 4 percent of vaudeville acts featured some form of mimicry, with one-third of those being gender impersonators. Impersonators almost always made clear that they were performing a role, which drew attention to their mimicry as a piece of acting. Male or female impersonators tended to act as though they were the sex they were assuming until the end, when they sang in a male or female voice or took off a wig to reveal their "true" sex. Mimics, in contrast, made clear from the start that they were impersonating someone else. Gertrude Hoffman would sometimes change costumes onstage, announcing that she was switching from one character to another. Other mimics, such as Terley, employed an assistant who named his subjects. Henry Lee, who impersonated men in the news and some historical figures—John D. Rockefeller, Andrew Carnegie, and Theodore Roosevelt—announced the characters himself. Impersonations became meaningless only when the characters depicted were not recognizable.[41]

In changing clothes in front of the audience, revealing disguises, and announcing their subjects, mimics were drawing attention to the difference between acting onstage and being themselves. This was why, when doing impersonations, it was important not to make the representation too close to life; it had to stand out for its lack of naturalness and be enjoyed for what it was: a performance. Henry Lee was sometimes criticized for forgetting this rule and losing "something of the popular appreciation he might gain by having a touch of caricature." Because they caricatured, rather than became, another character, the imitation itself could be parodied. Elsie Janis did such a funny version of Eddie Foy that Foy started doing impersonations of Janis impersonating him.[42]

Audience expectation that they would get "the real thing" from a player therefore provided a counterweight to the "performative." Impersonators made clear when they were becoming another character, thereby distinguishing themselves from the roles they played. The aesthetic of vaudeville, the centrality of actuality to the art, grounded players despite the theatricality of their work. The issue is complicated because as the mimic Juliet observed, "All actors are counterfeits," and vaudevillians merely made acting "appear to be the reality." We can't know how each of the thousands of vaudevillians felt about themselves or their values in this era of transformation, but we do know that a number of them described their work as an unselfconscious expression of their spirit. "Personality," Nora Bayes explained in 1917, is an "overused word"; successful performing was a matter of the artist's spiritual essence: "heart, faith and love for one's audience." Bayes was not alone in feeling this way; asked to explain the "tricks of her profession" by an Oakland reporter, Ada Reeve replied, "I don't think I have any." It is a fact, the reporter concluded, "being yourself is the staff of the stage and all that is not acting glitters." If vaudevillians were experiencing a crisis of self, they did not want spectators to know about it. Billie Burke summed it up well in maintaining that in entertainment one had to remain secure in one's core values. "We are simply the creatures of circumstance," she explained to an interviewer, "unless we . . . recognize the vital power of truth and falsehood[,] the two great forces upon which the morality of the world stands." Where the stage persona and the private one appeared to conflict, as it seemed to do in the case of Eva Tanguay, reporters suggested she might have a "dual personality," which they considered a psychosis.[43]

Vaudevillians wanted to appear as ordinary folks, unaffected by stage or success. This helps explain why celebrities invariably maintained that they were completely conventional in their private lives. Eva Tanguay responded to criticism by maintaining that she was misunderstood. She was a "careful and circumspect" hostess who lived quietly, enjoyed reading, and exercised "refinement and good taste." May Irwin similarly wrote that she loved nothing better than cooking a meal of beef stew or hash for her family, while Eddie Foy, the father of seven children, explained that his family afforded him more "comfort" than anything else in his life. Although many modern artists were concerned to show fractured perceptions and to understand impulses in new ways, as Douglas Mao points out, most people remained convinced of "the unviolated integrity" of the subject/object dichotomy.[44]

Mass entertainment's therapeutic function underlay the players' emphasis on their own homely authenticity. In truth, vaudeville was created just as the supposedly stable values on which people had built their self-identity were undergoing a tectonic shift. Behaviors once considered immoral—such as dancing and drinking and spending money on makeup—were now considered acceptable. Core principles were also in flux: divorce was not such a disgrace, and image was being sold as truth in advertising, as well as in mass entertainment. But the popular theater cautions us not to exaggerate the pace or scope of these changes. The great mass of Americans who attended vaudeville theaters appear not to have wanted to see modernity as emptiness, doubt, estrangement, and discontinuity, at least not when they went out for an evening of fun. Popular artists interested in exploring the conditions of modernity diverged most sharply from highbrow modernists. Vaudevillians wanted spectators to relax, recharge, and laugh; they didn't want to worry or discomfit them. In selling the modern character, as vaudevillians were doing, they declared it anchored in the integrity of the self. Modernists and their historians may grasp the bigger picture, but we should recognize that those in the frame wanted to be seen differently.

The optimism with which vaudevillians dealt with changes that we now see as destructive is noteworthy. Although they appreciated that technological and scientific discoveries were upending beliefs, performers showed audiences that space and time and electrical shocks could be overcome through training and willpower. The new, they seemed to say, was threatening only to those who didn't approach change with a positive attitude. The blithe insensitivity of vaudevillians to modernity's corrosive influence proved annoying to many intellectuals. Ordinary Americans seemed to want the appearance of reality, not the ugly truth, the writer O. Henry explained. Vaudeville was mere pasteboard and greasepaint: "The audiences reck not if the performing dogs get to the pound the moment they have jumped through their last hoop. They do not desire bulletins about the possible injuries received by the comic bicyclist who retires head-first from the stage in a crash of (property) china-ware. Neither do they consider that their seat coupons entitle them to be instructed whether or no there is a sentiment between the lady solo banjoist and the Irish monologist.... Let us have no lifting of the curtain upon a tableau," they seemed to say.[45]

It's hard not to agree with the writer. Despite their apparent actuality, variety acts were often banal, infantile, and schmaltzy. In vaudeville, wrote Michael Davis in 1911, "the humorous, sentimental, acrobatic and musical 'acts' pass in succession like the grinning figures at the shooting gallery.... Like the succession of city occurrences, vaudeville is stimulating but disintegrating; both excite and claim the mind of the beholder, and interest him only transiently; they do not recuperate or develop him; in the long run, they will cease to amuse him." But the blithe spirit of vaudeville was also an expression of modernism's cultural moment. The fantasy of its actuality may have been an illusion, but it was appealing to consumers, and in different guises it continues to be so. Moreover, the connection to modern life that Davis saw as "disintegrating" revealed an audience sensibility, a taste for modern things. As we have already seen, vaudeville in its prewar prime provided consumers access to new songs and fashions, movements and sounds. This, and the marketing of celebrities and styles which surrounded it, made the amusement a craze. But its addiction to the modern went further. As Davis recognized, vaudeville transferred the transient experience of modern life to the stage and challenged secure beliefs in the fixity of time, space, personality, and perception. The painter Marsden Hartley found the very thing Davis deplored to be the theater's primary attraction: "So brief they are [the acts], and like the wonders of sea gardens as you look through the glass bottoms of the little boats. So like the wonders of the microscopic, full of surprising novelties of colour and form. So like the kaleidoscope in the ever changing, ever shifting bits of colour reflecting each other, falling into new patterns with each twist of the toy."[46]

Vaudeville celebrated modernity and made the experience of it banal. This was, however, a no less noteworthy response to social and cultural change than the lamentations of conservative intellectuals or the muscular exertions of progressive reformers. It was racist to its core and accepted that white people could take anything they wanted from others, make it their own, and discard the rest. Its liberality was patriarchal, and it presented women's bodies as commodities that gained value the closer they approached masculine ideals of beauty or sexiness. Its innocence and its faults were, nonetheless, vibrant expressions of modernizing American life. The variety show displayed the chaos of the city, the dislocation of the real, the allure of speed, and the promise of technology, and it did so with surreal good humor. Vaudeville performers tried to make audiences feel better about their lives, and in doing so they urged audiences to get on in the new world and reassured them that everything would work out well if they just laughed more. They offered a democratic vision of cultural change and held out the hope that everyone could find modernity fun. This was part of its therapeutic appeal and was what made it such a vital expression of American optimism at a moment of disruptive change. Which brings us to a difficult question: If vaudeville exercised such a potent and reassuring influence, if it was so appropriate to its times, why did it decline?

CHAPTER FIVE

THE BUSINESS OF MASS ENTERTAINMENT

MASS ENTERTAINMENT—therapeutic, democratized, nationally distributed and celebrity-oriented—was a new thing in the 1890s, and none of its creators was working from a blueprint. The innovations that vaudeville entrepreneurs introduced were truly stunning in their originality, and in building vaudeville circuits, those impresarios laid the foundation for the modern entertainment industry. Vaudeville entrepreneurs were the first businesspeople to even attempt to provide amusement on a national scale to a majority of the people, and they did so without market research, in a face-to-face world of contracts and negotiations, where they depended on the telegraph and rail lines to place thousands of performers in the right theaters each week. Uncertainty about the market—the depth and durability of the public's taste for commercial amusement—dogged their advance. No one had experience managing the sudden popularity of the theater, no one knew what mass entertainment should look like, and its creators, not surprisingly, relied on strategies drawn from experience. Uncertainty produced in many vaudevillians a tendency to stick with formulas that seemed to work and a fondness for constraints that killed competition. Ultimately, their conservatism would serve to weaken the industry they created.

So far, this study has focused on the appeal of vaudeville: who went to it, what it offered spectators, and how it captured the spirit of its times. But vaudeville was also an industry that expanded quickly and then contracted with as great a speed. It grew ferociously from the mid-1890s to 1910, but by 1925 it was all but dead, surviving as a diversion in between film screenings. This chapter and the next explain why vaudeville lost its place on the cutting edge of entertainment, arguing that vaudeville declined for both business and cultural reasons. This chapter focuses on the business side and contends that the leading entrepreneurs who tried to restrict competition in vaudeville and skim off the cream for themselves pressed their rivals to secure low-cost content. The celebrities who embodied vaudeville's democratic, modern culture also came to symbolize the elitism and conservatism of a segment of the industry that called itself the big time. Control over the stars' appearances developed into a weapon that the big-time theaters were able to deploy to marginalize their opponents. But their effort to stratify the industry failed because it pushed their small-time competitors into the movies, even as it pressed up their own costs.

The most powerful entrepreneurs had trouble controlling variety entertainment at the point of sale because the retail side of the industry involved hundreds of small theaters dispersed around the country. It was at the wholesale or "booking" end—the supply and placing of acts—that vaudeville could be most effectively consolidated. Territorial monopolies, provided to theaters contracting all their bookings to a single supplier, were an inducement offered to get diverse retail operations to cooperate in their buying. The peculiarity in vaudeville was that the most predatory booking services were created and controlled by the major retail chains. Because of their influence over the supply of acts, those major chains were able to indirectly dominate much of the industry. They used their influence to fracture the industry into big-time and small-time (or family-time) chains. The booking services they controlled then denied the small-time houses access to headliners, and they manipulated performers through blacklists and predatory wages.

Big-time managers, who had oriented the industry around the stars, then used their control over supply to keep the most popular celebrities playing in their own theaters. They also attempted to preserve the vogue for vaudeville by adopting a more elitist approach to entertainment: building more regal theaters, charging reasonably high ticket prices, providing reserved seating, and concentrating on two shows per day. This strategy was based on the nineteenth-century idea that the market was deeply stratified and that consumers of different classes, ethnicities, and racialized identities preferred not to mingle. Since the market was viewed as deep rather than wide, catering to the more affluent was considered safer than selling to the masses. But one of the results of their policies was that working-class spectators moved over to cheaper entertainments that offered open seating. Small-time theater owners, who had no access to headliners, introduced movies and limited the number of live acts to reduce expenses and dodge the cartels' predatory policies. In short, although vaudeville pioneered the mass marketing of entertainment, the entrepreneurs who created the industry were not committed to the principle of equality.

Given the dominance of corporations in the Gilded Age and Progressive Era economies and our own tendency to associate the newest approaches with success, we are inclined to see mass entertainment as a product of big business. It wasn't. The men who created vaudeville (and from an ownership perspective, they were almost all men) were running small businesses organized as sole proprietorships or simple partnerships. Not until the 1920s, when vaudeville was disintegrating, did anyone issue publicly traded stock. That the first mass entertainment was created by small businesspeople is significant. It meant that vaudeville was more fluid and unstable than sectors dominated by big corporations. It also meant that the owners were primarily motivated by the desire to secure a stable supply of acts, to have freedom from competition from nearby theaters, and to employ a workforce willing to share their risk. Vaudeville never embraced the welfare capitalism that developed in big business during the Progressive Era. It became a highly centralized and coordinated industry because several of its leading entrepreneurs chose to combine to limit competition. In joining them, the majority of less assertive theater owners gained security, but at the cost of flexibility and independence. In the end, the choices they made when faced with the conflicting demands of centralization and freedom, stability and innovation, democracy and inequality, and cost and competition would prove destructive to the industry.

PROCTOR

Although a circus acrobat, Fred Proctor was no daredevil. Throughout his stage career he cleaved to practiced routines and relied on others only when absolutely necessary. For Proctor, going it alone was one of the ways he managed the insecurity of performing. "I like a free reign," he told a reporter, and "work better in single harness." Maybe it was his desire for independence that ultimately drew him out of the circus and into theater management. As an entrepreneur he kept insisting on his right to run his business in his own way, on his own turf, unencumbered by the constraints of both association and competition.[1] It was, however, a freedom that he was able to enjoy only intermittently. Entertainment was a business where limited resources and uncertainty drove people to partner, pool, and consolidate, and Proctor's theaters would eventually be scooped up not once but twice. However, Proctor was not the passive victim of corporate fratricide. Instead, he was instrumental in creating the business conditions that ultimately forced him to cash out. He provides a good example of the innovator who remained anchored to core business practices of an earlier era.

Proctor was born in Dexter, Maine, a lumber town tucked into a cleft in the highlands around Lake Wassookeag, in 1851. The son of a country doctor, he remembered his early childhood as privileged and happy, and he credited his father with inspiring his love of gymnastics. In 1860, Proctor's father died suddenly, and his mother returned to her family home in Lexington, Massachusetts. She sent her older children out to family, and nine-year-old Fred went to live with his older sister in Boston. A talented athlete, he joined the Tremont Club gymnasium (it was soon after incorporated into the YMCA), and at fourteen he was spotted by a circus acrobat looking for a new partner. The offer fired the boy's imagination, and, determined on making a career out of gymnastics, Fred quit his job in a dry goods store, teamed up with a fellow club member, and signed on with L. B. Lent's Circus as the Levantine Brothers. Through the late 1860s and 1870s the pair worked with various circuses and traveling shows. The Levantine Brothers were known for their jumping and tumbling, but Proctor's main specialty was Risley work, where he used his feet to juggle barrels, balance chairs, and toss his partner.

After fifteen years on the road and one successful European tour, Proctor, "with a heavy bankroll" in his pocket, quit the circus and took up the lease on the Green Theater in Albany, New York. A year later he opened a second business in Genesee Falls. Like most towns in the United States in the 1880s, both were underserviced when it came to entertainment. Albany had only the opera house, the Green Theater, and a museum (which had a stage) providing family entertainments to a population of over 100,000, while Genesee Falls, a summer tourist destination, had to put on shows in the park. Unfortunately, Proctor wasn't the only one to sense an opportunity in the local amusement industry. In 1884, H. R. "Harry" Jacobs, who had run museums in Brooklyn and Washington before becoming manager of "General" Tom Thumb's 1882–83 tour, also had a foothold in Albany. By the time Proctor leased his theater, Jacobs had museums in Montreal, Buffalo, Philadelphia, and Troy and was also running a traveling "dime museum" that circled the Northeast. Rather than fight such an expansive interest, Proctor decided to enter into a partnership agreement with his more experienced rival. The contract divided the territory, pooled the bookings for all six theaters, and allowed each partner to operate more or less independently.[2]

Proctor and Jacobs were part of a new generation of show business entrepreneurs who believed that the variety show could be cleaned up, removed from barrooms, and turned into a respectable family entertainment. Variety was an ideal form for businessmen with limited capital because the cost of developing, costuming, and touring acts fell on the performers. Managers needed only a stage and enough revenue from tickets to pay the performers their weekly salaries. Because a variety show was made up of individually contracted acts, theater managers were able to adjust costs and vary shows by mixing up the turns, adding cheaper or pricier ones as they became available. The most challenging aspect of the job was ensuring a large enough supply of acts to fill out the time.[3]

The question for these pioneering amusement entrepreneurs was this: would variety, with its saloon and dime-museum associations, manage to attract and maintain a respectable family audience when offered in a theater? Sensibly cautious investors, like Proctor and Jacobs, initially offered variety shows in conjunction with museums and alongside plays and musical comedies. The fixed displays gave people something to look at while waiting to get into a show, and the "stock" companies helped limit the theaters' dependence on acts bought on the open market. Proctor and Jacob's museum and theater in Albany, for example, featured a moss-haired Moorish lady and the elastic skin man and cages with bears, anteaters, and birds, as well as variety acts.[4] Paradoxically, Proctor was never fully convinced that variety could survive as a full-time stand-alone entertainment, and several of his theaters continued to offer it in alternation with musicals and melodramas.

Vaudeville, as opposed to variety, was a new type of entertainment when Fred Proctor entered the business. Vaudeville was created in the 1870s by entrepreneurs who, seeing the potential appeal of variety, separated the shows not just from the barrooms but also from plays and museum displays. "It used to be Variety," an Irish comic explained, summarizing the history, "but dey call it Vaudeville now. Dey give the same kinds of a show, only not so good." In New York City, the country's entertainment hub, there were only four vaudeville houses operating in 1880: Miner's, Aberle's, Fitzgerald's, and Pastor's. Three of these four had been recently founded by saloonkeepers who eliminated their barrooms and converted to family theaters. In Boston, dime-museum owner B. F. Keith established the first family-oriented variety theater in the city in 1886. Like other variety theater owners, Keith initially alternated variety acts with stock theater and operettas and committed to "continuous vaudeville" only when he leased the Bijou Theater, a new and bigger house in 1887.[5] More conservative than Keith, Proctor would adopt vaudeville in a few of his theaters only in the mid-1890s, once he was certain the audience was willing to accept the pure article. That change, as we have seen, occurred after variety's association with fashionable, bohemian fun had been established in the entertainment capital.

The idea of creating chains of theaters was also new in the 1880s, a response to the shortage of good variety acts. By establishing a chain of businesses, proprietors could entice the better performers with the promise of continual work as they moved from one theater to the next. Variety acts were normally booked at each theater for one week, at which point they were thought to stale, and the railroad was critical in providing players with other employment options. Naturally, actors—who had to pay their own travel between gigs—preferred short jumps to long ones, making work in a regional chain (such as the one Proctor and Jacobs created) highly attractive. Already in the 1870s, owners of individual theaters scattered around the trans-Appalachian west had started to pool their bookings, creating what were in fact chains of independently owned theaters. Establishing a centrally controlled loop of variety theaters that could carry a performer from a rail hub in a big city, be it Chicago or San Francisco or New York, through a circle of regional centers and then back to a major city was the next logical step. By 1888 Proctor and Jacobs were running sixteen museums and combination theaters in the Northeast. A performer employed in the Proctor-Jacobs circuit could follow the rails from New York City to Albany, then on to Troy, Utica, Syracuse, Rochester, and Buffalo, and then back through Newark to Philadelphia, or, alternately, from Albany to Lynn, Boston, Brookfield, Hartford, and Brooklyn.[6]

While Proctor and Jacobs agreed on much, they did not agree on how to sanitize the variety show and make it a family entertainment. Jacobs, who came from the dime museum business, believed that variety worked best as a cheap amusement with turns by acrobats, comedians, and singers leavening the "freak" acts and stuffed animals. He saw the main market for variety among the working class. Proctor, with his circus experience and middle-class background, wanted "to become manager of only first-class attractions" and favored the establishment of "combination houses." Combination theaters mixed variety acts with plays performed by a repertory company. Unlike conventional playhouses, which offered full-length dramas and comedies, combination houses presented local favorites in simpler, sometimes truncated productions. Keith first made enough money to open a vaudeville theater, for example, not with variety shows but with a pirated, trimmed-down version of Gilbert and Sullivan's *The Mikado*. Because conventional belief held that affluent people wanted amusements that involved mental and emotional effort and poorer and less educated ones preferred immediate gratification, commentators argued that the combination house appealed to everyone, attracting working people to the variety acts and middle-class audiences to the melodramas and comedies.[7]

"Though low-priced theaters are very popular," Proctor wrote, explaining his divergence from Jacobs, "and their patrons have been satisfied with a fair grade of companies, the novelty of the low price is past and dying out, [and] the audiences [are] desiring a better class of companies." Accepting their differences, in 1888 the partners amicably dissolved their partnership. Jacobs kept the northern and western New York theaters, as well as the anchors of the chain: the Continental in Philadelphia and New York City's Third Avenue Theater. Proctor retained ownership of the theater in Hartford and one in Bridgeport, Connecticut, as well as those in Lynn and Worcester, Massachusetts, one in Lancaster, Pennsylvania, the Brooklyn Criterion and Novelty theaters, and the Grand Opera House in Wilmington, Delaware, and he immediately secured his own anchor for his chain by leasing the 23rd Street Theater in Manhattan. Proctor established stock companies in all these theaters and raised the quality of the variety acts on offer. This pressed up the prices, and by the mid-1890s he was running the highest-priced popular theaters in the country, selling tickets ranging from twenty-five cents in the balcony to a dollar for a box seat (by contrast, Jacob's best seat cost fifty cents, as did one in Keith's Union Square).[8]

Over the next five years, Proctor made another critical decision. Determined on operating only high-class houses that could secure premium acts, he concentrated his investment in New York City and its immediate surroundings. The decision was in some ways a continuation of established convictions: he was going to charge higher prices and use the revenues to secure better acts, and he was going to make playing his houses attractive to performers by reducing the jumps between them. But it also represented a new idea about urban spectators: that they were inclined to go to shows in their neighborhoods rather than travel across town. Up until this point, theaters (including roof gardens) had located in downtown areas where they caught shoppers and businesspeople leaving work and customers traveling into town for an evening of fun. By moving into residential neighborhoods, Proctor was pioneering an idea that would become as essential to urban amusements as it was to the grocery business: bring the shop to the customer. By 1901 Proctor owned just seven theaters, four of which were in different neighborhoods of New York City. Four of his theaters were combination houses, with stock companies, and three offered only vaudeville. All of his theaters mounted three shows a day, in the early afternoon, the late afternoon, and the evening.[9]

In 1895 Proctor made an even more spectacular attempt to exploit the possibilities of variety when he opened his Pleasure Palace on 58th Street, in a fashionable residential area between Lexington and Third Avenue in New York.

Proctor's idea was to create a kind of vertical Coney Island playground, and the immense theater included a roof garden providing light meals, drinks, and a variety show, a main auditorium that alternated vaudeville and legitimate theater, a small concert hall, two themed cafés (one German, one "Oriental"), a bowling alley, archery and rifle ranges, and an ice-skating rink. One ticket bought a customer access to everything. Proctor apparently believed that he could charge higher ticket prices for vaudeville and secure the top acts by offering patrons something akin to a complete entertainment experience.[10]

The Pleasure Palace never did especially well, and Proctor gradually closed parts of it and converted others, but it was a sign that he was looking for ways to satisfy what he saw as a growing public appetite for commercial entertainment. He was more conservative in his approach than some of his rivals, including B. F. Keith and Tony Pastor, in that he remained unsure of the appeal of the variety show and wanted the security and status that he felt only the legitimate might provide. But unlike Jacobs, Keith, or Pastor, he saw variety as a middle-class entertainment rather than something for the masses. Where he made his great contribution was in imagining popular entertainment as something people would enjoy close to where they lived. In the Pleasure Palace, he even conceived of middle-class people going out for a full evening of varied fun in a theater near their homes.

An alternative, though equally innovative, approach was being developed in Boston by the former tent-show huckster B. F. (Benjamin Franklin) Keith. Like Jacobs, Keith started in business as a museum owner, but the store he leased was on Boston's most fashionable shopping street. In order to appeal to a more middle-class and female audience, Keith did what museum owners since Barnum and Moses Kimball had done and eliminated as much of the salubrious and lowbrow material as he could. In 1887 he then jumped in the opposite direction to Proctor. Since his clientele was made up of people on the go—shoppers, businesspeople, and children on their way home from school—he decided to offer his shows continuously. By running acts with no breaks, people could drop into his theater any time they wanted. Keith's Bijou presented what were, in essence, six shows a day in the 1880s and 1890s, with performers onstage from ten in the morning until ten at night. Continuous vaudeville was as new an idea as neighborhood theaters, but the two approaches suited different markets and developed out of different attitudes and experiences. The continuous was appropriate to theaters with a high customer turnover; the neighborhood house was designed to appeal to repeat customers living within walking distance. This is not to say that repeat customers didn't attend the continuous—in 1903 Keith's manager in Boston reported a conversation with a spectator who said he had been coming to the theater every week for the past nine years—but it did represent a different way of putting audiences in control of their entertainment consumption than they were in the neighborhood theater.[11]

Continuous vaudeville was first tried in New York by manager Frank Pilling at the National on the Bowery (renamed Pilling's Popular Theater) in 1889, where it failed. Four years later, Proctor experimented with it at his 23rd Street Theater, which stood in a commercial neighborhood close to the popular Chelsea Hotel and a block from the city's largest department store. Unlike Pilling, who ran a neighborhood house, Proctor understood that the continuous was appropriate to theaters serving a passing trade. Unfortunately, the continuous idea was unpopular with performers (who preferred three shows a day to as many as fourteen for the same money), and Proctor, who did not find it did much to boost sales, soon abandoned it. The experiment, however, shows that vaudeville did not arrive fully formed and that entrepreneurs in different locations were trying to figure out how best to supply consumers with amusement at a time or place they might find convenient.[12]

Vaudeville's distinctive features—it was cheap to put on, and its component acts were short and diverse—encouraged entrepreneurs to innovate. The amusement's connections to the museum and the saloon, which one might enter and leave at any point, led them to imagine continuous entertainment. The low cost and apparently endless diversity made them think in terms of repeat customers and convenient locations for their theaters. In introducing these innovations, men like Keith and Proctor were, despite their different approaches, creating a new idea in entertainment. They were designing an amusement that could be taken casually, without planning or forethought, at a time or in a place that suited the consumers' lifestyles. In imagining audiences purchasing leisure of this sort, vaudevillians did something remarkable: they laid the foundations for modern mass entertainment.

BIG TIME, SMALL TIME

At the turn of the twentieth century, Fred Proctor was the most important man in vaudeville, the owner of the classiest theaters in the nation's biggest and most trendsetting city. Over the next ten years, the industry expanded dramatically as vaudeville grew into America's favorite amusement. It spread into every part of the country, and by 1910 no city or town of any size (outside the South) was without a vaudeville theater. Many had three or four. Those theaters tended to be organized into chains that coordinated their bookings from head offices. Centralization allowed the booking agents to send acts from theater to theater, providing players with steady employment for weeks at a time. Vaudeville pioneered the idea that commercially produced leisure was an ordinary element in daily life; it first developed the notion that the consumer, rather than the producer, should determine when to take entertainment; it created the networks of theaters that would become the foundation of the motion picture industry; and it was the first entertainment to appeal to nearly all Americans. Vaudevillians were also among the first popular entertainment entrepreneurs to combine to prevent competition.

The model of mass entertainment Proctor favored was a conservative one based on the legitimate theater. His innovation in neighborhood venues did not prevent him from wanting to offer the best amusement in terms of the quality or number of his headlining features or from raising his ticket prices to pay for his stars, many of whom he recruited in Europe. Proctor did keep tickets at roughly half the price of those charged in the legitimate, but they were still two or three times higher than those charged by other vaudeville managers. His model of entertainment came, around 1909, to be called "big-time," and it was adopted by a number of other New York City entrepreneurs, including Percy Williams and Oscar Hammerstein.

The big time was, like everything else in this developing industry, a category that evolved over a span of years. It was rooted, however, in Proctor's desire to raise the status of his theaters by offering a higher cost, higher quality product to more discriminating customers. It arose out of the realization that vaudeville had become a craze because of its fashionable associations. Offering vaudeville along more conventional lines, Proctor's houses were reduced to two shows a day, a matinee and an evening performance. "Instead of filling in the time . . . with light wasted acts, it was better to have two shows a day and give ten all-star features, rather than twenty features in all with eight inferior attractions," a journalist reported after talking to Proctor about it. This rationalization reduced Proctor's weekly need for acts from ninety to twenty-four. Since he employed fewer performers, Proctor decided to focus on employing even more expensive acts in his shows. By 1900 his weekly bill cost $1,800; by comparison, the average vaudeville house was spending just $300 a week on performer salaries. As a sign of the high-status and middle-class appeal of his playhouses, he even contracted Lillian Russell, the country's most famous actress, to perform at the Palace.[13]

Fred Proctor, vaudeville's leading entrepreneur in the first decade of the twentieth century. Proctor's celebrity-driven approach to entertainment helped create the big time, while his chain of neighborhood theaters provided a model for the small. (National Vaudeville Artists, "Eighth Annual Benefit Program," 11 May 1924)

The big time became influential because a number of proprietors of vaudeville houses adopted Proctor's approach. In the West, Martin Beck, general manager of Morris Meyerfeld's Orpheum chain of five theaters, declared that he wanted "to make the Orpheum circuit bring the highest forms of art within reach of the people with the slimmest purses." "Slimmest" was a relative term. In 1900 the Orpheum in San Francisco, which had only recently stopped serving alcohol, charged a maximum admission of fifty cents; by 1906 customers could still buy a gallery seat for a dime, but the best seats now cost a dollar.

In 1910, the trade magazine *Variety* thought the Orpheum chain's thirty-two theaters had reached the "big time." Percy Williams, who ran a string of theaters in Brooklyn as well as the Bergen Beach amusement complex, also copied Proctor and competed with him for acts. He said his weekly payroll for artists in 1909 was $7,000 per house per week (Proctor's at this point would have been about the same), when the average theater owned by rival B. F. Keith was paying around $3,000 per week. According to Williams, the type of artists he wanted for his theaters commanded huge salaries, often because they were imported from overseas. In 1909, for example, Williams paid the Australian Annette Kellerman, who did a diving and swimsuit act, $1,500 a week, while the English cross-dresser Vesta Tilley, the highest paid performer in vaudeville at the time, earned a salary of $3,000 a week. Where most big theaters might employ just one headliner in a show, Williams, like Proctor, felt that this wasn't enough. Williams also adopted Proctor's approach in operating neighborhood, rather than downtown, houses. A vaudeville show, he explained, "cannot have a run like a play. You must change your bill constantly.... My plan was to build theaters in various localities and draw each week on the people of that section. I call my theaters neighborhood theaters." By 1909 Williams owned a couple of two-shows-per-day theaters in the Bronx, one in Harlem, one on the Upper West Side, one on the Upper East Side, two in Brooklyn, and one in Greenpoint. A contract with the Williams chain covered seven or eight weeks of employment as Williams shuffled the acts from one neighborhood of New York to another. Because each theater served a particular residential area, Williams, like Proctor, was not worried about reducing the drawing power of performers, even though he kept them working in the five boroughs for a two-month period.[14]

The alternative to the expensive neighborhood-based, two-a-day big time came to be known as the "small" or "family" time. The small time began with theaters in downtowns or "amusement districts" serving a drop-in trade. These theaters catered to an audience that wanted to pay less for entertainment and that accepted a show without celebrities or expensive props that was provided by low-paid performers. Where Williams, Beck, and Proctor sold tickets at $1 and even $1.50, the small-time houses charged 10 to 50 cents for admission. Insiders tended to categorize theaters by the cost of their weekly bill and the number of shows they offered per day. Small-time theaters, not surprisingly, paid their performers little and asked much more of them. In the early twentieth century, small-time theaters ran between three and eight shows a day, depending on the number of acts they employed. In the second decade of the century, small-time theaters increased this by adopting a "split week" principle whereby they changed their shows not weekly but twice a week. In 1919 the small-time Parlor Theater in Springfield, Illinois, was known as a three-a-day, $450-per-week theater. Where a soloist (or single) in the big time was paid a minimum of $100 per week, the Parlor generally hired singles at $20 per week but used them only every second day for three shows a day, meaning the theater paid around $8 per week to the players who worked three days of performances but kept them in town the whole week.[15]

Big-time managers were contemptuous of the small time and believed it degraded the entertainers who worked there. Performer salaries were determined by the status of the house, and according to the comic monologuist Frank Fogarty, if one moved from the big time to the small time, you couldn't "come back and expect to be the fellow you used to be . . . no more than I could play [small-time] Pantages, which I did . . . and expect to go into the [big-time] Orpheum Theater and be of the same value I was prior to playing Pantages. . . . The polish [will have] gone off of Fogarty." The problem, he thought, was that spectators were aware of where the performers were playing and would say, "We saw Fogarty last week for 15 cents admission, why should we now pay $1?" By the second decade of the century, performers maintained that it was almost impossible to graduate from the small time to the big time. "I think the atmosphere of the small time theater does not make for the development of high class vaudeville material. The atmosphere is different. The quality of the audience is different, and the entire entertainment of the small time theater is not conducive to it," observed one. The players were likely right. In their correspondence with booking agents, theater managers maintained that there were qualitative differences between the three-a-day and the two- or one-a-day acts. Big-time managers were scornful of agents who placed what they considered small-time acts in their houses. The elite atmosphere they promoted was how the big time justified higher seat prices, and they were so successful in their efforts that community boosters saw the securing of a big-time theater as a symbol of their city's maturity and cosmopolitanism.[16]

A fault line therefore opened in vaudeville in the first decade of the century as theater owners made choices about whether to go big-time or small. It was a conscious decision and involved divergent approaches to mass entertainment. Where the big time paid performers higher salaries and catered to the more limited pool of consumers willing to pay more, the small time made theater available at a low cost to a wide market but did so at the expense of the players. Moving from one approach to the other called for a profound change in marketing and management. The B. F. Keith chain, for example, transitioned from one to the other as the small time came to be distinguished from the big. The original Keith plan, instituted in Boston, was to run continuous shows. Tickets were sold at a maximum price of seventy-five cents, and they did not provide a reserved seat. Keith fiercely defended the idea of continuous, casual, inexpensive entertainment and regarded it as his particular invention. He expanded his business by doing what he had done in Boston: leasing theaters on busy shopping streets—such as the Union Square in New York and the Bijou in Philadelphia and in the downtowns of industrial towns across New England—and running continuous shows. His idea was to catch people on their way home from work or out shopping, to turn the audience over quickly, and to charge a modest amount to encourage customers to drop in for that part of the show that suited their schedules. In other words, everything about the early Keith chain pointed to what would soon be called the small time.

But Edward Albee, Keith's general manager—and, after the deaths of the founder in 1914 and of Keith's son in 1918, the owner of his chain—felt differently. Albee was twenty-eight when he joined Keith's theater/museum on Washington Street in Boston as its property manager. He was a wiry, hard-boiled, and smart superintendent who had gained his show business experience managing work crews in circuses. He later said that the problem Keith faced was that he was offering "a cheap show in an aristocratic neighborhood." Albee initially focused on the building itself and decided he needed to move Keith's theater from "cheap nonentity to refinement and excellence," though he admitted later that he and Keith were "absolutely different" in their attitudes. Albee, like Proctor and Williams, but unlike Keith, grew up in an urban middle-class family, and this may have influenced him to conceive of the theater as uplifting, refined, and educational. It was Albee who insisted on cleaning up the museum shows and eliminating the "freaks" on offer at Keith's in order to make vaudeville "more acceptable to the fastidious and religious. Offensive lines are being deleted from the acts.... We want to make vaudeville so clean that it will offend no one, and will be so nice that mothers can bring their children without any fear that they will see or hear anything they shouldn't."[17]

Albee's first independent management position was at Keith's Providence house in Rhode Island, which he started running as a combination theater in 1890. Providence became known as the most highbrow theater in the chain, and in 1900 Keith turned ownership of the building over to his general manager as a "gift." Albee also pushed Keith into expensive renovations to his new theaters in New York and Boston. He later boasted that he had even maneuvered Keith into making a half-million-dollar investment in the decorations at the new theater Keith built on the back of the Bijou, five times what the boss had hoped to pay (Keith's original theater had been valued at a mere $32,000 a decade before). When Albee took over management of the Union Square in New York in 1893, he quietly undermined Keith's philosophy by introducing a covert two-a-day policy. Albee essentially offered two performances—a matinee and an 8 p.m. show—but he filled in the time between with inexperienced performers who did not appear in the main show. This allowed the theater to follow Keith's cherished continuous policy without really doing so. In 1909, Albee convinced Keith to throw over the continuous altogether. Prices then went up and seat reservations were introduced. The process took time, and tickets at Keith theaters before 1910 still cost less than those at Williams and Proctor houses, and the bills featured fewer headliners. But under Albee's influence, the Keith chain moved by gradual stages into the big time.[18]

Historians often assume that the big time served the middle class and the small-time served working-class audiences. This is only partly true and for only part of the time. Both the big time and the small evolved in the first decade of the twentieth century as owners adapted their approach to their local market. This was never a stable industry. Although the big time originated with Hammerstein's, Proctor's, and Williams's neighborhood theaters, it started to move downtown in the second decade of the century under Albee's influence. Similarly, where the small time began as businesses catering to the passing trade, after 1910 it came to dominate the neighborhoods. As a result, the downtown big-time houses marketed themselves as theaters for all the people. "We open our doors," a Keith advertisement boasted, to everyone, "no favorites, no classes—all equal here."[19] By the same token, the conversion of many big-time to small-time houses placed the latter in middle-class neighborhoods. It's also important to remember that many communities had only one or two vaudeville theaters, and these catered to everyone. What distinguished the big and the small was price, headliners, reserved seating, and the cost of the bill. But despite the contempt shown for it by many influential managers, the small time was ultimately more true to the original spirit that built vaudeville. It was the small time that maintained vaudeville's focus on families wanting to drop into a theater for a part of an evening as repeat customers, and it was the small that kept pushing the idea of bringing the theater into every residential area. Small-time managers often complained that the big time was changing vaudeville by inflating the costs of acts to the point they could not afford them. They were not wrong; in following Proctor's model, it was big-time vaudeville that lost sight of innovations like affordable luxury and bringing the theater to the consumer.

B. F. Keith's opulent new theater in Boston, opened in 1894. The ornate facade featured a glass transom, stained glass doors, silver decorations, and a gold and ivory dome. The foyer and ticket booths were lined with a wainscot of Siena marble, and the floor was inlaid mosaic tile. (Author's collection)

No one was ever sure how many big- or small-time vaudeville theaters there were in America. Until the late 1890s, it was hard to sort the vaudeville theaters from the dime museums and saloons playing variety acts, the combination houses, and the music halls. After 1905 it was equally difficult to separate vaudeville theaters showing movies from cinemas offering some variety acts between pictures. James McIntyre, who spent half a century performing in the popular theater, remembered there being just 5 theaters in New York offering vaudeville by 1890. At that date, San Francisco had several variety saloons but only one—the Wigwam Garden—that did not serve liquor and that attracted families. In 1902 the *Chicago Tribune* counted only 43 theaters (rather than saloons or museums) in the United States devoted strictly to vaudeville, though it estimated that there were about 2,000 acts touring the country (which would have been enough to fill 150 houses). By the end of 1906, however, *Billboard* listed 557 vaudeville houses. In 1910, *Variety* reported that about a hundred vaudeville theaters were playing acts costing $2,000 a week or more, which would have been the big-time segment of the industry. In that year, one might reasonably estimate that there were 1,000 vaudeville theaters in the eastern United States and perhaps 600 in the West. The old South remained the most underserved market, containing only 5 percent of the country's vaudeville theaters, according to *Billboard*'s 1906 calculations.[20]

Vaudeville enjoyed its most explosive period of growth between 1905 and 1912. The number of big-time houses probably doubled or tripled in the first decade of the century, but it was the growth of the small time that really marked the industry's expansion. It was just so easy for "the man with a vacant store to erect a stage, place a few chairs, hang out his sign and then sit down and take in money." And as to talent, "every male or female regardless of age, that can sing a note, do a step or perform any kind of stunt is endeavoring to go into the business. . . . There never will be a scarcity of talent for the ten-cent vaudeville." New York's five boroughs boasted sixty-two vaudeville houses in 1914, with another twenty-one burlesque theaters and cinemas that offered at least some nights of vaudeville. Theater boosters looked at the numbers and concluded that the industry was growing from strength to strength. "It is immense today, compared with all the vaudeville in the past," explained an executive in 1919. It was a "constantly growing industry . . . the greatest form of entertainment in the world."[21] The anecdotal evidence certainly corroborated this view and points to a dramatic growth of the entertainment, though it also suggests that it never gained mature stability.

CARTELS

Vaudeville was a means of delivering variety entertainment. It was built on chains (sometimes called circuits at the time) that after 1900 mostly worked together in pools and cartels (sometimes called rings or trusts). A wide range of words were used, loosely and interchangeably, to describe combinations in the industry, but for our purposes a limited number of these will suffice. Chains were created when a single owner or partners controlled several theaters and booked acts for all of those theaters; circuits were formed when three or more separately owned theaters or chains combined for booking purposes but remained otherwise independent of each other; and circuits became cartels when the individual owners signed contracts with each other specifically designed to restrict competition through price-fixing or territorial monopolies.

The chains—such as the one created by Proctor and Jacobs—represented one of vaudeville's most impressive corporate innovations. The first theater chains were created only shortly after chains emerged in retail (the A&P dated to the 1860s, and F. W. Woolworth began organizing in the mid-1880s), and they were a novel idea in business, let alone entertainment. By the end of World War I the most extensive chains, in terms of the number of their theaters, were in the small time: Marcus Loew had 47 theaters in twelve states in 1918 and over 100 by 1920. In 1918 Alexander Pantages ran 26 small-time theaters in eight states, the B. S. Moss New York–based small-time chain had 16, and Gus Sun's Chicago business operated 17 houses. In the big time, the Proctor chain had 12 theaters in New York and New Jersey in 1910, and Percy Williams owned 8 when he sold out to Keith's in 1912. In 1913 the Orpheum included 32 theaters, and Keith's had 33. Although the individual chains were the most influential marketing operations, none of them had a dominant position in the industry. In 1914 there were over 250 theaters in the states in which the Orpheum chain operated, meaning it directly owned just over 12 percent of the total. Similarly, between 1900 and 1918, the Keith chain never owned more than 15 percent of the total theater stock east of the Mississippi.[22]

It was through circuit agreements and later cartel contracts that an industry of small- and medium-sized enterprises consolidated. Circuits were created through agreements among chains or independent theaters to combine their bookings. A few of these were run by artists' agencies, like William Morris's or Martin Klein's. Joining a booking circuit enabled independent theaters to secure performers who might not otherwise play those venues because it gave them higher profile booking services and turned them into a stop in a string of theaters without compromising much of their independence. A performer might even accept a lower salary to play a theater if it was in a convenient location or offered time that needed to be filled between more lucrative gigs.

The permeability of vaudeville as a business sector—the fact that entrepreneurs with limited capital needed only a rented space, the cost of developing and touring acts being borne by the performer—also created insecurity. Theater owners competed for acts and needed ways of increasing their attractiveness to performers; chains and pools were ways of securing the players whom theater managers wanted because they could offer longer contracts. Already, in the 1870s, managers reached informal booking agreements where they corresponded with each other and tried to place in each other's houses those acts they were interested in signing. But in the late 1890s, the voluntary booking pool idea grew stronger, and owners signed contracts agreeing to pay the same performer the same salary, to treat a performer who broke a contract the same way, and to follow the same practices when they canceled a performance.

There were fifteen major circuits in the early twentieth century, and they were much larger than the chains, which were mostly local or regional. The first was created west of the Mississippi in 1901 under the auspices of the Western Vaudeville Managers' Association (WVMA), though it used the Chicago booking office, management, and agents of its biggest member, the Orpheum. In 1912 around seventy-five theaters booked through the WVMA's Chicago agency. In the small time, circuits were less common as entrepreneurs like Marcus Loew and Alexander Pantages opted to build enormous chains of theaters they owned outright. One of the few small-time circuits was Gus Sun's, which included seventy-three theaters in eastern and midwestern states (including Sun's own chain). The primary draw of both vertically and horizontally integrated enterprises, whether circuits or chains, was the length of contract they offered. This is why, within the trade, the size of a circuit or chain was measured not by the number of theaters but by the number of weeks or "time" it offered. Most theaters booked an act for a week, so working "Orpheum time" in 1912 meant the act could be engaged for up to thirty-two weeks—one week at each of Orpheum's thirty-two theaters.[23]

As the number and size of theater chains and voluntary circuits increased, some entrepreneurs realized that "time" no longer provided them with enough of an edge in booking acts. This led entrepreneurs like Oscar Hammerstein and Fred Proctor, who owned relatively few theaters, to pay more than their rivals in the hopes of drawing the most appealing stars. To secure singular performers, these entrepreneurs also regularly traveled to Europe and recruited there. They also formed relationships with firms that managed artists, such as the William Morris Agency. Morris ran the largest and most respected booking agency in the United States. By 1906, Morris had developed a circuit of his own and was booking fifty weeks in a number of individually owned chains (like Proctor's or Sylvester Poli's), which made his time equivalent to that of his largest rivals. The strength of the independent theater/independent agency circuit approach lay in the prestige of Hammerstein's or Proctor's theaters and of agencies like Morris's; the weakness was that it depended on informal relationships, the prestige of the theater, and the cash reserves needed to buy the most expensive and exotic acts.

It was in order to fight the upward pressure on wages that the emerging big time created, and to preserve the advantage "time" had given them, that some chains began to discuss closer relationships—ones that would establish "territories" and would "blacklist" performers playing rival circuits. These practices were designed to prevent competition in the cost of the labor that theater owners bought. The collusive businesses that resulted were called "trusts" at the time; we would today see them as cartels. The most important cartel, the Vaudeville Managers' Protective Association (VMPA), was established east of the Mississippi in 1901 and reorganized as the United Booking Office (UBO) in 1906. Both iterations were under the management of Edward Albee and run out of B. F. Keith's booking offices. Eventually, the UBO would become a major influence in the East, handling eighty-five theaters, including almost all the big-time houses and a few of the small. As part of its cartel agreement, managers authorized the UBO to hire the artists who appeared in their theaters. The booking offices, in doing so, ignored ownership in preference of geography. The desks in the UBO were organized by area, and a performer was generally assigned to play up to a dozen theaters in a given district. For a booking agent, the crucial thing was to arrange a string of performances with reasonably short jumps between them. In the UBO, the agent responsible for "the Middle West" booked theaters in Cincinnati, Youngstown, Pittsburgh, St. Louis, Louisville, Dayton, Cleveland, Grand Rapids, Toledo, and Columbus. Although a good booking agent supposedly knew the tastes of his district, centralization did eliminate much of the individuality enjoyed by independent theaters. The trade-off was that each booking office gave a territorial monopoly to every theater in the cartel, meaning that two houses in Cincinnati were not bidding openly for the same act.[24] Cartel agreements also included provisions to blacklist performers working for rival chains, circuits, or cartels. One of the peculiarities about vaudeville is the way the biggest chains were members of the cartels. In retail, cartels (like Rexall or the Independent Grocers' Alliance) were created to allow independently owned businesses to combine their buying in order to combat the power of their bigger corporate rivals (like the A&P). But in vaudeville, the biggest chains used combination at the wholesale (booking) stage to manage a retail (theater) industry they lacked the financial power to otherwise control.

The first cartel emerged in a circuitous way. It grew out of an 1898 circuit agreement between three major competitors in the West, the Kohl-Castle, Hopkins, and Orpheum chains. Kohl-Castle and Hopkins had already decided to stay out of each other's "territory," or neighborhoods in Chicago, and the independents and chains that joined the western circuit were all operating theaters in different cities. In organizing a cartel to handle their bookings, the western managers said they were worried about rising costs and the way in which performers were using theater competition to "unscrupulously" drive up salaries, but they were also concerned about eastern chains moving west. When the booking office was finally launched in July 1901, the cartel was able to offer performers twenty-five weeks of time over circuits stretching from Buffalo to Los Angeles, but it also committed signatories to pay the same rate for acts and to keep out of each other's territory.[25]

The western managers wanted to extend their agreement, particularly regarding salaries, to the east. This was a big step as a traditional separation between eastern and western theaters existed, and most of the important eastern theaters disdained to even play acts that had made it big in the West. But in the western managers' eyes, it was the actions of big-time theater owners in New York—Percy Williams, Oscar Hammerstein, and most importantly Fred Proctor—backed by William Morris, that were responsible for the salary inflation. They found allies among eastern managers who resented the developing big time's effect on wages and their efforts to depict their rivals as second-class.

In May 1900, Charles Kohl, John J. Murdock of the Masonic Temple Theater, John D. Hopkins, and Martin Beck, the general manager of the Orpheum, met in Boston with Keith, J. H. Moore, who owned theaters in Rochester and Detroit, and the New York theater owner Louis Behman to discuss a national booking cartel. The idea was supported most energetically by Keith, who, as owner of a chain of low-priced continuous theaters, strongly opposed Proctor's move to create a high-priced, high-cost vaudeville. Managers like Keith hoped that if they created a national booking office, they would be able to offer enough weeks to make playing their houses more attractive to headliners, even at lower salaries than Proctor offered. This was a palpable threat to the big-time owners, and they refused to attend the Boston meeting. When it became clear, however, that the cartel was going ahead, they turned up for a subsequent meeting in Brooklyn and tried to get control of the process. They agreed to participate, with Proctor's decision to support the cartel being critical. Although the agreement prevented Proctor from paying higher salaries than anyone else, it included a territorial provision granting him almost exclusive control over vaudeville entertainment in Manhattan. B. F. Keith, whom Proctor seems to have intensely disliked, agreed that he would not expand beyond the two theaters he already operated in New York, and each of Proctor's theaters was given an extensive territorial monopoly.[26]

Performers and their agents were horrified by the idea that a national "vaudeville trust" had now emerged. Until the mid-1890s, theater managers secured acts by corresponding directly with artists, arranging their salaries and the dates they would appear. At a time when there were only a few dozen vaudeville theaters, such an informal system made good sense. But as the business expanded in the late 1890s and competition for acts increased, performers started to employ agents, mostly with offices in New York or Chicago, to correspond with the various theater managers, negotiate salaries, and set up a season of performances for them. By 1900, artists' agents, working on a percentage of salaries, were handling almost all of the big-name acts and a majority of the smaller. Managers estimated that by 1900 only about a quarter of all variety performers continued to handle their own contracts.[27]

Cartelization obviated the need for artists' agents because it pooled the individual theaters' booking offices, allowing the cartel to arrange performances for those wanting work. A performer simply needed to go into the cartel's booking office, and he or she could arrange an entire season's engagements without the help of a personal agent. On the other hand, the eastern and western booking offices reduced the negotiating power of the performer, and the cartel made no secret of the fact that salaries were going down. When the managers announced that they had reached an agreement to form a cartel, a significant number of the most highly paid artists organized a trade union, which they called the White Rats (a palindrome for "star"), and, with the financial support of their professional agents, went out on strike. The Rats announced that their main objective was "to down those managers who are getting rich by using us."[28]

As the strike developed in late February 1901, the fledgling cartel responded by blacklisting all the Rats, but the managers' unity quickly evaporated. Some theaters, including prominent ones like Tony Pastor's and Koster and Bial's, split from the trust, declared themselves White Rat houses, and paid performers the salaries they demanded. Rather than defy the players, Proctor suspended all vaudeville in his theaters and offered only stock-company plays. Accusations began to fly. According to Albee, Proctor was the "disturbing element" in the business, and he charged him with being "the main factor in bringing about the unpleasantness between the performers and the managers," meaning that he held Proctor responsible for driving up salaries in the first place by creating the big time. He also suggested that Proctor, backed up by Morris, had joined the cartel only in order to destroy it. Keith suspected that Morris and Proctor, and maybe others, were bankrolling the Rats. In an effort to shatter whatever remained of manager unity, the Rats set up their own booking office and promised houses that booked with them a complete bill of headliners. "Now that we have found we can play that game ourselves," declared the president of the union, George Fuller Golden, we are "going to have a little more of the money." The western managers had no stomach for the fight and agreed to most of the strikers' demands in early March 1901. By April, the eastern cartel gave way as well and agreed to the Rats' terms.[29]

The Rats still hoped to eliminate the cartel entirely, and they stayed the course, running their own booking office until the end of May 1901. For all intents and purposes, however, the players had already succeeded in smashing collusion in the industry. The owners' central booking offices in Chicago and New York survived, but most of the managers returned to their old method of securing acts. Performers continued to work through their agents, who booked them both independently and through the booking offices in New York and Chicago. The blacklist failed. But the fight, and the loss of their major vaudeville customers, transformed vaudeville. The agents now realized their vulnerability, and William Morris, in particular, started to think in terms of opening his own theater chain. Fred Proctor, disgusted by the association's failure to defeat the Rats, quit the cartel altogether. Performer salaries now rose unchecked. John Hopkins, the Chicago theater owner, declared in February 1902 that vaudeville was in disarray and that every manager was "out for himself and is acting independently of the others." In his view, "the actors are the only ones that are getting the best of it."[30]

Among the major eastern owners, only Keith and Albee remained faithful to the idea of cartelization. In 1901 Keith had not yet committed to the big time and still hoped to keep ticket prices and wages low. Consequently, he had been the most aggressive union buster among the industry leaders, and he blamed the other managers for giving in to the players. As the VMPA unraveled and other managers lost interest, Keith's control over what remained of the cartel increased. Albee managed the central booking office and gradually converted the Keith chain to the big time. He determined to use the VMPA service as a way of establishing a Keith-dominated circuit as a major player in the East. Soon, the independent managers who remained in the cartel were complaining that Keith was using the booking office to advance his own business interests. Several were disturbed that the old VMPA contract was being deployed to stop competitors opening in Keith territory. In fact, Percy Williams was thrown out of the organization in 1903 when he moved to buy the Circle Theater in Manhattan, reportedly a house that Keith was interested in securing. Williams retaliated by bidding against Keith bookings with higher salaries. There were also complaints that Keith used the booking office to place acts in which he had a financial interest, such as the Fadette Orchestra, an all-girl band, which he managed. Defections mounted, and by early 1906 the cartel was able to offer only forty-two weeks—fourteen of them in Keith houses.[31] But the financial strength of the Keith interests was growing not through theater expansion but through the profits made booking acts for the other houses in the VMPA.

The western association functioned much more harmoniously than the eastern. But it too quickly came under the control of its biggest members. In 1903 Martin Beck was asked by a reporter when the next meeting of the WVMA would take place, and he said the next time he and Charles Kohl were in a cab together. The western association remained a loosely organized circuit; it had no blacklist of performers who played rivals, and it maintained peaceful relations with the agents and players.[32] But harmony in the West was really built on the fact that there was no western Proctor, Hammerstein, or Williams to cause trouble.

Paradoxically, despite the failure of cartelization to control costs, vaudeville grew at its fastest pace in the decade following the White Rats strike. The Orpheum chain, for example, grew from seven houses in 1900 to ten in 1904 and twenty-seven by 1912. The small time expanded even more swiftly. As the craze for vaudeville waxed, theater profits rose to high levels, and salaries increased dramatically. Will Cressy, vaudeville's most successful sketch writer, observed in 1909 that he had heard that Hammerstein's Victoria Theater in New York cleared $200,000 in profit a year, the Orpheum in San Francisco made a similar amount, and one of Williams's theater in Brooklyn made $90,000 in its first year of operation. The writer Hartley Davis reported that Keith's in Philadelphia and the Brooklyn Orpheum (another Percy Williams house) each made $200,000 in net profit in 1907. These were piddling numbers compared to the profits in oil or mining, but they do suggest that the open market was a boon to the entertainment business.[33]

So profitable and disorganized was vaudeville that hungry outsiders began eyeing the entertainment. In 1906 the largest consortium of legitimate playhouses announced that it was interested in converting some of its less-successful theaters to vaudeville. Marc Klaw and A. L. Erlanger, who ran the "Theater Syndicate," as it was popularly known, looked to move into vaudeville by purchasing the struggling western-based Sullivan-Considine chain. Albee may have been involved in some way, as he had attempted, two years before, to convince Erlanger to enter vaudeville in the West. Consequently, when the Syndicate announced its move, Keith promptly proposed a massive merger of the booking operations of the Keith, Orpheum, and Klaw and Erlanger chains. Where this would have left other members of the eastern and western cartels is anyone's guess. It was a sign that the booking business was becoming the real source of profit in vaudeville as entrepreneurs were now willing to sacrifice the retail business to secure a monopoly in wholesaling. But whatever they were planning, the deal collapsed after four days of negotiations, apparently because the parties failed to agree on the allocation of stock.[34]

In the midst of this crisis, B. F. Keith had an unexpected turn of good luck. J. Austin Fynes, Fred Proctor's former general manager and a onetime employee of Keith's, advised him that the Gilsey estate, which held the lease on Proctor's Fifth Avenue theater, was interested in selling the property. With Keith's financial backing, Fynes quietly purchased the lease on behalf of Keith and, at the same time, transferred to his new associate a lot he owned in Harlem as well as the Bijou Theater in Jersey City, placing Keith in the territory of both Proctor and Williams. Since Proctor and Williams had quit the cartel, nothing protected them from Keith opening in their territory, but what the Gilsey purchase meant was that Proctor's bitterest rival was now his landlord as well as his probable competitor in neighborhoods he had long controlled. With talk of a massive Syndicate-Keith-Orpheum deal filling the papers, Proctor surrendered and agreed to a deal with B. F. Keith. The two established a new chain that included Proctor's theaters, Keith's Bijou, and Keith's Union Square. Proctor's contribution to the partnership, in terms of the market value of the theaters, was bigger, so the difference was capitalized and the shares divided equally. Under pressure from Keith, Proctor also agreed to stop booking through the Morris agency and to use the cartel's office; in exchange, Keith again sacrificed territory. He accepted Proctor's control over New York neighborhoods by agreeing not to expand his chain in Manhattan by building on the Harlem lot.[35] Keith knew what Proctor did not, which was that control over the supply of acts gave an entrepreneur more power in the theater business than any territorial monopoly.

The addition of Proctor's houses provided Keith's booking cartel with fifty weeks and made it the most powerful supplier of talent in the East. Having harmed his biggest rival in the supply business, the William Morris Agency, by capturing Proctor, Keith moved to absorb the growing Poli chain into the cartel. Sylvester Poli was an Italian immigrant who got his start in entertainment running a wax museum. In the late 1890s, he created a small chain of high-class vaudeville houses that ultimately included a dozen theaters in New York and New England. Poli, like Proctor and Williams and Oscar Hammerstein, had previously stepped around the Keith booking office and arranged his acts through Morris. Poli was small fry when Keith went after him, but the acquisition gave his booking office more time in the East. According to *Billboard*, Poli was brought in under intimidation, much as Proctor had been, when Keith agents secured options on theaters in New Haven and Hartford, Poli's two most profitable territories. Faced with the threat of having any act playing his houses blacklisted by the Keith booking service (which now included Proctor's houses), Poli agreed to a deal that saw him withdraw from Jersey City, and in exchange Keith agreed to close his theater in Worcester, Massachusetts, and to stay out of Hartford and New Haven. The new rule in vaudeville, Poli explained, was "protect your territory." But the most important condition of the arrangement was that Poli leave Morris and book acts through the cartel.[36]

By the summer of 1906, according to *Variety*, "most managers are frightened of the Keith office." But they were equally worried about handing their bookings over to him. "It is the fear of being buried alive and losing their individuality should they enter that booking agency that prevents the Keith threats from having the effect intended." The territorial agreements were, however, merely a way of rationalizing the booking business, by preventing competition for acts among the retail clientele. Having used a stick to force two rival chains to book acts through his office, Keith now used a carrot to bring in the other independents. In June 1906 Albee renamed the VMPA booking service the United Booking Office and announced that the profits from its operations would be shared on a proportional basis by all the businesses using its services. It continued, however, to employ Keith staff, to be located in a Keith building, and to be managed by Albee. Keith then forced Percy Williams into a territorial agreement by securing leases on properties close to his theaters in Manhattan and Brooklyn. Under their 1907 deal, Williams closed his theater in Philadelphia, which competed with Keith's, and in exchange Keith agreed to stay out of the territory of Williams's businesses in New York. Williams, who booked through the Morris agency, announced he was moving over to the UBO.[37]

William Morris was in serious trouble with the loss of the contracts for the Proctor, Poli, and Williams chains. In a rather desperate bid to reverse the tide of cartelization, he entered talks with the Klaw and Erlanger and Shubert chains of legitimate theaters about handling their bookings, should they convert some of their playhouses to vaudeville. Morris boasted that adding these theaters would restore his time to fifty-two weeks, but he was building castles in the air. As a trial, Klaw and Erlanger did open a dozen vaudeville theaters, which drew about 50,000 customers a week in the fall of 1907. But the real impact of the move was on overhead, as the Morris office bid performer salaries up in order to draw players away from the UBO.[38]

The financial panic that gripped Wall Street in October 1907 brought the feuding to an end as Klaw, Erlanger, and the other legitimate theater owners backed away from their risky vaudeville expansion. Apparently, Keith agreed to pay the leases and stock in Klaw and Erlanger's nascent vaudeville enterprise, and the UBO assumed the outstanding contracts for booked performers, reported later to total $1 million. It also paid Klaw and Erlanger and the Shubert brothers, Lee and Jake, $250,000 to stay out of vaudeville for ten years. The Morris agency was the real target and victim of the "vaudeville war." Morris survived, but the company's influence in vaudeville was broken. The Sullivan-Considine theaters and the remains of the Klaw-Erlanger-Morris circuit were soon bought up by Marcus Loew with Morris joining him as a partner. Loew was an ambitious new player in the industry who was rapidly creating an extensive small-time chain. Ironically, the Keith-OBU and Orpheum interests, so worried about the big-time threat of Proctor, Williams, and Klaw and Erlanger, paid almost no attention to Loew.[39]

Cartelization enabled two theater chains with limited financial resources and market share to control competition and divide territory. Initially created to preserve the mass market and keep costs low, the cartels became instruments for Keith and the Orpheum to enter the big time. Between 1901, when the first cartel failed, and 1907, when the second smashed its rivals, both chains had come to accept the Proctor model of entertainment. They competed with Hammerstein and Williams on salaries, abandoned the continuous show, and charged between one dollar and two for a reserved orchestra seat. Now, through cartelization, Keith and the Orpheum were able to prevent rival big-time theaters from securing better performers, paying different salaries, offering a more appealing product, and competing in the same territory. Although the cartels did not fix box office prices, they used the leverage they possessed by owning a limited number of theaters and the threat of dropping a noncompliant house into the "family time" division of their booking services (where it had no access to headliners) to exercise control. The cost of this was a sameness in vaudeville. Although the gap between big time and small widened, within each category the product was much the same, no matter where in the country one went. The same artists who appeared in Scranton played Buffalo or Louisville, in slightly different order, within weeks of each other. The chain and cartel booking offices maintained press or publicity bureaus that monitored local newspaper reviews and provided publicity to theaters for the acts being booked. Journalists across the country wanting more information on a performer would be referred to the booking offices in New York or Chicago. Because performer costs were largely fixed, ticket prices became standardized. Vaudeville remained an industry of independent proprietorships, but after 1910 the autonomy of the local theater was limited. Most theaters no longer advertised, booked their own acts, arranged their own bills, or determined the salaries they would pay.[40]

"COLORED VAUDEVILLE"

Until 1912, when the African American comedian Sherman H. Dudley organized the Colored Consolidated Vaudeville Exchange, vaudeville's chains, circuits, and cartels included only the managers of theaters serving predominantly white audiences. The small number of African American performers in the industry either booked directly with theaters or worked with one of the handful of independent agencies that accepted black clients. The founding of Dudley's booking service was therefore a significant moment in the history of African American entertainment as it demonstrated that commercial amusements had become sufficiently popular with black audiences to make coordinated action feasible. But the exchange's creation also signified a hardening of racial prejudice and evidenced a desire among white vaudevillians to do business separately. That the Dudley exchange eventually stirred a backlash among theater owners of Jim Crow theaters in the South is, perhaps, to be expected, but it was not Dudley's race that proved to be the paramount issue. Instead, the destruction of the Dudley booking agency by the Theater Owners' Booking Association (TOBA) represented another way of resolving the big questions in early mass entertainment: How would the industry be organized, and whose interests would it serve?

Sherman Dudley began his career with black-on-black minstrel shows (so called because the African American performers darkened their skin with black makeup), becoming a headliner in 1904 when he took over as lead in the Smart Set, a popular touring production company. Although the Smart Set played in some vaudeville theaters, the show was essentially a scripted musical in which performers played characters and acted out a loosely structured story or "book." Dudley did well with the Smart Set and invested his money profitably, becoming an affluent owner of theaters, apartment buildings, traveling shows, and racehorses. However, Dudley was not a theater owner when he organized his consolidated booking office—he would lease the Minnehaha Theater in Washington only in the spring of 1913—and he approached the booking business from the perspective of the agent, performer, and impresario.[41]

The Dudley circuit, as his exchange was popularly known, initially handled the bookings of seven small-time theaters serving African American communities in Washington and Virginia, but by 1917 it had grown to include a few in Tennessee, Kentucky, and North Carolina, most of whose owners, such as Anselmo Barrasso of the Metropolitan Theater in Memphis, were white. Colored vaudeville theaters generally offered a mix of road shows, like the Smart Set, traveling variety entertainments, like Sissieretta Jones's troupe, plays by stock companies, and vaudeville. Other than the Dudley circuit, the largest booking service for black artists was Martin Klein's actors' agency in Chicago.[42]

The development of African American commercial amusement depended both on there being enough consumers to support neighborhood theaters and on a steady supply of talent. The movement of black people from the countryside to cities in the South—20 percent of the African American population was urban by 1910—satisfied the first condition, and working-class consumers were able to afford the dimes and quarters needed for admission to small-time houses. By the turn of the century there were also a reasonable number of black performers, most of whom had learned their trade working in the black-on-black minstrel troupes that toured the southern countryside. Black-on-black minstrels traditionally specialized in grotesque and slapstick work where they exaggerated their mouths, their height, their slow-wittedness, or their ability to roll their eyeballs. For black audiences, laughing at crude racial stereotypes may have been a way of subverting the trauma those stereotypes expressed. For white audiences, however, outlandish black-on-black performers were widely taken as affirming their racial prejudices. As a *Chicago Inter Ocean* critic enthused of one black-on-black show, onstage one got to see "darkies by nature, precept and practice.... We get the original article without adulteration." Although there were a number of brilliant African American minstrels in the late nineteenth century, they were all expected to mug for the audience, to eschew sensitive feelings, and to act in outrageous and self-deprecating ways.[43]

The explosive talent of such black-on-black minstrels as Billy Kersands, Ernest Hogan, Ben Harney, and Dan Lewis was not, however, lost on variety theater owners serving a white clientele. In pursuit of a novelty, they began employing individual African American minstrels as singers or comedians, primarily in the winter months, which were the off-season for minstrel shows. Ernest Hogan, who was with Eaton and Farrell's Georgia Minstrels, started performing in predominantly white variety shows in the winter of 1892 and took to the road with "colored minstrel" troupes in the summer. Hogan, who lathered on the grease paint to make his skin darker, was billed as an "eccentric" or "grotesque" comedian whose "facial contortions" were considered immensely funny. Although he claimed to be "the only colored comedian" in mainstream vaudeville, he wasn't. Dan Lewis, another "grotesque" blackface minstrel, also performed periodically in variety shows from 1890, and he eventually joined Weber and Fields's touring burlesque entertainment.[44]

Between 1896 and 1910, around 200 acts with black performers broke into white vaudeville. The most popular acts were comedy and music pairs—Cole and Johnson, Williams and Walker, Avery and Hart, Carter and Bluford, Fiddler and Shelton, Cooper and Robinson, and Anderson and Goines—but there were also a number of dancers like Brown and Nevarro, the Brittons, and the buck-and-wing sextet the Dixie Serenaders. African American performers became prevalent enough that in 1899 the *San Francisco Call* would declare (though with considerable exaggeration) that "no bill nowadays is complete without a genuine colored team."[45]

Black performers were relatively inexpensive additions to a vaudeville bill, but many white performers, managers, and critics found their presence a sign that "novelty ... has become a nuisance." As early as 1898 some regional managers announced that they would not book African Americans, ostensibly because white audiences did not want them to. As an irate spectator in Cincinnati expressed it, he should "be allowed to enjoy a variety show without the disgusting cakewalk and the swelled headed niggers. . . . Put them in the coon companies where they may be avoided if desired." Chicot, the influential critic for the *New York Morning Telegraph*, agreed: "It is all well enough for the negro to become an actor if he can find a supporting clientele, but his place is in an octoroon company and not in a mixed bill." Although not openly discussed, a Pittsburgh paper reported, "There is a decided prejudice [against blacks] within the acting business." White performers apparently did not like working or traveling with them, and "dissensions are perpetual between the two races." The same animosity did not extend to the Irish, Jews, Latinos, or new Americans. The White Rats, for example, did not allow African Americans in the organization, but they had German- and Yiddish-language branches, and several Hispanics were members of the English-language union (Adgie the Mexican lion tamer was one). The managers probably did not help the cause of African American entertainment when Percy Williams created a company-union during the 1901 strike made up of those performers banned from membership in the Rats. Without much subtlety, he called his organization of strikebreakers the Black Cats.[46]

The strained relations between black performers and whites is illustrated by a story that circulated in the days after the New York race riot of 1900. According to the rumor, white mobs were screaming for the blood of African American vaudevillians Ernest Hogan, George Walker, and Bert Williams. While it is true that racist hooligans occupied the streets of the Tenderloin in New York, the heart of the city's African American community, following the killing of a white policeman by a black man, it is unlikely that they targeted black vaudevillians. The white gangs that roamed through the Tenderloin randomly beat and terrorized as many black persons as they could find, and the comedian Walker was pulled from a tram on Broadway and brutally beaten. But the story, which Hogan appears to have started, that "during the height of the riot the cry went out to 'get Ernest Hogan and Williams and Walker and Cole and [Billy] Johnson'"[47] was nowhere else reported. Its widespread acceptance among black performers, however, evidences the extremes of racism they had experienced at the hands of white coworkers and their misgivings about their primarily white audience.

In the wake of their strike, the White Rats, flush with success, took up the cause of the closed shop. The unionists' hope was that they might force managers to employ only Rats in their theaters, which would have pushed African American performers out of vaudeville altogether. Although the union failed to secure this demand, many vaudeville theaters did go "lily white." Increasingly, black entertainers found they could not secure enough weeks to make mainstream vaudeville a viable option. In 1902, approximately 2 percent of acts in primarily white vaudeville theaters were performed by African Americans; by 1905, that number had declined by more than half, and even in 1908, the best year for black representation before World War I, the number was only one in eighty. Because a standard show had eight to twelve acts, this means that only about one primarily white theater in ten would have featured an African American performer on any given night in the first decade of the twentieth century. After the White Rats strike, Chicot crowed, vaudeville had turned "a lighter shade."[48]

The hostility of white performers did not abate. In 1910 several white actors protested when Oscar Hammerstein headlined Bert Williams, the country's most successful black entertainer. Under pressure from white players, Hammerstein compromised by moving Williams's name down the list of performers in his promotional material while keeping his name in enlarged type. The *New York Age*, the city's leading African American newspaper, suggested that the Rats were behind this latest expression of racism, prompting Edward Albee of the UBO to reassure representative black performers of the managers' support. The Rats warned African American vaudevillians not to believe him and to create their own union. "Colored Artistes Beware" ran the headline in the Rats' newspaper. As the African American critic and sometime actor Sylvester Russell wrote, the sad fact was that "white actors and White Rats in some particulars have been the aegis of opposition [to black performers] more than the managers."[49]

As opportunities for work in white vaudeville declined, the most prominent black vaudevillians organized their own all-black musical comedies, modeled on those put on by the Smart Set, and took to the road. Their shows appeared in both segregated African American theaters and some "legitimate" houses serving white audiences. Williams and Walker moved into the traveling musical comedy business early, in 1899, when they launched the *Lucky Coon*. Bert Williams would continue his solo career in variety in between tours, but he was primarily a feature of the rooftops and revues rather than vaudeville. Similarly, Bob Cole and Rosamond Johnson, another headlining African American act, left vaudeville to create *The Shoo Fly Regiment* musical in 1906. Thereafter they appeared in vaudeville only infrequently, and their bookings were confined to a few theaters in major cities. As Cole explained in 1909, the "most painful" aspect of performing was "not being able to get employment because he is a Negro." This, he said, had driven him out of vaudeville, because "no matter how proficient" there was "an invisible barrier of prejudice."[50]

Segregated theaters grew in number as the supply of African American talent increased and the urban market expanded. They were all small-time houses and paid extremely low salaries, which is why big-name acts shunned them in favor of road shows, but the limited work and pervasive racism meant that the majority of performers, especially in the South, had few other options. Managers of "colored" vaudeville houses were notorious for canceling acts at the last minute without impunity, whenever they were able to secure something better or cheaper. Martin Klein's business was primarily in the Midwest, and he negotiated the highest salaries he could for his clients, but Dudley was operating a southern booking agency, and even he admitted that the conditions of work were appalling. His primary goal in establishing his own "circuit," he asserted, was to secure good and relatively remunerative work for black talent. All might not be "perfect," he apologized, and "he may not be paying his people all they ought to receive[,] but he is doing the best the business will stand in the present era of development; the more will come when the harvest grows richer."[51]

Unfortunately, talk like this was worrying to the owners of small-time Jim Crow theaters, and whenever Dudley tried to push up salaries for performers, he invariably ran into manager resistance. The fact is that while they wanted a reliable supply of acts, theater owners were reluctant to link themselves too closely to booking agents like Klein or Dudley. Unlike the cartels created in "white" vaudeville, which were initially designed to keep salaries low, the booking offices supplying "colored" houses were accused of favoring the performers and inflating wages. This was because in African American vaudeville, the cartels were organized by agents like Klein and Dudley, not by theater owners. Consequently, most managers of Jim Crow theaters preferred to book independently rather than use the centralized booking services run by Dudley and Klein. As late as 1917 even Klein was able to place a traveling show, like the Smart Set, only for sixteen weeks, and he offered just twelve weeks to individual vaudeville performers. In that year, the conflict between Dudley and the theaters in his exchange came to a head when he entered a fight with one of his clients, the New Howard Theater in Washington. The manager of the Howard complained that the acts Dudley booked for the venue were too expensive, and he broke the theater's contract with him in protest. Dudley blacklisted any performer working there, but he was playing a weak hand. The trouble was that most managers supported the Howard, not Dudley, in the salary dispute. In the three months following his fight with the Howard's management, over half of the nineteen theaters in Dudley's booking circuit defected.[52]

By December 1918, with his business in disarray, Dudley decided to sell out, merging his booking service with Martin Klein's and remaining on as Klein's southern regional manager. The new agency offered thirty weeks of what was now commonly called "Klein time." Unfortunately, Klein's penetration of the South provoked the managers of segregated theaters to further action. In August 1918, the owners of ten segregated theaters had joined together to form the Mutual Amusement Circuit. The Mutual offered lower wages than Klein but promised shorter jumps and represented more southern theaters. The managers complained that agents like Klein were more interested in getting high wages for performers than low costs for theaters. This was the same charge white theater managers leveled against William Morris and reflected a common desire on the part of small-time proprietors to push salaries down. Milton Starr, owner of the Bijou Theater in Kansas City and one of the founders of the managers' circuit, even predicted that the industry faced "impending disaster" thanks to "the gross mismanagement and unfair dealings of the booking agents, who, Kaiser-like, dominated the Colored vaudeville."[53]

Klein's agency attempted to fight the independents, and they responded by creating a cartel, the Theater Owners' Booking Association, which blacklisted anyone playing "Klein time." The combination of low salaries and the blacklist encouraged many of Klein's customers, including Sam Reevin, a Chattanooga theater owner and former treasurer of Klein's business, to defect to TOBA. In March 1921 Dudley attempted to mobilize the actors against the new cartel by establishing a union. But that effort was a belated one, and Klein's remaining theaters, even more worried now about the organization's direction, abandoned him en masse. In May 1921, Dudley and Klein accepted the inevitable and, at a meeting with their rivals in Chattanooga, agreed to merge their operations. Dudley became manager of the eastern office of TOBA, an organization that now handled the bookings for eighty Jim Crow theaters, "ending competitive bidding for acts" and promising to "stabilize figures" (meaning lower wages).[54]

Like the UBO and Orpheum cartels, TOBA was run by entrepreneurs struggling to keep live theater an inexpensive mass entertainment. The major difference was that in white vaudeville, leading chains (Keith's and the Orpheum) used the booking cartels to firm up the distinction between small- and big-time theaters. The big-time chains would use the UBO and Orpheum cartels to inflate the salaries they paid to keep performers from moving over to their small-time rivals. In contrast, TOBA was entirely made up of small-time managers who wanted player costs to be as low as possible. In both cases, the struggle to control wages was part of a broader effort to figure out how to create a mass entertainment. Managers experimented with a range of innovations—neighborhood theaters, continuous vaudeville, open seating, and centralized booking—that were designed to bring variety entertainment closer to where people lived, to make it suit the consumers' schedules, and to place well-known acts across the country. For many entrepreneurs, though not all, low ticket prices were an essential feature of mass entertainment, and they believed they could keep prices down only if they controlled performers' salaries. Prior to 1910, the approach introduced by Proctor, Williams, and Hammerstein and supported by most actors' agents, that audiences would attend higher-priced theaters to see the biggest stars, was not supported by most owners of houses serving primarily white audiences or any owners of segregated African American theaters. But as soon as Keith and the Orpheum had gained control over a substantial segment of the industry, the character of vaudeville changed as both chains shifted upmarket.

CONTRACTION

"Colored vaudeville" moved at a different pace, but its trajectory of development was initially not unlike that of mainline vaudeville. After a period of frenetic, competitive growth of relatively small, low-cost, neighborhood-oriented variety houses, the industry consolidated. Chains and cartels were organized and booking offices established, and the industry began to contract. Partially as a result of territorial arrangements and other collusive practices, the number of vaudeville theaters declined, competition was restricted, and blacklists were imposed. By 1912, in the West, the WVMA/Orpheum booking office, which Martin Beck managed, controlled the employment of artists in most of the big-time theaters west of the Mississippi. In the East, the UBO, a Keith functionary organization, controlled all the big-time bookings and some of the small. Together, the two offices booked 200 theaters in 1913 (around 15–20 percent of the total). TOBA's policy of strangling territorial competition also prevented growth. By 1925 only 50 houses remained in the TOBA circuit, and the black actors' union, which was still headed by Dudley, had only 250 members. But where the cartels in vaudeville serving primarily white audiences protected the big-time pretensions of their dominant members, the cartel in colored vaudeville fought to prevent the emergence of a high end. TOBA became notorious for its exploitation of African American players: there were complaints about the long jumps and the low wages and the poor treatment. But with few better jobs in entertainment to be had, there was little that African American performers could do. For those running the cartels, the actual operations of the individual theaters, including those owned directly by the Keith or Orpheum companies, were far less important and lucrative than the booking business.

Little competition existed within the cartelized segment of the industry. The booking offices of the cartels remained ostensibly separate, but the East Coast office of the Orpheum moved onto the same floor of the same building as the UBO. Beck, who was managing director of the Orpheum, joined the board of the UBO. As a sign of the peace now prevailing in vaudeville, Beck and Albee purchased shares in each other's chains. As Albee explained to the press, "The East and West will work absolutely together, having interests in each other's theaters and with their booking offices all on the same floor. Mr. Keith will have the entire control and management in the East and Meyerfeld and Beck west of Chicago."[55]

The constriction that cartelization placed on independent ownership was evidenced by Fred Proctor's unhappiness. Proctor had been one of the first victims of Keith's bid to revive the vaudeville cartel, and he was sufficiently miserable working in yoke with Albee that he handed over relations with the UBO to his seventeen-year-old son. In Proctor's case, the problem was that Keith seemed to be managing his theaters into obscurity. Keith boasted in 1910 that the new firm had quadrupled Proctor's 1907 sales, but each partner averaged net earnings of only $75,000 a year, the same amount that Proctor had made the year before amalgamation. Proctor's major complaint was that he had been forced to recast his theaters to suit Keith's move into the big time. His businesses were substantially renovated to make them more luxurious along the lines favored by Albee, something Proctor said was a waste of money. Proctor's stock companies were all let go and his houses converted, in what seems a malicious move, to small-time houses with three shows a day and thirty-cent admission for any orchestra seat. The UBO limited Proctor's access to headliners. For a time, the 23rd Street Theater was even returned to the continuous methods that Proctor had abandoned years before, and when that failed, it was turned into a cinema. By 1910 all the old Proctor houses, except the Fifth Avenue, were being run on the "10–20–30 cent plan" (ten cents for an upper balcony seat, twenty for a lower, and thirty for the orchestra), offering eight or nine unimportant acts plus films. Proctor later remarked that under Keith the "days of the headliner . . . when the public had come to expect the unusual at Proctor theaters" had passed. The emphasis, he complained, was being placed on the "good all-around program" rather than on the excellent one.[56]

The transformation of the Proctor chain gives insight into Keith and Albee's plans for vaudeville. They had come to accept the value of the big time but knew that higher ticket prices threatened the mass appeal of their theaters. They therefore elevated the Keith theaters in the UBO while trying to squeeze everyone else down into what they called "the family time." *The Player* magazine even reported that the Keith chain subsidized its bid for preeminence by secretly requiring performers to play Keith houses at lower rates than at the other theaters of the UBO, despite what their contracts said. But in Albee's view, there was a limited amount of room at the top. In 1911, Proctor managed to wriggle free of the partnership, but he lacked an alternative to the UBO. A malicious Albee adopted a vindictive booking policy, which *Variety* described as "Making Proctor the Goat," by denying his theaters any noteworthy acts. Proctor kept at it, however, though his houses no longer stood at the pinnacle of vaudeville.[57] Perhaps the old acrobat derived some pleasure from the fact that his vaudeville chain of eleven theaters, which he sold to RKO Pictures in 1929, survived Albee's by a year.

Centralized booking offices changed the face of vaudeville. They allowed two chains, which otherwise lacked market dominance, to prevent new firms from entering the industry and established ones from competing in salaries or quality. They obstructed innovations that might give one theater an advantage over another. Proctor complained that the proliferation of identical theaters under the UBO was what was overcrowding vaudeville, creating too much competition by making them all the same. "First class or 'big time' vaudeville," Proctor maintained in 1912, "needs new blood, new faces, new ideas and new acts, and it needs them now." Managers were in a squeeze, he insisted, but "with the speedy growth in the tone of vaudeville, it is getting correspondingly difficult to obtain high-class attractions."[58]

Paradoxically, the cartels, which were initially created to keep costs low and the entertainment accessible to the masses, were by World War I serving the interests of the Keith and Orpheum chains particularly. Once in control, the Keith and Orpheum chains repudiated many of the principles of mass entertainment. They ran their big-time theaters in downtown districts, offered two shows a day, provided reserved seating, and were relatively expensive. It was the small time that now preserved the idea of mass entertainment, not the big. Unfortunately, the small time also had less access to headlining acts and, as salaries rose, had to subsidize the cost of live entertainment with less expensive films.[59]

Vaudeville grew into a mass entertainment because it made tickets affordable and theaters accessible. It also paid low wages to performers and forced them to work long hours so that spectators could see them at their convenience. Big-time managers rejected aspects of this approach, arguing that vaudeville was sufficiently popular to bear elevation. Vaudeville had become a craze because of its fashionable associations, so why not develop that appeal? They therefore competed with the legitimate by running shows at fixed times, increasing ticket prices, and stratifying their seating. They drew audiences by heavily marketing their celebrities and the special atmosphere of the vaudeville show. They ensured their success by driving competitors out of business and creating cartels that prevented rivals from buying away their stars. Working in the big time was unquestionably more pleasant and remunerative for most performers. But in adopting this approach, vaudeville sacrificed an element of its innovative mass appeal. Small-time theaters tried to stick with the original formula, charging minimal amounts, running frequent shows, and ruthlessly exploiting players. The big-time booking cartels understood this and tried to make their small-time competitors as unattractive and unprofitable as they could by blacklisting any performer trying to cross from their side to the small. As it grew harder for small-time managers to secure players at a low enough price, they replaced them with movies. Was there a golden mean? As we will see, from a financial perspective, one might have been attainable, and a better balance of sales and costs was briefly found in 1918–20. But the revival was insufficient to drive vaudeville back into prominence. By the time managers and booking agents found a way of delivering celebrity-based live entertainment at a reasonable price, the craze for vaudeville had passed, new competitors had entered the leisure market, and vaudeville had fallen out of fashion.

CHAPTER SIX

THE HOOK

VAUDEVILLE MAKES ITS EXIT

SHORTLY AFTER Odell Williams died in 1902, a Boston spectator recalled a night when the popular comedian had unexpectedly walked onstage at Keith's and interrupted Nat Goodwin in the middle of his monologue with the bizarre line, "Mother wants to know if you will accept these frogs' legs?" As Goodwin stood there, not knowing what to say, the audience, most of whom appear to have recognized Williams, roared with laughter.[1] With this peculiar sentence Williams captured vaudeville's Dadaist irreverence, its fraternity of stars, its direct appeal, and its improvised feel. Qualities like these gave audiences the impression that they were eavesdropping on a great joke, and the sensation appealed to them. Early twentieth-century spectators flocked to the theater to experience vaudeville's casual style, comfortable chairs, glittery costumes, funny slang words, nimble dancers, and amazing acrobats. The vaudeville theater didn't have glamour, in a high-Hollywood sense, but in the first decade of the century it did have punch and pizazz. A great diversity of Americans enjoyed vaudeville because it offered them a feeling of belonging to a community of people with modern attitudes. Variety entertainment made them relax, detach, and laugh about the strenuous, chaotic world in which they lived. It served up a potent brew, but it wouldn't last. By the 1920s, vaudeville had come to look tawdry and tired; it was an industry going through the motions rather than buzzing with excitement. That indescribable quality of vitality—the swagger that comes from success—was now to be found in the movies, on the radio, in nightclubs, and in the musical theater.

As vaudeville declined, its owners came to increasingly rely on the appeal of the established stars whose contracts they controlled. Concerned over the apparent popularity of narrative entertainment, indicated by the development of feature films, the number of one-act plays rose sharply. Owners of big-time theaters tried to exploit the glamour of vaudeville and reduced the number of houses they operated while redecorating and expanding the ones they retained. The small-time chains chose a different route. Unable to afford the salaries that many headliners demanded and blocked by the cartels from hiring others, they chose to reduce their dependence on live entertainment by showing movies. By World War I, vaudeville was in flux. But as this chapter demonstrates, the entertainment's precipitous decline after 1912 was not preordained; it was produced by difficult circumstances combined with poor decision-making on the part of management, player resistance to change, and an approach to marketing that oversold those performers who enjoyed success.

Today, we are accustomed to seeing rapid, often catastrophic, changes in the entertainment sector. But in the first half of the twentieth century, the business of leisure was expanding, with the almost singular exception—at least among the newer mass entertainments—of vaudeville. Most historians attribute vaudeville's decline to the growing popularity of movies, and this makes sense given the large number of variety theaters that converted to cinemas. But as some scholars point out, vaudeville's great growth spurt coincided with the initial expansion of the film industry, between 1905 and 1912. Vaudeville and movies actually coexisted for a considerable period—in Boston, for example, as early as 1909, films were already drawing twice the attendance of vaudeville—but this did not reduce the variety theater's profitability.[2] Furthermore, while the business done by vaudeville houses fell after 1912, the industry recovered between 1916 and 1920. In fact, 1919 may have been vaudeville's single most profitable year. The renaissance was short-lived, however, and a misperception of its depth contributed to the collapse of the great chains. But vaudeville's recovery demonstrates that the industry was not undone merely by Hollywood. A more nuanced interpretation of vaudeville's decline, one that involves both the product on offer and the strategies used to put it before the public, is in order.

DECLINE AND REVIVAL

As we saw in the previous chapter, at the beginning of the twentieth century big-time vaudeville abandoned many of the innovations that made it so revolutionary: neighborhood theaters, the mix of expensive and inexpensive acts, the open-seating policy, low prices, and shows timed to suit customers. Between 1900 and 1916, many vaudeville managers were seduced by Edward Albee's design and built extravagantly appointed theaters located on major streets in commercial districts or middle-class neighborhoods, running two shows a day at standardized and reasonably high prices. Managers then used their influence over performers to diminish the competition, and they employed predatory practices to close markets and restrict capital for start-ups in their designated "territories." In effect, the men who controlled the big time wanted to consolidate the industry and move from a distribution model, based on bringing the product to the consumer and making it accessible, to one centered on creating the kind of upmarket buzz that would induce the spectator to accept higher prices, more restricted show times, and less convenient theater locations. The success of this strategy relied on vaudeville remaining in vogue, and this depended, it was believed, on the drawing power of the stars. The small time developed to fill the market niche vacated by the big time. But because the small time found it difficult to secure live entertainers with name recognition at a price that would allow them to sell tickets for less than a quarter, they filled in the time period between acts with movies. As the cost of labor rose, movies replaced more and more of the live acts.

Vaudeville therefore contracted in the early twentieth century for two reasons. First, the big-time cartels strangled the competition and drove up prices as they became increasingly headliner-oriented; and second, a great number of vaudeville businesses converted to cinemas or "pop" houses that offered a mix of live and prerecorded entertainment. The pattern of change makes it difficult to be precise with the numbers, as it was increasingly hard to distinguish vaudeville theaters from pop houses that were primarily showing films. Nonetheless, we can say with reasonable confidence that at the industry's peak, in 1910, there were 1,600 vaudeville theaters in the United States. Eight years later, the Internal Revenue office reported that there were 17,130 cinemas in the country, 10,000 legitimate and combination theaters, and 2,000 houses offering vaudeville, revues, or burlesque. Some industry pundits used this figure to suggest that vaudeville's growth was unstoppable, but the same year the tax office collected its data, the Vaudeville Managers' Association privately counted 907 actual vaudeville theaters, of which 485 booked through the two main cartels. In 1919, the *New York Tribune* estimated that there were only 750 vaudeville theaters left in the United States, and in 1920 the big New York and Chicago booking offices reported that there were about 60 big-time theaters and 500 small-time houses. According to a 1921 private investigation by the Shubert brothers (who owned a chain of legitimate theaters), the number of vaudeville theaters in the cartels had fallen to the point that only 112 houses booked through the United Booking Office and 62 through the western circuit.[3] What all this evidence shows, at the very least, is a significant drop in the number of vaudeville theaters between 1910 and 1920.

According to booking officers, the theater stock started to contract in smaller cities, and by 1914 they were suggesting that it no longer made sense to send acts out on the road in some districts with the same frequency. It was in towns like Des Moines and Duluth, they said, that vaudeville's decline first became apparent. Numbers in city after city confirm that impression. Smaller centers saw the number of vaudeville houses rise quickly and decline almost as fast in the first two decades of the century: Portland went from two theaters in 1900 to four in 1914 to three in 1919 and back to two by 1922, while Indianapolis went from one to five to three to two over these same years. Cities with one or two vaudeville houses in 1910 tended to have the same number a decade later, but very few—St. Louis being one, with four houses in 1910 and six in 1920—actually increased their stock of variety theaters. Numbers also declined in the major centers, but here enough "pop" and small- and big-time theaters remained that work was still reasonably plentiful. According to *Julius Cahn–Gus Hill* directory, which allowed businesses to describe themselves as movie, variety, or vaudeville houses, Chicago had three vaudeville theaters in 1900, forty-one in 1910, and eight in 1919; San Francisco had sixteen vaudeville theaters in 1905, nine in 1913, and five by 1919. Philadelphia had four vaudeville theaters in 1905, thirty-seven in 1912, and five in 1919. In New York City, the *Julius Cahn–Gus Hill* theater directory shows that the number of vaudeville houses rose from thirteen in 1896 to twenty-four by 1905 and to forty-eight by 1911, falling to twenty-eight vaudeville houses in 1919–20. How many theaters in these cities offered a pop mix of movies and variety remains unclear, but according to *Variety*, in 1921 there were twenty-two "part-time" vaudeville theaters in New York, which would make them about as numerous as dedicated vaudeville houses.[4]

Of course, big-time managers were happy to see the competition reduced. In fact, the cartel leaders used the leverage they gained from their control over bookings to drive rivals out of business. The decrease in the number of variety theaters was in part the fruit of a competitive policy sown between 1900 and 1912. The UBO, for example, had a strict policy of not allowing anyone who booked through it to play in the small time, which drastically reduced the talent available to those outside the cartel. Cartel members also mobilized to block rivals from encroaching on their territory. When William Fox constructed the Riverside in New York in 1911, the managers of nearby theaters objected, and Albee imposed a UBO boycott, threatened to open a rival theater nearby, and forced Fox to sell his house to the Keith interests.[5] But boycotts like this one were effective only so long as the opposition houses were in small chains or operated independently. Once they started colluding together and formed big cartels or chains of their own, their combined booking power and extensive circuits made them powerful competitors. To prevent this from happening, the UBO and Orpheum pursued a strategy of paying the highest wages as a way of discouraging players from defying their blacklist and moving over to a rival chain or cartel.

The strategy worked until around 1910, when the small time began to consolidate into substantial theater chains. Keith's cartel had cracked the opposition of Sylvester Poli and Fred Proctor and Percy Williams, but it could not cope with Marcus Loew or Alexander Pantages. Competitors of the big-time cartels traditionally worked with regional and local performers or with new acts or very old ones, which the big time ignored. This is why big-time managers referred dismissively to them as "small-time." What made them small wasn't the size of the theaters but the fact that they booked less prominent acts. Vaudeville was defined by its headliners, and anyone who couldn't afford the stars was regarded with disdain. Still, the growing number of small-time houses, their lower prices, and their impact on gallery ticket sales began to worry big-time managers around 1912. Facing competition from what Martin Beck called the "invasion of the small fry," big-time managers dug deeper into what they saw was their strength and promoted their players as celebrities that audiences could not miss.[6] As we have seen, the press agents of the booking cartels, chains, and larger theaters generated crucial hype for players and worked to build excitement over their appearance. Ominously, the big-time theaters' dependence on their stars deepened as their costs rose.

Small-time vaudeville grew in the entertainment space abandoned by the big time. Small-time theaters penetrated the neighborhoods and offered open seating and inexpensive tickets to people living within walking distance. They made their money by reducing their overhead and then selling tickets for fifteen to fifty cents. By 1920, in an effort to keep costs low, almost all of the small-time houses had become pop houses, offering variety turns as preludes to and breaks between silent movies. Small-time owners refused to compete with the big on salaries because it meant "our bills cost more, while the admission remains the same." In pop vaudeville, live entertainment was something, in the words of the *New York Times*, "sandwiched between films." Pop houses in working-class neighborhoods were often described as rowdy and dirty, not unlike the segregated theaters in the South; in fact, one vaudevillian referred to them as "broken bottle places." Some variety performers complained that they were "not vaudeville theater[s] at all, except Sundays," meaning they featured films during the week and live acts on weekends.[7] Moreover, many of the small-time combination cinema/theaters no longer featured much range in terms of live acts and concentrated on singers and comedians who could perform in front of the curtain. Still, because of their low prices, continuous hours of operation, and convenience, pop vaudeville proved an appealing combination for consumers.

The fastest growing of the small-time chains was Loew's, which by 1921 included 127 houses. Two-thirds of these were cinemas only, but the others offered "entertainment divided [more equitably] between motion pictures and a minor grade of vaudeville." Marcus Loew was born in New York's Alphabet City in 1870 and grew up in the German Jewish community of the Lower East Side. After selling newspapers and working in a printing firm, he settled into the fur business. Like many small businesspeople, he also invested in real estate and soon owned several tenements near Union Square. Inspired by his friend and fellow furrier Adolph Zukor, and in partnership with the actor David Warfield, in 1899 Loew bought a penny arcade on 14th Street. The arcade made money, and Warfield and Loew opened a second one in Cincinnati. It was there that Loew first saw a motion picture, and he quickly introduced such pictures in his arcades. By 1907, Loew owned a chain of forty small storefront and arcade cinemas, called at the time "nickelodeons," in recognition of their cost. Most of Loew's cinemas were in the working-class immigrant neighborhoods on the Lower East and West Sides of New York.[8]

Few people before 1910 considered movies to be a prestige entertainment. Consequently, when Loew decided to make his move up in the amusement industry, he thought in terms of vaudeville, the trendiest form of theater. In 1907, Loew leased Watson's Cozy Corner Theater, a vaudeville house formerly operated by Oscar Hammerstein near Borough Hall in Brooklyn. Watson's was in a prestigious neighborhood that had deteriorated as the subway and the Brooklyn Bridge increased the traffic and congestion. Unfortunately, Loew didn't appear to have done any market research because, after enlarging the theater from 700 to 2,000 seats and renaming it the Royal (evidencing his ambitions), he installed an Italian opera company in the house. Within three months he had switched to straight vaudeville, but the business still failed, taking with it much of his fortune. Remarkably, the entrepreneur did not give up, as Hammerstein had done, but tried again.[9]

"Everything changes," Loew told the press, and "one must keep moving." Intent on making the Royal work, the entrepreneur turned it into a combination vaudeville and movie house, the first "pop" theater. The Royal operated

Marcus Loew transformed vaudeville by creating a vast chain of neighborhood small-time "pop" theaters. Loew pioneered the use of movies to keep down the cost of live entertainment. ("The Small Time King," *Theater Magazine* 19, no. 157 [March 1914])

continuously, offering two truncated five-act shows a day, and between them one- and two-reel films. At a time when movies were moving over to longer format features, vaudeville became a market for less expensive shorts, especially comedies. Thanks to the low rental costs on these films and his employment of less well known vaudeville entertainers, Loew was able to sell tickets for ten cents. Seating at the Royal was open, though black customers were forced up into the gallery. Loew did extraordinary well with his pop vaudeville formula, and the Royal made $35,000 in its first year in operation. In 1914, after a few more experiments with the format in New York, Loew pushed the new pop vaudeville idea nationwide and purchased the sprawling Sullivan-Considine circuit, which had recently been at the center of the big time's war with William Morris and Marc Klaw and A. L. Erlanger. Although only a half-dozen Sullivan-Considine houses were still making any money when Loew secured them, acquiring the chain expanded his circuit to eighty-six theaters in New York, thirty-seven in the Northeast, and twenty-six in the West. Loew then applied the same pop formula he had developed at the Royal to several of Considine's 1,000- and 2,000-seat theaters while continuing to run his other theaters as cinemas. By this point, admission to Loew's cinemas was a dime, with a quarter buying a ticket to one of his pop theaters. Marcus Loew, a journalist declared shortly after the Sullivan-Considine purchase, was becoming "supreme in vaudeville," and he would, the paper predicted, soon supplant Albee and Beck as its "king."[10]

The cartels initially ignored the growth of pop vaudeville, as their eyes were fixed on the threat posed by agents like William Morris and the interlopers from the legitimate. But after 1912 they began to take notice as their working-class audiences slipped away and their galleries emptied. Although the loss of a few hundred fifty-cent tickets to the gallery may not seem altogether serious, prewar vaudeville operated on relatively slim margins. According to court records submitted at its disaggregation in 1911, the Keith-Proctor circuit's net profits averaged $150,000 a year between 1907 and 1910. That was a tidy sum, to be sure, but it meant that the chain's net profit was being produced by the sale of less than a hundred fifty-cent tickets per show. A relatively slight dip in ticket sales could severely impact profits. Hartley Davis calculated, after interviewing several managers, that a big-city vaudeville house typically had to sell $7,000 a week, and theaters outside the metropolis $5,000 a week, to be profitable. A 2,000-seat metropolitan theater with fourteen sold-out shows during the week could expect revenue of $17,000. This meant that it would need to run at 40 percent capacity through the week to be profitable. Even in the good times this was a difficult proposition. A 1911 study estimated that the average vaudeville theater in New York City sold 60 percent of its seats in a week, or 750,000–800,000 seats out of a 1.3-million-seat capacity. It was the same elsewhere. Detroit's five vaudeville houses, all of which were located in the downtown, were reported to average a little over 50 percent of capacity attendance in 1913 (which was not as good as the 70 percent attendance estimated for the city's three burlesque houses). In 1914, Indianapolis had seven vaudeville and burlesque houses with a combined capacity of 9,400 per night. Weekly attendance was estimated at 75,000, which would keep them (for theaters offering two or three shows per day) hovering a touch above 50 percent occupancy. In other words, the margin separating profit from loss in a 2,000-seat urban vaudeville theater was an average of 100 mid-priced tickets per show. This is why the loss of revenue for the gallery seats mattered.[11]

As pop vaudeville ate into sales, the big-time chains responded with an effort to reduce costs rather than prices. In 1914, they announced a blanket 15 percent cut in performer salaries as well as a salary cap of $500 a week, though they were careful to exclude players "of such magnitude that this sum would not be a living wage." However, even big stars, like Nora Bayes, who returned to the United States from Europe in September 1914, saw her salary cut from $2,500 a week to $1,500. The problem for the big-time cartels was that they were unable to squeeze the pop houses as they did other rivals, because the inexpensive theaters did not compete with them for acts or territory. Paradoxically, as the cartels cut salaries, it was Marcus Loew and the other small-time chains that reaped the reward. The wage cut not only placed some big-time performers in the reach of small-time employers but also angered players, and some of them crossed over to the pop side. Soon, small-time chains like Loew's were strong enough that they began blacklisting performers who appeared in rival small-time chains, though they kept open the road to the big time. As Loew chortled, there was increasingly "no difference except price" between the shows in his small-time houses and those offered "by the best in the land." He may have been right. In a remarkably candid statement, totally at variance from its usual boosterism, the UBO announced in 1915 that the industry was in crisis. Big-time vaudeville profits, the cartel admitted, had been diminishing for several years—down 50 percent from the 1910–12 average—even though it hastened to add, "The business is still profitable." The cause of the slump, the owners insisted, was that vaudeville actors had "pushed their salaries up to big figures," and the "old scale will have to go or managers will find it necessary to close their theaters."[12]

The problem was, how could the big time respond to the threat from the small? Managers wanted to monopolize the stars and pay lower salaries without anyone drifting off to the pop circuits. But it simply wouldn't work. And so, in a truly bold move, Albee in 1915 decided to take the battle to the enemy with an experiment launched in Dayton, Ohio, and a few months later in B. F. Keith's prestigious Boston theater. In an unexpected retreat from the big time, Keith's theaters switched to a five–fifteen–twenty-five-cent scale, halving the number of vaudeville acts and introducing more films. Soon almost all the Keith theaters were running on a small-time scale, offering what was essentially pop vaudeville. Other chains, including the Orpheum, followed suit. A 1916 survey of the twelve vaudeville houses in west Harlem and the Upper West Side in New York found that all but the 81st Street and the Alhambra were now being operated as pop houses. The three surviving "old time" vaudeville theaters had, however, all adopted the lower scale of prices: the Harlem Opera House was a ten- and fifteen-cent theater, while the Alhambra sold tickets for a maximum of thirty-five cents on weekdays and seventy-five cents on weekends.[13] In other words, by the time America entered the war, the hard-fought distinction between small-time and big-time vaudeville was disappearing.

The scale reductions and salary cuts had a demoralizing impact on performers. Players who had formerly been given preferential treatment resented the high-handed methods of the cartel agents, their exclusive contracts, and their salary manipulations. Much of the hostility toward Albee expressed by players like Groucho Marx in their memoirs date to this period. Less famous and older acts that had lost their star appeal were particular victims of the new regime. Joe Fox and Bill Ward, a blackface comedy team with a successful history playing minstrel shows dating back to the 1880s, stormed in a letter that "after our visit to those few Booking Offices we were disgusted and especially Ward for we never in all our Professional career did We ever meet with such— Contemptible Mean & Scornful Agents, or Managers or anything else you want to call or Name them in the show business if they condescend to see you when you approach they don't look at you explain to them the nature of your visit and when they do speak it's in an insulting contemptible way as if to convey to you that I'm Monarch here—you only a Slave." In the old days, Fox continued, "it was the artist first and from what we hear thats the way it is in Europ at the present time we might say before . . . there was respect for a Performer."[14]

Not surprisingly, as big-time vaudeville returned to its roots, performers revived the moribund White Rats organization. The union reflected the changing character of the profession, and unlike the first union, it was now dominated by players who felt stuck in low-wage work. Membership figures are not especially reliable, but the union claimed 9,000 members in June 1914 and 14,000 one year later, which, while inflated, indicate significant unhappiness among vaudeville performers over the salary cut and the surrender of the big time to small-time pricing. Unfortunately, the Rats' support among the most expendable players also meant that the union had little leverage, as few but the major stars could expect a withdrawal of their labor to be noticed. In order to buttress their power, the Rats again demanded that vaudeville become a closed shop, but the managers responded in the established fashion: blacklisting performers active in the union. By early 1916, the mood in the industry had turned very dark. "A Person must be Very careful what they say these days out side of their own homes," Bill Ward observed.[15]

When stagehands and musicians in Oklahoma City went on strike over wages in the fall of 1916, the Rats decided to join them by declaring a sympathy strike. The union executive urged performers to refuse to play in houses operating with scab labor, and the Rats then called on local managers to accept the closed shop. But the attempt to piggyback the Rats' demands on top of those of their fellow workers in the name of labor solidarity failed. The Oklahoma City strike lasted about five months and petered out slowly with several managers in the city agreeing to employ only unionized musicians and stagehands, while others gave up on vaudeville altogether. None, however, surrendered to the White Rats' demands for a closed shop. The stagehands and musicians went back to work with agreements that gave them much of what they wanted, shrugging off the support they had received from the Rats.[16]

Over the next few months, the Rats made sporadic attempts to force small-time owners to accept their demands. In February 1917 a strike against the Gordon Brothers' pop houses in Boston and Lynn was called, and there were efforts to have actors walk out of theaters in St. Louis and Chicago. Few responded. Ward and Fox, who were with Lew Dockstader's show in Boston at the time of the strike, observed sadly that "the White Rats are still on Picket but . . . they never will accomplish anything by it. Just as we all said, the People with the Capitol [sic] will rule." In March 1917, the Rats called a strike against the Poli circuit and then the Loew chain, but at Poli's only seven out of eighty acts booked that week responded, and only three struck against Loew. According to *Variety*, which was initially sympathetic to the union, by the spring of 1917, 85 percent of performers were opposed to the Rats. "The whole thing is a joke," Marcus Loew told the *New York Times*, and he added that none of those who walked out would ever work for him again. In April, the Rats officially called off all strike actions.[17]

The second strike in vaudeville was a cataclysmic failure. The support of independent managers and the Morris agency had been critical to the first strike's success, and that situation had changed. By 1917 the independents were gone, and consolidated booking offices (whether small-time chain offices or big-time cartels) were now in complete control. Moreover, the union did not secure the support of any headliners and remained anchored in the most replaceable workers in the industry. So minimal was the threat from the players that in 1919 the big-time cartels even lifted their lifetime ban on blacklisted Rats. By that date, the union had held its last meeting. A representative of the UBO later testified to the Federal Trade Commission that he believed the labor unrest of 1916–17, limited though it had been, drove revenues of some theaters down about $1,800 a week. The bad publicity it generated, he felt, cost vaudeville as a whole $200,000 in revenue, which was a significant amount, but not enough to change management practices.[18]

The unfortunate truth is that vaudeville profits revived once owners had broken the resistance of their workers and introduced lower ticket prices and more movies. Attendance rose steadily during the war for the first time since 1912. In 1919, despite the flu pandemic, the post-Christmas week smashed all records in several vaudeville theaters. Keith's flagship business, the Palace in New York, reported gross receipts of $40,000 and an average of 10,000 customers per day, the highest attendance and receipts ever recorded in vaudeville. The queen of the Orpheum chain, the State-Lake Theater in Chicago, similarly reported attendance topping 11,000 on Boxing Day. This was icing on the cake of a terrific year in vaudeville. The State-Lake, for example, reported having sold 3.7 million tickets in 1919–20, which meant it was regularly sold out. The small time also enjoyed spectacular returns. Loew's twenty-six houses in New York reported they were "jammed at every performance," and the company made $1.2 million net profit for the fiscal year 1919–20 and optimistically projected a profit of $3 million in 1920–21. Vaudeville, the critic Walter Kingsley declared, "is just now on the crest of a tremendous wave of popularity." Vaudeville's ebullience came in part from the gradual spread of state and local prohibition during the war and the legislation of national prohibition in 1919. Cabarets and restaurants had been offering floor shows for more than a decade, cutting into theater revenues. In response to prohibition, these businesses canceled their variety shows and introduced dance bands instead, and customers who wanted to watch rather than dance returned to vaudeville. "Good-Bye to Cabarets," *Variety* chuckled happily in 1920, openly embracing the cause of prohibition. For the first time since well before the war, there was talk that major cities were "under theatered" and needed more vaudeville houses. Chicago, the trade press reported, had only one vaudeville theater seat for every 226 inhabitants; it could use one for every 50![19]

With almost all vaudeville theaters, big-time and small-time, now competing in the under-a-dollar market and with almost all using some mix of movies and live entertainment, competition heated up. Once costs and prices had been reduced, owners returned to the trusted approach of consolidation, building bigger theaters and establishing neighborhood monopolies. As Loew explained it, "The best way to make this business profitable is by big houses with big capacity, that will swallow up the all the trade in the neighborhood at our prices." Securing the best movies became increasingly important, and here the small-time chains, like Loew's, held the decisive advantage: they offered more screens and had already developed close relations with the producers and distributors. Moreover, the small-time chains, with their hundreds of outlets, were better placed to catch movie stars who might choose to sell a feature by making a vaudeville appearance. The big time tried to use this advantage too and advertised exclusive rights to movies made by performers like the Castles, who had signed contracts with them. In fact, the strength of the big-time chains increasingly came to reside in their monopoly on older headliners. As the general manager of the Orpheum circuit boasted, the big time offered "the best . . . on the vaudeville circuit. [Their players] will not be fillers, but will be real acts, acts which will cost us large sums in salary." In contrast, for Loew, the movies were the core of the business, and he offered "just that little touch of song and dance that kept his houses full." Arguably, their reliance on existing celebrity assets, most of whom had become famous before the war, made the big-time chains appear more dated than the movie-centered pop houses. The reason big-time vaudeville was on a "downward toboggan ride" in terms of influence, the *Los Angeles Times* theater critic observed, was because managers were still relying on "old women with frowsy clothes and rough voices." The movies, he noted, had the corner on youth and beauty. His comments might have been motivated by the fact that female headliners at the Los Angeles Orpheum Theater in 1926 included Trixie Friganza, Alice Lloyd, Nora Bayes, Ruth Roye, Elsie Janis, Adele Rowland, and Rae Samuels, all of whom became headliners before the war and most in the early years of the century. Indeed, the big-time theaters began promoting their shows as featuring "good old vaudeville kind of fun" and "veteran performers."[20]

Nonetheless, the apparent revival of vaudeville at the end of the war inspired all the chains to engage in a massive reinvestment in building stock. The high profits enjoyed by the State-Lake and the Palace, two mammoth new downtown theaters, undoubtedly made owners think that a facelift would be good for business. In 1919 construction began on a large number of new theaters, and many others were overhauled. Ten new ones were built in Brooklyn alone—all seating between 2,000 and 4,000 spectators—seven of them small-time and three big-time houses. The big-time chains were especially aggressive in their expansion. Albee opened a new theater in Providence in 1919 and planned three new 3,000-seat ones in Cleveland, razed and rebuilt the company's theater in Cincinnati, and drew up plans for new houses in Columbus, Dayton, Indianapolis, Toledo, Richmond, Atlanta, and Syracuse. The Orpheum invested in new theaters in San Francisco, Los Angeles, Oakland, Kansas City, and Minneapolis. Fred Proctor even stirred himself from semiretirement and built a new theater in Schenectady. These new theaters represented a sizable investment: the Dayton house reportedly cost Keith $2 million, while the Palace in Cleveland was built at a cost of $5 million. Investments on this scale drained reserve funds, and the chains looked for new ways of raising money. In 1919, the Orpheum reorganized as a publicly traded company to raise $10 million toward new theater construction, while the Morgan Bank managed a $20 million stock issue by Loew's for the same purpose. *Variety* noted that, for the first time, Wall Street money was "pouring" into vaudeville to support its expansion plans.[21]

The timing could not have been worse. The economic bubble of 1916–19 burst in 1920–21, as the government pulled money out of circulation and the wartime economy crashed. Production slowed, 5 million people lost their jobs, and Charles Dow's index of stock prices fell from 120 to 64. Although brief, the depression of 1920–21, and the collapse in ticket sales, drove a number of unprofitable theaters, especially in the Midwest, out of business. In response, the vaudeville chains introduced further reductions in ticket prices of 25 percent in an effort to retain customers. But investor panic dragged down Loew's and the Orpheum's stock, placing both companies in severe difficulty. Loew's managed to appease investors with a dividend in 1920, though it was half of what had been projected. Even so, Loew had to institute an employee stock option and to offer new shares on a layaway plan to raise enough money to meet his company's obligations. The Orpheum was not so fortunate; it suspended dividend payments through 1921 and watched helplessly as the value of its stock plummeted. For all theaters, the only way to pay shareholders or meet obligations to builders was to cut costs. It was at this point that most of the vaudeville chains, including the Orpheum, converted their theaters to cinemas. By 1926 only a dozen houses in the country continued to offer pure vaudeville entertainment, though a large number of pop houses still provided a limited number of musical or comedy acts as preludes to their features or, like the Empire in Salem, Massachusetts, on Sundays.[22]

The decline of vaudeville was more complicated than consumers preferring movies to live entertainment. Admittedly, there was a price the public was willing to pay for different forms of amusement, and when vaudeville grew too expensive, as happened in the big time before 1915, a segment of its audience sought cheaper options. Consumers still went out to vaudeville shows, but the industry had to fill at least 50 percent of the seats to remain profitable, and as it made itself into more of a luxury, a substantial number of spectators turned to ten-cent movies. Since vaudeville operated on reasonably slim margins, the loss of even a portion of its audience was problematic. Big-time vaudeville revived when it narrowed the price gap with movies, but the high cost of live theater meant that all houses, big-time and small-time, could afford this only by mixing variety acts and films. The formula proved successful, however, and the chains grabbed some of the easy money generated during the war and expanded, only to find themselves saddled with crushing overhead when the market suddenly contracted. Reducing overhead to meet financial obligations led most of the chains to convert their newly built temples to variety into picture palaces.

Democratic mass entertainment in the early twentieth century was grounded in low prices and neighborhood theaters. This was the niche that big-time vaudeville abandoned and that the pop houses and cinemas occupied. The big time responded by relying on the drawing power of its celebrities to justify greater inconvenience and higher prices. Protecting that asset became the big-time cartel's primary function, even though it imprisoned vaudeville in its past successes as much as it kept headliners away from the competition. Untimely investments compounded this fundamental problem.

Nonetheless, vaudeville would have better weathered the financial storms and preserved its market had enough people continued to find it chic. By 1923, according to the critic Bland Johaneson (Elizabeth Bland Gaynor), sophisticates believed that "all vaudeville performers are born with no foreheads and full sets of gold teeth, and that the base individuals who are amused by their offensive antics are the hard-boiled gentry of bootleggers, ticket-scalpers, song-pluggers, turf-touts and their nocturnal lady-friends."[23] To be fair, it was not easy remaining in vogue, especially when new forms of entertainment were emerging that seemed more trendsetting and magical. Vaudeville's tired response to the threat of cabarets, revues, and movies was very much a part of the story of its decline. The big-time owners were certainly complacent and responded sluggishly to the competition of the pop houses. They misread a temporary revival as a full recovery. But managers and players also seemed unsure of how to keep the entertainment fresh and preserve its fashionable cachet. As new entertainments emerged, they simply tried to assimilate and emulate them, and as they did so vaudeville lost the novelty that first placed it on the cutting edge of amusement.

NARRATIVE

Will Cressy wrote his first work for the stage—a blackface comedy routine presented at a fundraiser for yellow fever victims—in 1888. The Bradford, New Hampshire, native was twenty-five years old at the time and working as a grain buyer, a profession in which tall tales came with the territory. Even then, Cressy carried a notebook with him in which he wrote down the sayings, expressions, and jokes of the farmers that would remain central to his playwriting. In 1889, he joined a touring theater company and there met Blanche Dayne, whom he married the next year. Dayne specialized in playing plucky young women, individuals more convinced of their independence and abilities than was warranted. Cressy first attracted positive notice when he played a crusty New England farmer in Denman Thompson's touring production of *The Old Homestead*, a role that he would reprise throughout his career. In 1898, in between tours of *The Old Homestead*, Cressy and Dayne secured a place on the bill at Keith's Union Square performing in a one-act play (what vaudevillians later called a sketch) called "Grasping an Opportunity," that he had written. The story featured a young professional city reporter visiting a town in New Hampshire collecting the reminiscences of old-timers. She arrives to interview Cressy, flirts nonchalantly with him, and the old man gets carried away, becomes "foolishly fresh," and kisses her. As he does so, she snaps a photo and then blackmails him out of fifty dollars to keep the picture from "going public." The play ends with Cressy putting the photo in a sock, adding a brick, and throwing it down a well. Dayne was apparently pert and piquant as the "slick" young woman (though one reviewer found her insufficiently "brazen and audacious" in her exploitation of the "good old gentleman"), while Cressy played a crusty but lovable New Englander. The play was a hit with Union Square audiences and went out on the Keith circuit. Cressy and Dayne never returned to the legitimate. Chicot, the theater critic of the *New York Morning Telegraph*, predicted that Cressy and Dayne's sketch, one of the first one-act plays to be featured in vaudeville, represented "an art that will be of great service." He was right. Over the next decade sketches would transform vaudeville, and they would become so important to the big time that managers felt the variety theater could not survive without them.[24]

Vaudeville managers were continually in pursuit of the new and unusual that might keep the entertainment in vogue. Ragtime, auto-defying, slang, and the shimmy were only a few of the novelties vaudeville employed to remain fresh. The sketch was initially introduced as just another original feature, but it quickly became something more. It came to serve, at least in the minds of many vaudeville managers, as a crutch for an entertainment in which they never placed great faith. For Edward Albee and Fred Proctor, the sketch "was the future of vaudeville" and manifested their goal of improving the variety show and rivaling the perceived quality of the legitimate. Skits would act as a "lever on

Narrative penetrated the variety theater thanks in part to the success of Will Cressy and Blanche Dayne's "Grasping an Opportunity" of 1898, one of the first sketches performed in vaudeville. (Library of Congress Prints and Photographs Division, Theatrical Poster Collection, no. 4573)

popular taste," the *Chicago Tribune* predicted, educating a population suckled on incoherent and disintegrating variety to appreciate the feast of narrative. "I cannot keep my houses open without the one-act plays," Brooklyn chain owner Percy Williams explained, as "I can't get acts enough without them." As B. F. Keith observed, he turned to plays because "there is bound to be a certain monotony about singing, dancing and acrobatic acts. The sketch is the only one that can change indefinitely."[25]

In many ways, the sketch and vaudeville were an odd fit. Some managers and commentators felt that plays would not work in variety because of the inattentiveness of audiences, the immensity of vaudeville houses, and the tradition of the direct appeal. Those observers appear to have been in the minority. Between 1904 and 1922, some 10 to 15 percent of vaudeville acts were sketches, and the number remained reasonably constant until 1920, when the entertainment was in precipitous decline. Between 1910 and 1918, the big time was all but drowning in sketches, often two per show, and because they lasted on average twice as long as the usual variety act, their importance exceeded their number. In some ways, film augmented a narrative content that had already been introduced through the sketch, representing a cheaper alternative (first for the small time, later for everyone) to one-act plays. Moreover, sketches established a new relationship between managers and performers and harmed the independence and flexibility of the industry.

Unlike variety performers, whose acts managers booked, the sketch was the property of the theater. Playwrights were contracted to write sketches, and theaters hired actors to play in them. Auditions were held at designated "showing houses" in New York and Chicago, which managers, agents, and booking officers attended. The managers and agents suggested changes to the sketches during these auditions, involving themselves even more directly as producers. Managers also organized a Stock Producing Managers' Association in 1908 whose members circulated reviews of the plays they had featured or had seen auditioned. Sketch writing became a lucrative business for people like Cressy and New York–based Aaron Hoffman, who sold their work directly to performers or theaters for $500 and up. In 1910 Cressy claimed to have written 132 sketches since 1900 and boasted that he had made well over $50,000 from the work (on top of the $500 a week he and Dayne were paid for performing in the ones they kept for themselves).[26]

The introduction of skits changed vaudeville by placing stories at its center. Traditionally, vaudeville was not so much opposed to narrative as "indifferent" to it (or so Wilfred Clarke wrote in 1906). Vaudeville had "no time for plot." As we have seen, vaudeville performers did not present themselves as actors; rather, they were imagined as "personalities" who sang or danced or told jokes. Sketches and films, no matter how rudimentary, the *Chicago Tribune* pointed out in 1903, rested on "impersonations and situations.... [They] depend on acting." Audiences may have continued to see the singer, acrobat, or comic monologuist "playing" themselves differently from the actor filling a part, but there is evidence to suggest that attitudes to vaudeville were gradually changing. A phrase search of daily newspapers shows that "vaudeville performer" appeared over twice as often as "vaudeville actor" between 1901 and 1910. But between 1911 and 1920 the phrase was used only 20 percent more often, and from 1921 to 1930 "vaudeville actor" surpassed "vaudeville performer" in frequency of use by 21 percent. This suggests that the perceived uniqueness of vaudeville was diminishing as acting a role gradually became more common in variety than performing an authentic self. Feeling "retrospective," Jen Powers, a character comedian active in the 1890s, wrote a friend in 1915 that where vaudevillians used to "put on ad lib," today "how many can you find ... that can create a part without lines[?]" The mix of films, plays, and traditional performances, together with the employment of vaudevillians in movies, may have been responsible for this shift. It might also have made people more critical of the way variety performers acted. The use of skits and films invited comparisons, and these did not tend to go in vaudeville's favor. Even the president of the White Rats revealed that he thought the vast majority of those "now appearing in so-called first-class vaudeville theaters are bad actors."[27]

Vaudevillians performing sketches did have less material to work with than their colleagues in the legitimate. With only twenty minutes to develop and resolve a story, there was little time for character or plot development. Writers of sketches mostly began with the climax and worked backward in order to keep the momentum flowing forward. Action, rather than dialogue, Will Cressy advised the would-be playwright, was critical: "Instead of the characters telling the audience what they are going to do, have them do it. This is absolutely necessary to get the mind of the audience away from the scenery and the impression left by the previous performance." Given the constraints, it is not surprising that, in the early years especially, good sketches were considered extremely rare. Plays before 1910 were often interrupted by singing or dancing turns to stop them from dragging ("When an actor gets a good sketch he hangs onto it like a shipwrecked sailor clinging to a floating spar," a reporter laughed). As early as 1905, one reviewer commented, "the audience knows the chances against the sketch being clever" were so good that "it always flinches when the stage appears set in that manner peculiar to sketches."[28]

A typical example of the hackwork used in vaudeville before the war was the Miller-Browning Company's 1906 production of "Caught." The story involved a young man down on his luck who turns to burglary. On his first job he is caught by a servant girl who turns out to be his sweetheart. A policeman then appears who, as chance might have it, is his brother. The policeman lets the burglar go after he promises to give up crime, and the lovers announce they will get married. According to *Variety*, the "acting is poor. The police officer is so heavily made up that his appearance is ludicrous. The girl is too hysterical. The story is not well told."[29] Small wonder audiences winced when sketches like this were announced.

Forced to create and resolve situations quickly, vaudeville sketches often relied on stereotypical devices, like mistaken identities, to accelerate the story and create opportunities for comedy. In a typical sex farce by George Neville and Co. called "The Cold Deal," a man masquerades as a woman so that he and his friend, whose wife is absent, can go to a fancy-dress ball. When the wife turns up inopportunely, the female impersonator hides in the icebox. The struggle of the husband to keep his wife in ignorance of the ball, and the efforts of the friend in the icebox to escape before he freezes, furnished the comic material. The identity-switching employed in sketches like this was completely implausible. In "All the World Loves a Lover," a man doesn't recognize his fiancée, who shows up for dinner pretending to be a chorus girl. Similarly, in the Mollie Fuller vehicle "On the Beach," a woman in a provocative swimsuit puts a dummy in a wheelchair, dressed up as her father, and brings it to the beach to stop men from harassing her. A young man who is courting her switches places with the dummy, and she, not recognizing the difference, reveals her love for the young man to the supposed mannequin.[30] What is striking is the way in which sketches transformed a theater that so valued actuality into one that was completely artificial and contrived.

Prior to 1905, almost all vaudeville sketches were comedies, but in response to film, action adventures became increasingly common. According to theater managers in towns as unlike as Johnstown, Pennsylvania, and Brooklyn, New York, patrons preferred dramatic sketches to farces. Oddly enough, knockabout comedies were never significant, perhaps because slapstick as a whole had migrated to the movies. Westerns, on the other hand, were very popular, just as they were in film. In the Middleton-Spellmeyer sketch "A Texas Wooing," an innocent young woman is searching for her father, who is missing in Texas. A treacherous Indian lures her to his hut promising to show her where her father is, and she is spared a sexual assault only by the timely arrival of a Texas Ranger who shoots the villain and rescues the girl. Thrillers like "The Motor Duel" were also popular and similar in many ways to the Westerns. Here a wicked European count intent on rape ("having his way," as it was euphemistically described) kidnaps a beautiful American heiress and drives off with her. Dick Manley, the splendidly named American hero, comes to her rescue and, after a car chase against a moving panorama, catches up to them. *Variety* breathlessly summarized the rest: "A terrific duel with swords then ensues as the autos are abreast. Dick climbs into the Count's machine and the struggle continues. Dick throws the Count back into his machine, it blowing up directly afterward. The Heiress and Dick then speed on. Vigorous applause. One of the most stupendous acts attempted on stage."[31]

Serious dramas with clear moral lessons also became more common. "At the Threshold," for example, opened with a young married woman about to leave her aged husband and run off with a young lover. They are discovered in her home by a burglar, who frustrates their attempt to escape and, in the ensuing action, reveals the young man to be a cad. The burglar not only threatens to kill the bounder but also compels him to listen to his own confession, in which he tells the harrowing story of how he pursued and ultimately murdered the man who stole his wife away. After the unnerved would-be lover flees, the burglar recognizes the wife as his long-lost daughter. "It is a sombre sketch," *Variety* observed, but because "the logical points are admirably blended and [there is] some reflections of comedy interspersed in places, it should serve well in vaudeville."[32] Sometimes, however, in the drive for the cinematic, vaudevillians misjudged their audience, as we saw in the case of "The Submarine."

There was something unsatisfying about vaudeville sketches, which reviewers characterized as "cheap." That impression grew as film effects became more eye-catching and their stories more engrossing. Sketches gradually lost favor in vaudeville, press agent S. L. Harris explained in 1921, because "of the better way a story is told in pictures."[33] But there had been a problem even from the start. The sketch sacrificed vaudeville's most distinguishing feature, its direct appeal, in favor of narrative. Sketches imposed order and dispelled the impression of vitality, spontaneity, and chaos. Actors delivered lines in sketches, and hard as they might try to be natural, they did not interact with audiences in the way vaudeville performers could. The impression of community suffered.

The turn to narrative was a sign that all was not well in vaudeville, even in its prime. The introduction of sketches in 1898 reflected a concern among managers that audiences would soon tire of variety. Even in their triumph, as they created a new mass entertainment, entrepreneurs were worrying that it couldn't last, and they turned toward what they knew and revered—narrative theater—for security. What seems ironic is that plays represented a move away from many of the characteristics that made vaudeville singular and cost-effective in the first place. Unlike variety acts, which performers sold to theaters, most sketches were the property of the chains. Moreover, the variety act and the direct appeal were what made vaudeville distinct; sketches were simply movies with live actors. The derivative impulses of vaudevillians grew, however, as competition from other entertainments increased. Just as performers and managers adapted plays and movies to variety through the sketch, after the war they assimilated such new entertainments as jazz and the revue. As with the proliferation of sketches, the attempt to incorporate rival amusements demonstrated a lack of innovation in vaudeville. It marked a shift in variety's character as it became a repository of everything new rather than something with its own distinctive aesthetic. "There is very little in the vaudeville world that is actually new," the critic for the African American newspaper the *Chicago Defender* remarked in 1913, "and the reason for this state of affairs is plagiarism."[34] This derivative quality suggests that, despite the industry's brief revival from 1916 to 1920, vaudeville had already lost its place on the leading edge of entertainment by the time war began in Europe.

THE JAZZ AGE

Ragtime was at the jittery heart of vaudeville's popularity in the first decade of the twentieth century. One critic even believed the theater had been built on a "ragtime aesthetic."[35] Under ragtime's influence, the variety theater became the primary show business medium for promoting new cultural forms. So dominant did ragtime become that the nonmusical acts declined over the first two decades of the century. The proportion of singers and those offering song/comedy acts more than doubled from 1902–6 to 1917–21. Where 17 percent of vaudevillians were singing in 1905, ten years later 38 percent of them were doing so. Other genres—acrobatics, magic, impersonation, novelty work, and the rest—shrunk in importance. Roughly 50 percent of acts in the early twentieth century contained no stage (as opposed to pit) music; by World War I that proportion had fallen to 25 percent. In the first decade of the century, no other venue offered audiences the chance to hear the newest songs by the leading popular composers of the era. Songwriters like Harry Von Tilzer and Irving Berlin not only wrote for vaudeville performers but also toured big-time theaters promoting their compositions. Music came to dominate variety shows because vaudeville theaters monopolized its professional performance, at least in terms of the mass audience.

Unfortunately, what was true in the ragtime era was not the case in the jazz age. The difference in the way the two musical genres became popular illustrates the degree to which vaudeville's status as the country's leading cultural pastime had faded. But it was not just competition from other entertainments that led to the theater's declining influence in American popular music life. Variety was itself slow to accept the racialized sounds of urban America.

Jazz first attracted national attention during the war. For many who first heard it, jazz was simply another way of "embroidering" instrumental parts to produce what band leader James Reese Europe called "new [and] peculiar sounds." Commentators focused on the methods used by jazz musicians, such as placing mutes and tin cups on the ends of horns, spinning bass fiddles, and making whirling motions with the tongue when playing brass instruments. "Jazz ragtime," a critic wrote in 1917, was merely a cacophony of sound. An Atlanta critic thought jazz was a form of contortion. But playwright and humorist George S. Kaufman came closer to accurately describing it by using a modernist analogy, calling it "cubistry into music." Although "it is all done to correct time," a critic wrote, it strained one's definition of music: "The clarinet is yelping like a dog that hasn't fletcherized a bone sufficiently. This inspires the cornetist to frenzy.... The ensuing noise is something like the buzzing rattle of a machine gun, only not so musical. Not to be outdone, the trombonist inserts the end of the instrument into a large tin can.... The pianist beats the baby grand into insensibility; the drummer vents his spleen on the cymbals ... and the selection expires in a grand final cataclysm." There seemed to be "no coordination" in jazz; the cornetist generally carried the melody, but all the other performers sounded like they were doing whatever they pleased.[36]

All of this should have made jazz a natural fit with vaudeville. Wacky variety musicians had long waged war on their instruments. The Howard Brothers, for example, juggled their banjos, while Clyde Darrow played a trombone with her feet; Volant played a piano while both instrument and performer were suspended in the air and swinging from the flies. In keeping with this, a "Creole Orchestra," which may have played jazz (as well as "plantation melodies" and ragtime), appeared in vaudeville in 1914–16. Reviewers noticed the weird sounds the orchestra made—one said it was discordant enough to wake the dead—and treated the music as a form of comedy. Most serious ragtime musicians rejected jazz like this as a passing fad. Even Bee Palmer, who within a year would be closely associated with the dissemination of the new music, maintained in 1919 that "jazz is a lot of noise. It is a sort of an all-over-the-place affair[,] brassy and loud. Syncopation is rhythm, moving the body in perfect harmony with the tones of the music. My specialty is syncopation. Jazz doesn't appeal to me at all." Some performers even denied any connection between ragtime and jazz. Ragtime, they argued, putting another twist into the knotty problem of authenticity, was the "expression of the simple life and jovial spirit of the negro," but jazz was cacophony, nothing more than "weeping and wailing," with roots in slapstick comedy. One of the few vaudevillians to champion the new music was Nora Bayes, who introduced what appears to have been vaudeville's first self-proclaimed jazz band in April 1917. When the Dolly Sisters added a jazz band to their vaudeville act later in the year, one reviewer deemed it an "unforgivable assault on the ears."[37]

Before 1918, jazz bands were uncommon in mainstream vaudeville, and even on the Jim Crow circuit they were a decided novelty. It was through restaurants like Reisenweber's in New York and the Belvedere in Chicago, as well as cabarets like the Clef Club, that jazz first became a big-city fad. Vaudevillians made fun of the new music and its associations with untheatrical settings, liquor, and eccentricity. *Variety* in 1919 dismissed cabaret singers as inappropriate to vaudeville because they have "no voice." The songs they sing, the reviewer added, sound as though they "had been written while a party sat around a table in a restaurant." In a 1917 musical sketch, set in a cabaret called Café de Luxe, which toured Poli's and Loew's circuit, an (all white) jazz band, dancing girls, and two female jazz singers turn the cabaret into a scene of drunken excess. Ironically, because of their crazy gags and habit of "getting confidential" with the audience (the direct appeal), some jazz bands playing clubs and restaurants advertised their work as "Jazz Vaudeville."[38] In a revealing twist, jazz musicians were appropriating vaudeville's reputation for fun, using it to characterize the work they did in other venues. "Vaudeville jazz," however, was slower to gain acceptance.

Cabarets and restaurants provided new competition for theaters and attracted some of their more affluent spectators. Where the dance halls of the early twentieth century popularized ragtime, reinforcing vaudeville's appeal, the clubs and restaurants had floor shows featuring musical and comedy acts that competed directly with the variety stage. By 1914, even smaller cities like Scranton had cabarets serving an estimated 2,000 people per week. Chicago had 230 cabarets by 1918, and New York had scores of restaurants with floor shows as well as night clubs like the Little Club, the Rendezvous, the Gypsy Land, Palais Royale, the Plantation, and the Club Gallant. Late in 1914, jazz became the newest craze thanks to these hot spots, with "its wailing syncopation" being heard "in every gin mill where dancing holds sway." By the end of the war, New York seemed to be "going crazy.... The average citizen has found that his digestion will work only to the wild-beating of the tom-tom and the mad shriek of the jazz.... People who never patronized the jazz joints are now flocking to them."[39]

The cabarets and clubs continued to be more closely associated with jazz than was vaudeville right through the war years. When the Navy Jazz Orchestra toured the Keith circuit as part of a Liberty Loan drive in 1918, the advertisement noted that it played "mostly ragtime numbers" along with some of the "jazzier actions" that "cabarets boast of." Similarly, when Ruby Norton and Sammy Lee returned to vaudeville in 1919 after three years in the cabaret revues, *Variety* felt that the audience at the Riverside in New York liked their music only because the theater was full of people familiar with their club work. Vaudeville resisted the new music for many reasons. Many in the audience didn't like it, and some managers reported that when jazz bands played, spectators walked out. This probably inclined managers to be more conservative in their choice of performers, and it is notable that jazz in vaudeville was closely associated with older singers like Sophie Tucker, Blossom Seeley, and Rae Samuels. Blues numbers, which were less peppy than jazz, were somewhat more popular, but not blues singers. Marion Harris, who had established her popularity as a blues singer on record, first appeared in vaudeville in 1921 and was considered a flop. Her turn was "monotonous," the *Dramatic Mirror* reported, "owing to the lack of variety. . . . For vaudeville one or two Blue numbers would be sufficient." From the performers' perspective, touring a vaudeville circuit was also less palatable than working in a cabaret. Nick La Rocca of the Original Dixieland Jazz Band said in 1917 that his band might go into vaudeville one day, after playing in the cafés, but only as a way of boosting their popularity and selling records. Similarly, in 1925 Marion Harris, who lived in Beverly Hills, turned down a vaudeville tour so that she could remain at home. She accepted an extended contract to sing at the nearby Café Lafayette.[40]

Even more than ragtime, jazz was understood to be the music of African Americans. This diminished its influence in vaudeville as the theater, since the turn of the century, had provided limited opportunities to black performers. White musicians and audiences alike knew, however, as the musician Johnny Lala remarked, that the music they played and heard "was not as hot as the negroes[']." Many vaudevillians, including Sophie Tucker, therefore tried to learn jazz from African American musicians by attending black-and-tan clubs and cabarets. A few creole and black jazz artists, such as trombonist Santo Pecora, violinist John Robichaux, and clarinetist Leon Roppolo, did work at least some of the time in the house bands of vaudeville theaters, but very few were accepted in, or accepted the offer to work in, white vaudeville. Racism was a factor. Comedians Van and Schenk tried unsuccessfully to hire Barney Bigard to accompany them on the circuit, but most white musicians, including Bee Palmer, refused to perform with African Americans. Popular black recording artists like Bessie Smith and Ethel Waters, who had many white fans, followed the accepted practice of organizing their own touring shows or playing night clubs rather than appearing as an individual act in white vaudeville. When they did perform as soloists, it was on the Theater Owners' Booking Association circuit.[41]

The unwillingness of white vaudeville theaters to engage popular black artists is made clear by the case of Mamie Smith, whose 1920 recording of "Crazy Blues" sold more than a million copies. Smith was extremely popular with white audiences, but she performed exclusively on TOBA's circuit before organizing her own jazz revue, which toured white legitimate theaters (not vaudeville). Only in the fall of 1922, when her success with white audiences was undeniable, did Loew's offer her a contract. The African American jazz artists most likely to receive their own billing (as opposed to backing up a white performer) were dancers, such as John Bubbles and Bojangles Robinson. Bubbles was performing in Jim Crow theaters when he was taken on by the white vaudeville producer Nat Nazarro. Nazarro put Bubbles in an act with two grotesque African American dancers, and he introduced them himself as curiosities so that they didn't offend white sensibilities. Bubbles maintained that he was often told that white audiences and players didn't want any black jazz performers in vaudeville. Wanting African American music but unwilling to open the door to a new generation of performers, vaudeville managers tried marketing old favorites from the ragtime era, like Rosamond Johnson or Seymour and Jeanette James, as jazz musicians. Still, as Mary Lou Williams, who made it into white vaudeville in the mid-1920s with Seymour and Jeanette's Syncopaters, noted, there were no more than twenty-one black acts on the white circuit at that time.[42]

After the war, jazz was a synonym for peppy, and vaudeville did have its jazz juggler (Joe Madden), jazz comedian (Hank Mann), jazz circus animals (Camilla's Birds and "Jim," a bear that did a shimmy), jazz ballet dancers (Stone and Delehanty), and jazzed opera arias (George White's "aesthetic jazz"). But until the early 1920s, few musicians performed actual jazz. The most notable exception was the white dancer Joe Frisco, who began his career in clubs before making the transition to vaudeville. Frisco burst onto the scene in 1918 after Flo Ziegfeld saw him at the small-time Fulton Theater and hired him to dance in his Frolics and later in the year in his Follies. Albee managed to buy him away from the Follies, and he entered vaudeville in the fall of 1918 with a comedy dance routine accompanied by Loretta McDermott fronting Bert Kelly's jazz ensemble. Like other "jazzists" in vaudeville, Frisco's was a novelty turn laced with comedy. He didn't really dance, observed one critic; he "just steps around in a queer sort of fashion" with a derby on his head and a cigar in his mouth. His high-stepping, shaking, and jumping—which the critic called "the delirium tremens of syncopation"—did, however, prove highly influential in jazz dance.[43]

Frisco was rare in being a headliner whose success was linked to "hot" jazz. In most vaudeville theaters, when jazz bands were featured, they filled marginal spots on the bill, as the dumb act that either got audiences seated or closed the show. Unlike ragtime, which infused and described vaudeville, jazz remained peripheral. The manager of Keith's Theater in Providence was convinced that jazz was "pretty well played out" as early as 1920. Only when they were backing up a singer or dancer—as the Original Dixieland Jazz Band did in 1920 when it toured with Gilda Gray, or as Santo Pecora's group did with Bee Palmer, or as Eddy Edwards's did with dancer Johnny Muldoon—did jazz bands receive noteworthy billing. The Orpheum theaters in Chicago started placing jazz bands in prominent spots on the bill in 1920, but it wasn't until 1923, by which time jazz was culturally pervasive, that Keith's first presented the Billy Sharp Orchestra as a headliner. Sharp was a former blackface minstrel, and his six-piece band (which included a female violinist "who can't keep still") played "conventional" jazz music while three girls danced, a tenor soloist sang, and Sharp did a soft-shoe.[44] Vaudeville seemed incapable of adapting quickly or effectively to the rise of jazz as serious music rather than farce. Times were changing, however, and well-to-do white people were increasingly slumming in cabarets where they could drink, eat, dance, and listen to hot bands. Vaudeville, stuck in its past successes, moved only cautiously into this new age. It was further evidence that the theater's days on the cutting edge of fashion were over.

Significantly, Al Jolson, who was billed as "America's Greatest Jazz Entertainer," rarely brought his art to vaudeville. After World War I, Jolson was popularly regarded as the country's leading singer, largely because of his records; composer Irving Berlin said his voice was the perfect jazz instrument. Jolson made his name in variety, and he continued to employ the direct appeal in his theater and film work, but at the close of the 1909–10 season he left vaudeville and joined the Shubert organization. For the next fifteen years Jolson would be the star of the Shuberts' Winter Garden Theater, performing in a series of hit musical comedies and revues.[45] His abandonment of vaudeville was a sign of changing times. It was not just that musical comedies and revues paid better salaries; they were also the new entertainment fad of the century's second decade. Because the currency of the music in revues and musicals was part of their appeal, it was there, not in variety acts, that composers married jazz with Tin Pan Alley. The big-time cartels may have succeeded in blocking entrepreneurs like the Shuberts and Klaw and Erlanger from entering vaudeville, but those entrepreneurs responded by creating revues and touring musical comedies that appeared in the chains of legitimate theaters they owned. Their productions—the *Passing Show*, *Scandals*, the *Follies*, *Sinbad*, and a host of others—integrated jazz and became the cutting edge of entertainment in the years surrounding World War I.

The revue was derived from a nineteenth-century French entertainment (hence the exotic spelling) traditionally offered at season's end, in which events and shows of the previous year were parodied. It was a clever way for audiences to recall the fun of the season and for performers to derive additional work burlesquing their colleagues. A revue was not a random collection of scenes, however. Unlike vaudeville, the music was mostly written for the particular show; it had a "book," or story; and it moved through the acts and within them, toward a climax. Revues were better able than variety shows to engineer song hits by using casting, placement, and framing to enhance their effect.[46]

The first American revue was mounted by George Lederer, the manager of the Casino Theater, in 1894. The Casino served New York's most fashionably decadent fun-lovers; in fact, an upstate newspaper called it a place "at odds with all decent public sentiment . . . the fountainhead of the sewage that inundates the stage." The revue, which Lederer called the *Passing Show*, featured topical skits on current events, politics, and entertainment. The book, written by Sydney Rosenfeld, was, like those in all subsequent revues, a thin excuse on which to hang the musical, topical, and satirical numbers. But the *Passing Show*'s actors still played characters, and they delivered scripted lines to each other. It was not vaudeville, even though the variety theater provided both the talent and topicality for revues. For example, in the *Man in the Moon* revue of 1899, vaudeville stars Sam Bernard and Ferris Hartman played Conan Doyle and Sherlock Holmes, while Walter Jones, the vaudeville tramp comedian (who was rumored to be Lillian Russell's lover), did an impersonation of vaudeville entrepreneur Fred Proctor.[47]

Revues began as year-end reviews, but in the early twentieth century the term expanded to include a wide range of loosely organized book musicals. What came to unite them wasn't the burlesque of the year's events but the imperceptibility of their story line and the attention given to choreography and dance. Revues employed lavish sets, extravagant costumes, and elaborate choreography, and the most beautiful of the revues, the Ziegfeld *Follies*, was particularly known for its stylistic coherence and the attractiveness of its chorines. Florenz Ziegfeld, an agent and impresario, mounted his first Follies in 1907, in the roof garden atop the New York Theater. Emma Carus and Nora Bayes headed the cast, which included fifty high-stepping, tightly corseted chorines (the Anna Held Girls). Ziegfeld famously costumed his chorines in real furs and sprayed them with expensive French perfumes to make them "feel like royalty," a verisimilitude that the majority of vaudevillians could not afford. The revues went further than variety in almost every way. Ziegfeld was one of the first to have his chorus unlace, and by World War I his "girls" had become models of tasteful nudity (like a nice salad, one reviewer wrote, they looked good dressed or undressed). The objectification of women in revues was even more striking than it was in vaudeville. Ned Wayburn, a choreographer and producer who worked for both the Shuberts and Ziegfeld, said that in revues, chorines were hired according to type: "fulsome beauties"; "lightweights," "chickens," or "squabs"; "medium heavyweights" or "peaches"; and "dainty girls," "ponies," or "pacers" there for "decorative" work. Wayburn further classified the girls he hired according to their sexual appeal, such as "BQ," meaning low-class or "burlesque," and "TW," signifying "high-end" or "train wreckers."[48]

Jazz and revues were a natural fit because revues were predicated on being what vaudeville had once been: "swiftly volatile, racy, witty and up to the minute." Because of the need to sound topical, as early as 1918 Ziegfeld featured a jazz song, picking up on the music's insipient popularity. Gilda Gray made her first sensational appearance not in vaudeville but in the *Follies* in 1919, where she introduced a blues song, "a form of art new to Broadway." Gray shimmied as she sang, showing "complete control over the swaying muscles" while she "mechanically kept on staring ahead of her.... The lyrics were incomprehensible.... The singer fairly froze in the atmosphere of red lights," but "her minor notes tore at the auditory nerves."[49] It proved a sensational hit and, more than any other performance, awakened white Americans and white composers to the possibilities of the blues. As with Frisco and other jazz artists, vaudeville booking agents moved on Gray only after she had established her star power in the revue.

In their casting, revues may have been "nothing more or less than vaudeville and burlesque of the highest class," but the shows differed in critical ways. They were, in the first place, more expensive to attend. Tickets were twice the price of the highest class in vaudeville, and some spectators reportedly paid twenty dollars for seats near the stage at the Ziegfeld Follies. Unlike vaudeville, which was mostly made up of acts sold to a theater, the book for a revue was generally written after the cast was hired, as the skits contained in it were designed to showcase the performers. "The whole secret of the revue," a producer explained, "lies in the blending of the scenes in such a way that, though there is no very definite story, there is almost a logical continuity." Much of that continuity came through the scenic designer/choreographer who stamped his character on the whole. "The theatergoer of yesterday ... seldom stopped to consider the importance of the stage director.... The mounting of the production was, in his eyes, of the least consequence.... Today conditions are different. The name of the stage manager ... ranks equally and occasionally far above the author.... The stage director is everything nowadays!" a critic remarked. In the *Follies* of 1917, for example, Ned Wayburn created flow by first having Bert Williams sing a solo, and then following him with a Mississippi levee number featuring the chorus dressed in antebellum costumes. Next was a series of Stephen Foster songs sung by a duo in blackface. This sequence formed the center of the show and created what Wayburn said was an homage to minstrelsy. This was the kind of coherence no variety show could match, though it evidently did not please Williams. Unhappy with Wayburn's direction and possibly with the show's white racial nostalgia, Williams quit the *Follies*, returning only when the director was gone. Wayburn, who began his career as a blackface minstrel on vaudeville and a writer of "coon" songs, did not seem unhappy to lose the comic.[50]

Revues may have popularized some up-and-coming jazz musicians, but when it came to their regular headliners, they were parasitical, grabbing stars who had attracted public attention over the previous year. Before the war, they ran in the summer months because that was when most theaters closed, allowing revues to secure stars like Eddie Foy and Emma Carus. Like many parasites, as they grew stronger, they reduced their host's fitness, affecting both vaudeville's headliners and its audiences. After the war, producers began touring revues during the regular theater season and playing them in legitimate theaters in competition with vaudeville. The Ziegfeld *Follies* touring company appeared in Klaw and Erlanger theaters, while the Shuberts offered the *Passing Show* and the *Greenwich Village Follies*. Shut out of vaudeville by the UBO and Orpheum but eager to cash in on the popular theater market, the big interests from the legitimate crept in by way of the revue, a hybrid of vaudeville and musical comedy. Revues not only used vaudeville talent but packaged it in ways that made the stars more classy and upscale. Middle-class spectators at a revue didn't have to sit through acts designed to please the gallery. Revues never tried to be mass entertainment; they were satisfied to secure part of vaudeville's market: its highest spenders. In so doing, revues made vaudeville look second-class. Even as movies snatched away vaudeville's working-class audience, revues and cabarets lured away the more fashionable.

As had been their practice with sketches, vaudeville managers belatedly tried to get control of the revue phenomenon by organizing their own revues and integrating them into their shows. They commissioned music; hired directors, set designers, and choreographers; and cast the shows in-house. Although the revue, like the sketch, represented the antithesis of vaudeville's production model, its numbers grew between 1915 and 1920 and then declined in the early 1920s. In effect, revues began to be offered when vaudeville was in financial trouble and the industry was struggling to reestablish itself. Unfortunately, because they cost on average $10,000 to stage, their numbers declined sharply after 1920 as their high cost contributed to the chains' difficulties.

The revue was only one of a series of new competitors that emerged in the early twentieth century to challenge vaudeville's monopoly on entertainment. Variety seemed increasingly tired and derivative as it struggled to keep up with the changes in culture and entertainment. Edward Albee defiantly maintained that one should not confuse seasonal swings in taste with an overall disaffection with vaudeville. "There is always talk of the decline of vaudeville," he maintained, none of which had proved true in the past. But vaudeville, as he'd designed it, was fading. The public, a reporter in the *Los Angeles Times* concluded in 1920, was already bored with the old-style comics, the singing soubrettes, the "silly tricks and gabble, the silly patter." Audiences wanted novelty, not the "dreary rounds" of the average vaudeville show. "Vaudeville needs an injection of originality," the critic from the movie city concluded. The trouble was, no one knew where to find it.[51]

OH! MISTER GALLAGHER

Edward Gallagher died broke and forsaken in a sanatorium in Queens in 1929, his house and furniture seized and his wealth "wastefully dissipated." Since he was penniless, the National Vaudeville Artists fund paid for his burial. Only a handful of people attended the funeral, though one of them was his former stage partner, Al Shean. Shean, who a few months before had tried to sue Gallagher for $10,000 in royalties he claimed his partner stole from him, told a reporter that death "wipes the slate clean." Gallagher's pauper's death was not unlike that of many thousands of small-time vaudevillians, people who had scraped out modest incomes, run up debts, and never managed to build savings. But Ed Gallagher was different. Only a few years before, he was one of the most popular and highly paid performers in the country, pulling in $750 a week. In 1921, he and Shean signed a contract worth $250,000, committing themselves to perform for a year with a touring revue company. His long preparatory career, brief moment of extraordinary success, and rapid decline into obscurity is an apt metaphor for vaudeville's surprising career. "Many will ask why there are not more here to pay a last tribute to him," Henry Chesterfield, the executive secretary of the artists' fund noted in the eulogy. "It is because we are all actors, children more or less, irresponsible. . . . We forget easily . . . [and] soon we are all forgotten."[52]

Tall, thin Edward Gallagher was a comedian known primarily for his puns. He was born in San Francisco in 1873 and first entered the theater as an "Irish punster" in 1889, playing museums and small theaters for several years. He was, according to a press release, "almost unable to converse without perpetrating a pun," something that his wife said during their divorce proceedings made living with him unbearable. In 1892 he began singing as well as telling jokes, and in 1895 he added impersonations. In 1908, Gallagher wrote an Irish comedy sketch, "The Battle of Too Soon," which featured J. J. Barrett as a character whose "blunders" occur in "bewildering profusion," and took it into vaudeville. In 1910, after performing for two years with Barrett, he was hired as an Irish comedian to play alongside Al Shean, who did a Dutch act. Like Gallagher, Shean was a trouper who had been on the stage for more than two decades, enjoying modest success and a pay of $75 a week. A colleague later said Shean did a Dutch act about as well as a "hod-carrier could carve a beautiful work of art out of an oyster shell." Still, the pair continued to act together and even appeared in a musical comedy, *The Rose Maid*, where they were cast against type as Jewish moneylenders. When that show closed in 1912, the pair drifted apart, resuming their individual careers in vaudeville and burlesque as ethnic impersonators.[53]

By World War I, Gallagher's career had stalled. He was getting older, his hair was thinning, he wore thick glasses, and he projected an owlish urbanity. His estranged second wife complained that there was never much money and that he was on the road continually, though it spared her listening to the puns. Then in 1921 Gallagher's luck suddenly changed. He bought a song from Eddie Foy's son Bryan for fifty dollars and approached his old partner, Al Shean, to try it in a vaudeville act.[54] In the song, the men addressed each other with comic politeness, employing their own names and often ending stanzas with the lines "Positively, Mister Gallagher; / Absolutely, Mister Shean." The tune was inconsequential, but the words could be indefinitely altered to keep the song topical. It was essentially a comic conversation set to a slight jingle:

> Shean: Oh! Mister Gallagher,
> Oh! Mister Gallagher,
> If you're a friend of mine,
> You'll lend me a couple of bucks.
> I'm so broke and badly bent,
> And I haven't got a cent.
> I'm so clean you'd think
> That I was washed with Lux.

> Gallagher: Oh! Mister Shean,
> Oh! Mister Shean,
> Do you mean to say
> You haven't got a bean?
> On my word as I'm alive,
> I intended touching you for five.
>
> Shean: Oh! I thank you Mister Gallagher.
> Gallagher: You are welcome Mister Shean.[55]

Unsure of how to stage the act, Gallagher and Shean initially appeared against the incongruous backdrop of the pyramids, with Shean in a fez and Gallagher sporting a pith helmet. They later set it outside a Paris café with Shean in a beret and Gallagher in a straw boater. Both outfits seemed designed to convey an image of dingy sophistication, something reinforced by the politeness of the conversation.

No one could explain why, but the act "caught the fancy of the audience" when it premiered at the Palace in August 1921. Although placed in an inconsequential spot, late in the program, the old comedians stopped the show. Within a week they were headlining at the Riverside Theater and then at the Orpheum in Brooklyn. They were considered "side-splittingly" funny when they appeared in Brooklyn and had to sing verse after verse of their song, the audience calling them back so many times that in the end the manager was forced to ring down the drop curtain. They eclipsed even Sophie Tucker and her jazz band.[56]

Success hit them like a blast from a furnace. Gallagher and Shean went out on the UBO circuit in the fall and winter of 1921–22, reaching Chicago in March. The *Tribune* had trouble explaining the sensation. The critic remembered Shean as a "furtive" figure in vaudeville and had no recollection whatsoever of Gallagher. "They do no more than stand in front of an absurd curtain and bandy nonsensical observations on this and that, some set to music, some not." Shean played "the complacent picture of inane innocence," Gallagher "the domineering wise guy." It was "endless" and "quite idiotic," but, the critic added disbelievingly, "I have never heard an anthem so insistently encored." Records were made by Victor and Edison. Fox made a film of the duo. The song's publisher, who apparently sold a million copies of the sheet music, declared it one of the biggest hits in a generation, and it was estimated to have brought the pair $75,000 in royalties by December 1922. Impersonators proliferated.

But vaudeville was failing in 1921. It could no longer hold onto a successful

Gallagher and Shean's sprightly and inane musical conversation of 1921 proved a surprising hit. It took the country by storm but was repeated so often that the public soon tired of it. (Edward Gallagher and Albert Shean, "Oh! Mister Gallagher; Oh! Mister Shean" [New York: Jack Mills, 1922]).

act on this scale. In the early 1920s, the financial crisis had become pronounced, and the chains could not pay the kinds of salaries available in the movies, on Broadway, or in the touring revues. The Shuberts came forward with an offer of $1,500 a week for Gallagher and Shean's appearance that lured them away from the UBO. Then Ziegfeld stole them from the Shuberts with an offer of $2,000 a week to play the *Follies*.[57]

Shean appears to have kept his head amid the sudden success, but not Gallagher. A notorious womanizer, he started to be seen in New York cabarets with a chorine from Ziegfeld's Follies. After his second wife divorced him, he married an actress in her early twenties whom he met on the set of Fox Pictures. They were together only a few months before she also divorced him on grounds of infidelity. He drank heavily, absorbed massive divorce settlements, spent lavishly on luxuries, and seemed to believe there could be no end to the song's success. In November 1923 the appellate court reversed a lower court ruling and ordered the pair to pay damages to the Shuberts for jumping to Ziegfeld. By the summer of 1925, Shean had become fed up with his partner's behavior, and when Gallagher began another affair with a chorine, he quit the act. Soon after, Gallagher fell ill and was hospitalized, ostensibly having suffered a mental breakdown. He was unable to keep working, but his expenses continued to pile up, and by 1928 he was broke and sequestered in a sanatorium. He never recovered.[58]

Even before Shean and Gallagher parted, there were signs that the popularity of the pair was fading. In 1924 they moved from performing in big cities to touring the regional circuit, but audiences were tiring. The duo could be heard on the radio and on record, and their act lost its freshness. The song was subjected to multiple covers: by a saxophone group, by the Paul Whiteman band, by the Sousa Orchestra. There was a comic strip and an exhausting number of parodies. Old-style vaudevillians to the last, Gallagher and Shean just kept plugging their hit, happy in the publicity and convinced the audience wanted to see the stars in the flesh. One Pittsburgh writer complained he was so fed up hearing the song on the radio he didn't want to watch them in the theater. As they toured with the *Greenwich Village Follies* in early 1924, reviewers noted that the novelty of their act had totally worn off and they were "falling short of expectations." Even in Bismarck, North Dakota, they secured less applause than many of the other acts in the revue.[59]

In so many ways Gallagher and Shean followed the course of vaudeville's decline. A spectacular and unexpected craze, they initially thrilled audiences, and their salaries skyrocketed. They played themselves, acted naturally, and sang conversationally. The pair, Oscar Hammerstein's son Arthur explained, were poor actors and the song was bad, but they were popular and "that's what counts" in vaudeville. A direct "ratio existed between personality and bank accounts," the showman explained, but the material they worked with was limited. As Hammerstein pointed out, the song was "commonplace and because it had no root it withered away.... It was decidedly low brow stuff and there is nothing so uncertain as low brow stuff. Also, there is nothing quite so dead as low brow comedy." Gallagher and Shean never claimed they had any talent. In fact, their defense in the lawsuit Lee and Jake Shubert brought against them for breach of contract was that they were "hams" and "rotten actors." Will Rogers, the laconic comedian, testified that he didn't think much of the pair and that they could be easily replaced in any vaudeville bill. The performers turned the joke on the public. As Shean laughed to a reporter after the lower court ruled in the contract dispute with the Shuberts, "We're willing to be rotten actors, so long as it doesn't hurt the bank account." That was the sentiment of a true vaudevillian, but in the early 1920s it no longer washed.[60]

CURTAINS

Shifting gears is not easy in the entertainment industry. Cultural commodities sometimes lose popularity suddenly, but more usually portions of the audience looking for something new drift away, leaving the media to the diminishing number who like the old product and want to keep getting it. This undoubtedly made it harder for vaudeville managers to exploit such novelties as jazz. Many members of the audience deplored the new music, and "progressivists" were inclined to go to clubs to hear the hottest sounds. Vaudeville managers therefore secured toned-down versions of the music, relying on well-known stars to put it over. "A vaudeville manager takes little or no risk," a critic remarked, as they put their shows together on the bases of "successes." But a large segment of the audience was getting tired of the predicable lineup of familiar stars. Vaudeville managers recognized this and "will tell you what they need are new faces." It continued, in other words, to be stuck on the idea that celebrities sold the show. But the problem, the critic concluded, was that vaudeville "doesn't want new faces. Vaudeville wants new ideas."[61]

Vaudeville's financial health began to suffer even before the war, when the big time rejected the fundamentals of the mass market and adopted an approach based on the gravitational pull of the stars. It vacated an entertainment niche that the small time filled with movies, and the cartels' efforts to control their neighborhood competitors proved unsuccessful. While this was happening, white vaudevillians pushed African Americans out of the mainstream and helped propel the development of the segregated circuit. Belatedly, the big time responded to the growth of a low-priced, neighborhood-oriented competition by reducing costs through salary caps and reduced ticket prices. "We have been talking for some time about our empty galleries and our emptying balconies," a manager in Oregon lamented in 1915, "but now we must wake up and face the music. It isn't any longer a matter of galleries and balconies. Our public isn't beginning to go away from us. It has gone and now we must win it back." The way to do this, in his view, was to recover vaudeville's excitement: "We must give them light, color, sound, romance and poetry.... We must offer the appeal of the voice."[62] Big-time vaudeville did recover once it adopted some of the successful practices of the small time, but it never recaptured the light and sound and excitement it possessed when it was in vogue. In fact, by the early 1920s vaudeville could no longer pay the salaries needed to retain star performers like Gallagher and Shean. And yet, like the ill-fated pair, vaudevillians refused to believe that they were a fad whose time had passed.

There was an economic logic to vaudeville's decline, but there was also a change in taste. Americans did not simply embrace movies and turn away from live entertainment. Nightclubs, cabarets, and touring revues all emerged in the postwar years as spunky, variety-based competitors to vaudeville; in some ways, movies were easier for vaudeville to assimilate than these rival amusements. What revues and nightclubs did was challenge vaudeville's status as the country's premier live entertainment, the place where spectators went to see the biggest stars or experience the latest songs, fads, and fashions. Vaudeville entrepreneurs and players never knew how to respond to their waning cultural influence. Having built what they imagined was a quality product for a broadly based audience, they couldn't understand why the public didn't want to pay for it.

Vaudeville, like cinema, depended on a vast and variegated mass of repeat customers, but it also remained stuck in a nineteenth-century approach to the appreciation of theater, one that reflected class, gender, and racial hierarchies. Managers and owners were initially contemptuous of the small time and then scrambled to catch up and recover their dominance. But they failed to respond adeptly to the changes rocking the leisure industries or even see how they could adapt to meet them. Emulation and assimilation were the responses of businesspeople no longer keeping ahead of the pack. As the former *Variety* editor Abel Green and the onetime monologuist Joe Laurie wrote, vaudeville simply "watched the crowds go by in doddering bewilderment. Too rigid to change, too incredulous to believe its day was over."[63]

Still, unlike one of Will Cressy's sketches, we shouldn't write vaudeville's history backward. The first mass entertainment should be remembered as a vital and creative industry that democratized leisure at a time when no one knew what an amusement for everyone might look like. It carried the marks of its transitional and experimental birth. As with modernism in the refined arts, it was a response to a rapidly changing society, and it developed as a way of providing a friendly and undemanding amusement to a public believed to be exhausted by modern living. Entrepreneurs brought the theater to their customers and, as far as the technology of the time allowed, offered amusement on-demand. While the radio transported show business into people's homes, vaudeville pioneered the fundamental idea of consumer-controlled entertainment that the radio embodied. The shows themselves were designed to make people feel as though they were among friends. Performers talked to the audience, explained what they were doing, laughed at each other's jokes, and generally kidded around. They presented contemporary issues in ways that engaged audiences rather than threatened them. They were marketed not just as performers but as celebrities. Vaudevillians also broke conventions of good behavior and encouraged a democratization of taste and style. They made glibness and spontaneity into signs of urbanity. Considered in its totality, vaudeville cultural and commercial contributions were remarkable.

Democratized leisure did not, however, escape the confines of early twentieth-century American culture and economics. The small businesses that created vaudeville lost much of their independence when they accepted, or were pressured into entering, the booking cartels. Proprietary capitalism failed in mass entertainment, even though many independent theaters survived, and all managers enjoyed some local autonomy. Shows also embodied the racial and gender prejudices of their era. Sexism and racism were always far more obvious in vaudeville than were the efforts of some notable performers to discredit the pernicious stereotypes.

Moreover, vaudeville was less the discursive democracy that some historians imagine it to have been than a theater that engaged audiences in a pseudo-dialogue. Spectators did not actually determine what jokes they would hear or how the acrobat would do her stunts. In vaudeville, the animal performers were carefully trained, the dancers' steps were memorized and executed, the singers' songs rehearsed. Audiences did participate by expressing their pleasure or disfavor: they laughed or failed to do so, sang along, applauded, or "sat on their hands." Sometimes spectators guyed performers, but more often, unhappy customers simply walked out. In making their direct appeal, performers employed language that implied that everyone had gathered in the theater to laugh together, as participants rather than as customers. But that was no less a gimmick than the advertising copywriters' friendly address to readers. The flow of material was largely unidirectional. Granted, many spectators did consume press releases about the private lives and tastes of vaudeville's stars, and some may have dreamed of becoming or knowing a celebrity. Their reimaging of entertainment as part of a private, rather than a public, sphere does show the problems consumers experienced connecting in a mass society, but it does not make them actual participants in a conversation with the stars.[64]

In its various dimensions, vaudeville embodied the dynamism and constraints of turn-of-the-century American democracy. It was ebullient and optimistic, open to innovation and transfixed by novelty. But it was also deeply divided by race and class and gender, and its most successful practitioners struggled to restrict access to its riches and to deter rivals. The more predictable and secure vaudevillians made the industry, the more space they left for competitors to exploit the opportunities they spurned. Although vaudeville expanded rapidly when it became a craze, the quixotic nature of its appeal left it vulnerable to other forms of entertainment, some of which, like movies and records, made use of new technologies, while others, like revues and cabarets, managed to associate themselves with more risqué pleasures than vaudeville would countenance. Unfortunately, because variety theaters had high expenses, they could not afford to lose part of their market to the movies and another to night clubs, musicals, and revues. In the end, vaudeville did not so much die as erode. The tension here between inclusiveness and hierarchy, order and instability, predictability and innovation, was fundamental to the country and the times.

Of course, vaudevillians would not want us to remember them as transitional figures in the history of mass entertainment. I am fairly certain that they would resist the effort made here to rationalize their work and to fault some of the choices they made. They would point to the happiness they brought to millions of Americans and the creativity they showed in much that they produced. They would insist that they offered the public new ways of looking, sounding, and being seen. Their gimmicks did what many performance artists still want to achieve: they made less visible the theater's fourth wall. And they would not be wrong. It was, without question, the jokes and tunes and stars and gowns that mattered most to the people who watched variety shows. But the happiness vaudevillians generated is difficult for us to grasp today, let alone meaningfully render. Where pain is universal and empathy-inducing, humor is culturally very specific. Our world is so different from theirs that it is hard to appreciate the sensational appeal of people like Gallagher and Shean or Trixie Friganza. The exasperating pun, on which so much of their work turned, has, particularly, lost much of its appeal. But why not give it a try and allow a pair of vaudevillians the final word as the curtain falls?

> Hunting dogs, Dutch comic Dave Ferguson tells his partner, Harry Frey, recognize a fox by its scent:
> Frey: The fox has got money?
> Ferguson: De fox ain't got no money.
> Frey: De fox ain't got a cent?
> Ferguson: No, de fox ain't got a cent.
> Frey: So what has he got?
> Ferguson: He's got a scent.
> Frey: How can he have a cent when he ain't got a cent?...
> Ferguson: If I only had in my head half of what you ain't got in yours...
> Frey: Aw, you talk so sensible, I'm ashamed of you.[65]

Time for the hook.

NOTES

ABBREVIATIONS

BRTD	Billy Rose Theatre Division, New York Public Library
CDT	*Chicago Daily Tribune*
CT	*Chicago Tribune*
K-AVC	Keith-Albee Vaudeville Collection, University of Iowa Archives
LAT	*Los Angeles Times*
NA, FTC	National Archives, Federal Trade Commission, Docket 128, *Federal Trade Commission v. Vaudeville Managers Protective Association*
NUSC	Northwestern University, Special Collections
NYC	*New York Clipper*
NYMT	*New York Morning Telegraph*
NYS	*New York Sun*
NYT	*New York Times*
NYTr	*New York Tribune*
PI	*Philadelphia Inquirer*
SFC	*San Francisco Call*
UASC	University of Arizona Special Collections
WP	*Washington Post*

INTRODUCTION

1. Michael Davis Jr., *The Exploitation of Pleasure: A Study of Commercial Recreation in New York City* (New York: Sage Foundation, 1911), 32; "Harlem Opera House," *Variety*, 29 October 1915; "Grand Opera House," *Pittsburgh Press*, 26 August 1915; "Proctor's 23rd St.," *Variety*, 16 December 1905; "Colonel Gaston Bordeverry," *Variety*, 23 December 1905; "His Bullets Take Lady's Dress Off," *LAT*, 29 March 1905; William Grimes, "Bringing Vaudeville Back from the Wings," *NYT*, 23 November 1997.

2. Trav S. D. (stage name of Donald Travis Stewart), *No Applause—Just Throw Money: The Book That Made Vaudeville Famous* (New York: Faber and Faber, 2005). Also recommended are Bernard Sobel, *A Pictorial History of Vaudeville* (New York: Citadel Press, 1961), and Douglas Gilbert, *American Vaudeville: Its Life and Times* (New York: McGraw-Hill, 1940).

3. On Americanization, see Matthew Frye Jacobson, *Whiteness of a Different Color:*

European Immigration and the Alchemy of Race (Cambridge, Mass.: Harvard University Press, 1998), and David R. Roediger, *Working toward Whiteness: How America's Immigrants Became White; The Strange Journey from Ellis Island to the Suburbs* (New York: Basic Books, 2005). In the past two decades several historians have taken Progressive Era efforts to enhance democracy more seriously. Robert D. Johnson, "Re-democratizing the Progressive Era: The Politics of Progressive Era Political Historiography," *Journal of the Gilded Age and Progressive Era* 1, no. 1 (January 2002): 69–92, traces the shift in the literature. Meg Jacobs, *Pocketbook Politics: Economic Citizenship in Twentieth Century America* (Princeton: Princeton University Press, 2005), and Kathleen Donohue, *Freedom from Want: American Liberalism and the Idea of the Consumer* (Baltimore: Johns Hopkins University Press, 2003), present expanding consumption as a central tenet of American liberalism, a cause that bound together diverse constituencies. Social historians have been more cautious in their treatment of the link between consumerism and democracy. Roy Rosenzweig, Kathy Peiss, and Nan Enstad, for example, maintain that consumerism reinforced class and gender divisions, even as it helped mobilize and empower workers: Roy Rosenzweig, *Eight Hours for What We Will: Workers and Leisure in an Industrial City, 1870–1920* (Cambridge: Cambridge University Press, 1983); Kathy Peiss, *Cheap Amusements: Working Women and Leisure in Turn-of-the-Century New York* (Philadelphia: Temple University Press, 1986); Nan Enstad, *Ladies of Labor, Girls of Adventure: Working Women, Popular Culture, and Labor Politics at the Turn of the Century* (New York: Columbia University Press, 1999).

4. *The Julius Cahn Official Theatrical Guide, 1910–11* (New York: Julius Cahn, 1910).

5. On the nineteenth-century variety show, see Gillian M. Rodger, *Champagne Charlie and Pretty Jemima: Variety Theater in the Nineteenth Century* (Urbana: University of Illinois Press, 2010); and David Monod, *The Soul of Pleasure: Sentiment and Sensation in Nineteenth-Century American Mass Entertainment* (Ithaca: Cornell University Press, 2016).

6. Michael Tueth, *Laughter in the Living Room: Television Comedy and the American Home Audience* (Bern: Peter Lang, 2008), chapter 2; Gerald Nachman, *Right Here on Our Stage Tonight! Ed Sullivan's America* (Berkeley: University of California Press, 2009); Gerald Nachman, *Raised on Radio* (Berkeley: University of California Press, 1998).

7. "Keith Houses Heavily Hit," *Variety*, 22 May 1914.

8. Producerist ideas dominated nineteenth-century economic thought. See Donohue, *Freedom from Want*, chapters 1 and 2. The idea of tailoring a product to a market, through research into tastes, appears to have first developed in the genteel goods industries, like glassware and ceramics, and the idea spread only slowly. Even though department stores in the nineteenth century were temples to consumption, they specialized in displaying objects, as though the attractiveness of the goods would create their own demand. John Lauer, "Making the Ledgers Talk: Customer Control and the Origins of Retail Data Mining, 1920–1940," in *The Rise of Marketing and Market Research*, ed. H. Berghoff, P. Scranton, and U. Spiekermann (New York: Palgrave Macmillan, 2012), 153–69. In the nineteenth century, cartels were ubiquitous. They were common in oligopolistic industries such as railroads, shipping, and sugar, but they also occurred in industries consisting of hundreds of small competing firms, like insurance. They came under attack in the

United States in the 1890s, and antitrust policies helped push American business away from cartel agreements toward combination in the form of merger. Gerald Berk, *Alternative Tracks: The Constitution of American Industrial Order, 1865–1917* (Baltimore: Johns Hopkins University Press, 1994); John Binder, "The Sherman Antitrust Act and the Railroad Cartels," *Journal of Law and Economics* 31 (1984): 443–68; Richard Sicotte, George Deltas, and Konstantinos Serfes, "American Shipping Cartels in the Pre–World War I Era," *Research in Economic History* 19 (1999): 1–38 ; Dalit Baranoff, "A Policy of Cooperation: The Cartelisation of American Fire Insurance, 1873–1906," *Financial History Review* 10, no. 2 (2003): 119–36.

9. Herbert Marcuse, "The Affirmative Character of Culture," in *Negations: Essays in Critical Theory* (London: Penguin Books, 1968), 86; Gunther Barth, *City People: The Rise of Modern City Culture in Nineteenth Century America* (New York: Oxford University Press, 1980), chapter 6; Robert Snyder, *The Voice of the City: Vaudeville and Popular Culture in New York* (New York: Oxford University Press, 1989).

10. David Nasaw, *Going Out: The Rise and Fall of Public Amusements* (New York: Basic Books, 1993); Richard Butsch, *The Making of American Audiences: From Stage to Television, 1750–1990* (New York: Cambridge University Press, 2000); M. Alison Kibler, *Rank Ladies: Gender and Cultural Hierarchy in American Vaudeville* (Chapel Hill: University of North Carolina Press, 1999); Nicholas Gebhardt, *Vaudeville Melodies: Popular Musicians and Mass Entertainment in American Culture, 1870–1929* (Chicago: University of Chicago Press, 2017), 74.

11. Shannon Jackson, *Professing Performance: Theatre in the Academy from Philology to Perfomativity* (New York: Cambridge University Press, 2004), esp. chapter 1.

12. Much of this work shows the influence of Eric Lott's landmark study of nineteenth-century blackface, which he saw being adopted by working-class entertainers in the nineteenth century to expose class resentments and sexual anxieties. Eric Lott, *Love and Theft: Blackface Minstrelsy and the American Working Class* (New York: Oxford University Press, 1993). Henry Jenkins, *What Made Pistachio Nuts? Early Sound Comedy and the Vaudeville Aesthetic* (New York: Columbia University Press, 1992), 34–35; Rick DesRochers, *The New Humor of the Progressive Era: Americanization and the Vaudeville Comedian* (London: Palgrave Macmillan, 2014), chapter 2; Susan Glenn, *Female Spectacle: The Theatrical Roots of Modern Feminism* (Cambridge, Mass.: Harvard University Press, 2000); Andrew Erdman, *Blue Vaudeville: Sex, Morals and the Mass Marketing of Amusement, 1895–1915* (Jefferson, N.C.: McFarland, 2004); Sharon R. Ullman, *Sex Seen: The Emergence of Modern Sexuality in America* (Berkeley: University of California Press, 1997).

13. Paul Duncum, "Towards a Playful Pedagogy: Popular Culture and the Pleasures of Transgression," *Studies in Art Education* 50, no. 3 (Spring 2009): 232; Mikhail Bakhtin, *Problems of Dostoyevsky's Poetics*, trans. Caryl Emerson (Minneapolis: University of Minnesota Press, 1984), 127; Walter Benjamin: *Towards a Revolutionary Criticism* (London: Verso, 1981), 148; Kathleen Casey, "Sex, Savagery, and the Woman Who Made Vaudeville Famous," *Frontiers: A Journal of Women Studies* 36 (2015): 104 and 86.

14. Richard Schechner, *Performance Studies: An Introduction* (New York: Routledge, 2006), 1–2. For a less historically informed view, see Peggy Phelan, *Unmarked: The Politics*

of Performance (New York: Routledge, 1993); Camille Forbes, "Dancing with 'Racial Feet': Bert Williams and the Performance of Blackness," *Theater Journal* 56, no. 4 (December 2004): 603–25; and Geraldine Maschio, "Effeminacy or Art? The Performativity of Julian Eltinge," *Journal of American Drama and the Theater* 10, no. 1 (1998): 28–38.

15. "The 5th Avenue," *Variety*, 17 April 1909; "Bertie Herron," *Variety*, 28 March 1919; "Bertie Herron Is a Woman Minstrel," *Muncie (Ind.) Star Press*, 18 December 1904.

16. Because the trade press was concentrated in New York, and because the surviving internal records for vaudeville theaters cover the Northeast, that region dominates this study. This did, however, reflect a business reality. Most acts were booked in New York or Chicago, and appearing in those cities was a sign that an act had made it. In the early twentieth century, as Karl Hagstrom Miller points out, New York–based businesses so shaped American commercial entertainment that even the sound images southerners formed of their own region were "heard by way of New York." Karl Hagstrom Miller, *Segregating Sound: Inventing Folk and Pop Music in the Age of Jim Crow* (Durham: Duke University Press, 2010), 134.

17. "Ruby Norton and Sammy Lee," *Variety*, 24 January 1919.

18. Edmund Wilson, "Gilbert Seldes and the Popular Arts," in *The Shores of Light: A Literary Chronicle of the Twenties and Thirties* (New York: Farrar, Straus and Young, 1953), 163; Henry McBride, "An Adventurer in the Arts," *The Dial*, December 1921, 706; Mary Cass Canfield, "The Great American Art," *New Republic*, 22 November 1922, 355; Marsden Hartley, *Adventures in the Arts* (New York: Boni and Liveright, 1921), 155.

19. Kathryn Oberdeck, *The Evangelist and the Impresario: Religion, Entertainment, and Cultural Politics in America, 1884–1914* (Baltimore: Johns Hopkins University Press, 1999), 418. I use the term "actuality" as developed by June Deery in *Reality TV* (Malden, Mass.: Polity Press, 2015), 29; see also David Pattie, *Rock Music in Performance* (Basingstoke: Palgrave Macmillan, 2007). Weaver cited in Denise Mann, "The Spectacularization of Everyday Life: Recycling Hollywood Stars and Fans in Early Television Variety Shows," *Camera Obscura* 6 (1988): 49.

20. Larry May, *Screening Out the Past: The Birth of Mass Culture and the Motion Picture Industry* (New York: Oxford University Press, 1980), 114; Rene Girard, "Hunger Artists: Eating Disorders and Mimetic Desire," in *The Body Aesthetic: From Fine Art to Body Modification*, ed. Tobin Siebers (Ann Arbor: University of Michigan Press, 2000), 194; Marsha Cassidy, *What Women Watched: Daytime Television in the 1950s* (Austin: University of Texas Press, 2005), 22–23.

21. "Hoey and Lee," *Scranton Republican*, 23 October 1910; "Hoey and Lee," *Variety*, 6 December 1918. As Jeffrey Melnick points out, performers like Eddie Cantor and Al Jolson retreated from their Jewishness when they removed their blackface; see Melnick, *A Right to Sing the Blues: African Americans, Jews, and American Popular Song* (Cambridge, Mass.: Harvard University Press, 1999), 112. For a different interpretation, see Michael Rogin, *Blackface, White Noise: Jewish Immigrants in the Hollywood Melting Pot* (Berkeley: University of California Press, 1996).

22. NA, FTC, Cross-Examination of Patrick Rooney, 14 October 1919, 2501.

23. Arthur Wertheim, *Vaudeville Wars: How the Keith-Albee and Orpheum Circuits Controlled the Big Time and Its Performers* (New York: Palgrave Macmillan, 2006).

CHAPTER ONE

1. "Entrance Guards Carried Away," *NYT*, 26 November 1895; "Hammerstein's Big and Gorgeous Olympia Opened Wide," *NYS*, 26 November 1895.

2. Lloyd Spencer, "It Is the Craze," *Burlington (Iowa) Evening Gazette*, 26 January 1907; *NYMT*, 1 September 1912, cited in Arthur Wertheim, *Vaudeville Wars: How the Keith-Albee and Orpheum Circuits Controlled the Big Time and Its Performers* (New York: Palgrave Macmillan, 2006), 98; "Vogue of Vaudeville," *Boston Transcript*, 8 October 1907.

3. Susan Strasser, *Satisfaction Guaranteed: The Making of the American Mass Market* (New York: Pantheon Books, 1989); Andrew Heinze, *Adapting to Abundance: Jewish Immigrants, Mass Consumption and the Search for American Identity* (New York: Columbia University Press, 1990); William Leach, *Land of Desire: Merchants, Power and the Rise of a New American Culture* (New York: Pantheon Books, 1993); T. Jackson Lears, *Fables of Abundance: A Cultural History of Advertising in America* (New York: Basic Books, 1995).

4. Marlis Schweitzer, "'The Mad Search for Beauty': Actresses' Testimonials, the Cosmetics Industry, and the 'Democratization of Beauty,'" *Journal of the Gilded Age and Progressive Era* 4, no. 3 (July 2005): 255–92; and, more generally, Schweitzer, *When Broadway Was the Runway: Theater, Fashion, and American Culture* (Philadelphia: University of Pennsylvania Press, 2009).

5. "Philosophy of the Ad," *New Orleans Times-Democrat*, 29 August 1908; K-AVC, Managers' Reports, 21 September 1903–14 March 1904, Keith's Bijou Show, Philadelphia, week of 23 November 1903.

6. Albee quoted in "Growth of Vaudeville," *NYTr*, 15 September 1912; K-AVC, Scrapbook #140, "Press Release: Violinist Tells Why She Would Be Vaudeville Headliner," n.d.

7. Parker R. Zellers, "The Cradle of Variety: The Concert Saloon," *Educational Theater Journal* 20, no. 4 (December 1968): 578–85; William Lawrence Slout, *Broadway below the Sidewalk: Concert Saloons of Old New York* (San Bernardino: Borgo Press, 1994); Brooks McNamara, *The New York Concert Saloon: The Devil's Own Nights* (New York: Cambridge University Press, 2002); David Monod, *The Soul of Pleasure: Sentiment and Sensation in Nineteenth-Century American Mass Entertainment* (Ithaca: Cornell University Press, 2016), chapter 4.

8. Alan Gevinson, "The Origins of Vaudeville: Aesthetic Power, Disquietude, and Cosmopolitanism in the Quest for an American Music Hall" (Ph.D. diss., Johns Hopkins University, 2007); Monod, *Soul of Pleasure*, chapters 5–6.

9. "Enforcing the Excise Law," *NYT*, 11 November 1877; "Lights in the Fog," *M'lle New York*, 23 August 1895, 17; "Clara at the Ball," *Atlanta Constitution*, 26 December 1886.

10. "Lights in the Fog," 10; "Editorial Notes: Music and Drama," *Bachelor of Arts: A Monthly Magazine Devoted to University Interests and General Literature* 3 (December 1896), 859.

11. "Trouble at Koster & Bial's," *NYT*, 17 March 1882; letter to the editor, "How New York Women Drink," *Boston Gazette*, 5 August 1879; Clara Belle, letter to the editor, *WP*, 26 December 1886; "What Changed His View?," *NYT*, 22 August 1889.

12. Rudolph Aronson, *Theatrical and Musical Memoirs* (New York: McBride, Nast,

1913), 57–64. For Koster and Bial's troubles with licensing, see Gevinson, "Origins of Vaudeville," 356–57.

13. Stephen Burge Johnson, "The Roof Gardens of Broadway Theaters, 1883–1941" (Ph.D. diss., New York University, 1983), 124–57; "Manhattan Opera House," *NYC*, 29 July 1893.

14. "Around the Theaters," *New York Evening World*, 19 July 1890; "News of the Theaters," *NYS*, 22 May 1892; "On the Roof Gardens," *NYT*, 2 July 1893.

15. Gevinson, "Origins of Vaudeville," 24, 241, and 326, describes the roof garden audience. Paul van du Zee, "New York's Roof Gardens," *Godey's Magazine*, August 1894, 211; "Music Hall Crusade," *NYT*, 29 December 1895; "A City under One Roof," *Scientific American* 6, no. 70 (10 February 1894): 211; Harry Mawson, "Al Fresco in New York," *Harper's Weekly*, 9 July 1892, 654; "The Week at the Theaters," *CT*, 6 May 1895; "The Variety Stage," *Atlanta Constitution*, 26 May 1895; "Roof Garden," *WP*, 14 March 1896; "Variety on the Union Roof Garden," *WP*, 17 July 1898.

16. Percy Williams, "Vaudeville and Vaudevillians," *Saturday Evening Post*, 5 June 1909, 16.

17. "News of the Theaters," *CDT*, 2 January 1906; "New Orpheum's Bright Birth," *LAT*, 27 June 1911; BRTD, Emerson Collection on Vaudeville, box 2, folder 23, Hurtig and Seamon's Harlem Music Hall at 7th and 125th, 25 October 1897; "Orpheum Theater Kansas City," *Kansas City Sun*, 19 December 1914.

18. "A Venture in Vaudeville," *FRA: A Journal of Affirmation* 5, no. 3 (June 1910): 66; "In the Vaudevilles," *NYT*, 9 June 1901; "Opening of Summer Season," *WP*, 14 May 1901; "News of the Theaters," *CDT*, 2 January 1906; Albee quoted in Frank Copley, "The Story of a Great Vaudeville Manager," *American Magazine*, December 1922, 47.

19. BRTD, ZAN T274, E. W. Sargent Scrapbook, clipping 14 August 1899; BRTD, Robinson Locke Collection, envelope 2053, Lala Selbini, clipping *New York Globe*, 8 June 1906.

20. UASC, MS 421, Vaudeville Collection, box 60, files "House Rules of Gem Concert Hall" and "High Class Vaudeville," ca. 1904; Williams, "Vaudeville and Vaudevillians," 16; "Gallery Gods," *Freeport (Ill.) Journal-Standard*, 14 September 1922; LSHS, PN1968 U5 H45 1915z, "Orpheum Circuit of Vaudeville Theaters," memorandum, 1915.

21. *Keith's News*, 4 September 1922; "Gallery God Fined," *Scranton Republican*, 30 April 1908; "Gallery Gods in Fight," *Buffalo Courier*, 1 May 1906; "Plays and Players," *San Francisco Chronicle*, 3 April 1904; "Noisy Critic Disturbs Play," *Los Angeles Herald*, 21 January 1907.

22. "An American Institution," *Buffalo Courier*, 14 October 1899; "Chase's," *WP*, 26 May 1907; "Polite Vaudeville," *Boston Daily Globe*, 19 July 1898.

23. BRTD, E. W. Sargent Scrapbook, clipping "Sam T. Jack," 26 September 1898.

24. "Footlight Favorites," *Boston Sunday Post*, 10 December 1911; Caroline Caffin, *Vaudeville* (New York: Scurfield, 1914), 17; Campbell MacCulloch, "Vaudeville, Drama and Opera in Tabloid Form," *NYTr*, 4 June 1905.

25. "Vogue for the Vaudeville," *Brooklyn Daily Eagle*, 29 October 1899; Michael Davis Jr., *The Exploitation of Pleasure: A Study of Commercial Recreation in New York City* (New York: Sage Foundation, 1911), 32; Francis North, *A Recreation Survey of the City of Waltham, Massachusetts* (Waltham: E. L. Barry, 1913), 46; William Trufant Foster,

Vaudeville and Motion Picture Shows: A Study of Theaters in Portland, Oregon (Portland: Reed College Social Service Series, 1914), cited on 34; Caffin, *Vaudeville*, 16. Images of New York vaudeville houses often show men outnumbering women; see, for example, the one in Israel Zangwill, "The Future of Vaudeville in America," *Cosmopolitan* 2 (1897): 643; and "View of Proctor's Pleasure Palace and Garden of Palms," in James S. Moy, "Proctor's Pleasure Palace and Garden of Palms, 1895–1898," *Nineteenth Century Theater Research* 8, no.1 (Spring 1980): 23. BRTD, Robinson Locke Collection, series 3, vol. 387, Wellington Cross file, clipping "Fine Vaudeville," 21 January 1914.

26. "125th Street," *Variety*, 6 June 1907; "News of the Local Theaters," *Saint Paul Globe*, 27 May 1902.

27. "Here's the Brooklyn Matinee Girl," *Brooklyn Daily Herald*, 22 November 1908; "At the Play," *PI*, 30 April 1899.

28. Caffin, *Vaudeville*, 17; MacCulloch, "Vaudeville, Drama and Opera in Tabloid Form"; "Behold the Actorettes," *Akron Weekly Pioneer Press*, 30 June 1911; "Miss Fallon Takes Note of Her Wednesday Matinee Audience," *NYS*, 10 May 1901.

29. Levera Berlew, *Recreation Survey of Scranton during July and August 1913* (Scranton: Playground Association, 1913), 9; North, *Recreation Survey of the City of Waltham*, 46; Michael Davis Jr., *The Exploitation of Pleasure: A Study of Commercial Recreation in New York City* (New York: Sage Foundation, 1911).

30. "Theaters This Week," *Brooklyn Daily Eagle*, 13 April 1909; "Ticklish Piece of Dramatic Work," *Louisville Courier-Journal*, 25 April 1909.

31. "Hebrew Actors and Managers Agree," *The Player*, 28 March 1913.

32. "Yiddish Theater," *New York Evening Sun*, 18 May 1903; BRTD, MWEZ+ n.c. 14339, W. C. Crowley Collection of Vaudeville Clippings, "Vaudeville in Yiddish," 18 May 1903; "Seen on the Yiddish Rialto," *NYTr*, 5 November 1905; "Vaudeville in Yiddish," *NYS*, 24 November 1902; for Italian-language vaudeville, see Harvard Theatre Collection, Houghton Library, "Vaudeville and Variety, 1891–1900," clipping "Night Life in the Bend," 1899.

33. Berlew, *Recreation Survey of Scranton*, 4, 6, 8; "Musical and Dramatic," *Chicago Defender*, 9 April 1910.

34. "Music and the Stage," *New York Age*, 10 January 1910; "National and Local Theatrical News," *Salt Lake City Broad Ax*, 3 February 1912.

35. Stephen K. Huff, "The Urban Geography of Theater in a New South City: Memphis, 1890–1920" (Ph.D. diss., City University of New York, 2012); BRTD, MWEZ+ n.c. 2203, Scrapbook Relating to New York Theater, clipping "Burlesque and the Colored Audience," *The Billboard*, 1922; "New Theater for New York," *Salt Lake City Broad Ax*, 9 December 1911; "There Are Many Colored Thespians," *PI*, 17 September 1922; J. Wilson, letter to the editor, *Kansas City (Mo.) Sun*, 5 February 1916; "An Audience Reacts," *New York Age*, 9 February 1935; "Pictures, Music, Drama," *Los Angeles Eagle*, 25 January 1929; Jines quoted in "What Do They Want?," *Chicago Defender*, 5 April 1924; Whitney quoted in "Compliments His Race," *The Tennessean* (Nashville), 28 February 1912.

36. George Jean Nathan, *The Popular Theater* (New York: Alfred A. Knopf, 1918), 221; Mae West, *Goodness Had Nothing to Do with It* (New York: Prentice Hall, 1959), 50; Friganza quoted in "Some inside Vaudeville," *NYT*, 22 March 1914.

37. Richard Dyer, *Stars* (London: British Film Institute, 1979); Richard Schickel,

Intimate Strangers: The Culture of Celebrity (New York: Doubleday, 1985); Richard de Cordova, *Picture Personalities: The Emergence of the Star System in America* (Urbana: University of Illinois Press, 1990); Richard de Cordova, "The Emergence of the Star System in America," in *Stardom: Industry of Desire*, ed. Christine Gledhill (New York: Routledge, 1991), 17–29.

38. Valeska Suratt, "The Easy Way to Make Your Wrinkles Vanish," *Salt Lake Herald-Republican*, 7 November 1915.

39. "The Booth Family," *NYTr*, 25 April 1865; Armond Fields, *Lillian Russell: A Biography of "America's Beauty"* (Jefferson, N.C.: McFarland, 1998), 36–49. Lillian Russell was considered America's most beautiful woman and, as such, a source of national pride. "For a nation to have one beautiful woman in a century means a great deal," observed one fan. "The Virtue of Patriotism," *Pittsburgh Press*, 31 January 1897. On media see David Giles, *Illusions of Immortality: A Psychology of Fame and Celebrity* (Basingstoke: Macmillan, 2000), chapter 2.

40. Gerald Baldasty, *The Commercialization of News in the Nineteenth Century* (Madison: University of Wisconsin Press, 1992), 123–24; Ellen Gruber Garvey, *The Adman in the Parlor: Magazines and the Gendering of Consumer Culture, 1880s to 1910s* (New York: Oxford University Press, 1996), 5.

41. Karen Halttunen, *Confidence Men and Painted Women: A Study of Middle-Class Culture in America, 1830–1870* (New Haven: Yale University Press, 1983); James V. Catano, *Ragged Dicks: Masculinity, Steel, and the Rhetoric of the Self-Made Man* (Carbondale: Southern Illinois University Press, 2001); John G. Cawelti, *Apostles of the Self-Made Man* (Chicago: University of Chicago Press, 1965); Irvin G. Wyllie, *The Self-Made Man in America: The Myth of Rags to Riches* (New Brunswick: Rutgers University Press, 1954); K-AVC, Scrapbook #140, Rae Eleanor Ball press release, n.d.

42. "The Press Agent," *The Tennessean*, 23 August 1908.

43. On Held's milk bath, see Eve Golden, *Anna Held and the Birth of Ziegfeld's Broadway* (Lexington: University of Kentucky Press, 2000), 31; "Alexander Pantages," *System: The Man of Business* 37 (March 1920): 502; "Eva Tanguay," *Muncie Star Press*, 26 September 1913; "Joe Frisco," *NYTr*, 18 April 1920; "Eva Tanguay Proud of Her Home," *Muncie (Ind.) Evening Press*, 1 October 1913.

44. "Tale of Tanguay," *Pittsburgh Press*, 19 November 1911; "Where Belle Baker Started," *Brooklyn Daily Eagle*, 1 August 1915; "Belle Baker," *Detroit Free Press*, 21 November 1915.

45. "Irene Franklin Heads Good Bill," *Brooklyn Daily Eagle*, 3 October 1911; "Two Little Romances," *The Tennessean*, 18 February 1912. Barnard appeared at the Union Theater in October 1912. K-AVC, Managers' Reports, vol. 14, Union Theater Show, 7 October 1912.

46. Daniel J. Boorstin, *The Image: A Guide to Pseudo-Events in America* (New York: Vintage Books, 1962), 217; "King's Highway Congregational Church Strawberry Festival," *Brooklyn Daily Eagle*, 19 June 1906; "Armory Show," *Brooklyn Daily Eagle*, 11 February 1907; "Montgomery Wins Cup," *Brooklyn Daily Eagle*, 3 August 1908; "Montgomery Creates a Furore," *Wilmington Evening Journal*, 20 May 1909.

47. "Eva Tanguay Proud of her Home"; "Lucre Lures to Vaudeville," *Wichita Daily Eagle*, 31 December 1911; "Big Salaries for Big Acts in Vaudeville," *Wilkes-Barre (Pa.) Times Leader*, 7 November 1908; "Eva Tanguay," *Variety*, 15 June 1907.

48. Alexander Klein, "Personal Income of U.S. States: Estimates for the Period

1880–1910," *Warwick Economic Research Papers*, no. 916, Department of Economics, University of Warwick (table 9); Bureau of the Census, *Historical Statistics of the United States* (Washington: Government Printing Office,1960), Series D 699–684; BRTD, MWEZ + n.c. 19456, Will Cressy Scrapbook, clipping "Vaudevillians Get Big Salary," 1910.

49. "Boom in Vaudeville," *CDT*, 21 April 1902; BRTD, MWEZ+ n.c. 19457, Will Cressy and Blanche Dayne Pressbook, clipping "The Truth at Last Concerning Vaudeville Salaries," 1910; NA, FTC, Cross-Examination of Edward M. Fay, 26 March 1919, 810.

50. "Boom in Vaudeville"; "With the Men and Women of the Twice-a-Day," *NYT*, 6 May 1906; NA, FTC, Examination of Pat Casey, 3 February 1919, 298, and 6 February 1919, 306.

51. NA, FTC, Examination of Pat Casey, 6 February 1919, 258 and 300; Final Arguments, 3356; and Brief of FTC Attorneys, 9; "Vaudeville Situation," *Billboard*, 18 October 1919; NA, FTC, Examination of Frank Fogarty, 28 March 1919, 1185 and 1216; Managers' Brief, 6–7, 11, 12 and R 300–1, Examination of Patrick Rooney, 14 October 1919, 2490.

52. BRTD, Robinson Locke Collection, NAFR+, series 2, vol. 297, clipping "Eva Tanguay" and clipping "Eva Tanguay," *Dramatic Mirror*, 29 January 1915; Dorothy Dix, "Eva Tanguay," *Salt Lake Herald Republican*, 5 June 1910; "The Theater," *Pittsburgh Post-Gazette*, 2 May 1915; "Eva Tanguay," *Baltimore Sun*, 21 February 1915; Eva Tanguay, letter to the editor, *CDT*, 2 April 1911.

53. "The Truth about Eva Tanguay," *Pittsburgh Daily Post*, 5 May 1912.

CHAPTER TWO

1. Marketing experts refer to "Type Authenticity"; see B. Kovacs, G. R. Carroll, and D. W. Lehman, "Authenticity and Consumer Value Ratings: Empirical Tests from the Restaurant Domain," *Organizational Science* 25, no. 2 (2014): 458–78; and Michael Hughes, "Country Music as Impression Management: A Mediation on Fabricating Authenticity," *Poetics* 28 (2000): 188. For different approaches to authenticity in performance, see H. Quirko, "Consumer Authentication of Popular Music in the Global Postmodern Popular Music," *Society* 37, no. 3 (2014): 291–312; and Bruce Baugh, "Authenticity Revisited," *Journal of Aesthetic Art Criticism* 46, no. 4 (1988): 477–87.

2. Peter van der Merwe, *The Origins of the Popular Style: The Antecedents of Twentieth-Century Popular Music* (New York: Oxford University Press, 1989); Nicholas Tawa, *The Way to Tin Pan Alley: American Popular Song, 1866–1910* (New York: Schirmer Books, 1990); Charles Hamm, *Yesterdays* (New York: W. W. Norton, 1983); Peter C. Muir, *Long Lost Blues: Popular Blues in America, 1850–1920* (Urbana: University of Illinois Press, 2009). On songsters, see Leslie Shepard, *The Broadside Ballad* (Hatboro, Pa.: Legacy Books, 1978).

3. Felix McGlennin and Monroe Rosenfeld, "Her Golden Hair Was Hanging Down Her Back" (New York: Leo Feist, 1892).

4. Michael J. Pfeifer, *Rough Justice: Lynching and American Society, 1874–1947* (Urbana: University of Illinois Press, 2004); William Cohen, *At Freedom's Edge: Black Mobility and the Southern White Quest for Racial Control, 1861–1915* (Baton Rouge: Louisiana State University Press, 1991); Howard Rabinowitz, *Race Relations in the Urban South, 1865–1890* (New York: Oxford University Press, 1978).

5. "Louisville Originated Rag Time," *Louisville Courier-Journal*, 5 February 1902; "Origins of Rag-Time," *Detroit Free Press*, 30 June 1901; "Ben Harney and Rag Time," *Chicago Inter Ocean*, 17 May 1897.

6. "Several Good Entertainments," *Louisville Courier-Journal*, 20 May 1895.

7. Charles Trevathan, "May Irwin's Bully Song" (New York: White-Smith Publishing, 1896).

8. Research for this study revealed that less than 1 percent of singers were identified as presenting "coon" songs, but the vaudevilleamerica.org database covers the period after 1902, at which point "coon" songs were no longer especially popular. Karl Hagstrom Miller, *Segregating Sound: Inventing Folk and Pop Music in the Age of Jim Crow* (Durham: Duke University Press, 2010), 33 and 41; "A Colored Composer," *Chicago Inter Ocean*, 26 November 1897.

9. Ashton Stevens, "The Good 'Coon' Song," *SFC*, 13 February 1898; "A Colored Composer," *Chicago Inter Ocean*, 26 November 1897; "Opening of the Theaters," *Brooklyn Daily Eagle*, 6 September 1896; BRTD, MWEZ+ n.c. 10841, Sophie Tucker Scrapbook, clipping *Pittsburgh Dispatch*, ca. 1915.

10. "Elizabeth Murray," *Pittsburgh Daily Post*, 14 April 1917; BRTD, Robinson Locke Collection, envelope 1575, Elizabeth Murray, clipping 20 April 1913; BRTD, MWEZ+ n.c. 10834, Sophie Tucker Scrapbook, clippings *Show World*, 29 September 1909, and *Los Angeles Record*, 26 September 1910.

11. Artie Hall may have been the first white female vaudevillian who donned blackface to sing "coon" songs, and Tucker appears to have copied her practice of removing a glove to show that she was white. "May Irwin and Her Ghost," *Minneapolis Star Tribune*, 29 April 1899.

12. "Ragtime and Comedy Sketches at Orpheum," *SFC*, 18 April 1899.

13. BRTD, ZAN T274, E. W. Sargent Scrapbook, clipping "Campbell Is Shy."

14. Susan Bordo, *Unbearable Weight: Feminism, Western Culture and the Body* (Berkeley: University of California Press, 1993), 190–91; BRTD, Aaron Hoffman Papers, box 20, "Levinsky at the Party," 8; Lyla Kavenaugh, "Tights and Their Lovely Wearers," *New York World*, 15 October 1893.

15. "The Bully Song, Fun by May Irwin," *CT*, 18 April 1898.

16. James McIntyre (of McIntyre and Heath) claimed to have first performed a rag at Pastor's in 1879, and McIntyre maintained Harney once admitted to having copied him. BRTD, MWEZ+ n.c. 10446, McIntyre and Heath Scrapbook, clipping *New York Review*, 4 November 1916; NUSC, MS 133, McIntyre and Heath Collection, box 4, James McIntyre to *Variety*, 25 February 1916. Ragtime scholars have traditionally put some distance between ragtime and the "coon" shout. They have described ragtime as piano music rather than theater music and have traced its birth to composers like Scott Joplin rather than Ben Harney and Charles Trevathan. The piano theory of ragtime's origins is presented in John Edward Hasse, ed., *Ragtime: Its History, Composers and Music* (New York: Schirmer Books, 1985); and in Eileen Southern, *The Music of Black Americans* (New York: W. W. Norton, 1971), 312. Singer Ada Lewis traced the origin to the expression "my rag" in "Evolution of Slang," *Zanesville (Ohio) Times Signal*, 11 January 1925. See also "Green Room Gossip," *New Orleans Times-Picayune*, 23 July 1899.

17. "A Novelty," *Livingston (Ala.) Journal*, 17 January 1873; "The Cake Walk," *CT*,

15 December 1880; "Cake-Walk," *Argos (Ind.) Reflector*, 6 September 1888; Eden Elizabeth Kainer, "Vocal Racial Crossover in the Song Performance of Three Iconic American Vocalists: Sophie Tucker, Elsie Janis and Ella Fitzgerald" (Ph.D. diss., University of Wisconsin, 2008), 149–50; Charles Hamm, "Genre, Performance and Ideology in the Early Songs of Irving Berlin," *Popular Music* 13, no. 2 (1994): 150. Many of the most popular songs that were considered rags by vaudevillians, including "Hello! Ma Baby" and "When the Midnight Choo-Choo Leaves for Alabam," made limited or no use of syncopation.

18. "Sophie Tucker," *Ragtime Review* 1, no. 3 (March 1915), 6; Indiana University, Archives of Traditional Music, Elmer Teflinger, interview by Jared Carter, 13 April 1979; "About the Christensen System," *Ragtime Review* 1, no. 3 (March 1915): 3.

19. "De Wolf Hopper's Round Dollars," *San Francisco Examiner*, 6 December 1895; "Hopper and Casey," *CT*, 2 February 1898.

20. BRTD, Robinson Locke Collection, envelope 1575, Elizabeth Murray, clippings *Cleveland Leader*, 15 September 1918, and *New York Mail*, 10 April 1917.

21. Irving Berlin, "Words and Music," *Green Book Magazine*, July 1915, 104–5.

22. "Clarice Vance," *SFC*, 18 April 1899; "Amusement Notes," *PI*, 22 April 1900; "Clarice Vance," *Newport (R.I.) Daily News*, 14 July 1903; "Miss Clarice Vance," *Indianapolis News*, 7 November 1903; "Vaudeville at the Grand," *Indianapolis Journal*, 10 February 1903; "How to Sing a Ragtime Song," *Detroit Free Press*, 27 January 1907.

23. Tucker explained in 1915 that it was difficult transitioning from the "coon" shout because she felt she needed to rely on her volume to get the music across. As she told an interviewer, when she first sang quietly or was "just talking along," she would periodically "break out ... and yell. I'd see people down in front put their hands over their ears and I'd think I'd spoiled everything." As tastes changed, Tucker began singing more of what people in the business called "Mammy numbers," which she delivered more emotionally than "coon" songs and much "softer, to get the rhythm of syncopation." BRTD, MWEZ+ n.c. 10853, Sophie Tucker Scrapbook, clipping *Fresno Bee*, 21 September 1923.

24. "Blanche Ring," *Variety*, 11 December 1909; Blanche Ring, "How to Put 'Em Across," *Green Book Magazine*, July 1912, 45–47; "Popular Air Has Appeal," *LAT*, 20 July 1924; Nora Bayes, "Why People Enjoy Crying in a Theater," *American Magazine*, April 1918, 33–35.

25. "Nichols Sisters," *Indianapolis Star*, 16 February 1904.

26. "Have You a Good Voice?," *Buffalo Enquirer*, 29 August 1918; Margarete Matzenauer, "The Vaudeville Voice," *Musical Courier* 74, no. 1 (4 January 1917): 164.

27. K-AVC, Managers' Reports, vol. 1, Chase's Empire, Cleveland, week of 9 March 1903; Willis Steell, "A Picturesque Clubland," *New York Herald*, 6 April 1919.

28. Owen Kildare, "The Jargon of Low Literature," *The Independent*, 19 July 1906, 139; "Manufacturing Stage Slang," *NYT*, 18 September 1910; Fred Niblo, "English and American Audiences," *Variety*, 15 December 1906.

29. H. L. Mencken, *The American Language* (New York: Alfred A. Knopf, 1919), 27; "Manufacturing Stage Slang," *NYT*, 18 September 1910.

30. "Movies and Dance Halls," *NYT*, 27 April 1913; "Social Sets," *WP*, 8 February 1913; "Investigation Report of the Committee of Fourteen," 9 November 1912, cited in Danielle Robinson, "Performing American: Ragtime Dancing as Participatory Minstrelsy," *Dance Chronicle* 32, no. 1 (2009): 96.

31. BRTD, Blossom Seeley clipping file, clippings "Blossom Seeley Dancing the Texas Tommy" and "Little Miss Fix-It," 10 September 1912. The Tommy apparently originated at Purcell's Dance Hall, an African American business, in San Francisco. A. H. Hallett, "The Old Barbary Coast," *Variety*, 26 December 1919.

32. "Take It from Bee Palmer," *Los Angeles Sunday Times*, 2 November 1919; Bert Williams, "The Comic Side of Trouble," *American Magazine*, January 1918, 34; Lynn Abbott and Doug Seroff, *The Original Blues: The Emergence of the Blues in African American Vaudeville, 1899–1926* (Jackson: University of Mississippi Press, 2017), 116–18. Despite Gray's insistence that she originated the dance, it was almost certainly African American in origin. Nonetheless, Bee Palmer, who was Gray's main rival for the title of "Shimmy Queen," was also widely credited with inventing the dance. She usually accepted the compliment but on occasion did acknowledge that the dance was what she called an African American "folk dance." The name of the dance came from a popular rag of 1916, "Shim-Me-Sha-Wabble," which described a new dance step in which one bounces and shakes like a rubber ball. Spencer Williams, "Shim-Me-Sha-Wobble" (New York: Joseph W. Stern and Co., 1917). "Few of Gilda Gray's Admirers Know," *The Tennessean*, 30 March 1941; "Former Dance Sensation Dies," *New Orleans Times Picayune*, 23 December 1959; Rutgers University, Institute of Jazz Studies, Marshall Stearns Papers, box Dance Material, file Shimmy, clippings *Time*, 4 January 1960, 43, and "Gilda Gray Tells Her Story," *Muncie Star Press*, 18 April 1926. Mae West later claimed she invented the shimmy and introduced the dance on Broadway in 1918; see Rutgers University, Institute of Jazz Studies, Marshall Stearns Papers, box 7, file 38, clipping *New York Mirror*, 31 October 1959.

33. BRTD, MWEZ+ n.c. 19080, Will Cressy Scrapbook, clipping 12 July 1888; BRTD, Robinson Locke Collection, envelope 125, Charmion, clipping "Perfect Athletic Girl," *Denver Post*, 9 October 1904; BRTD, E. W. Sargent Scrapbook, clipping 11 October 1899; BRTD, MWEZx n.c. 21049, Ned Wayburn Scrapbook, clipping *Indianapolis News*, 17 May 1898; "May Irwin and Her Ghost," *Minneapolis Star Tribune*, 29 April 1899.

34. BRTD, Hoffman Papers, box 24, Joe Watson "Solly the Salesman," August 1915, 25 and 33.

35. "She Discovered an Obesity Cure," *Chicago Inter Ocean*, 10 July 1904; "Stories about Players," *Salt Lake Herald*, 3 July 1904; BRTD, MWEZ+ n.c. 10836, Sophie Tucker Scrapbook, clipping *Chicago Sunday Examiner*, 16 April 1911; BRTD, Hoffman Papers, box 21, "Manna Falls for Moses," 1913, 11; "Emma Carus No Longer Fat Like a Baby Elephant," *Philadelphia Evening Ledger*, 20 January 1916; "Rival Devils Create Sensation," *Salt Lake Herald*, 23 August 1908; BRTD, MWEZ+ n.c. 10841, Sophie Tucker Scrapbook, clipping "At the Majestic," ca. 1915; Eva Tanguay, *Minneapolis Star Tribune*, 22 September 1922; "Blanche Ring," *Indianapolis Star*, 23 October 1910.

36. *Hippodrome News*, March 25, 1908, cited in "Clarice Vance," http://www.tinfoil.com/cv-bio.htm; "Miss Friganza's Remedy for Fatness," *PI*, 27 December 1908.

37. Emma Carus, "How I Lost 62 Pounds," *Detroit Free Press*, 27 October 1918.

38. "Emma Carus in Blue Tights," *NYMT*, 16 March 1901; "Emma Carus Refuses Tights," *Buffalo Courier*, 6 April 1900; "Hammerstein and Emma Carus Part," *NYMT*, 20 June 1904; "The Theater," *NYMT*, 22 June 1904.

39. BRTD, MWEZ+ n.c. 1406, Valeska Suratt Scrapbook, clippings "Vaudeville at the

Temple," *Detroit Free Press*, 27 March 1906; "The Stage," *Cincinnati Times-Star*, 22 March 1906; and "Says Our Girls Shocking," *LAT*, March 1907.

40. K-AVC, Managers' Reports, vol. 14, Union Theater Show, 7 October 1912; "House Scarcity Drove Me Back on Stage," *Los Angeles Herald*, 16 June 1920. An excellent study of thinness and feminism is Katharina Vester, "Regime Change: Gender, Class and the Invention of Dieting in Post-bellum American," *Journal of Social History* 44, no. 1 (Fall 2010): 39–70.

41. BRTD, Robinson Locke Collection, envelope 1110, La Sylphe, clipping "Not Enough of Costume to Worry About"; "Charmion," *Des Moines Register*, 9 December 1908; BRTD, MWEZ+ n.c. 18770, Evelyn Law Scrapbook, clipping 17 December 1920 and clipping "Boston," 5 November 1921.

42. "Lalla Selbini," *Variety*, 9 June 1906; BRTD, Robinson Locke Collection, envelope 903, Annette Kellerman, clipping *Syracuse Post Standard*, ca. 1909.

43. "In the Spotlight's Rays," *Cincinnati Enquirer*, 9 November 1924.

44. Marshall D. Beuick, "The Vaudeville Philosopher," *The Drama* 16 (December 1925), reprinted in *American Vaudeville as Seen by Its Contemporaries*, ed. Charles W. Stein (New York: Alfred A. Knopf, 1984), 329–30.

45. Robert C. Toll, *Blacking Up: The Minstrel Show in Nineteenth-Century America* (New York: Oxford University Press, 1974); Eric Lott, *Love and Theft: Blackface Minstrelsy and the American Working Class* (New York: Oxford University Press, 1993); Dale Cockrell, *Demons of Disorder: Early Blackface Minstrels and Their World* (New York: Cambridge University Press, 1997); William John Mahar, *Behind the Burnt Cork Mask: Early Blackface Minstrelsy and Antebellum American Popular Culture* (Urbana: University of Illinois Press 1998).

46. BRTD, MWEZ+ n.c. 2550, George Gouge Scrapbook, clippings "Billy Rice Sees War Enthusiasm" and "Lothrop's Opera House"; "Billy Rice," *Washington Times*, 4 December 1898; Mark Twain, *Autobiography* (Madison: University of Wisconsin Press, 1990), 175.

47. "Dan Emmett the Author of Dixie," *Buffalo Courier*, 23 June 1895; "Ethiopian Minstrelsy," *Brooklyn Daily Eagle*, 1 September 1901; Harvard Theatre Collection, Houghton Library, American Minstrel Show Collection, series 3, file 636, "History of Negro Minstrelsy," 24 July 1854; BRTD, MWEZ+ n.c. 10446, McIntyre and Heath Scrapbook, typescript of interview with Charles Salisbury, 1910.

48. K-AVC, Managers' Reports, vol. 1, Boston Show, week of 15 December 1902; BRTD, Robinson Locke Collection, envelope 529, Gene Greene, clipping 8 April 1916; Krystyn R. Moon, *Yellowface: Creating the Chinese in American Popular Music and Performance, 1850s-1920s* (New Brunswick: Rutgers University Press, 2005), 134–36 and 160; "Frank Wilson Trio," *San Antonio Light*, 19 November 1905; "Flying Dancer," *Variety*, 20 September 1912.

49. K-AVC, Managers' Reports, vol. 8, Boston Show, week of 4 November 1907. In an instructive case, Al Blanchard, who previously performed in whiteface, adopted blackface for his comedy routine. In the act, Blanchard flirted with his partner, Al Warren, who was dressed as a "wench." Although the manager in Boston preferred the new act to the old, he said, "I do not think that any audience wants to see a white man making love to a negro." They soon changed the act and both performed in blackface.

50. K-AVC, Managers' Reports, vol. 6, Keith's Cleveland, week of 16 October 1905; Lori Harrison-Kahan, *The White Negress: Literature, Minstrelsy and the Black-Jewish Imaginary* (New Brunswick: Rutgers University Press, 2011), 33; "Artie Hall," *Variety*, 23 December 1905.

51. "A Colored Composer," *Chicago Inter Ocean*, 26 November 1897; "Orpheum," *Los Angeles Sunday Times*, 22 August 1897; "Klondike Lyre," *Los Angeles Herald*, 16 December 1895; advertisement, *Brooklyn Daily Eagle*, 7 February 1897; "The Audience Was Large," *Ottawa Journal*, 7 June 1898; "Amusements," *Bridgewater (N.J.) Courier-News*, 18 November 1897; "Amusements," *Oshkosh Daily Northwestern*, 11 March 1899; "At Keith's," *NYT*, 27 October 1903; K-AVC, vol. 3, Hyde and Behman's Show, Brooklyn, week of 11 April 1904.

52. "On the Variety Stage," *CDT*, 24 May 1902; "At Keith's."

53. Karen Sotiropoulos, *Staging Race: Black Performers in Turn of the Century America* (Cambridge, Mass.: Harvard University Press, 2006), 46–47; "Williams and Walker," *Variety*, 22 February 1908; "Cole and Johnson," *Colored American* (Washington, D.C.), 1 November 1902; "Keith's," *Boston Daily Globe*, 15 July 1902; "Two Negro Song Writers," *NYT*, 3 May 1903; Lester Walton, "Music and the Stage," *New York Age*, 6 October 1910.

54. "What Williams and Walker Think of *The Clansman*," *Chicago Inter Ocean*, 24 June 1906; Ziegfeld quoted in Esther Romeyn, *Street Scenes: Staging the Self in Immigrant New York, 1880–1924* (Minneapolis: University of Minnesota Press, 2008), 187.

55. "What Williams and Walker Think of *The Clansman*"; K-AVC, Managers' Reports, vol.1, New York Show, week of 29 September 29 1902; Romeyn, *Street Scenes*, 134–56; Paul Distler, "Exit the Racial Comics," *Educational Theater Journal* 18, no. 3 (October 1966): 247–54; M. Alison Kibler, *Censoring Racial Ridicule: Irish, Jewish, and African American Struggles over Race and Representation, 1890–1930* (Chapel Hill: University of North Carolina Press, 2015).

56. BRTD, Hoffman Papers, box 24, Joe Watson "Solly the Salesman," August 1915, 1, 25, 31, and 33; BRTD, Robinson Locke Collection, envelope 2528, Joe Welch, clipping "Modern Theater."

57. BRTD, MWEZ+ n.c. 4564, Edward Harrigan Scrapbook, clipping "Joe Welch Doesn't Eat"; "Joe Welch," *Oakland Tribune*, 10 July 1911; BRTD, Robinson Locke Collection, envelope 2528, Joe Welch, clipping Joe Welch, "Abraham Jacobson"; "National Theater," *Suburbanite Economist* (Chicago), 24 November 1916; BRTD, Hoffman Papers, box 19, Joe Welch monologue "I Got Troubles," 5–6. The *New York Dramatic Mirror* was particularly scathing: BRTD, Robinson Locke Collection, envelope 2528, Joe Welch, clipping "Joe Welch and Company," 9 April 1910.

58. Grace Kingsley, "Flashes," *LAT*, 11 December 1923. W. C. Handy thought that people hearing Harris's recordings would think she was black, something that, by the time he said it, had become a compliment to a jazz singer. W. C. Handy, *Father of the Blues* (New York: Da Capo Press, 1969), 199–200; "Willis P. Sweatnam," *New York Dramatic Mirror*, 31 May 1911.

59. George Antheil, "The Negro on the Spiral," in *Negro: An Anthology*, ed. Mary Cunard (1934; New York: Negro Universities Press, 1969), 3; "Nora Bayes as a Star," *Baltimore Sun*, 8 April 1913; Carus's story recounted in "When Marie Dressler Gets Chatty,"

NYMT, 11 April 1902; BRTD, Robinson Locke Collection, envelope 2414, Clarice Vance, clipping "Blues Go Jazz One Better," *Lansing (Mich.) State Journal*, 10 July 1923.

60. Historians debate about just what was going on. Some see blackface as an assumed mask, others as what Ann Douglas called a "mongrelization." On masking, see Michael Rogin, *Blackface, White Noise: Jewish Immigrants in the Hollywood Melting Pot* (Berkeley: University of California Press, 1996); and Michael North, *The Dialect of Modernism: Race, Language and Twentieth Century Literature* (New York: Vintage Books, 1993). The idea of creolization or mongrelization is presented as positive in Ann Douglas's *Terrible Honesty: Mongrel Manhattan in the 1920s* (New York: Farrar, Straus and Giroux, 1995). Like Charles Hersch, I see both the overcoming of race in the theory of "mongrelization" and the self-conscious assumption of it as an external mask to be problematic concepts. See Hersch, *Subversive Sounds: Race and the Birth of Jazz in New Orleans* (Chicago: University of Chicago Press, 2007), 8–9.

61. K-AVC, Managers' Reports, vol. 6, Cleveland Show, week of 7 May 1906; "Gene Greene," *Fort Wayne Journal-Gazette*, 8 May 1916; "Fontaine Ferry," *Louisville Courier-Journal*, 19 May 1910; "Gene Greene," *Variety*, 7 April 1916; K-AVC, Managers' Reports, vol. 1, Chase's Empire Theater Show, Cleveland, week of 10 November 1902; "Dan Emmett Minstrel," *New York Sunday Telegram*, 29 June 1902.

62. "Origins of the Turkey Trot," *Louisville Courier-Journal*, 14 May 1911; Lester Walton, "Music and the Stage," *New York Age*, 6 October 1910; "The Brittons," *New York Age*, 16 April 1908.

63. "The Shimmy," *NYTr*, 1 February 1920.

CHAPTER THREE

1. Advertisement for Marino, *NYC*, 17 November 1906; "Marino Tells of His Thrilling Act," *Altoona (Pa.) Times*, 10 December 1906.

2. "Hammerstein's," *Variety*, 17 November 1906. Among other auto-defiers were Maximus the Great, who claimed to have invented "the exhilarating sport," and Zenda the strongman. Both were critical of Marino for allowing the car to pass over his back rather than over his stomach. "Maximus the Great," *Variety*, 30 March 1907; "Zenda, Auto-Defier," *Variety*, 1 December 1907.

3. Frederick Crum, "Street Traffic Accidents," *American Statistical Association* 13, no. 103 (September 1913): 6. For a railway or trolley company to be found at fault in a streetcar collision, a failure of machinery or official practice had to be determined. Conductor error or distraction was an individual, not a company, problem. Wex Malone, "American Fatal Accident Statutes: Part 1," *Duke Law Journal*, no. 4 (Autumn 1965): 673–719; BRTD, Aaron Hoffman Papers, box 17, monologue by Milt Collins, 27 September 1913.

4. K-AVC, Managers' Reports, vol. 6, Philadelphia Show, week of 7 January 1907; "Volta," *Variety*, 5 January 1907; "St. Louisans Amazed by Remarkable Feats," *St. Louis Post-Dispatch*, 24 March 1907.

5. K-AVC, Managers' Reports, vol. 1, Keith's [Bijou] Theater, Philadelphia Show, week of 6 August 1903.

6. Classic studies of the active audience are Stuart Hall, "Encoding/Decoding," in

Culture, Media, Language, ed. Stuart Hall, Dorothy Hobson, Andrew Lowe, and Paul Willis (London: Hutchinson, 1980), 128–38; and David Morley, *The "Nationwide" Audience: Structure and Decoding* (London: British Film Institute, 1980). "Audience" even moved from noun to verb: John Fiske, "Audiencing: A Cultural Studies Approach to Watching Television," *Poetics* 21 (1992): 345–59; George Gottleib, "Psychology of the American Vaudeville Show," *Current Opinion* 60 (April 1916): 257–58.

7. Marc Vernet, "The Look at the Camera," *Cinema Journal* 28, no. 2 (Winter 1989): 53, makes the point about the absent audience. For the "look at the camera," see Jim Collins, "Towards Defining a Matrix of the Musical Comedy: The Place of the Spectator within the Textual Mechanisms," in *Genre: The Musical*, ed. Rick Altman (London: Routledge, 1981), 134–45. Tom Gunning argues that early film was a "cinema of attraction" that ruptured the fourth wall just as vaudeville was doing; Gunning, "The Cinema of Attraction: Early Cinema, Its Spectator and the Avant-Garde," *Wide Angle* 8, no. 3 (1986): 57. For more, see Tom Brown, *Breaking the Fourth Wall: Direct Address in the Cinema* (Edinburgh: Edinburgh University Press, 2012), 2.

8. "Gallery Gods of Other Days," *Topeka Daily Capital* (30 October 1910); "Gallery Gods Must Be Suppressed," *Philadelphia Ledger*, 5 October 1902; Frances Trollope, *Domestic Manners of the Americans* (New York: Dodd and Mead, 1901), 187.

9. "The Human Note in Vaudeville," *NYS*, 29 November 1908.

10. Owen Kildare, "Behind the Scenes in Vaudeville," *Washington Evening Star*, 16 September 1906.

11. K-AVC, Managers' Reports, vol. 5, Philadelphia, Show, 26 March 1908; "Vaudeville in Yiddish," *New York Evening Sun*, 18 May 1903.

12. BRTD, ZAN T274, E. W. Sargent Scrapbook, "Williams and Walker's Farce," 20 November 1899. Unfortunately, the best study of the segregation of leisure facilities does not discuss theaters: Victoria W. Wolcott, *Race, Riots and Roller Coasters: The Struggle over Segregated Recreation in America* (Philadelphia: University of Pennsylvania Press, 2012).

13. "Vaudeville," *Philadelphia Public Ledger*, 11 October 1921; "Vaudeville's Thorny Road," *Scrap Book* 1, no. 6 (August 1906): 1082.

14. Edward Albee, "Twenty Years of Vaudeville," *Variety*, 6 September 1923; "Boston's News: $2,000,000 Theater," *Boston Globe*, 21 January 1916; "New Columbia Theater Opens," *Davenport (Iowa) Daily Times*, 18 December 1913; "New Orpheum's Bright Birth," *LAT*, 27 June 1911; "Opening of Summer Season," *WP*, 14 May 1901.

15. "Keith's Newest Theater," *PI*, 9 November 1902; Caroline Caffin, *Vaudeville* (New York: Scurfield, 1914), 10–11; "Seen from the Stage," *WP*, 9 May 1909; "The Vaudeville Look," *CDT*, 3 May 1906.

16. Indiana University, Archives of Traditional Music, Bea Walker, interview by John Hasse, 17 July 1979; B. F. Keith, "The Vogue of Vaudeville," *National Magazine*, November 1898, 146; Marsden Hartley, *Adventures in the Arts* (New York: Boni and Liveright, 1921), 173; William Dean Howells, "On Vaudeville," *Harper's Monthly Magazine*, April 1903, 813.

17. *Indianapolis Freeman*, 19 September 1914, cited in Lynn Abbott and Jack Stewart, "The Iroquois Theater," *Jazz Archivist* 9, no. 2 (December 1994): 8. The Pekin was founded by Robert T. Motts in 1905, and he made an effort to attract "the very best people" to his

theater; "Captain Rufus Makes Them Laugh," *New York Age*, 15 August 1907. Motts was a former saloon owner and associate of D. S. "Patsy" King, a white saloonkeeper who ran one of the biggest numbers games in Chicago. Motts also played the numbers and had a policy bank where customers gambled; "Must Have Held Some Bad Cards," *CDT*, 24 November 1894, and "Eye Open for Fraud," *CDT*, 21 November 1897. When authorities closed Motts's lottery business, he moved his barroom into the Pekin Theater. Lynn Abbott and Doug Seroff, *The Original Blues: The Emergence of the Blues in African American Vaudeville, 1899–1926* (Jackson: University of Mississippi Press, 2017), 57–60; Edward A. Robinson, "The Pekin: The Genesis of American Black Theater," *Black American Literature Forum*, Winter 1982, 136–38; "Only Colored Theater to Pass Over to Whites," *Pittsburgh Courier*, 8 September 1912; H. G. Wells, *The Future in America: A Search after Realities* (New York: Harper and Brothers, 1906), 196.

18. Michael Davis Jr., *The Exploitation of Pleasure: A Study of Commercial Recreation in New York City* (New York: Sage Foundation, 1911), 32–33; "Vaudeville Look"; Caffin, *Vaudeville*, 85; "The Other Side of Vaudeville," *Christian Science Monitor*, 31 August 1920, 10.

19. P. B. Chase, "Why Polite Vaudeville Is Popular," *Washington Times*, 20 June 1902.

20. U.S. Census, table 1027, motor vehicle registrations, http://www.allcountries.org/uscensus/1027_motor_vehicle_registrations.html; Thomas Bender, *The Unfinished City: New York and the Metropolitan Idea* (New York: New York University Press, 2007), 35–38; Joseph Korom Jr., *The American Skyscraper: A Celebration of Height* (Boston: Branden Books, 2008), 494–506; Paul Bourget, *Outre-mer: Impressions of America* (London: T. Fisher Unwin, 1895), 118.

21. "Pressing Darragh Hard," *NYS*, 22 April 1909; Robert Stuart, "Reducing the Costly Percentage of Failure Due to Our Eyes," *Health* 61, no. 11 (November 1911): 257; "Some Twentieth Century Advice," *Atlanta Constitution*, 1 February 1901.

22. William Crary Brownell, "New York after Paris," in *The Oxford Book of American Essays*, ed. Brander Matthews (New York: Oxford University Press, 1914), 446; W. R. Gowers, "Fatigue," *Eclectic Magazine of Foreign Literature* 144, no. 3 (March 1905): 347; J. H. Girdner, "The Plague of City Noise," *North American Review* 163, no. 478 (September 1896): 298; Bourget, *Outre-mer*, 27. See also Emily Thompson, *The Soundscape of Modernity: Architectural Acoustics and the Culture of Listening in America, 1900–1933* (Cambridge, Mass.: MIT Press, 2002), chapter 4.

23. David Shuster, *Neurasthenic Nation: America's Search for Health, Happiness, and Comfort, 1869–1920* (New Brunswick: Rutgers University Press, 2011), especially chapters 3 and 4; John Quackenbos, "Causes and Recent Treatment of Neurasthenia," *Medical and Surgical Reporter* 78, no. 4 (30 April 1898): 146 and 148.

24. F. G. Gosling, *Before Freud: Neurasthenia and the American Medical Community, 1870–1910* (Chicago: University of Chicago Press, 1987); Barbara Will, "The Nervous Origins of the American West," *American Literature* 70, no. 2 (1998): 293–316.

25. Arnold Daly, "The Vaudeville Audience and Bernard Shaw," *New York Evening Telegram*, 3 November 1906; BRTD, Robinson Locke Collection, Envelope 1575, Elizabeth Murray, clipping "Elizabeth Murray and Getting Over in Vaudeville," *New York Dramatic Mirror*, 1914; "The Vaudeville Patron," *Puck* 81, no. 2090 (24 March 1917): 19; "The Human Note in Vaudeville," *NYS*, 29 November 1908.

26. "Konorah Lightning Calculations," *Variety*, 7 September 1907; "Vaudeville No Refuge," *New York Herald*, 9 October 1921; BRTD, MWEZ+ n.c. 19064, Blanche Ring Scrapbook, clipping *San Francisco Examiner*, 27 April 1911; "Adele Rowland," *CDT*, 2 May 1909; "May Robson in New Comedy," *NYTr*, 5 September 1905.

27. "Press Eldridge Confesses," *NYT*, 28 February 1904; BRTD, Robinson Locke Collection, vol. 496, clipping "Waltz Me Professor"; "Imro Fox Dies in Hotel Chair," *NYMT*, 5 March 1910.

28. "Dunn Sisters," *Variety*, 30 July 1910; Henry Evans, "Adventures in Magic, the Chinese Question," *The Sphinx*, 18 September 1919, 160–61; "Massey and Kramer," *Variety*, 28 April 1906; "Emma Carus," *Variety*, 12 September 1908; "Riene Davies," *Variety*, 1 January 1910; "The Passing Show," *Washington Times*, 4 November 1900.

29. "This Knocks Them Out of Their Seats in Vaudeville," *CDT*, 28 March 1906.

30. BRTD, MWEZ+ n.c. 14339, W. C. Crowley Collection, clipping "Time Worn Witticism"; "Welch, Francis and Company," *Variety*, 1 February 1908; "Philadelphia Shows," *Variety*, 25 January 1908; "Hammerstein's," *Variety*, 13 January 1906.

31. Walter Benjamin, "The Work of Art in the Age of Mechanical Reproduction," in *Illuminations* (New York: Schocken Books, 1986), 233; "Amusements," *Pine Bluffs (Ark.) Daily Graphic*, 8 March 1908.

32. Caffin, *Vaudeville*, 27–29; "Harlem Opera House," *Variety*, 3 November 1906; "How to Make a Hit in Vaudeville," *Broadway Weekly*, 28 September 1904.

33. "Miss Billie Burke," *SFC*, 10 October 1909; Caffin, *Vaudeville*, 53–54; Nora Bayes, "Holding My Audience," *Theater Magazine*, September 1917, 128.

34. "Personality in Vaudeville," *NYT*, 19 June 1912; "Grace Edmonds," *Wilmington Evening Journal*, 5 February 1910.

35. BRTD, MWEZ+ n.c. 21050, Ned Wayburn Scrapbook, clipping *Waterbury Republican*, 4 February 1912.

36. Owen Kildare, "Behind the Scenes in Vaudeville," *Washington Evening Star*, 16 September 1906.

37. "Public Is Blamed," *SFC*, 13 February 1909; BRTD, MWEZ+ n.c. 2203, Scrapbook Relating to New York Theater, clipping "Manager Miner's Views"; Walter De Leon, "The Wow Finish," *Saturday Evening Post*, 14 February 1925, reprinted in Charles W. Stein, ed., *American Vaudeville as Seen by Its Contemporaries* (New York: Alfred A. Knopf, 1984), 199–200.

38. "A Crushed Actor Detective," *NYS*, 1 May 1901; K-AVC, Managers' Reports, vol. 1, New York Show, week of 2 March 1903; "Cissy Loftus Outwitted," *Boston Globe*, 19 May 1901.

39. George Fuller Golden, *My Lady Vaudeville and Her White Rats* (New York: White Rats of America, 1909), 67; NUSC, MS 133, McIntyre and Heath Collection, box 5, file 20, Foster Feltmore to McIntyre and Heath, 9 April 1928; "Fifth Avenue," *Variety*, 18 April 1908. Alice was preferred in America to her sister, Marie, who was the more popular in England. Some spectators thought Marie depended too much upon suggestiveness: K-AVC, Managers' Reports, vol. 6, Boston Show, week of 2 December 1907.

40. BRTD, MWEZ+ n.c. 19702, Irene Bordoni Scrapbook, clipping "Bordoni Sings," *Cleveland News*, 9 November 1921; "Did You Hear?," *New York Herald*, 13 November

1921; Forrest Davis, "Americans the Best Audience in the World," *New York Herald*, 10 September 1922; Caffin, *Vaudeville*, 20.

41. "Laurant Describes a Magician's Profession," *Lyceum News*, November 1914; "The Elevation of Magic," *M-U-M,* December 1912; Jean-Eugène Robert-Houdin, *Secrets of Conjuring and Magic or How to Become a Wizard*, trans. Louis Hoffman, (New York: Cambridge University Press, 2011), 43.

42. "Eva Fay," *Variety*, 15 April 1911; K-AVC, Managers' Reports, vol. 6, Philadelphia Show, week of 26 February 1906; Harry Ransom Center, University of Texas, Harry Houdini Papers, box 1, Professor De Louie, undated playbill, and box 2, promotional circular for Eva Fay, 11 July 1926; K-AVC, Managers' Reports, vol. 7, Philadelphia Show, week of 24 September 1907.

43. "Laurant Describes a Magician's Profession"; on the popularity of magicians, see Robert Toll, *The First Century of Show Business in America* (New York: Oxford University Press, 1976), 284.

44. "Cleverness," *M-U-M* 2, April 1914; "Elevation of Magic"; "Professional Ethics," *M-U-M* 1, December 1911; "Laurant Describes a Magician's Profession."

45. "Music and Stage," *LAT*, 28 March 1912; K-AVC, Managers' Reports, vol. 11, Hudson Theater Show, Union Hill, week of 6 February 1911.

46. *Chicago Sunday Tribune*, 2 October 1909; "Pauline the Hypnotist at Fulton Theater," *Brooklyn Standard Union*, 7 September 1909; "Polis and Old Dr. Pauline," *Bridgeport (Conn.) Times and Evening Farmer*, 17 September 1915; K-AVC, Managers' Reports, vol. 9, Grand Opera House, Pittsburgh, week of 14 October 1908.

47. "Hammerstein's," *Variety*, 1 February 1908; Caffin, *Vaudeville*, 32–35.

48. Bayes, "Holding My Audience," 128.

49. Bert Williams, "The Comic Side of Trouble," *American Magazine*, January 1918, 33; K-AVC, Managers' Reports, vol. 9, Philadelphia Show, week of 30 November 1908; "Eva Tanguay," *Variety*, 28 January 1908.

50. "Four Georgia Belles," *Variety*, 13 July 1907; "Lincoln Square," *Variety*, 17 October 1908.

51. BRTD, Robinson Locke Collection, NAFR+, series 2, vol. 297, Eva Tanguay, clipping "Undone by a Song," *Theater Magazine* 37, no. 147 (May 1913), and clipping *Cleveland Leader*, 12 October 1913.

52. "Vaudeville's Thorny Road," 1082; Henry Jenkins, *What Made Pistachio Nuts? Early Sound Comedy and the Vaudeville Aesthetic* (New York: Columbia University Press, 1992), 61; Caffin, *Vaudeville*, 21.

53. Henry James, "Baltimore," *North American Review* 183 (August 1906): 264; BRTD, Hoffman Papers, box 21, Palace Theater version of Lew Dockstader's monologue "My Policies," 3 August 1914, 8.

54. Robert Grant, "The Tired Business Man," *Yale Review* 7 (October 1917): 65, 68–69, and 71.

55. "Work and Then Some!," *Oakland Tribune*, 21 December 1912; "Back to Vaudeville," *Brooklyn Daily Eagle*, 12 September 1915; "William Hammerstein, the Vaudeville Epicure," *New York Evening Telegram*, 3 November 1906.

CHAPTER FOUR

1. Anne Witchard, "Introduction: The Lucid Atmosphere of Fine Cathay," in *British Modernism and Chinoiserie*, ed. Anne Witchard (Edinburgh: Edinburgh University Press, 2015), 15; Lloyd Spencer, "It Is the Craze," *Burlington Evening Gazette*, 26 January 1907; "Houses, Prices and Plays," *Brooklyn Daily Standard Union*, 13 September 1903.

2. "Fashion Letter," *Lincoln (Neb.) Courier*, 11 January 1900.

3. Richard Pells, *Modernist America: Art, Music, Movies and the Globalization of American Culture* (New Haven: Yale University Press, 2012), x; "Back to Vaudeville," *Brooklyn Daily Eagle*, 12 September 1915.

4. Alison Lee, *Realism and Power: Postmodern British Fictions* (Abingdon: Routledge, 1990), 5.

5. "Orpheum in Peoria," *Peoria Journal*, 26 April 1912; Sherry Lee, "The Other in the Mirror, or Recognizing the Self: Wilde's and Zemlinsky's Dwarf," *Music and Letters* 9, no. 2 (May 2010): 198–223; K-AVC, Managers' Reports, vol. 5, Philadelphia Show, week of 26 March 1906.

6. Tim Armstrong, *Modernism: A Cultural History* (London: Polity, 2005); Tom Gunning, "Chaplin and the Body of Modernity," *Early Popular Visual Culture* 8, no. 3 (2010): 237–45; Johnathan Goldman, *Modernism Is the Literature of Celebrity* (Austin: University of Texas Press, 2011), 111.

7. As Louis Menard pointed out, the "It" in "Make It New" was "the old." Louis Menard, "The Pound Error: The Elusive Master of Allusion," *New Yorker*, 9 June 2008; BRTD, Aaron Hoffman Papers, box 25, file Squidgulum (1915), 6; "At the Varieties," *NYT*, 25 May 1910.

8. "American Roof," *Variety*, 9 March 1917.

9. "Pastor's," *Variety*, 27 July 1907. It was not an uncommon trick—in 1911 Bauman and Sturn had an act where one appeared as the theater manager to reported that he'd called the booking agent for a replacement act and immediately a sprightly fellow appeared who, unbeknownst to the supposed manager, was a plumber who'd been palmed off on them because the agent had no acts available. "Bauman, Stern and Co.," *Variety*, 8 January 1910.

10. BRTD, Aaron Hoffman Papers, box 25, file Squidgulum (1915), 18.

11. "Cameron and Flanagan," *Variety*, 22 December 1906; K-AVC, Managers' Reports, vol. 10, Pittsburgh Show, week of 20 June 1909; "5th Avenue," *Variety*, 22 December 1906.

12. K-AVC, Managers' Reports, vol. 2, Chase's Theater Show, week of 4 January 1904; "Blessed A Sues Babing Wabe," *NYS*, 21 July 1904; K-AVC, Managers' Reports, vol. 10, Philadelphia Show, week of 15 February 1909; "Minstrel Misses Are the Maids for Me," *NYMT*, 25 June 1903; "Bertie Herron," *Variety*, 15 December 1906; "Shea's Theater," *Buffalo Courier*, 15 August 1909; K-AVC, Managers' Reports, vol. 11, Bijou Theater Show, Woonsocket, week of 7 March 1910; "Playhouses," *Albany Times Union*, 22 July 1913.

13. Woods cited in Miriam Hansen, *Babel and Babylon: Spectatorship in American Silent Film* (Cambridge, Mass.: Harvard University Press, 1991), 37.

14. T. S. Eliot, "The Metaphysical Poets," in *Selected Prose of T. S. Eliot*, ed. Frank Kermode (London: Faber and Faber, 1975), 65.

15. "The Theater in Current Print," *Theater Arts Monthly* 13, no. 1 (January 1929): 63.

16. "The Romance of the Zancigs," *Decatur Herald*, 9 February 1902; "Space and

Walls No Barrier," *PI*, 24 February 1907; "American Thought Readers," *The Tennessean*, 15 March 1907.

17. "The Mysterious Howards," *Variety*, 24 November 1906; "Why?," *CT*, 7 January 1912; "Analysis of a Problem," *Winnipeg Tribune*, 1 March 1904; "Telepathic Problems Carefully Analyzed," *Bakersfield (Calif.) Morning Echo*, 15 October 1903.

18. "New Ideas in Conjuring," *Minneapolis Journal*, 9 November 1913; Henry Whitely, "Horace Goldin's Program," *The Sphinx*, 3 January 1905, 138; BRTD, Robinson Locke Collection, envelope 514, Horace Goldin, clipping *Minneapolis Journal*, 10 November 1915, and unmarked clipping dated 28 October 1913. "Horace Goldin has a remarkable mysticism act ending in the apparent shooting of the woman into a trunk across the heads of the audience." Ernest Waitt, "Boston," *Variety*, 15 February 1908.

19. "Bills of the Week," *Omaha Daily Bee*, 19 February 1911; "Hammerstein's," *Variety*, 16 January 1909; "Hymack Has Big Spectacular Act," *SFC*, 11 December 1910; "A Vaudeville Oddity," *Washington Herald*, 9 May 1909.

20. K-AVC, Managers' Reports, vol. 11, Providence Show, week of 10 April 1911; "Konorah's Lightning Calculations," *Variety*, 7 September 1907; K-AVC, Managers' Reports, vol. 8, Keith and Proctor's 125th Street Show, week of 5 January 1908; "Woman of Mystery," *Variety*, 5 October 1907.

21. Armstrong, *Modernism*, chapter 6.

22. Djuna Barnes, "Interviewing Arthur Voegtlin Is Something Like Having a Nightmare," in *I Could Never Be Lonely without a Husband: Interviews by Djuna Barnes*, ed. Alyce Barry (College Park, Md.: Sun and Moon Press, 1985), 81; Djuna Barnes, "Superstitions of Sensible New Yorkers," *NYTr*, 20 February 1916; Margaret Bockting, "Performers and the Erotic in Four Interviews by Djuna Barnes," *Centennial Review*, 41, no. 1 (Winter 1997): 183–95; Kathleen Spies, "Girls and Gags: Sexual Display and Humor in Reginald Marsh's Burlesque Image," *American Art* 18 (Summer 2004): 35–58; Peter Nicholls, *Modernisms: A Literary Guide* (London: Palgrave Macmillan, 1995), 193–222.

23. "The Submarine," *New York Dramatic Mirror*, 21 November 1908; "Stage Comings and Goings," *NYS*, 25 April 1909; "Colonial," *Variety*, 14 November 1908.

24. BRTD, MWEZ+ n.c. 19457, Will Cressy and Blanche Dayne Pressbook, clipping "Vaudeville." On censorship in the legitimate theater, see John H. Houchin, *Censorship and the American Theater in the Twentieth Century* (New York: Cambridge University Press, 2003), chapter 2; Theresa Saxon, "Sexual Transgression on the American Stage: Clyde Fitch, Sappho and the 'American Girl,'" *Literature Compass* 10, no. 10 (October 2013): 744; K-AVC, Managers' Reports, vol. 9, Boston Show, week of 5 October 1908 and week of 12 October 1908; "Vaudeville Managers Unite," *NYT*, 2 March 1911; and Andrew Erdman, *Blue Vaudeville: Sex, Morals and the Mass Marketing of Amusement, 1895–1915* (Jefferson, N.C.: McFarland, 2004), chapter 2. Maybeth Hamilton, *When I'm Bad I'm Better: Mae West, Sex and American Entertainment* (Berkeley: University of California Press, 1997), 32–37, suggests managers constrained sexual play in vaudeville and that the theater was more conservative than its audiences. BRTD, Robinson Locke Collection, envelope 2050, Blossom Seeley, clipping *Vanity Fair*, 1 March 1911.

25. "The Vaudevilles," *Louisville Courier-Journal*, 22 March 1908; "Colonial," *Variety*, 25 January 1908; "Eva Tanguay," *Minneapolis Star Tribune*, 22 September 1913.

26. "A Chorus of Chimpanzees," *Washington Times*, 24 January 1904; BRTD,

MWEZ+ n.c. 19064, Emma Carus Scrapbook, clipping (January 1904?); Gus Edwards and Will Cobb, "In Zanzibar (My Little Chimpanzee)" (New York: Shapiro, Remick and Co., 1904).

27. K-AVC, Managers' Reports, vol. 10, Keith's Hippodrome Show, Cleveland, week of 20 February 1909; for more on Shaw see M. Alison Kibler, "Nothing Succeeds Like Excess: Lillian Shaw's Comedy and Sexuality on the Keith Circuit," in *Performing Gender and Comedy: Theories, Texts and Contexts*, ed. Shannon Hengen (Amsterdam: Gordon and Breach, 1998), 59–80. K-AVC, Managers' Reports, vol. 10, Boston Show, week of 10 May 1909.

28. William Trufant Foster, *Vaudeville and Motion Picture Shows: A Study of Theaters in Portland, Oregon* (Portland: Reed College Social Service Series, 1914), 10 and 36. John C. Burnham ("The Progressive-Era Revolution in American Attitudes toward Sex," *Journal of American History* 59 (March 1973): 885–908) thought there was a sexual revolution in the Progressive Era. In more recent years the emphasis shifted, and progressivism came to be seen as successfully repressing the public display of "vernacular sexuality." Andrea Friedman, *Prurient Interests: Gender, Democracy and Obscenity in New York City, 1909–1945* (New York: Columbia University Press, 2000); Barbara Meil Hobson, *Uneasy Virtue: The Politics of Prostitution and the American Reform Tradition* (Chicago: University of Chicago Press, 1990), chapter 6; David Langum, *Crossing over the Line: Legislating Morality and the Mann Act* (Chicago: University of Chicago Press, 1994); Michael Trask, *Cruising Modernism: Class and Sexuality in American Literature and Social Thought* (Ithaca: Cornell University Press, 2003), chapter 1. Even more recent works argue that the dichotomy between sexual freedom and bourgeois repression has been drawn too starkly. As Leigh Ann Wheeler observes, "The liberalizing sexual trend emancipated even the women it horrified, because the same sexual freedom that encouraged sexual expression released women to speak openly against sexual amusements." *Against Obscenity: Reform and the Politics of Womanhood in America, 1873–1935* (Baltimore: Johns Hopkins University Press, 2007), 182–83.

29. [Percy] Hammond, "Billie Burke," *CT*, 28 November 1909; "Hammerstein's," *Variety*, 21 April 1906; "Grecian Dancing Girls," *Variety*, 21 January 1911.

30. The best history of the Salome phenomenon is Larry Hamberlin, "Visions of Salome: The Femme Fatale in American Popular Songs before 1920," *Journal of the American Musicological Society* 59, no. 3 (2006): 631–96; see also Isabel Joyce, "Sinuous Salome," *Washington Times*, 26 July 1908. Reporters were curious to know what it felt like to have her body so exposed onstage, and La Sylphe reassured them that she wore a corset under her bodice and that she was "cased in silk tights from her shoulder to her midleg." BRTD. Robinson Locke Collection, envelope 1110, La Sylphe, clipping "La Sylphe to Do Her Salome"; "Her Sheath Gown Nothing but Slits," *New York Telegram*, 18 July 1908.

31. BRTD, Robinson Locke Collection, envelope 1110, La Sylphe, clipping "125th Street Theater."

32. BRTD, Princess Rajah clipping file; K-AVC, Managers' Reports, vol. 10, Maryland Theater Show, Baltimore, week of 30 August 1909.

33. "Vampire Dance," *Detroit Free Press*, 2 January 1910; "Vampire Dance," *Jackson (Miss.) Daily News*, 8 April 1911; for managers' opinions of the dance see K-AVC, Managers' Reports, vol. 10, Columbus Show, week of 30 January 1909, and Maryland Theater Show, Baltimore, week of 30 September 1909.

34. "Ada Lewis," *Oakland Tribune*, 4 October 1925; "New York Notes," *SFC*, 27 May 1891; "Ada Lewis," *SFC*, 14 September 1900.

35. BRTD, NAFR, series 2, Robinson Locke Collection, vol. 298, Adele Rowland, clipping "Way with a Woman," 28 November 1909; Castle cited in Lisa Tickner, "The Popular Culture of Kermesse: Lewis, Painting and Performance, 1912–13," in *In Visible Touch: Modernism and Masculinity*, ed. Terry Smith (Chicago: University of Chicago Press, 1998), 161.

36. In 1902 the American Mutoscope and Biograph Company filmed someone named "Kid" Foley, who may have been the boxer, doing a "tough dance" with a performer called Sailor Lil. As was typical of these dances, the two performers approached each other from opposite directions, and the man began the act by slapping the woman, then throwing her to the floor. The dance itself involved little more than some jerky jumping, though in the filmed version both performers end by tumbling on the floor and rolling over each other. The film ends with Foley lying on top of Lil, in a probable reference to sex.

37. "5th Avenue," *Variety*, 2 October 1912; "Swelldom Smitten with Fascination of Wiggle Dances," *Oakland Tribune*, 25 June 1911; "Texas Tommy Dancers," *Variety*, 20 April 1912. The group later boasted that it did "graceful executions" of the dance; "Texas Tommy Dancers," *Oakland Tribune*, 19 December 1911.

38. Anthony Giddens, *Modernity and Self-Identity: Self and Society in the Late Modern Age* (Cambridge: Polity Press, 1991); T. J. Jackson Lears, *No Place of Grace: Antimodernism and the Transformation of American Culture, 1880–1920* (New York: Pantheon, 1981), 35–37; Susan Glenn, "'Give an Imitation of Me': Vaudeville Mimics and the Play of the Self," *American Quarterly* 50, no. 1 (1998): 61; Warren I. Susman, "'Personality' and the Making of Twentieth Century Culture," in *Culture as History: The Transformation of American Society in the Twentieth Century* (New York, 1973), 222–86.

39. "Ada Reeve," *SFC*, 11 December 1911; Caffin, *Vaudeville*, 164–65; "London Stage Songs," *SFC*, 10 July 1892.

40. Caffin, *Vaudeville*, 165–66; Leo Levy, "Ada Reeve Is Merely—Ada Reeve," *Oakland Tribune*, 22 January 1912; "A Happy Marriage Is My Secret," *Buffalo Enquirer*, 23 October 1912.

41. "National," *Variety*, 5 September 1908; "Hyde and Seeman's," *Variety*, 14 April 1906.

42. "Twenty-Third Street," *Variety*, 9 June 1906; "Eddie Foy," *Variety*, 19 May 1906.

43. Juliet, "How We Imitate Actors Like You," *Green Book Magazine*, December 1912, 1064–69; Nora Bayes, "Holding My Audience," *Theater Magazine*, September 1917, 128; "Ada Reeve," *Oakland Tribune*, 22 January 1912; Hammond, "Billie Burke." See, for example, "The Truth about Eva Tanguay," *Pittsburgh Daily Post*, 5 May 1912.

44. "The Truth about Eva Tanguay"; "May Irwin," *Kenna (N.M.) Record*, 27 June 1913; "Eddie Foy," *Pittsburgh Press*, 22 March 1908; Doulas Mao, *Solid Objects: Modernism and the Test of Production* (Princeton: Princeton University Press, 1988), 11.

45. O. Henry, *Cabbages and Kings* (New York: McClure, Phillips and Co., 1904), 341.

46. Michael Davis Jr., *The Exploitation of Pleasure: A Study of Commercial Recreation in New York City* (New York: Sage Foundation, 1911), 32–33; Marsden Hartley, "Vaudeville," *The Dial*, March 1920, 343, in Harvard Theatre Collection, Houghton Library, file Vaudeville and Variety, 1920.

CHAPTER FIVE

1. William M. Marston, *F. F. Proctor: Vaudeville Pioneer* (New York: R. R. Smith, 1943), 114.

2. "F. F. Proctor Once Acrobatic Performer," *Brooklyn Daily Eagle*, 8 September 1929; "A Mad Actor," *Detroit Free Press*, 11 May 1881; "F. F. Proctor," *NYC*, 21 January 1888; "Regional News," *NYC*, 26 April 1884; "New Jersey News," *NYC*, 26 January 1884; advertisement, *NYC*, 8 September 1883; "Albany News," *NYC*, 14 June 1884; "H. R. Jacobs Dead," *NYC*, 9 January 1915.

3. On variety saloons, see David Monod, *The Soul of Pleasure: Sentiment and Sensation in Nineteenth-Century American Mass Entertainment* (Ithaca: Cornell University Press, 2016), chapter 4; Gillian Rodger, *Champagne Charlie and Pretty Jemima: Variety Theater in the Nineteenth Century* (Urbana: University of Illinois Press, 2010); and Brooks McNamara, *The New York Concert Saloon: The Devil's Own Nights* (New York: Cambridge University Press, 2002). On museums, see Andrea Stulman Dennett, *Weird and Wonderful: The Dime Museum in America* (New York: New York University Press, 1997).

4. "Albany News," *NYC*, 1 November 1884.

5. NUSC, MS 133, McIntyre and Heath Collection, box 6, "A Trial Marriage" (typescript 1916), 5; NA, FTC, Direct Examination of James McIntyre, 14 October 1919, 2654; UASC, MS 421, American Vaudeville Museum Collection, box 1, file 9, clipping J. J. Murdock, "The Evolution of Vaudeville"; Albert McLean, "Genesis of Vaudeville: Two Letters from B. F. Keith," *Theater Survey* 1 (1960): 82–95; "B. F. Keith," *NYC*, 1 December 1888.

6. "New York News," *NYC*, 25 December 1886; "Albany News," *NYC*, 17 November 1888.

7. "Albany News," *NYC*, 17 November 1888. "A New Departure at Proctor's," *New York Dramatic Mirror*, 1 November 1892, names the most successful plays put on by Proctor's stock company; most were melodramas. On the idea that combination catered to all tastes, see "The Howard Athenaeum," *Boston Daily Globe*, 11 August 1874; and Timothy D. Connors, "American Vaudeville Managers: Their Organization and Influence" (Ph.D. diss., University of Kansas, 1981), 25–27.

8. "Dramatic and Musical Notes: Letter from Proctor," *NYC*, 24 November 1888; "Dissolution of a Theatrical Firm," *Brooklyn Daily Eagle*, 15 November 1888; "Managers Proctor and Jacobs Trying to Outdo Each Other," *New York Evening World*, 25 January 1888; see, for example, advertisements in the *New York Sun*, 11 December 1898.

9. "A Talk with J. Austin Fynes," *New York Dramatic Mirror*, 20 July 1901; "F. F. Proctor," *NYTr*, 8 May 1900; advertisement for Proctor's, *NYS*, 7 April 1901.

10. "Manager Proctor's New Theater," *NYT*, 4 November 1894; "Manager Proctor's New Theater," *NYT*, 28 July 1895; "Proctor's Pleasure Palace," *NYC*, 27 July 1895.

11. For the early history of Keith's, see Arthur Wertheim, *Vaudeville Wars: How the Keith-Albee and Orpheum Circuits Controlled the Big Time and Its Performers* (New York: Palgrave Macmillan, 2006), 4–13. NA, FTC, Examination of James McIntyre, 14 October 1919, 2653; Harry Scott, "Origin of the Continuous," *New York Dramatic Mirror*, 7 December 1895; Murdock, "Evolution of Vaudeville"; K-AVC, Managers' Reports, vol. 3, Boston Show, week of 27 April 1903.

12. "Pilling's Popular Theater," *NYC*, 5 October 1889; "New York News," *NYC*,

21 January 1893. An acrobat recalled playing fourteen shows in one day at Huber's Museum in the 1890s; see NA, FTC, Examination of Charles Grapewin, 19 October 1919, 2541.

13. "F. F. Proctor," *NYC*, 29 June 1912; "Chicot" [Epes Sargent] "Vaudeville Artists Will Have to Work for Smaller Salaries," *New York Morning Telegraph*, 29 July 1901; NA, FTC, Cross-Examination of Daniel Hennessy, 27 March 1919, 978; "Lillian Russell Signed," *NYS*, 5 August 1905.

14. Beck cited in Wertheim, *Vaudeville Wars*, 63; Orpheum ticket prices from advertisements in *SFC*, 1 January 1906; Percy Williams, "Vaudeville and Vaudevillians," *Saturday Evening Post*, 5 June 1909, 16–17.

15. NA, FTC, Examination of Bernard Myers, 6 February 1919, 503; and Cross-Examination of Daniel Hennessy, 27 March 1919, 983. The average Loew's house in 1918 spent around $1,600 a week on acts, a year when the average big time was spending $5,000–6,000: Examination of Fred C. Schanberger, 16 October 1919, 2906 and 2909.

16. NA, FTC, Cross-Examination of Frank Fogarty, 28 March 1919, 1235; FTC, Cross-Examination of James William Fitzpatrick, 22 May 1919, 2079; K-AVC, Managers' Reports, vol. 8, Keith Theater, Providence Show, week of 2 March 1908; "Atlanta Entitled to the Best in Vaudeville," *Atlanta Constitution*, 3 December 1920.

17. "Edward F. Albee," *Brooklyn Daily Eagle*, 15 March 1923; Richard Allen, *Horrible Prettiness: Burlesque and American Culture* (Chapel Hill: University of North Carolina Press, 1991), 184–85; Frank Copley, "The Story of a Great Vaudeville Manager," *American Magazine*, December 1922, 47. Albee's father was a shipwright who later joined the police force; they lived in a well-to-do neighborhood. "The Life Story of E. F. Albee," *Boston Sunday Post*, 16 January 1901.

18. "Boston News," *NYC*, 16 September 1893; "B. F. Keith's Gift," *PI*, 2 June 1900; "E. F. Albee Had Given Fifty Years to the Theater," *NYMT*, 24 December 1922; Murdock, "Evolution of Vaudeville"; "Keith Abandons Continuous Vaudeville," *Billboard*, 24 April 1909; "The Vaudeville Situation," *New York Dramatic Mirror*, 12 September 1908.

19. Poem written on opening of Keith's Boston, cited in Wertheim, *Vaudeville Wars*, 83.

20. NUSC, MS 133, McIntyre and Heath Collection, box 1, "Memoirs of James McIntyre" (typescript), 5; "Early San Francisco Variety Theaters," *New York Dramatic Mirror*, 1 January 1910; "Boom in Vaudeville," *CDT*, 21 April 1902; "Vaudeville Theater List," *Billboard*, 15 December 1906; "$2,000 Pop Show," *Variety*, 16 April 1910.

21. "Ten Cent Vaudeville," *New York Dramatic Mirror*, 1 July 1905; Alfred Bernheim, "The Facts of Vaudeville," *Equity News*, September–November 1923, reprinted in *American Vaudeville as Seen by Its Contemporaries*, ed. Charles W. Stein (New York: Alfred A. Knopf, 1984), 129; NA, FTC, Re-direct of Daniel Hennessy, 27 March 1919, 999; "Variety Theaters in Greater New York," *Variety*, 4 September 1914.

22. NA, FTC, Brief for Attorneys for the Federal Trade Commission, 25 June 1918, 120; United States, *Hearings before the Committee on the Judiciary*, ser. 7, vol. 3, part 21 (Washington: Government Printing Office, 1914), 1240–41; NA, FTC, Final Arguments, 16 February 1920, 3355.

23. "United Booking Offices, Eastern Office," *Variety*, 16 March 1907; NA, FTC, Brief of the Attorneys for the Federal Trade Commission, 25 June 1918, 3–4, and Final Arguments, 16 February 1920, 3248; "$725,000 a Week," *Shreveport Times*, 14 December 1913;

NA, FTC, Examination of Pat Casey, 3 February 1919, 303, and Examination of S. K. Hodgdon, 6 February 1919, 513; Vaudeville Managers Protective Association, *Year Book 1912* (Chicago: General Publicity Service, 1912), 21.

24. NA, FTC, Examination of Pat Casey, 3 February 1919, 47, and Examination of S. K. Hodgdon, 6 February 1919, 520.

25. "Managers George Castle and John D. Hopkins," *NYC*, 24 July 1897; "Big Western Combine," *New York Dramatic Mirror*, 3 December 1898; "Great Theater Combine," *NYTr*, 30 May 1900; "Illinois News," *NYC*, 3 February 1900; "Plan Hits the Actor's Pay," *CDT*, 21 May 1900; "Chicago News," *NYC*, 3 February 1900; "Another Vaudeville Trust," *NYT*, 15 July 1901.

26. McIntyre remembered the London Theater being the only one willing to play "Western acts"; NUSC, MS 133, McIntyre and Heath Collection, box 1, "Memoirs of James McIntyre," 69. "Massachusetts News," *NYC*, 26 May 1900; "The Vaudeville Managers," *NYTr*, 22 May 1900.

27. NA, FTC, Examination of S. K. Hodgdon, 6 February 1919, 568 and 545.

28. The Rats claimed a membership of 500 at the time of the strike. "White Rats to Admit Women," *New York Dramatic Mirror*, 26 January 1901; "Theaters Bar the White Rats," *CDT*, 23 February 1901; "White Rats Strike," *Baltimore Sun*, 22 February 1901.

29. "Vaudeville Managers Decide to Abolish All Commissions," *NYT*, 7 March 1901; "F. F. Proctor Draws Out," *NYTr*, 22 April 1901; "White Rats Unable to Use an Opportunity," *CDT*, 26 April 1901; "Commission Abolished Here," *Chicago Inter Ocean*, 7 March 1901; "White Rats Victory," *Chicago Inter Ocean*, 9 March 1901.

30. "What the White Rats Want," *Washington Evening Times*, 1 March 1901; "F. F. Proctor Draws Out"; "Col. Hopkins New Policy," *NYMT*, 12 February 1902.

31. "Rumored Split in Vaudeville," *NYMT*, 27 April 1904; Chicot, "Now the Question Arises—What Is the Vaudeville Managers Association Anyway?," *New York Morning Telegraph*, 8 March 1903; "Percy G. Williams Stands Trial," *New York Dramatic Mirror*, 28 March 1903; "Percy G. Williams Is Out," *New York Dramatic Mirror*, 19 April 1903.

32. Chicot, "Now the Question Arises."

33. "Here with Cash," *Minneapolis Journal*, 12 January 1904; "Will Cressy Talks of Modern Vaudeville," *New York Star*, 23 January 1909; Hartley Davis, "The Business Side of Vaudeville," *Everybody's Magazine*, October 1907, 528.

34. "Orpheum Circuit," *Winnipeg Tribune*, 16 November 1912; "New Combine Born in Theater Land," *NYT*, April 28, 1907; Sime [Sime Silverman], "The Question of Combination," *Variety*, 5 May 1906; "The Usher," *New York Dramatic Mirror*, 12 May 1906; "New Syndicate Afoot," *NYT*, 1 May 1906.

35. Fynes and Proctor ostensibly parted amicably, but the *Clipper* reported that their relationship had been strained for a year: "Fynes and Proctor Part," *NYC*, 16 December 1905. See also "Mr. Fynes Out for Himself," *NYT*, 11 March 1906; "Proctor's Fifth Avenue Sold," *NYS*, 26 April 1906; and "The Proctor Keith Deal," *Variety*, 5 May 1906. According to *Variety*, it was Keith who orchestrated the moves of 1906, not Albee. "B. F. Keith Declared Himself," *Variety*, 1 September 1906.

36. "S. Z. Poli Dies," *Brooklyn Daily Eagle*, 1 June 1937; "The Poli-Keith Deal," *Variety*, 5 May 1906; "The Vaudeville Situation Assumes Definite Shape," *Billboard*, 26 May 1906;

Nina Purdy, "You've Got to Have Nerve," *Everybody's Magazine*, November 1925, cited in Wertheim, *Vaudeville Wars*, 120.

37. "The Big Merger Completed," *New York Dramatic Mirror*, 23 June 1906; "The Situation" and "Keith Reported after More," *Variety*, 22 September 1906; "Vaudeville Combination Effected," *Billboard*, 23 February 1907.

38. "Vaudeville War Now On," *NYT*, 17 February 1907; "Vaudeville War Ends," *Brooklyn Daily Eagle*, 8 November 1907. The best survey of the struggle is Wertheim, *Vaudeville Wars*, part 4.

39. "New Vaudeville War," *NYT*, 8 November 1907; UASC, MS 438, Arthur Frank Wertheim Collection, box 4, file 16, photocopy B. F. Keith to Lee and Jacob Shubert, 10 April 1913. The amount of the payoff (slightly inflated) was eventually revealed in a trial in 1922; Douglas Gilbert, *American Vaudeville: Its Life and Times* (New York: McGraw-Hill, 1940), 238. The figures presented here were different from the ones reported at the time: "Keith and Proctor Get Control of Vaudeville," *PI*, 15 November 1907; "Loew-Sullivan-Considine Deal," *The Player*, 14 April 1911; "Heavy Losses in Vaudeville Field," *San Francisco Chronicle*, 15 November 1907.

40. UASC, MS 421, American Vaudeville Museum Collection, box 1, file 14, New Orpheum Theater, *Orpheum Circuit of Theaters* (New York: Orpheum Theater and Realty Company, 1909), 14. Standardized prices led to regionally coordinated price increases; "Price Raise Is Uniform," *Elmira (N.Y.) Star-Gazette*, 22 September 1923.

41. *New Orleans Daily Picayune* cited in Lynn Abbott and Doug Seroff, *Ragged but Right: Black Traveling Shows, "Coon Songs," and the Dark Pathway to Blues and Jazz* (Jackson: University of Mississippi Press, 2007), 86; "S. H. Dudley Is Man of Wealth," *Pittsburgh Courier*, 25 September 1926.

42. Athelia Knight, "In Retrospect: Sherman H Dudley: He Paved the Way for T.O.B.A.," *Black Perspective in Music* 15, no. 2 (Autumn 1987): 165–72; Stephen K. Huff, "The Urban Geography of Theater in a New South City: Memphis, 1890–1920" (Ph.D. diss., City University of New York, 2012); "New Theater for New York," *Salt Lake City Broad Ax*, 9 December 1911; "There Are Many Colored Thespians," *PI*, 17 September 1922.

43. "The Amusements," *Chicago Inter Ocean*, 11 May 1877; Lynn Abbott and Doug Seroff, *Out of Sight: The Rise of African American Popular Music, 1889–1895* (Jackson: University of Mississippi Press, 2002); Abbott and Seroff, *Ragged but Right*; Monod, *Soul of Pleasure*, chapter 7.

44. "Hogan Engaged," *Anaconda (Mont.) Standard*, 28 April 1893; "Back Again," *Anaconda Standard*, 28 October 1893. For example, in 1884 Lewis performed at the Tivoli in Sacramento; "Tivoli," *Sacramento Record-Union*, 5 April 1884. "Weber and Fields," *Chicago Inter Ocean*, 9 January 1898.

45. "The Stage," *Colored American*, 25 May 1901; Ernest Hogan, "The Negro in Vaudeville," *Variety*, 15 December 1906; "The Orpheum," *SFC*, 16 April 1899.

46. BRTD, ZAN T274, E. W. Sargent Scrapbook, clipping *New York Telegram*, 30 October 1898; "The Stage," *Pittsburgh Press*, 21 October 1898. On the Black Cats, see "The Stage," *Colored American*, 16 March 1901; "Black Cats," *Baltimore Sun*, 25 February 1901; and "Black Cats Combine to Fight White Rats," *Brooklyn Daily Eagle*, 23 February 1901.

47. Hogan's story appeared in the *New York Journal*, quoted in Henry T. Samson, *The*

Ghost Walked: A Chronological History of Blacks in Show Business, 1865–1910 (Metuchen, N.J.: Scarecrow, 1988), 222. James Weldon Johnson, *Black Manhattan* (New York: Alfred A. Knopf, 1930), 127–28. On the riot, see Gilbert Orofsky, "Race Riot 1900: A Study in Ethnic Violence," *Journal of Negro Education* 32, no. 1 (Winter 1963): 16–24; and Martha Hodes, "Knowledge and Indifference in the New York City Race Riot of 1900: An Argument in Search of a Story," *Rethinking History* 15, no. 1 (March 2011): 61–89.

48. BRTD, ZAN T274, E. W. Sargent Scrapbook, clipping 30 October 1902. The Rats claimed that colored performers worked for considerably less than white ones.

49. "A Word of Warning," *The Player*, 24 March 1911; "White Rats Did Not Object," *NYT*, 25 April 1925; "Colored Artistes Beware," *The Player*, 7 April 1911; "Musical and Dramatic," *Chicago Defender*, 19 November 1910.

50. "The Duquesne," *Pittsburgh Post-Gazette*, 18 February 1899; "Music and the Stage," *New York Age*, 15 April 1909.

51. "An Evening with the Boss of the Dudley Circuit," *Nashville Globe*, 17 August 1917.

52. "Mr. Dudley and Vaudeville," *Nashville Globe*, 18 January 1918; "An Evening with the Boss of the Dudley Circuit," *Nashville Globe*, 17 August 1917; "National and Local Theatrical News," *Salt Lake City Broad Ax*, 30 September 1911; "All Bets Off," *Nashville Globe*, 31 August 1917.

53. "Milton Starr Makes Statement," *Chicago Defender*, 12 February 1912. On TOBA see Lynn Abbott and Doug Seroff, *The Original Blues: The Emergence of the Blues in African American Vaudeville, 1899–1926* (Jackson: University of Mississippi Press, 2017), 231–44.

54. Abbott and Seroff, *Original Blues*, 244–48; "Colored Actors' Union Growing" and "Signs of Truce," *Billboard*, 28 May 1921; "TOBA Absorbs the Consolidated," *Billboard*, 4 June 1921; "Improvements and Benefits Promised," *Variety*, 25 March 1925.

55. NA, FTC, Examination of Irving Weingart, 16 October 1919, 2818; "$725,000 a Week," *Shreveport Times*, 14 December 1913; "Keith Buys into Beck and Beck Buys into Keith," *The Player*, 22 July 1910; "Williams Sells His Theaters to B. F. Keith," *NYS*, 29 April 1912.

56. "Keith and Proctor Plans," *New York Dramatic Mirror*, 11 August 1906; "The Keith & Proctor Disagreement," *NYC*, 25 February 1911; "Keith-Proctor Up Against the Loew and Fox Houses," *Variety*, 6 May 1911; "F. F. Proctor: The Future of Vaudeville," *Muncie Evening Press*, 23 October 1915.

57. "Making Proctor the Goat," *Variety*, 6 December 1912; "Two and Two Make Four," *The Player*, 7 January 1910; NA, FTC, Cross-Examination of Frank Fogarty, 28 March 1919, 1268.

58. "Beck Denies Everything," *Variety*, 22 April 1911; NA, FTC, Examination of Edward Fay, 6 February 1919, 736; "Proctor's Hunt for Artists," *NYT*, 5 February 1912; NA, FTC, Cross-Examination of Frank Fogarty, 28 March 1919, 1268.

59. On Casey and Pantages, see "Western States Circuits," *Variety*, 18 April 1908; "United Will License Agents," *Variety*, 19 December 1908; "Small United Managers," *Variety*, 6 March 1909; "Flood of Small Time," *Variety*, 29 May 1909; and NA, FTC, Examination of Loney Haskell, 14 October 1919, 2605.

CHAPTER SIX

1. "The Iconoclast," *Boston Post*, 3 May 1903.
2. Drama Committee of the Twentieth Century Club, *The Amusement Situation in Boston* (Boston: Twentieth Century Club, 1910), 7–9.
3. "29,130 Theaters in the U.S.," *Variety*, 21 February 1919; NA, FTC, Final Arguments, 16 February 1920, 3383–84; "Big Managers Block Peace," *NYTr*, 4 September 1919; "Conditions in Vaudeville," *The Billboard*, 22 September 1920; UASC, MS 438, Arthur Frank Wertheim Collection, box 20, file 1, list of vaudeville theaters appended to letter from Ray Leason to Lee Shubert, 11 September 1920; Alfred Bernheim, "The Facts of Vaudeville," *Equity News*, September–November 1923, reprinted in *American Vaudeville as Seen by Its Contemporaries*, ed. Charles W. Stein (New York: Alfred A. Knopf, 1984), 129. None of these figures included African American theaters.
4. "Orpheum Drops Three Towns," *Variety*, 23 July 1915; *The Julius Cahn–Gus Hill Theatrical Guides* for 1897–98, 1900–1901, 1905–6, 1912–13, and 1919–20. The figures provided in the *Julius Cahn–Gus Hill Theatrical Guide* were checked against those in *Variety* surveyed for the years 1900, 1910, and 1919. Where there was a discrepancy between the Cahn-Hill figures and *Variety*'s, I used the higher numbers for all years on the assumption that it was easier to miss including a theater than to list one that did not exist.
5. "Watching Small Time," *Variety*, 12 January 1919; NA, FTC, Examination of Loney Haskell, 14 October 1919, 2605.
6. "Martin Beck Talks on the Future," *New York Dramatic Mirror*, 16 July 1913.
7. "How He Runs 127 Theaters," *NYT*, 4 September 1921; "Another Manager Banquets Actors," *The Player*, 12 January 1917.
8. "How He Runs 127 Theaters"; "Loew after Opposition," *Variety*, 9 December 1911; Gabriel Mendoza, "An Idea Made Marcus Loew," *Brooklyn Daily Eagle*, 3 May 1925; David Warfield, "Marcus Loew," *Harrisburg Telegraph*, 9 May 1927.
9. "Italian Theater for Brooklyn," *NYS*, 22 August 1907. Watson's Cozy Corner had been a burlesque house with a cabaret in the basement, but it was often in trouble with the police because it did not stop customers from carrying drinks into the theater from the bar downstairs. In 1905 the Hammersteins bought it and changed its name to the Nassau Theater but failed to make it work as a vaudeville house and sold it after a year. "Nassau Theater," *NYTr*, 5 January 1906
10. Mendoza, "Idea Made Marcus Loew"; "Theater News," *Harrisburg Telegraph*, 15 December 1924; "Carry the Fight to Brooklyn," *New York Age*, 23 November 1911; "To Amuse the Public," *Anaconda Standard*, 21 June 1914; "The Story of Marcus Loew," *Anaconda Standard*, 26 April 1914; "Marcus Loew Takes Over Considine Circuit," *Fort Wayne Journal-Gazette*, 9 August 1914.
11. "The Keith & Proctor Disagreement," *NYC*, 25 February 1911; Hartley Davis, "The Business Side of Vaudeville," *Everybody's Magazine*, October 1907, 530; Michael Davis Jr., *The Exploitation of Pleasure: A Study of Commercial Recreation in New York City* (New York: Sage Foundation, 1911), 25; Rowland Haynes, *Recreation Survey: Detroit, Michigan* (Detroit: Detroit Board of Commerce, 1913), 47; Francis North, *Indianapolis Recreation Survey* (Indianapolis: Indianapolis Chamber of Commerce, 1914), 44.

12. "Salary Cutting Sole Topic," *Variety*, 17 October 1914; "Vaudeville Salaries," *New York Evening World*, 10 October 1914; "Moss Bookings Banned," *The Player*, 26 January 1917; "New York Stage Awhirl," *LAT*, 1 November 1914; "Growing Chary of Conditions," *Variety*, 18 September 1914; "Vaudeville Opens at the Lyric," *Allentown (Pa.) Morning Call*, 12 November 1913; "Vaudeville Salaries," *Louisville Courier-Journal*, 1 August 1915.

13. "Boston's Biggest Theater," *Variety*, 28 May 1915; "Prices Fall," *Variety*, 14 January 1916.

14. Andrew Erdman, *Blue Vaudeville: Sex, Morals and the Mass Marketing of Amusement, 1895–1915* (Jefferson, N.C.: MacFarland, 2004), 45; Groucho Marx, *Groucho and Me* (New York: Random House, 1959), 181; BRTD, Emerson Collection on Vaudeville, box 2, file 89, Fox and Ward to Al Fostell, 20 October 1916. Ward added that "he never seen so many Jews in one bunch as he did in Loew's Booking Office something he'll never forget. He had to laugh when telling his wife about it and she had to laugh."

15. "Vaudeville Actors," *NYT*, 26 October 1914; "White Rats," *Variety*, 7 January 1916; BRTD, Emerson Collection on Vaudeville, box 2, file 89, Fox and Ward to Al Fostell, 14 April 1917.

16. Kerry Segrave, *Actors Organize: Union Formation Efforts in America, 1880–1919* (Jefferson, N.C.: McFarland, 2007), chapter 7; "Oklahoma City Strike," *Variety*, 3 November 1916; "Editorial," *Variety*, 16 March 1917; "Oklahoma Strikers Abandon Metropolitan," *Variety*, 6 October 1916.

17. "Rats Win First Fight," *The Player*, 9 March 1917; "Vaudeville Actors Wait Strike Order," *Boston Daily Globe*, 26 December 1916; "White Rats Strike," *The Player*, 9 February 1917. The Gordon Brothers houses may have been selected because the owners had not joined the managers' association and as a result players who walked out of their houses would not be blacklisted elsewhere. "Threatened Strike in Vaudeville," *New York Star*, 14 February 1917; "Three Actors on Picket Arrested," *Boston Daily Globe*, 7 February 1917; BRTD, Emerson Collection on Vaudeville, box 2, file 89, Fox to Fostell, 14 April 1917; "Rats Awful Flop in St. Louis," *Variety*, 23 February 1917; "Rats v Poli," *Variety*, 9 March 1917; "Strike Fails Says Loew," *NYT*, 10 March 1917.

18. "White Rats End Strike Because of the War," *Boston Daily Globe*, 11 April 1917; "Failure Again," *Variety*, 9 February 1917; "Vaudeville Managers Purchase Assassins," *The Player*, 23 February 1917; NA, FTC, Examination of Pat Casey, 3 February 1919, 262 and 270.

19. "All Vaudeville Box Office Records Smashed," *Variety*, 2 January 1920; "State-Lake's Huge Year," *Variety*, 19 March 1920; "Loew Circuit Reported," *Variety*, 31 October 1919; Walter Kingsley, "Vaudeville Volleys," *New York Dramatic Mirror*, 25 January 1919; "Good-Bye to Cabarets," *Variety*, 6 February 1920; "Chicago Seats," *Variety*, 9 January 1920.

20. "Loew after Competition," *Variety*, 9 December 1911; "Boston Notes," *The Player*, 19 January 1917; "Orpheum Circuit," *San Francisco Chronicle*, 27 March 1922; "Loew Maintained," *Vaudeville News*, 26 December 1924; "The Lancer," *LAT*, 27 September 1926; "Majestic," *Harrisburg Telegraph*, 28 October 1920; "Old Vaudeville Days," *Brooklyn Daily Eagle*, 13 January 1918; Robert Allen, *Vaudeville and Film, 1895–1915: A Study in Media Interaction* (New York: Arno Press, 1980), 298.

21. "Brooklyn's Ten New Theaters," *Variety*, 25 April 1919; "Keith's Extensive Building," *Variety*, 16 May 1919; "Martin Beck Makes Statement," *New York Star*, 3 December 1921;

"Proctor's New Theater," *Washington Times*, 29 August 1920; "Reorganized Orpheum Circuit," *Variety*, 10 October 1919.

22. "Vaudeville Houses to Close," *Variety*, 15 April 1921; "Famous Reports," *Variety*, 18 March 1921; "Loew's and Orpheum Are Down," *Variety*, 25 June 1920; "Loew's Profits," *Variety*, 23 July 1920; "Orpheum Earnings," *Variety*, 4 February 1921.

23. Bland Johaneson, "Vaudeville," *Theater Magazine*, August 1923, 42.

24. BRTD, MWEZ+ n.c. 19080, Will Cressy Scrapbook, clipping *Boston Journal*, 21 February 1899, clipping *Providence News*, 29 December 1898, Keith's Union Square Program, week of 19 December 1898, and clipping *New York Morning Telegraph*, 20 December 1898. The first sketch in vaudeville featured actors from the legitimate theater Hugh Stanton and Francesca Redding. The play was called "For Reform" and debuted at Keith's Philadelphia in 1894. Over the next five years other sketches appeared with actors like Robert Hilliard, Elvira Croix, Digby Bell, and Louise Thorndyke Boucicault. BRTD, MWEZ+ n.c. 19456, Will Cressy Scrapbook, Will Cressy, "History of the One-Act Play," ca. 1910.

25. BRTD, NAFR, series 2, Robinson Locke Collection, vol. 298, clipping Charles Ross, "The Building and Repairing of Vaudeville Sketches," *New York Dramatic Mirror*, 5 July 1911; BRTD, MWEZ+ n.c. 19456, Will Cressy Scrapbook, Will Cressy, "History of the One-Act Play," ca. 1910; "The Vaudeville Sketch," *CDT*, 5 October 1903.

26. Sarah Williamson, "Building a Vaudeville Sketch," *SFC*, 9 May 1909; NA, FTC, Cross-Examination of Daniel Hennessy, 27 March 1919, 938–40. K-AVC contains a volume of reports of managers regarding sketches that they auditioned, mostly for stock company use; see "Stock Managers Incorporate," *Baltimore Sun*, 21 March 1909; "Theater News," *Los Angeles Herald*, 13 August 1909; and BRTD, MWEZ+ n.c. 19457, Will Cressy and Blanche Dayne Pressbook, clipping "The Truth at Last Concerning Vaudeville Salaries."

27. Wilfrid Clarke, "Vaudeville Novelty," *Variety*, 12 December 1906, cited in Rob King, *The Fun Factory: The Keystone Film Company and the Emergence of Mass Culture* (Berkeley: University of California Press, 2009), 108–9; "The Vaudeville Sketch," *CDT*, 5 October 1903; search of approximately 1,500 daily newspapers 1901–10, of 1,300 newspapers 1911–20, and of 1,100 newspapers 1921–30 on newspapers.com, accessed 5 April 2017; BRTD, Emerson Collection on Vaudeville, box 2, folder 93, Jen Powers to Al Fostell, 3 April 1915; NA, FTC, Cross-Examination of James William Fitzpatrick, 22 May 1919, 2060; "Boston Notes," *The Player*, 12 January 1917.

28. BRTD, MWEZ+ n.c. 19456 Will Cressy Scrapbook, clipping Will Cressy, "The Market for Vaudeville Sketches," ca. 1909; "New Bill at Poli's," *Hartford Courant*, 24 October 1911; "A Good Vaudeville Sketch," *St. Louis Post-Dispatch*, 9 May 1905.

29. "Caught," *Variety*, 17 March 1906.

30. K-AVC, Managers' Reports, vol. 6, Philadelphia Show, week of 18 June 1906, and Keith's Theater Providence, week of 18 November 1906; "Mollie Fuller and Co.," *Variety*, 16 December 1905.

31. K-AVC, Reports on Plays, "At the White Horses Tavern," Crescent Theater Brooklyn, and "When We Were Twenty-One," Majestic Theater, Johnstown; "The Human Note in Vaudeville," *NYS*, 29 November 1908; "The Motor Duel," *Variety*, 12 May 1906.

32. "At the Threshold," *Variety*, 24 August 1907.

33. "Vaudeville as It Is," *New York Star*, 5 January 1921.

34. "Musical and Dramatic," *Chicago Defender*, 26 July 1913.

35. Johaneson, "Vaudeville," 42.

36. Grenville Vernon, "That Mysterious Jazz," *NYTr*, 30 March 1919; "Keith's Lyric," *Atlanta Constitution*, 7 February 1922; George S. Kaufman, "Broadway and Elsewhere," *New York Tribune*, 11 March 1917, cited in E. Douglas Bomberger, *Making Music American: 1917 and the Transformation of Culture* (New York: Oxford University Press, 2018), 50; Tulane University, Hogan Jazz Archive, Larroca Collection, clipping "Jazz, Ragtime By-Product," *NYS*, 4 November 1917.

37. On the Creole Orchestra, see Lawrence Gushee, *Pioneers of Jazz: The Story of the Creole Band* (New York: Oxford University Press, 2005). "Orpheum," *Oakland Tribune*, 6 September 1914; "Take It from Bee Palmer," *Los Angeles Sunday Times*, 2 November 1919; Estrella Hailey, "Jazz Is a Prostitution of a Fine Art," *El Paso Herald*, 28 January 1919; advertisement for the 39th Street Theater, *New York Dramatic Mirror*, 19 May 1917; "Heard on the Rialto," *New York Dramatic Mirror*, 25 August 1917.

38. On nightclubs, see Burton Perretti, *Nightclub City: Politics and Amusement in Manhattan* (Philadelphia: University of Pennsylvania Press, 2007); and Lewis A. Erenberg, *Steppin' Out: New York Nightlife and the Transformation of American Culture* (Chicago: University of Chicago Press, 1981). "5th Avenue," *Variety*, 4 April 1919; "The Palace," *Hartford Courant*, 18 May 1917.

39. "What Clamping on Lid Means," *Scranton Republican*, 7 January 1914; "Cabaret Facts," *CDT*, 24 March 1918; Gordon Seagrove in the *CT*, 11 July 1915; O. O. McIntyre, "New York Day-by-Day," *Buffalo Enquirer*, 13 May 1919 and 22 May 1919.

40. "Navy Jazz Music," *New York Herald*, 16 April 1918; K-AVC, Managers' Reports, vol. 22, Philadelphia Show, week of 9 August 1919, and vol. 23 Bijou Theater Show, Woonsocket, week of 11 October 1920; "The Riverside," *Variety*, 24 January 1919; "Marion Harris," *Dramatic Mirror and Theater World*, 28 May 1921; Tulane University, Hogan Jazz Archive, Larroca Collection, clipping "Jazz, Ragtime By-Product," *NYS*, 4 November 1917; "Hollywood Becomes Capital of Jazz," *LAT*, 13 December 1925.

41. Tulane University, Hogan Jazz Archive, interview with Johnny Lala, 24 September 1958, and interview with Willie Hightower, 3 June 1958; Nanette Kutner, "The First Jazz Dance to Dance Music," *Dance Lovers Magazine*, October 1924, 58; Tulane University, Hogan Jazz Archive, interview with Norman Mason, 6 February 1960; Sanford Josephson, *Jazz Notes: Interviews across the Generations* (Santa Barbara: Praeger, 2009), 81; "Bessie Smith to Play South," *Pittsburgh Courier*, 12 September 1925; "Entertain at Midnight Show," *Pittsburgh Courier*, 16 February 1924; "Ethel Waters at the Grand," *Greensboro (N.C.) Daily News*, 25 May 1922. Waters also appeared in touring revues.

42. "Mamie Smith and Jazz Hounds," *Dramatic Mirror and Theater World*, 18 December 1920; Rutgers University, Institute of Jazz Studies, interview with John Bubbles, 8 December 1979; "Jazz King at Orpheum," *Des Moines Register*, 8 July 1923; Linda Dahl, *Morning Glory: A Biography of Mary Lou Williams* (Berkeley: University of California Press, 1999), 53.

43. "New York Day by Day," *Washington Herald*, 9 August 1918; "Palace," *Variety*, 31 January 1919; BRTD, NAFR+, series 3, Robinson Locke Collection, vol. 504, Frisco, clipping

Toledo Blade, 13 September 1921. Members of Kelly's all-white ensemble were responsible for much of the jazz featured in vaudeville at the end of the war. Kelly's group had grown from the nucleus of Brown's Band from Dixieland, one of the first New Orleans bands to move north, which became the house orchestra in Lamb's Café in Chicago in 1915. With Kelly as bandleader, the musicians moved to New York for a stint at Reisenweber's restaurant, and he then took on a few months of work in vaudeville backing up Frisco. Cornetist Raymond Lopez, who first muted his cornet with his derby hat, was an original member of Tom Brown's band and joined Blossom Seeley's group in 1917; he would remain with her for four years. Walter Kingsley, "Vaudeville Volleys," *Dramatic Mirror*, 14 December 1918.

44. K-AVC, Managers' Reports, vol. 23, Providence Show, week of 27 October 1920; "B. F. Keith's," *Cincinnati Enquirer*, 1 May 1923; "Poli's," *Scranton Republican*, 11 March 1922.

45. Berlin quoted in "A Jazz Opera," *St. Louis Star*, 12 March 1922.

46. The best history of the revue is Jonas Westover, *The Shuberts and Their Passing Shows: The Untold Tale of Ziegfeld's Rivals* (New York: Oxford University Press, 2016). On creating a song hit in a revue, see Jonas Westover, "Shaping a Song for the Stage: How the Early Revue Cultivated Hits," *Studies in Musical Theater* 6, no. 2 (2012): esp. 166–69.

47. "The Casino," *Rochester Democrat and Chronicle*, 30 July 1898; "The Casino," *NYT*, 17 April 1894; "Musical and Dramatic," *NYT*, 25 April 1899.

48. "The Follies of 1912," *Brooklyn Daily Eagle*, 22 October 1912; Richard Ziegfeld and Paulette Ziegfeld, *The Ziegfeld Touch: The Life and Times of Florenz Ziegfeld, Jr.* (New York: Harry N. Abrams, 1993), 49; Lee Davis, *Scandals and Follies: The Rise and Fall of the Great Broadway Revue* (New York: Limelight Editions, 2000), 98; advertisement for Leubrie Hill's *Darktown Follies*, *Pittsburgh Daily Press*, 16 March 1918; BRTD, MWEZ+ n.c. 21063, Ned Wayburn Scrapbook, clipping *Atlantic City Gazette Review*, 6 June 1917; Barbara Cohen-Stratyner, *Ned Wayburn and the Dance Routine: From Vaudeville to the Ziegfeld Follies* (Madison: University of Wisconsin Press, 1996), 53–54.

49. "Revue: The Most Hopeful Sign on the Dramatic Horizon," *Current Opinion*, November 1918, 304; Ann Ommen van der Merwe, *The Ziegfeld Follies: A History in Song* (Plymouth, UK: Scarecrow Press, 2009), 119; "Outlaw Songs," *Current Opinion*, September 1919, 165.

50. "Interview with Albert de Courville," *The Observer* (London), 19 September 1920; "Revue," *Music Trade Review*, 9 December 1911; "Bert Williams Quits the Follies," *New York Age*, 22 June 1918.

51. BRTD, E. W. Sargent Scrapbook, clipping *New York Telegram*, 25 May 1899; "Behold the Great Change Wrought by the Review," *NYS*, 4 January 1920; "Strenuous Silliness," *LAT*, 24 November 1920.

52. "At Funeral of Ed Gallagher," *Wilkes-Barre (Pa.) Evening News*, 1 June 1929; "They May Be Worth It," *PI*, 17 February 1924.

53. See advertisements for the Eden Museum, *Omaha Daily Bee*, 26 January 1890, for Keith's Bijou, *PI*, 10 July 1892, and for the Palace Theater, *Boston Post*, 28 May 1895; "Hart's Novelty," *Scranton Republican*, 21 November 1908; "The Call Boy's Chat," *PI*, 8 April 1923; "Orpheum," *Brooklyn Daily Eagle*, 9 April 1911; "Girly Show at Casino," *PI*, 30 August 1910; "The Rose Maid," *Washington Herald*, 8 October 1912.

54. "Gallagher and Shean," *Indianapolis Star*, 18 June 1922; "Gallagher and Shean Suit," *Music Trade Review*, 1 July 1922.

55. Edward Gallagher and Albert Shean, "Oh! Mister Gallagher; Oh! Mister Shean" (New York: Jack Mills, 1922).

56. "Gallagher and Shean," *NYTr*, 16 August 1921; "The Orpheum," *Brooklyn Daily Eagle*, 30 August 1921; "The Orpheum," *Brooklyn Daily Eagle*, 8 November 1921.

57. "Here and There in the Theaters," *CT*, 8 March 1922; "Gallagher and Shean Popular," *Music Trade Review*, 17 March 1923; "Gallagher and Shean Sued," *Pittsburgh Daily Post*, 13 December 1922; "No Pikers," *Houston Post*, 18 March 1923. The peculiarity of their popularity drew comparisons with another bizarre song that took the country by storm in 1922, Eddie Cantor's "Yes, We Have No Bananas." Jack Mills, Inc., the music publisher, ran a national contest for the best new verses to the song, offering $5,000 to the winner. "Gallagher and Shean Contest," *Music Trade Review*, 31 March 1923.

58. "Ed Gallagher," *Bridgewater Courier News*, 1 June 1929; "Gallagher and Shean Sued on Salaries," *Brooklyn Daily Eagle*, 23 November 1923; "Gallagher Divorce," *Indianapolis Star*, 19 July 1925.

59. "The Tuning Troubles of Gallagher and Shean," *Pittsburgh Daily Post*, 25 July 1923; "Greenwich Village Follies," *Harrisburg Telegraph*, 6 June 1924; "News of the Stage," *Chicago Sunday Tribune*, 5 October 1924; "Follies Send Big Audiences Away Pleased," *Bismarck Tribune*, 3 June 1925; "The Theater," *Richmond Times*, 4 March 1923; "Absolutely!," *Cincinnati Enquirer*, 2 March 1923.

60. "Suit against Messrs. Gallagher and Shean," *Alton (Ill.) Evening Telegraph*, 27 February 1923; "Curtain for Mr. Gallagher," *Rochester Democrat and Chronicle*, 31 May 1929; Edward Thiery, "Hams? Not Us," *Danville (Tenn.) Bee*, 13 March 1921.

61. "The Stage," *Dramatic Mirror and Theater World*, 20 August 1921.

62. "Public Tastes Have Changed," *Oregon Daily Journal* (Portland), 7 February 1915.

63. Abel Green and Joe Laurie, *Show Biz: From Vaude to Video* (New York: Henry Holt, 1955), 113.

64. On the male gaze, see Laura Mulvey's landmark essay "Visual Pleasure and Narrative Cinema," *Screen* 16 (1975): 6–18.

65. BRTD, Aaron Hoffman Papers, box 18, skit for Frey and Ferguson, ca. 1905.

INDEX

Page numbers in italics refer to illustrations.

acrobat, 12, 13, 25, 31, 52, 53, 70, 73, 76, 133, 146, 152, 204, 208
Adgie (Castillo), 178
advertising, 4, 39–43, 49, 64, 91, 141, 142, 176, 179–80, 185, 199, 224; banned from acts, 23
Albee, Edward Franklin, 21, 25; biography, 163–63, 194–95; business, 30, 97, 110, 168, 170–71, 172–74, 180, 183–84, 190, 199, 212; opinions, 23, 188, 196, 202, 217. *See also* Keith, Benjamin Franklin
Alexander the Great, 111
Anderson and Goines, 178
animal trainers, 2, 12, 53, 76, 92, 105, 125, 224
Antheil, George, 86
Aronson, Rudolph, 27–28
audience: actuality and, 52, 124–26, 143–144; African American, 37–38, 96–97, 99–100, 177, 193; attention and engagement, 13, 63, 66, 93–95, 100, 103–4, 107, 110–11, 113–16, 131–32, 205, 207, 224–25; behavior, 21, 32, 94, 96–98, 109–10; class, 6, 25–26, 28–29, 35–37, 39, 99–100, 150, 154, 163, 194, 216, 154, 156; ethnicity, 35–37, 83, 96, 150; female, 13, 25, 27, 30, 48–49, 54, 70, 98–100, 121, 133, 136; matinee girls, 33–34, 98; music hall, 25–29, 31, 39, 55, 59, 94, 96, 99, 130, 164; relationship with stars, 39, 41–42, 49, 54, 70, 107, 110–11, 114, roof garden, 27–29, 31, 53, 155, 156, 164, 214; tyranny of, 61, 63, 70, 114–15; urbanity, 5, 6, 9, 19, 25, 34–35, 68, 98, 100–101, 104, 155;

vaudeville's decline, 10, 200–201, 221, 222, 223. *See also* celebrity; vaudeville: popularity of
Aug, Edna, 123
authenticity, 12–14, 52–53, 63–64, 75–76, 89; aesthetics, 12, 125, 144; in performance, 105–9, 128, 143, 204; modernism and, 127, 141–3, 146; race and, 57, 77, 78, 80–82, 209
auto-defying, 91–92, 95, 202
Avery and Hart, 80, 178

Baker, Belle, 43–44, 45, 65
Baldwin, S. S., 132
Barnard, Sophye, 44, 45, 73
Barnes, Djuna, 132
Barnum, P. T., 128, 156
Barrasso, Anselmo, 177
Barret, J. J., 218
Barrison Sisters, 25
Bayes, Nora, 23, 65–66, 83, 86, 107, *108*, 114, 144, 195, 199, 209, 214
Beatty, Maud, 135
Beck, Martin, 4, 159, 160, 169, 172, 183, 191, 194
Bedini and Arthur, 23
Behman, Louis, 169
Benny, Jack, 93
Bergère, Valerie, 67
Berlin, Irving, 43, 64, 66, 208, 213
Bernard, Sam, 214
Bernhardt, Sarah, 10
bicyclist, 12, 53, 75, 92, 146
Bigard, Barney, 211

Biller, John, 57
Billy Sharp Orchestra, 213
blackface, 14, 36, 60, 66, 80, *127*, 196, 201, 215–16; actuality and, 16, 55, 77–81; black-on-black, 81–83, 176, 177–78; female, 8, 60, 80, 86, 126; minstrel, 54, 56, 62, 76–78, 80, 177; number of acts, 14, 77; whitewashing of, 80, 87, 125–27, 211. *See also* impersonation; race
Black Patti Company, 37
Boltwood, Bertram Borden, 128
Booth, Edwin, 14, 41
Bordeverry, Gaston, 1
Bordoni, Irene, 110
Brittons, the, 178
Brown and Nevarro, 178
Brownell, William Crary, 101
Bubbles, John, 212
Burke, Billie, 107, 136, 145
Burke, Dan, 135

Caffin, Caroline, 33, 98, 100, 107, 111, 116, 143
Cahill, Marie, 59, 60, 66
Calvé, Emma, 10
Cameron, Tudor, 125–26
Camilla's Birds, 212
Canfield, Mary Cass, 11
Carpenter, John Alden, 11
Carter, Lucille, 110–11
Carter and Bluford, 178
Carus, Emma, 47, 60, 71, 72, 86, 105, 134–35, 137, 140, 214, 216
Caruso, Enrico, 60
Castle, Vernon and Irene, 86, 140, 199
celebrity, 2, 22–23, 48–49, 63, 115, 141–42, 146, 221, 224–25; decline of vaudeville and, 17–18, 184, 191, 199, 201, 223; defined, 10, 39, 41; importance of, 10, 48, 50, 187, 189; publicity, 39–40, 42–45, 49; rags to riches, 10, 43–45, 49, 119, 145. *See also* consumerism
censorship, 133–34, 136, 137–38, 162
Chaplin, Charlie, 122
Chapman, Etta, 60–61

Charmion, 70, 73, 133
Chase, P. B., 100
Chesterfield, Henry, 217
Christensen, Axel, 63
cinema, 94, 158, 189; decline of vaudeville and, 16–17, 149–50, 187, 189–90, 195, 198, 200, 201, 207, 216, 222, 225; number of, 189; "pop" theaters, 48, 164–65, 189–93, 198–99, 201; RKO Pictures, 184; vaudeville stars and, 199, 205, 219
Clancy, Gertrude, 44
Clarke, Wilfred, 204
Cliff, Laddie, 113–14
Cobb, Will, 134
Cohan, George M., 72
Cole, Bob, and J. Rosamond Johnson, 81, *82*, 178, 179, 180
Collins, Arthur, 56
comedian, 1, 16, 46, 47, 52, 63, 67, 87, 131, 154, 204, 217; ethnic, 14, 36, 178; monologue, 4, 12, 53, 105, 110, 119, 135, 187, 204, 223; number of, 53
commodification: of race, 16, 58–60, 66–67, 77, 83, 85–86, 126, 133, 177; of style, 14, 16, 22–23, 50, 53, 87; women's body ideals, 69–73, 117, 139
Comstock, Mrs. A, 136
consumerism, 5, 9, 19, 22–24, 31, 39–40, 64, 141, 146; fashions and goods, 10, 11, 14, 34, 61, 70–75; pursuit of pleasure, 18, 21, 88–89; the self and, 141–42; sexiness and, 71, 72–76, 136, 147; women and, 23, 41, 46–47, 73. *See also* celebrity; modernity
contortionist, 1, 137–38
Cooper and Robinson, 178
Creole Orchestra, 209
Cressy, Will, 46, 172, 201–2, *203*, 204, 205, 223
Crum, Frederick, 92

Dalton, Emmett, 109
Daly, Arnold, 103–104
dance and movement, 4, 68–71; actuality and, 81, 107; angular, 113–14; in "coon"

performance, 60–61; number of dance acts, 69; prewar dance craze, 68–69; ragtime, 62, 64, 65, 69, 71, 202; revues and, 214
dance halls, 12, 68–69, 210
dances, types of: Apache dance, 139–40; Boston dip, 69; buck-and-wing, 16, 62, 80, 87, 178; cakewalk, 62, 78, 81, 86, 178; Elgin movements, 69; fox-trot, 69; Dance of the Seven Veils, 136; gigolette, 137, 140; grizzly bear, 73, 88; Salome, 72, 88, 136–37, 139; shimmy, 69–70, 74, 89, 113–34, 202, 212, 215; soft-shoe, 16, 213; Texas tommy, 69, 71, 140–41; todolo, 69, 134; "tough" dances, 65, 78, 137, 139, 140; turkey trot, 69, 75, 78, 87; two-step, 68–69, 87, 139; vampire dance, 139; waltz, 54, 55, 62, 69, 140
Darrow, Clyde, 209
Davies, Riene, 105
Davis, Hartley, 172, 194
Davis, Michael, 1, 7, 19, 33, 146
Dayne, Blanche, 202, *203*, 204
Demuth, Charles, 11, 132
De Vine, Harry, 106
dime museum, 2, 5, 24, 28, 31, 94, 113, 152, 153, 154, 164
diver, 12, 23, 47, 72, 75, 160
Dix, Dorothy, 48
Dixie Serenaders, 178
Dixon, Frank, 123
Dockstader, Lew, 62, 78, 116, 197
Dolly Sisters, 209
Dresser, Louise, 70
Dressler, Marie, 115–16
Dudley, Sherman H., 176, 177, 180–82, 183; Dudley circuit, 177, 180
Duncan, A. O., 46
Dunn, Maud, 105

Eaton and Farrell's Georgia Minstrels, 177–78
Edwards, Eddy, 213
Edwards, Gus, 134
Einstein, Albert, 128

Eldridge, Press, 105
Eliot, T. S., 127
Emmett, Dan, 77–78, 87
entertainment (non-vaudeville): cabaret, 18, 65, 198, 201, 209–11, 213, 216, 221, 223, 225; clubs, 28, 140, 141, 187, 209, 210, 211, 225; concert saloons, 2, 4, 5, 13, 14, 24, 29, 39, 54, 94, 97, 111, 153, 157; legitimate, 10, 29, 32–34, 127, 136, 158, 185, 189, 205, 216
Erlanger, A. L., 172–73, 174–75, 193, 213, 216
escape artist, 52, 92, 112
escapism, 2, 5, 7, 97, 117
Europe, James Reese, 208
European association/influence, 27–28, 39, 71, 213; actuality and, 52; European acts, 4, 25, 46, 55, 91, 107, 110–11, 115, 122, 129, 130, 134, 139, 158, 160, 167, 226; European audiences, 99, 111; European Tours, 137, 152, 195; race and, 78, 99–100; theater experience and, 29

Fadette Orchestra, 34, 172
Fay, Eva, 111
Feist Music Publishers, 56
Ferguson, Dave, 226
Fiddler and Shelton, 178
Fields, Gracie, 136
Fields, W. C., 46
Flanagan and Edwards, 123, 125
Flying Dancer, the, 78
Fogarty, Frank, 161
Foo, Ching Ling, 105
Ford, Paul, 99
Foster, Stephen, 55, 216
Foster, William Trufant, 135–36
Fox, Imro, *15*, 105, 106
Fox, Joe, 196, 197
Fox, William, 190
Foy, Bryan, 218
Foy, Eddie, and the Foys, 46–47, 144, 145, 216, 218
Francis, Kitty, 106
Frank, Harry, 28

Franklin, Irene, 44, 47
Frank Wilson Trio, 78
Freud, Sigmund, 132–33
Frey, Harry, 226
Friganza, Trixie, 39, 72, 199, 225
Frisco, Joe, 43, 212, 215
Fuller, Mollie, 206
Fynes, J. Austin, 173

Gallagher, Edward, 217–22, *220*, 223, 225
Garvey, Ellen Gruber, 41
Gaylord, Bonnie, 126
George Neville and Co., 205
Golden, Billy, 59
Golden, George Fuller, 46, 62, 110, 171
Goldin, Horace, 130, 131
Goldwyn, Sam, 22
Goodwin, Nat, 187
Gordon Brothers, 197
Gottleib, George, 93
Gould, Billy, 73
Graham, Lillian, 109
Grant, Robert, 117
Gray, Gilda, 69–70, 89, 133–34, *142*, 213, 215
Great Hermann, the, 111
Green, Abel, 223
Greene, Gene, 49, 65, 66, 86–87
Greenway, Ned, 140–41
Greenwich Village Follies, 216, 221
Guilbert, Yvette, 46

Hall, Artie, 80
Hammerstein, Arthur, 221
Hammerstein, Oscar, 72, 91, 192; business, 28–29, 31, 158, 163, 167–69, 172, 174, 175, 182, 179, 182; opinions, 21, 24–25
Hammerstein, Willie, 91, 118
Harney, Ben, 57, 58, 59, 61–62, 177
Harris, Charles, K., 55
Harris, Marion, 86, 211
Harris, S. L., 207
Hartley, Marsden, 11, 99, 146–47
Hartman, Ferris, 214
Held, Anna, 37, 42, 49, 60, 214

Hemingway, Ernest, 11
Henry, O., 146
Herbert, Victor, 25
Herron, Bertie, 8, 126
Hitchcock, Raymond, 44
Hoey, Charles, and Harry Lee, 14–15, 83
Hoffman, Aaron, 204
Hoffman, Gertrude, 144
Hogan, Ernest, 58, 62, 80, 177–78, 179
Hopkins, John D., 169, 171
Hopper, DeWolf, 63–64
Houdin, Jean-Eugène-Robert, 111
Houdini, Harry, 52
Howard Brothers, 209
Howards, the, 129
Howe and Scott, 78
Howells, William Dean, 99
Hubbard, W. L., 100
Hurtig and Seamon's, 29, 96–97
Hymack, Mr. (Quentin McPherson), 130–31, 132
hypnotist, 113, 131

immigrants, 3, 6, 7, 35–36, 37, 85, 87, 173, 192
impersonation, 16, 86, 143–44, 214, 218; actuality and, 16, 55, 60, 66, 80, 83, 84, 144; African American, 58–59, 61, 65, 77, 78, 87; "Dutch," 218; female and male, 1, 144, 160, 205–6; Irish, 83, 217; Italian, 84; Jewish, 14–15, 36, 66, 78, 83–85, *84*, 105, 218; mimics, 144; naturalizing stereotypes, 16, 57, 60, 66, 80, 83–85; number of, 53, 144; "oriental," 111–12; slang and, 67. *See also* blackface
Irwin, May, 57, 58–59, 60, 61, 64, 66, 70, 145

Jack, Sam, 32–33
Jackson, Joe, 107–8
Jacobs, H. R. "Harry," 152–55, 156, 166. *See also* Proctor, Fred
James, Henry, 116
James, Seymour and Jeanette, 212
Janis, Elsie, 144, 199

Jardon, Dorothy, 10
jazz, 11, 16, 18–19, 43, 132, 207, 208–13; African Americans and, 211–12; revues and, 215–16; types of acts, 212; vaudeville resistance to, 210–11, 222. *See also* music
"Jim" the shimmying bear, 212
Jines, Henry "Gang," 38
Johnson, Billy, 81, 179
Johnson, J. Rosamond, 81, *82*, 180, 212
Jolson, Al, 213
Jones, Sissieretta, 177
Jones, Walter, 214
Joyce, James, 127
juggler, 1, 23, 46, 53, 122–23, 152, 209, 212
Juliet, 144

Kaufman, George, S., 209
Keaton, Buster, 122
Keith, Benjamin Franklin, 25, 182, 190, 191, 203; biography, 153, 154, 169–75, 200; business, 21, 29, 32, 47, 98, 156–57, 160, 161–62, 166, 184, 194, 195, 198; opinions, 162–63, 183, 185
Kellar, 111
Kellerman, Annette, 23, 39–*40*, 47, 75, 88, 160
Kelly, Bert, 212
Kendall, Ezra, 46
Kersands, Billy, 177
Kildare, Owen, 67, 95–96, 109
Kilties Highland Band, 32
Kimball, Moses, 156
Kingsley, Walter, 198
Klaw, Marc, 172–73, 174–75, 193, 213, 216
Klein, Martin, 166, 177, 180, 181, 182
Kohl, Charles, 169, 172
Konorah, Mrs., 104, 131–32
Koster, John, and Albert Bial, 25–*26*, 27, 94, 170

La Belle Dazie, 136–37
Lala, Johnny, 211
La Rocca, Nick, 211

La Sylphe (Edith Lambelle Langerfield), 73, 137, *138*, 139
Lauder, Harry, 14, *15*, 107, 115
Laurant, Eugene, 112
Laurie, Joe, 223
Lavine, Edward, 122–23
Law, Evelyn, 74
Lederer, George, 214
Lee, Henry, 144
Lee, Sammy, 11, 210
Leonard, Eddie, 79
Leslie, Bert, 67–68
Levi, Leo, 143
Lewis, Ada, 139
Lewis, Dan, 177, 178
Lewis, Henry, 122, 124–25
Lloyd, Alice, 110, 199
Loew, Marcus, 5, 166, 167, 175, 191, 192–94, *193*, 195, 198, 199–200, 212; Loew's Circuit, 29–30, 37, 192, 210
Loftus, Cissy, 70, 110
Lo Lo, 131

Madden, Joe, 212
magician/illusionist, 1, 2, 4, 14, 53, 105, 111–12, 125, 129–31, 208; actuality and, 112–13
Maitland, Sybil, 136
Mann, Hank, 212
Marino, 91, 93, 95
Marsh, Reginald, 132
Marx, Groucho, 93, 196
Mason, Homer, 109
mass entertainment, 2–3, 5, 13–14, 19, 22, 45, 88–89, 145, 149–50, 157, 161, 182, 185, 207, 223; critique of, 5, 100, 117
Massey and Kramer, 105
Matzenauer, Margarete, 67
May, Butler "String Beans," 69
McAvoy, Charles, 14
McBride, Henry, 11
McDermott, Loretta, 212
McIntyre, James, and Thomas Heath, 77, 123, 165
Mencken, H. L., 68

Meyerfeld, Morris, 159, 183
Miller-Browning Company, 205
Miner, Harry, 109
Minstrel Misses, 126
modernity, 2–3, 9, 11–12, 88–89, 117, 127–28, 141–42, 187; cities and, 100–104, 116; dangers of, 91–93, 101, 141; modernism, 11, 119–23, 132–33, 135, 136, 139, 145–47, 224–25; ragtime and, 53, 64; science and technology and, 91–92, 100–101, 121, 128–30, 146, 147, 225; self and, 141, 145–46; sensory damage from, 100–104, 116, 120; slang and, 67–68, 119; style of, 10, 13–14, 31, 50, 76, 89, 146; violence and primitivism, 121, 135–40, 211–12. *See also* consumerism
Modjeska, Helena, 14
Moeller, Molly, 135
Montgomery, Marshall, 44–45
Moore, J. H., 169
Morris, William, 166, 167–68, 169, 170–71, 173–75, 181, 193, 194, 197
Moss, B. S., 166
Muldoon, Johnny, 213
Murdock, John J., 169
Murray, Elizabeth, 59, 64, 104
music: blues, 211, 215; musicians (instrumental), 2, 4, 25, 53, 81, 105, 113, 208; ragtime, 53, 59, 62–64, 69, 208; singers and songwriters, 55, 208. *See also* jazz; song and speech
musicals/musical theater, 18, 54, 153, 176, 180, 187, 213, 214
Mutual Amusement Circuit, 181

narrative: as element in show, 19, 187, 203–5, 207; in song, 55–56, 59, 60, 64. *See also* sketches
Navy Jazz Orchestra, 210
Nesbit, Evelyn, 109
Nazarro, Nat, 212
Niblo, Fred, 68
Nichols Sisters, 66–67, 106
North, Bobby, 65, 83

North, Francis, 33
Norton, Ruby, 11, 210

O'Connor, Johnny, 123
Original Dixieland Jazz Band, 211, 213

Palmer, Bee, 69, 209, 211, 213
Pantages, Alexander, 42, 117, 166, 167, 191
Pastor, Tony, 156
Pauline, 113
Paul Whiteman Band, 221
Pecora, Santo, 211, 213
performer and performance: actors and, 204; actuality, 12–16, 39, 42, 51–52, 54, 64–66, 78, 86, 92–93, 123–25, 126–27, 146, 187, 218–19; African American, 57, 69, 78–83, 114, 177–81, 183, 211–12; danger in, 91–93; direct appeal, 13, 64, 66, 95–96, 104–11, 114, 125, 207, 210, 224; fourth wall, 93, 95, 115, 225; managerial influence on, 109–10; number of performers, 47–48; personality, 10, 11, 42, 48–49, 53, 63–66, 68, 75, 104, 106–8, 114, 141; sexuality, 7–8, 24, 25–26, 28, 31, 33, 38, 55–56, 61, 69–70, 73–75, 89, 132–40, 142, 143, 147, 206, 214–15. *See also* blackface; dance and movement; song and speech
Pilling, Frank, 157
Poli, Sylvester, 167, 173–74, 191, 197
Pound, Ezra, 119
Princess Rajah, 137–38
Proctor, Fred, 24–25, 28–29, 32, *159*, 162, 214; biography, 151–57, 199–200; business, 4, 158–60, 163, 166, 167–75, 182, 183–85, 191, 194; opinions, 202
Powers, Jen, 204–5

Quigley Brothers, 83

race, 37–38, 60, 65–66, 114–15, 211–12, 216; "colored vaudeville," 176–82; modernity and, 78, 80, 87–88; racism, 177–80, 83, 114, 215–16. *See also*

blackface; commodification: of race; impersonation
radio, 3, 4, 5, 13, 19, 187, 221, 224
Raymond and Caverly, 46
Reeve, Ada, 142–143, 145
Reevin, Sam, 182
Reményi, Ede, 25
revues, 18–19, 189, 207, 213–17
Rice, Billy, 76–78, 85
Rice, Dan, 77
Ring, Blanche, 66, 71, 104
Robertson, Forbes, 34
Robichaux, John, 211
Robinson, Bill "Bojangles," 212
Robson, May, 104–5
Rogers, Will, 222
roller skater, 12, 53
Rooney, Pat, 16, 48
Roppolo, Leon, 211
Rosenfeld, Sydney, 214
Rossow's Midgets, 121
Rowland, Adele, 49, 65, 66, 104, 140, 199
Roye, Ruth, 199
Russell, Lillian, 41, 70, 72, 158, 214
Russell, Sylvester, 37, 180
Ryley, Thomas, 133

salaries, 18, 46–47, 50, 158, 160–61, 165, 170–72, 184, 185, 188, 194–96, 199, 217, 220; African American performers', 180–82, 183. *See also* celebrity
Samuels, Rae, 65, 199, 211
Sargent, Epes (Chicot), 70, 96, 178, 179, 202
Scheff, Fritzi, 10
Schwartz, Louis, 123–24
Seely, Blossom, 69, 134, 140–41, 211
Selbini, Lalla, 75
Seldes, Gilbert, 11
Seymour and Jeanette's Syncopaters, 212
Shaffer, Vi, 86
Shaw, Lillian, 83, 135
Shean, Al, 217–22, *220*, 223, 225

Shekla, 112
shootists, 1, 92, 131
Shubert, Lee and Jake, 174, 175, 189, 213, 215, 216, 220, 221, 222
Shuster, David, 103
Simon, Louis, 123
sketches, 4, 53, 124, 172, 202–5, *203*; actuality and, 206; film and, 203–4, 206–7; format of, 205–6; genres, 206–7; number of, 203; propriety, 204; sketch performers, 105. *See also* narrative
Smart Set, 38, 176, 177, 180, 181
Smith, Bessie, 211
Smith, Joseph, 139–40
Smith, Mamie, 211
Solomon, Edward, 41
song and speech: ragtime and jazz, 59, 64–66, 75, 86–87, 209, 210, 212; shouting "coon" style, 56–63, 65, 66, 72, 81; slang, 67–68; syncopated, 62, 66–67, 69, 209, 210
Sothern, E. H., 34
Sousa Orchestra, 221
Spencer, Lloyd, 21, 119
Starr, Milton, 181
Stein, Gertrude, 133
Stevens, Ashton, 58
Stock Producing Managers Association, 204
Stokes, W. E. D., 109
Stone and Delehanty, 212
Strauss, Richard, 136
strongman, 52, 91
Sullivan-Considine, 172, 175, 193–94
Sully, Lew, 87
Sun, Gus, 166, 167
Suratt, Valeska, 23, 40, 42, 60, 71, 73, *74*
Sweatnam, Willis, 86

Talking Tea Kettle, 1
Tanguay, Eva, 7, 43–44, 45–46, 48–49, 71–72, 105, 110, 114, 115, 134, 136, 137, 145
television, 3, 4, 5, 13–14, 19

Teller, Maud, 135
Templeton, Fay, 10, 71
Terley, 144
Texas Tommy Dancers, 141
Theater Owners Booking Association (TOBA), 176, 182, 183, 211, 212
theaters: Aberle's, 153; Academy, 98; Alhambra Theater, 195–96; American, 98; American Roof, 123; Americus, 98; Barnum's, 24; Bijou, 153, 173; Bijou Kansas City, 181; Bronx Theater, 111; Brooklyn Criterion, 155; Casino Theater, 27–28, 214; Chase's theater, 29, 32, 98; Chelsea Hotel, 157; Circle Theater, 172; Colonial, 133; Columbia Theatre, 70; Continental, 155; Crescent, 38; 81st Street Theater, 195; Ellis, 98; Empire Theater Salem, 200; Empire Theatre Cleveland, 32; Empress, 98; Fifth Avenue, 173, 184; Fitzgerald's, 153; Fulton Theater, 212; Gem Concert Hall, 31; Grand Opera House, Pittsburgh, 113; Grand Opera House, Wilmington, 155; the Grand Theater, 38, 98; Green Theater, 152; Hammerstein's, 21, 22, 28, 31, 46, 91, 106, 113, 136, 172; Harlem Opera House, 195–96; Hippodrome, 132; Iroquois Theater, 99; Jefferson Theatre, 37; Kedzie, 98; Keith's Theaters, 47, 65, 79, 92, 98, 99, 110, 125, 135, 155, 156, 162, 163, *164*, 172, 173, 195, 200, 202, 212–13; Lafayette Theater, 99; Lincoln Theatre, 38, 132; Loew's Orpheum, 97; Lothrop's Opera House, 77; Lyceum, 112; Lyric, 37; Macauley's, 57; Madison Square Garden, 27–28; Majestic Theater, Chicago, 29; Majestic Theatre, Nashville, 38; Masonic Temple Theater, 169; McVickers, 106; Metropolitan, 136, 177; The Midway, 98; Miner's, 153; Minnehaha Theater, 177; Monogram, 38; the Monroe, 98; Moulin Rouge, 140; National, 157; New Apollo, 98; New Columbia Theater, 97; New Howard Theater, 181; New Variety Theatre, 28; New York Theater, 214; Novelty, 155; Odd Fellows' Hall, 141; 125th Street Theater, 137; Oriental Music Hall, 36; Orpheum chain, 29, 32, 97, 159–60, 161, 166, 167, 169, 172–73, 175, 182, 183, 185, 191, 195, 198, 199–200, 213, 216, 219; the Palace, 93, 158, 198, 199, 200, 219; Pantages, 161; Parlor, 161; Pastor's, 123, 153, 170; Pekin, 38, 99; Pilling's Popular Theater, 157; Plantation, 210; Pleasure Palace, *30*, 155–56; Riverside, 190, 210, 219; Royal, 192–94; Savoy Hotel, 86; Third Avenue Theater, 155; Tony Pastor's, 123; 23rd Street Theater, 155, 157, 184; Union Station, 28; Walker, 38; Watson's Cozy Corner Theater, 192; Wigwam Garden, 165; Winter Garden, 213

Thumb, "General" Tom, 152
Tilly, Vesta, 160
Tilzer, Harry von, 86, 208
Tin Pan Alley, 213
"tough girl," 65, 139–40
Trevathan, Charles, 57
Trollope, Frances, 94
Tucker, Sophie, 7, 47, 59, 60, 62, 65, 71, 80, 211, 219
Twain, Mark, 77

Ullman, Sharon, 7
unionization, 110, 170, 182, 196–97; Black Cats, 176, 178–79, 183; strikes, 170–71, 172, 178–79, 196–97; White Rats, 36, 47, 170–71, 172, 178–79, 180, 196–97, 205
United Booking Office (UBO), 168, 174–75, 180, 182, 183–85, 189–91, 195, 197, 216, 218, 219, 220

Van, Billy B., *79*, 86
Van, Charles and Fannie, 123–24, 125, 126
Van and Schenk, 211
Vance, Clarice, 59, 65, 72, 86

Vance, Eunice, 56
Van Hoven, 123
Vaudeville: African Americans and, 37–38, 96, 99–100, 177, 180–82, 183, 211–12; amenities, 28–30, 97–98, 184, 188; big time, 17, 48, 150, 158–61, 163–65, 166, 168, 169, 175, 182, 183, 184, 185, 189, 190, 191, 195–96, 199, 200, 201, 223; business culture, 4–5, 6, 17, 150–51, 154–55, 158, 161, 162–63, 168–69, 172, 174, 178, 185, 195, 224; cartelization, 166, 168–72, 175–77, 181–82, 183–85, 189, 190–91, 194, 195–96; chains and circuits, 2, 5, 154–55, 166–68; continuous vaudeville, 153, 156–57, 162, 163, 182; cost (tickets), 5, 17–18, 21–22, 150, 155, 158, 160, 161–63, 171, 175–76, 182, 184, 185, 188, 191, 192, 193–95, 198, 200; decline of, 16–19, 149–51, 175–76, 182–86, 188–91, 194–96, 200–201, 217, 223; defined, 4, 153; as democratizing agent, 2–3, 9, 10–11, 18, 23, 44–46, 54, 75–76, 119, 122, 128–29, 147, 223; foreign language theatres, 36–37; location of theaters, 34, 98–99, 156–57; morality and, 133–34, 135–36; neighborhood theaters, 96, 98–99, 155–57, 158, 160, 163, 177, 182, 183, 188, 191; novelty and, 119, 122, 201; number of theaters, 3, 38, 150, 153, 157, 164–65, 172, 183, 189–90, 200; "pop" vaudeville, 17, 189–90, 191–95, 197, 199, 200; popularity of, 3, 16, 18, 21–22, 25, 39, 49, 117, 146, 158, 172, 185–86, 189–90, 225; postwar revival, 199–200, 208; profits/revenue, 172, 184, 187, 193, 194–95, 197–98, 200–201; small time/family time, 17, 47, 86, 97, 150, 160–61, 163–64, 165, 166, 172, 175, 180, 182, 183, 184, 190, 191, 196–97, 198, 199, 223; as therapy, 2, 5, 103–4, 116–17, 145; as transgression, 6–9, 11, 13
Vaudeville Managers Protective Association (VMPA), 47, 100, 168, 171, 172, 174, 189

Victoria, Vesta, 134, 140
Volant, 209
Volta, 92, 93

Walker, George, 79, 80–82, 96, 178, 179, 180. *See also* Williams, Bert
Ward, Bill, 196–97
Warfield, David, 192
Waters, Ethel, 211
Watson, Joe, 70–71, 83
Wayburn, Ned, 8, 109, 126, 215–16
Weaver, Sylvester, 13
Weber, Joe, 2
Weber and Field's, 178
Weill, Kurt, 11
Welch, Joe and Ben, 83–85
Wells, H. G., 99
West, Mae, 39
West, Nathanael, 132
Western Vaudeville Managers' Association (WVMA), 167, 172, 183
White, George, 212
Whitney, S. Tutt, 38
Williams, Belle, 106
Williams, Bert, 37, 60, 69, 79, 80–81, 82, 83, 114, 179–80, 215–16. *See also* Walker, George
Williams, Mary Lou, 212
Williams, Odell, 187
Williams, Percy, 28–29, 158, 160, 162, 163, 166, 169, 171–74, 178, 182, 191, 203
Wilson, Edmund, 11
Wilson, Francis, 105
women's rights, 64, 73–75, 135
Woods, Frank, 127

Zancig, Agnes and Julius, 129, 130, 132
Zemlinsky, Alexander, 121
Ziegfeld, Florenz, 83, 135, 212, 214, 215, 220, 221
Ziegfeld Follies, 53, 212, 214, 215, 216, 220, 221
Ziegfeld Frolics, 212
Zukor, Adolph, 192

www.ingramcontent.com/pod-product-compliance
Lightning Source LLC
Chambersburg PA
CBHW030530230426
43665CB00010B/833